March 21–23, 2012
Bengaluru, India

Association for Computing Machinery

Advancing Computing as a Science & Profession

ICIC'12

Proceedings of the 4th International Conference on
Intercultural Collaboration

Sponsored by:
ACM SIGCHI

Association for Computing Machinery

Advancing Computing as a Science & Profession

The Association for Computing Machinery
2 Penn Plaza, Suite 701
New York, New York 10121-0701

Copyright © 2012 by the Association for Computing Machinery, Inc. (ACM). Permission to make digital or hard copies of portions of this work for personal or classroom use is granted without fee provided that copies are not made or distributed for profit or commercial advantage and that copies bear this notice and the full citation on the first page. Copyright for components of this work owned by others than ACM must be honored. Abstracting with credit is permitted. To copy otherwise, to republish, to post on servers or to redistribute to lists, requires prior specific permission and/or a fee. Request permission to republish from: permissions@acm.org or Fax +1 (212) 869-0481.

For other copying of articles that carry a code at the bottom of the first or last page, copying is permitted provided that the per-copy fee indicated in the code is paid through www.copyright.com.

Notice to Past Authors of ACM-Published Articles
ACM intends to create a complete electronic archive of all articles and/or other material previously published by ACM. If you have written a work that has been previously published by ACM in any journal or conference proceedings prior to 1978, or any SIG Newsletter at any time, and you do NOT want this work to appear in the ACM Digital Library, please inform permissions@acm.org, stating the title of the work, the author(s), and where and when published.

ISBN: 978-1-4503-0818-2 (Digital)

ISBN: 978-1-4503-1723-8 (Print)

Additional copies may be ordered prepaid from:

ACM Order Department
PO Box 30777
New York, NY 10087-0777, USA

Phone: 1-800-342-6626 (USA and Canada)
+1-212-626-0500 (Global)
Fax: +1-212-944-1318
E-mail: acmhelp@acm.org
Hours of Operation: 8:30 am – 4:30 pm ET

Printed in the USA

Foreword

It is our great pleasure to welcome you to the *4th* Association for Computing Machinery's *International Conference on Intercultural Collaboration – ICIC 2012.* This conference is a continuation of ICIC'10, which was held at Copenhagen Business School in Copenhagen, Denmark; IWIC'09 which was held at Stanford University in Palo Alto, USA; and IWIC'07, which was held at Kyoto University in Kyoto, Japan. The mission of the conference is to bring together researchers from a variety of disciplines and provide a forum to discuss research related to international and intercultural collaboration, from technical, linguistic and socio-cultural perspectives. We hope that the conference proceedings will serve as a valuable reference for researchers interested in various theoretical and methodological approaches to intercultural collaboration.

Putting together *ICIC 2012* was a team effort. We would like to thank the authors and panelists for providing the content of the program. We would also like to express our gratitude to the program committee and external reviewers, who worked hard in reviewing papers and providing suggestions for their improvement, and the entire conference committee for all of their efforts over the last months. Thanks also to staff members at the Indian Institute of Science (IISc) who assisted with various aspects of conference planning. Finally, we would like to thank our sponsor, ACM SIGCHI, for support of this conference, and the organizations whose generous donations made this conference possible.

As you will see from looking through the program, the conference offers many opportunities for coming into contact with a variety of researchers from different walks of life and to network with those who have shared interests. We encourage you to engage with all of these to enjoy the full richness of the conference.

We hope that you will find the ICIC 2012 program interesting and thought-provoking and that the conference will provide you with a valuable opportunity to share ideas with other researchers and practitioners from institutions around the world.

Ravi Vatrapu
ICIC 2012 General Co-Chair
Copenhagen Business School

Vanessa Evers
ICIC 2012 General Co-Chair
University of Twente, The Netherlands

K.B. Akhilesh
ICIC 2012 General Co-Chair
Indian Institute of Science, India

Program Chairs' Welcome

We are pleased to present the technical program for the International Conference on Intercultural Collaboration, ICIC 2012. The call for papers resulted in 31 regular submissions and 9 late-breaking submissions from Asia, Europe, North America, the Middle East and Latin America. The program committees accepted 15 regular papers and all late-breaking papers. In addition to these papers, the conference also included two keynote speakers and two panels. The members of the Program Committee and all of the reviewers are listed elsewhere in these proceedings. We are grateful for the careful attention they gave to the submissions and their hard work in making careful assessments on the submissions. We are delighted that so many people are willing to help it along.

We hope that these proceedings, along with those from the previous conferences, will constitute a rich resource for those interested in intercultural collaboration. The diversity of topics demonstrates what a lively and growing area this is. We hope you find the program useful and inspirational as you engage the complex issues involved in intercultural collaboration. We welcome your presence and participation here in Bengaluru.

Bonnie Nardi
ICIC 2012 Program Co-Chair
University of California, Irvine
USA

Martha Maznevski
ICIC 2012 Program Co-Chair
International Institute for Management Development
Switzerland

Table of Contents

ICIC 2012 Conference Organization ... vii

Session 1: Learning

- Global E-Mentoring: Overcoming Virtual Distance for an Effective Partnership ... 1
  Nancy Philippart, Julia Gluesing *(Wayne State University)*

- Building a Mexican Startup Culture Over the Weekend ... 11
  Ruy Cervantes, Bonnie Nardi *(University of California, Irvine)*

Session 2: Bridging Cultures

- Sources of Miscommunication: Searching for Contextual Information in Communication between Chinese and Danish Collaborators ... 21
  Renée Korver Michan, Pernille Bjørn *(IT University of Copenhagen)*

- Bridging Cultures via an Online Business Simulation over Different Time Zones ... 31
  Iris Fischlmayr *(Johannes Kepler University)*

Session 3: Social Media

- Using Social Networks for Multicultural Creative Collaboration ... 39
  Foad Hamidi, Melanie Baljko *(York University)*

- Supporting Collaboration in Wikipedia Between Language Communities ... 47
  Ranjitha Gurunath Kulkarni *(Carnegie Mellon University)*,
  Gaurav Trivedi, Tushar Suresh *(National Institute of Technology Karnataka)*,
  Miaomiao Wen, Zeyu Zheng, Carolyn Rose *(Carnegie Mellon University)*

- Analysis of Discussion Contributions in Translated Wikipedia Articles ... 57
  Ari Hautasaari, Toru Ishida *(Kyoto University)*

Session 4: Intercultural Communication

- Computational Representation of Discourse Practices Across Populations in Task-based Dialogue ... 67
  Elijah Mayfield, David Adamson, Alexander I. Rudnicky, Carolyn Penstein Rosé *(Carnegie Mellon University)*

- Studying the Influence of Culture in Global Software Engineering: Thinking in Terms of Cultural Models ... 77
  Hina Shah, Nancy J. Nersessian, Mary Jean Harrold, Wendy Newstetter *(Georgia Institute of Technology)*

- "Are You a Trustworthy Partner in a Cross-Cultural Virtual Environment?" Behavioral Cultural Intelligence and Receptivity-Based Trust in Virtual Collaboration ... 87
  Ye Li *(University of Mannheim)*, Hui Li *(Tsinghua University)*, Alexander Mädche *(University of Mannheim)*,
  Pei-Luen Patrick Rau *(Tsinghua University)*

Session 5: Teams

- Trust and Surprise in Distributed Teams: Towards an Understanding of Expectations and Adaptations ... 97
  Ban Al-Ani, Erik Trainer, David Redmiles *(University of California, Irvine)*, Erik Simmons *(Intel Corporation)*

- Offshoring Attitudes and Relational Behaviours in German-Indian Offshoring Collaborations. Reflections from a Field Study ... 107
  Angelika Zimmermann *(Loughborough University)*

Session 6: Work and Home

- Domestic Artefacts: Sustainability in the Context of Indian Middle Class ... 119
  Dhaval Vyas *(University of Twente)*

Session 7: Intercultural Communication, Virtual Teams, and Technology

- **An Exploratory Analysis of Effective Indo-Korean Collaboration with Intervention of Knowledge Mapping** 129
  Indumathi Anandarajan, K.B. Akhilesh *(Indian Institute of Science)*

- **Knowing Me Knowing You: Exploring Effects of Culture and Context on Perception of Robot Personality** 133
  Astrid Weiss *(University of Amsterdam & University of Salzburg)*,
  Betsy van Dijk, Vanessa Evers *(University of Twente)*

- **Now That's News: Substitution and Culture in Electronic Newspaper Adoption in Scandinavia** 137
  Nicolai Pogrebnyakov, Mikael Buchmann *(Copenhagen Business School)*

- **A Conceptual Framework of Information Learning and Flow in Relation to Websites' Information Architecture** 141
  Ather Nawaz *(Copenhagen Business School)*

- **Networks in Equity and Sustainability: A Preliminary Tool for Intercultural Analysis and Discussion** 145
  Arlene Ducao, Alexander Simoes *(Massachusetts Institute of Technology)*, Ilias Koen *(The DuKode Studio)*,
  Henry Holtzman, Cesar Hidalgo *(Massachusetts Institute of Technology)*

- **Cultural Differences across Governmental Website Design** 149
  Nitesh Goyal, William Miner, Nikhil Nawathe *(Cornell University)*

- **Detecting Value Differences behind Intercultural Meetings** 153
  Naomi Yamashita *(NTT Communication Science Labs)*, Hideaki Kuzuoka *(University of Tsukuba)*

- **An Intercultural Study of HCI Education Experience and Representation** 157
  José Abdelnour-Nocera, Mario Michaelides, Ann Austin, Sunila Modi *(Univesity of West London)*

Author Index 161

ICIC 2012 Conference Organization

General Chairs: Ravi Vatrapu *(Copenhagen Business School, Denmark)*
Vanessa Evers *(University of Twente, The Netherlands)*
K.B. Akhilesh *(Indian Institute of Science, India)*

Program Chairs: Bonnie Nardi *(University of California Irvine, USA)*
Martha Maznevski *(International Institute for Management Development (IMD), Switzerland)*

Late Breaking Papers Chairs: Naomi Yamashita *(NTT Communication Science Labs, Japan)*
Girish Prabhu *(Srishti School of Art, Design & Technology, India)*

Demonstrations Chairs: Ari Hautasaari *(Kyoto University, Japan)*
Sameer Patil *(Indiana University, USA)*

Proceedings Chair: Jose Abdelnour Nocera *(University of West London, United Kingdom)*

Treasurer: Naomi Yamashita *(NTT Communication Science Labs, Japan)*

Student Volunteers Chairs: Ather Nawaz *(Copenhagen Business School, Denmark)*
Nitesh Goyal *(Cornell University, USA)*

Website Manager: Rieko Inaba *(Kyoto University, Japan)*

Program Committee: Cris Gibson *(University of Western Australia)*
Julia Gluesing *(Wayne State University)*
Sameer Patil *(Indiana University, USA)*
Nimmi Rangaswamy *(Microsoft, USA)*
Anne-Marie Soderberg *(Copenhagen Business School, Denmark)*
Naomi Yamashita *(NTT Communication Science Labs, Japan)*
Yang Wang *(Carnegie Mellon University, USA)*

Additional Reviewers:

- Payal Arora
- Xianghua Ding
- Yucong Duan
- Jennifer Gibbs
- Tijana Gonja
- Ari Hautasaari
- Brent Hecht
- Ryuichiro Higashinaka
- Laura Huang
- Yun Huang
- Rieko Inaba
- Aditya Johri
- Hideaki Kuzuoka
- Mark Levy
- Ye Li
- Mihir Mahajan
- Arvind Malhotra
- Chris Miller
- Harekrishna Misra
- Sumitra Nair
- Jahnavi Phalkey
- Kenneth Riopelle
- Sandhya Sastry
- Taryn Stanko
- Revi Sterling
- Alex Taylor
- Hao-Chuan Wang
- Takashi Yoshino
- Qiping Zhang

Sponsor: SIGCHI

Global E-Mentoring: Overcoming Virtual Distance for an Effective Partnership

Nancy Philippart
Industrial and Systems Engineering
Wayne State University
Detroit, MI 48201 USA
President, NLP Solutions, LLC
+1 248 497 3665
nancy.philippart@wayne.edu

Dr. Julia Gluesing
Industrial and Systems Engineering
Wayne State University
Detroit, MI 48201 USA
President, Cultural Connections, Inc.
+1 248 210 7640
j.gluesing@wayne.edu

ABSTRACT
The benefits of being mentored to one's career development and advancement have been recognized both anecdotally and through academic research. A new model of mentoring enabled by technology that works not only across organizational but geographical and cultural boundaries has emerged to meet the needs of today's complex, fast changing, global workplace. Although e-mentoring has several advantages over traditional mentoring, the absence of regular face to face interactions requires different strategies to develop an effective partnership. Additional complexities arise when this virtual mentoring is global. This paper uses both participant observation and pilot data to develop a conceptual framework that examines intercultural collaboration issues and enablers in global e-mentoring partnerships. The framework is derived from Sobel Lojeski's [28] virtual distance model augmented with a new construct, cultural intelligence that more thoroughly explores the intercultural aspect of the partnerships. The authors also describe a more comprehensive, planned mixed-methods research study to validate the proposed e-mentoring conceptual model. This work makes an important contribution to the literature beyond the application to e-mentoring since one-on-one virtual collaboration is also an essential component for effective global leadership.

Author Keywords
e-mentoring; intercultural collaboration; virtual distance; e-leadership

ACM Classification Keywords
K.3.1. Computer uses in education: Collaborative learning.
K.4.3. Organizational impacts: Computer-supported collaborative work.

INTRODUCTION
Mentoring has been shown both anecdotally and through academic research to enhance employee's career development and advancement [7, 12, 13]. The traditional mentoring model, whether formal or informal, involves an experienced executive 'teaching' a high potential junior associate how to successfully perform in the organization. Today, forces such as globalization, elimination of lifetime employment expectations and consequent mobility of employees in and out of organizations as well as technology-enabled ways of doing work have made the traditional mentoring model not only appear quaint but ill suited to current business realities. At the same time, given the complexities of business, mentoring has never been so important for the development of the next generation of global leaders.

A more relevant model of mentoring facilitated by technology is now available that not only works across organizational boundaries but geographical and cultural ones as well. Referred to in the literature by such names as CMC (computer mediated communication), virtual, on-line, cyber or e-mentoring, this type of mentoring, although relatively new, eliminates or significantly reduces face-to-face interactions between mentor and protégé and instead relies on electronic and other virtual media to carry on the mentoring partnership [3]. Virtual mentoring has several advantages over traditional mentoring including greater mentor-mentee access, reduced costs, decreased emphasis on geography, equalization of status, and better records of interactions [15]. However, the single biggest obstacle to virtual mentoring is building a relationship of trust in the absence of face-to-face meetings. Trust building obstacles include:

- Partners may never have the opportunity to meet in person during the mentoring process requiring different strategies for developing a comfortable, trusting partnership.

- National cultural differences are present in addition to gender differences in the national business context.

- Time zone differences may challenge the partnership particularly in the mentor's ability to 'observe' the mentee in action.

This 'psychological separation' created by physical, operational, cultural and social distance between partners can inhibit development of an effective mentoring partnership. Called virtual distance, this phenomenon was first described by Sobel Lojeski and Reilly [28] as they studied virtual work teams and observed the 'psychological separation' between people that built over time due to a combination of 'physical separation, technology mediation and disconnected relationships'. Virtual distance has been shown to impact such outcomes as work performance, trust, job satisfaction, goal and role clarity and behavior [28, 29] and is hypothesized by the authors of this paper to be an impediment to effective intercultural e-mentoring. Although research has explored ways that leaders can reduce virtual distance in non co-located work teams, little research is available on virtual mentoring across national borders. This paper attempts to fill this gap by using participant observation and pilot study data guided by the framework of virtual distance to develop a conceptual model to better understand global e-mentoring relationships and enablers for successful outcomes. This is a critical issue for any organization interested in global talent development.

LITERATURE REVIEW

Definition of Mentoring

The literature provides a multitude of definitions of mentoring. Hunt & Michael [19] define mentoring as 'a dyadic relationship in which a mentor, a senior person in age or experience, provides guidance and support to a less experienced person, a protégé.' Zey [33] provides a more functionally focused definition of a mentor as 'someone who overseas the career and development of another person, usually a junior, through teaching, counseling, providing psychological support, protecting and at times sponsoring.' Bierema & Hill [3] assert that 'mentors have existed throughout history in the form of a wiser, older person who's job is to guide a mentee's or protégé's development', whether career, academic or personal. From their extensive investigation of the mentoring literature, Bierema & Merriam [4] conclude that the definition and function of mentors vary widely, ranging from career sponsor to coach to classical mentor who facilitates all aspects of a mentee's development.

Despite varying definitions of mentoring, there is general agreement in the literature about the ways mentors support their mentees. Mentors many provide vocational support that augment a mentee's career enhancement such as career advice, information and feedback, challenging assignments, training, increased visibility, exposure to senior management thinking, sponsorship and even political protection [3, 9, 12]. Mentors may also provide psychosocial support to mentees through counseling, encouragement and even friendship [9] often functioning as a sounding board or shoulder to cry on. Finally, mentors may demonstrate appropriate organizational behavior either explicitly or implicitly for their mentees [7, 20, 27], thereby functioning as role models.

Definition of Virtual Mentoring

Given the lack of a common mentoring definition in the literature and the infancy of non face-to-face mentoring, one can hardly expect agreement on a definition of 'virtual mentoring'. There is not even consensus on how to refer to this type of mentoring. The terms CMC (computer mediated communication), virtual, on-line, cyber or e-mentoring are used to refer to this relatively new type of mentoring that eliminates or significantly reduces the face-to-face interactions between mentor and mentee and instead relies on electronic and other virtual media to carry on the mentoring partnership [3]. But contrary to expectations, definitions of what will be referred to as e-mentoring in this paper, are more similar than those describing traditional mentoring. E-mentoring characterizations in the literature have several attributes in common – one, the utilization of electronic technology to facilitate the partnership, is not surprising given the rapid growth and deployment of electronic communication tools. For example, O'Neill et al. [25] assert e-mentoring is the 'use of email or computer conferencing systems to support a mentoring relationship when a face-to-face relationship would be impractical.' Likewise, Boyle Single & Miller [5] describe it as a computer mediated relationship between a senior individual who is the mentor of a lesser skilled protégé with the goal of developing the protégé in a way that helps him or her to succeed.'

But there is a second similarity in the more recent virtual definitions that differs from traditional face-to-face mentoring descriptions – that is, convergence on the concept of mentoring as a mutually beneficial relationship for mentor and mentee, a partnership with shared support that is more egalitarian and less paternalistic. Bierema & Merriam [4] define e-mentoring as 'a computer mediated, mutually beneficial relationship between a mentor and protégé which provides learning, advising, encouraging, promoting that is often boundary less, egalitarian and qualitatively different than traditional face-to-face mentoring.' According to Hunt [18], 'utilizing technology, e-mentoring is the process by which two people assist each other to grow in a safe and supportive relationship.' These definitions are consistent with the new leadership models [12, 21, 29] necessary for success in today's increasingly complex, globally connected workplace. It is important to note, however, that the literature on e-mentoring is still theoretical with limited rigorous empirical substantiation.

Virtual Mentoring Benefits and Challenges

An extensive survey of the literature shows that virtual mentoring is qualitatively different from traditional face-to-face mentoring relationships [3]. This 'qualitative difference' arises from the asynchronous nature of the relationship, the lack of proximity, the increased flexibility and the lower social presence of e-mentoring relationships and has the potential to provide the following benefits compared to traditional partnerships [18].

- The asynchronous nature of email allows people time for reflection before responding.
- The need to write out a message drives clarity and greater depth of communication.
- Location is not an issue.
- Gender, race, power and other barriers are reduced.
- Time is easier to manage and virtual meetings are not costly.
- A record of discussion often exists for later reflections and learning.
- There is opportunity for greater and wider participation.

E-mentoring creates 'unparalleled opportunities' due to its affordability, time independence and use of multiple media including email, chat groups, intranet and computer conferencing [3]. It can facilitate both synchronous and asynchronous communication and support a 'reflective learning environment where mentoring pairs can explore their values, feelings and objectives at their own pace and more freely than in face-to-face communication, which can be pressurized through the need to respond immediately' [24]. This environment can also be enhanced through the use of on-line resources [15].

The lack of place dependency in e-mentoring means that mentors and mentees can literally be around the world from each other. This virtuality has and will continue to make e-mentoring more 'egalitarian' with the potential for mentoring to be more available to people customarily underrepresented in traditional mentoring, particularly women and people of color [3]. The utilization of computer mediated communication tools can break down barriers that prevent would be mentees from obtaining a mentor due to organizational, professional, industry or geographical boundaries [9, 15]. Moreover, research has shown that e-mentoring also transcended functional, hierarchical and demographic barriers making mentoring, typically restricted to an elite group of senior women managers, more widely accessible [14, 32].

Finally, the lower social presence of computer mediated communication can actually work to advantage collaboration [24]. Virtual mentoring can reduce the impact of status differences between mentor and mentee, thereby improving communication [5]. The partnership becomes more two way with less emphasis on seniority, hierarchical position and age allowing each partner to bring their strengths and experiences to the relationship.

Despite its benefits, e-mentoring is not without challenges. Several challenges are similar to those encountered in traditional mentoring. These include effectively matching mentors and mentees so chemistry will form to enable development of comfortable, mutually respectful, confidential and trusting relationships [3, 15]. Making the mentoring relationship a priority with frequent and regular interaction despite the time constraints of work and personal responsibilities is critical. Both parties and their organizations must be equally committed to the collaboration [4].

E-mentoring, however, has some additional challenges. First, mentors and mentees must have access to technology and skills to competently utilize the technology. In global relationships, where significant time zone differences occur, access to technology from one's home is critical. This may result in additional access costs. Overcoming distance to develop trust can often prove difficult and requires specific strategies beyond those used in face-to-face collaboration [29]. Creating the right match between mentoring partners becomes even more important virtually [3]. Training partners in techniques to overcome 'virtual distance' and facilitate understanding of each other's environmental and cultural contexts is often necessary. Intercultural competencies and the ability to make context explicit are especially critical to achieving mentoring benefits appropriate to the cultural business contexts [10]. Finally, overcoming privacy concerns when at least some mentoring interactions are documented electronically can also be a potential issue [3, 18].

Global Virtual Mentoring
Relatively little research is available on virtual mentoring across national borders beyond focus on career development for expatriates during international assignments [6]. The situation where mentoring occurs between individuals with different national origins, from different organizations working in different countries that may or may not be their countries of origin is not addressed in the literature. This paper and the subsequent research proposition attempt to address this gap.

Mentoring and Leadership
Mentoring is an effective component of contextual leadership development [2, 7]. In a survey of over 350 companies conducted by Giber et al. [12], mentoring programs were reported as some of the most successful in leadership development. In particular, the opportunity to interact with senior management was cited as a critical component of mentoring as it helped mentees develop a 'more sophisticated and strategic' leadership perspective. Along with such tools as 360 degree feedback, executive coaching, networking, developmental job assignments and action learning projects, mentoring is a leadership development best practice recognized and utilized by organizations [2, 13, 16]. However, the effectiveness of mentoring for leadership talent development is highly dependent on 'quality of the relationship, type of program and manner in which the program is developed and

maintained' [13]. Additionally, trust between both organization and individuals and between individuals has been identified as a key success factor in mentoring relationships [26, 30].

Just as mentoring is a key leadership competency, e-mentoring and one-on-one cross cultural collaboration skills are key global e-leadership competencies. This paper is intended to better understand the impact of virtual distance on e-mentoring partnerships and what interventions can help improve effectiveness.

RESEARH QUESTION AND PROPOSITION

The problem of interest in this interdisciplinary research[1] is whether the construct of virtual distance is useful for global e-mentoring partnerships. Specifically, there are three related questions:

- To what extent is virtual distance present in global e-mentoring partnerships?
- How does virtual distance impact the outcomes of the partnership?
- Are there interventions that can reduce virtual distance in global e-mentoring partnerships?

The word partnership is used in this paper to describe mutually beneficial interaction between mentor and mentee. In other words, the partnership is intended to enhance the learning of both partners. The terms partnership, relationship and collaboration are also used interchangeably.

Sobel Lojeski and Reilly [28] first conceived virtual distance after researching the issues encountered by geographically dispersed work teams. The physical distance among team members, their reliance on technology for communication and task achievement and the disconnected relationships as a result of limited face to face interaction created a dynamic that over time led to a type of 'psychological' separation amongst people. This separation or virtual distance is comprised of three major components illustrated in the model in Figure 1.

Virtual Distance Model components include:

- Physical distance – factors based on actual location differences in time and geography but can also include sense of separateness due to different functional or organizational affiliations

---

[1] The authors bring different disciplinary perspectives to this proposition. One author is an engineer with extensive executive management experience at a global company who is currently working on a non-traditional doctorate in industrial and systems engineering; the other author is a business anthropologist who works with and studies cross functional participants in global collaborations.

- Operational distance – psychological separations that occur due to everyday challenges in the workplace resulting from communication distance, task overload, waiting for support and irregular resource allocation
- Affinity distance – emotional distance between distributed team members due to cultural or social distance, failure to invest in team relationships or lack of commitment to the team

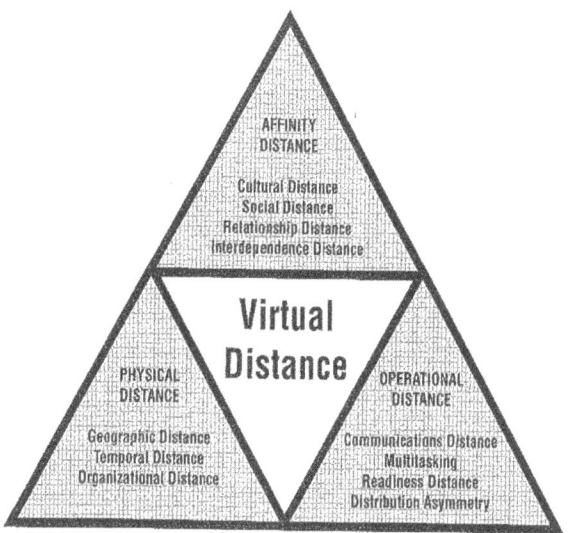

Figure 1. Virtual Distance Model [28]

Virtual distance has been shown to negatively affect team performance and competitive advantage as measured by outcomes in over 500 project teams from multi-national companies [28]. These negative outcomes include a:

- 90% reduction in innovation severely impacting competitive advantage
- 80% decline in trust amongst team members
- 80% drop in job satisfaction
- 70% decline in good citizenship behaviors
- 60% reduction in goal and role clarity
- 50% reduction in on-time/on-budget performance costing millions of dollars

Furthermore, several other critical insights were revealed. First, virtual distance cannot only be measured but predicted, and as such, can be mitigated with proper planning and intervention. Second, virtual distance is not solely confined to teams where people are distributed but frequently occurs within co-located teams. Finally, leader actions and behaviors significantly impact virtual distance and can both contribute to or reduce it amongst subordinates [29]. Leaders who value techno-dexterity, the ability to use the most appropriate communication mechanism for message delivery and who use technology to create context for virtual workers, form communities and co-activate distributed leaders can help reduce virtual distance experienced by teams [29].

Global e-mentoring partnerships share some but not all attributes of globally dispersed teams [11]. In many ways, collaboration is less complex since it primarily focuses on one-on-one vs. multiple person interactions. However, it can be argued that the trust and rapport required for an effective partnership must be greater than that for teams working on project task completion so that the existence of psychological separation between partners is more consequential. Other challenges comparable to those experienced by global teams include time zone and geographical distance, organizational and functional differences, time constraints and task overload, social and cultural diversity, lack of goal and role clarity, lack of commitment to the partnership or unwillingness to invest in the relationship. These similarities prompted the authors of this paper to postulate that the virtual distance construct can be adapted to measure and predict virtual distance in global e-mentoring partnerships. As with global teams, the authors reason that virtual distance will negatively impact partnership effectiveness but that recognizing and understanding virtual distance will result in identification of enablers to reduce its effects. In particular, the use of mechanisms and technologies that help to create context and community between partners should support improved intercultural collaboration.

Both the one-on-one and intercultural aspects of e-mentoring partnerships necessitate thoughtful consideration of the construct used to represent cultural distance. The virtual distance model uses differences in national origin to measure culture. The authors postulate a more sophisticated approach and propose using a construct of cultural intelligence to assess the ability of partners to work interculturally.

The literature is rich with information on cultural intelligence and how to measure and assess it [1, 8, 23, 31]. Earley and Ang [8] define cultural intelligence as a person's capability for successful adaptation to new cultural settings, that is, for unfamiliar settings attributable to cultural context. They postulate four aspects to cultural intelligence: both cognitive and metacognitive skills to help one conceptualize and understand how to function in a new culture as well as gain culture specific knowledge, motivation to want to engage with a new culture, and capabilities to engage in adaptive behaviors. Similarly Thomas and Inkson [31] define cultural intelligence as the capacity to interact effectively with people from different cultural backgrounds, that which enables one to recognize cultural differences through knowledge and mindfulness and gives one the propensity and ability to act appropriately across cultures. Cultural intelligence leads to competence in responding effectively to people of all cultures, languages, races, classes, ethnic backgrounds, religions and other diversity attributes in ways that recognize, affirm and value their dignity [8]. It is this competency and its contribution to virtual distance rather than merely national origin that the authors seek to explore in global e-mentoring partnerships.

RESEARCH METHODOLOGY FOR CONCEPTUAL MODEL CONSTRUCTION

A conceptual model that relates virtual distance and partnership effectiveness was developed using data from global e-mentoring partnerships facilitated by a mentoring service and support organization, Menttium.[2] Menttium's core mentoring program matches high potential mentees, sponsored and funded by their organizations, with experienced male or female executives in other organizations who volunteer their time and expertise to support the development of emerging female talent and contribute to increased diversity within corporate leadership ranks. Formal partnerships are in place for one year. Although virtual mentoring has been a component of Menttium's program for over ten years, *global* e-mentoring was first piloted in 2006/7 at the request of the organization's multinational clients who were seeking talent development support for high potential non-US nationals working in their overseas subsidiaries. One of this paper's authors served as a mentor in that pilot and continues to mentor cross culturally. These mentoring experiences provided a rich opportunity for participant observation. Patterns observed across multiple relationships sparked a desire to more formally explore the dynamics of intercultural e-mentoring partnerships. Sobel Lojeski's virtual distance model [28] provided a framework and defined constructs for physical, operational and affinity distance that appeared consistent with many of the author's participant observations. This led to the development of a pilot survey intended to collect directional data on whether virtual distance was a feasible construct for e-mentoring and to support the construction of a specific conceptual model for this application.

Four mentees from global partnerships with the author between 2006 and 2010 completed the pilot survey. The number of participants in this pilot survey was intentionally kept small because of the researchers' initial concern about limited population of *global* partnerships available for the main study sample. For purposes of this study, a global partnership was defined as one in which the mentor and mentee were from differing national origins, who identified with different cultures and lived and worked in different countries. Mentees in the pilot were females from Europe, the Middle East and Asia and worked in Europe or Asia. Two of the four mentees did not live and work in their country of origin. The mentor was a female U.S. executive with extensive global business experience.

---

[2] Menttium has been in existence for over twenty years and has enabled over 50,000 cross company partnerships between emerging female business leaders and senior executives from hundreds of companies around the world.

The pilot survey was used to gather data on demographics, as well as information related to the development of cultural intelligence such as working and travelling outside one's country of origin, global professional responsibilities and foreign language proficiency. Details of each partnership were examined including partnership goals, methods and frequency of communication, mentoring practices utilized, resources used during partnership and types of difficulties encountered. Finally, partners were asked to evaluate overall effectiveness of the partnership, mentoring techniques used, available support and resources, mentor-mentee matching process and whether the partnership helped their career or personal development. Each respondent was contacted for an interview after completing the pilot survey and asked to briefly discuss reasons for partnership effectiveness ratings and given the opportunity to make any other comments. As previously stated, the pilot survey and interview data were intended for directional purposes only to explore application of the virtual distance construct for global e-mentoring and more importantly to investigate enablers to help reduce virtual distance and increase partnership effectiveness.

Participant observation and pilot survey and interview data also assisted the authors in the construct of a more comprehensive quantitative and qualitative study to be fielded later this year. This study will sample mentors and mentees from the over 180 global partnerships facilitated by Menttium since 2006. The redesigned survey aligns with several of the relevant constructs for virtual distance but includes a more comprehensive approach to cultural intelligence. A subset of this sample will also participate in semi-structured interviews to increase the richness of responses. This study is intended to test the conceptual model described below.

CONCEPTUAL MODEL CONSTRUCTION

Both participant observation and pilot data suggest that physical, operational and affinity distance exist in global e-mentoring partnerships.[3] Physical distance was present in all partnerships as mentees and mentors were located in different countries in different regions of the world across different time zones and worked for different organizations. Operational distance varied across partnerships but was primarily influenced by communication issues created by language difficulties and discomfort with use of communication technologies. Affinity distance also varied as a function of partners' cultural intelligence, clarity around partnership goals and commitment to the collaboration. The measure of partnership effectiveness utilized in the pilot was the subjective assessment by both mentor and mentee of the effectiveness of the collaboration and whether goals were achieved.[4] Not surprisingly, participant observation and pilot survey data support the premise that the greater the virtual distance, the less effective the collaboration according to ratings by both partners. The more important insight, however, comes from understanding the factors that contributed to virtual distance in the relationship and how these can be avoided or reduced. Four mechanisms were identified in the pilot as impacting virtual distance between mentor and mentee: the partner matching process, partnership goal clarity and alignment, mentoring practices and support and technology usage. The proposed conceptual model shown in Figure 2 illustrates this relationship.

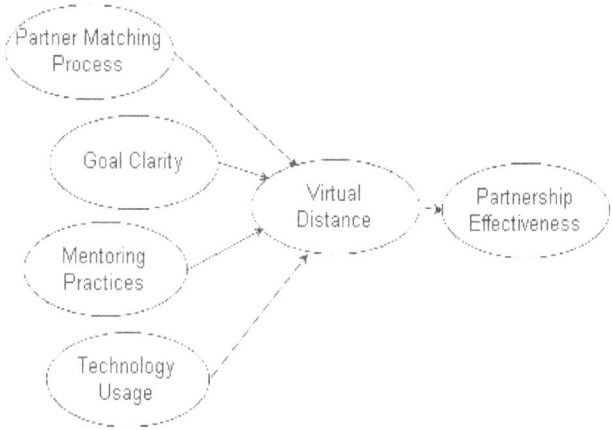

Figure 2. Proposed Conceptual Model

Partner Matching

The 'right' partner match appears to be one way to mitigate virtual distance initially within a partnership. For our sample, the mentor and mentee matching was and will continue to be completed by Menttium using the following process. Mentors complete an on-line profile and are interviewed by Menttium staff to ascertain professional and business experience and skills, leadership skills as well as personal and family interests. Mentees who are nominated for the program by their employer also complete an on-line profile and interview that focuses on their developmental needs. Menttium staff use interview and profile information, mentee development needs and a fair amount of judgment to assign mentors that they believe will best enable mentees to meet their goals. Historically, matching focused on compatibility of professional skills and relevant business experience as well as personal compatibility – sharing some common personal and/or family interests can help to develop rapport. A good matching process can begin to reduce virtual distance and help diminish initial awkwardness in a new relationship. One mentee

---

[3] Pilot data was not collected to replicate the exact measures of Sobel Lojeski's virtual distance as this information is proprietary. Sobel Lojeski has permitted use of applicable virtual distance constructs for the next phase of study.

[4] This assessment is part of Menttium's process at the conclusion of the formal partnership.

commented that "being matched with a mentor that could relate to the challenges I'm facing (both professionally and personally) helped to immediately develop trust".

Global mentoring has made the matching process more complex. National cultural differences add a new dimension to mentor-mentee matching and contribute to increased virtual distance beyond geography. As shown in Figure 3, cultural distance significantly varies by country cluster and illustrates the additional challenge of global partnership matching [17]. Mentors involved in global partnerships must have international work experience so in theory they have some familiarity with working cross culturally. Per Menttium, mentors are typically American senior executives who have worked internationally but still have limited language proficiency beyond English. Mentees, however, can exhibit wide variability in the extent of their global experience and cultural knowledge. In three of the four partnerships in the pilot rated as highly effective, mentees were culturally intelligent with some international business and travel experiences. One mentee, born and educated in Romania and currently living in Belgium had worked extensively in Eastern and Western Europe for both European and American companies, was fluent in five languages and was well traveled. She had global job responsibilities; virtually managed small teams of people located in Europe, Middle East and Africa and visited these locations frequently. A second mentee, born and raised in Iran, was educated in France, currently lived in the Netherlands, had lived and worked in other areas of Europe and the United States over the course of her career and was also fluent in five languages. Even the third mentee, who was born, educated and had worked her entire career in India was well travelled and visited the U.S. frequently because her children were in college there. Given the global experience and cultural intelligence of these three women, national culture did not appear to unduly widen affinity distance between them and their mentors. This is in contrast to the fourth mentee, who was born, educated and worked in Spain. Although an American company employed her, she had not travelled outside Spain for work and her personal travel experiences were confined to Mediterranean Europe. Although rated by her mentor as proficient in English, she was uncomfortable and apologetic speaking the language. Despite being well matched professionally and personally with her mentor, she cited language as a barrier in the partnership. Her mentor did not speak Spanish and believed had she even had limited competency to help bridge the affinity distance, it may have supported a more comfortable and trusting partnership.

Partnership Goal Clarity and Alignment
Data showed that aligning partnership goals with mentor expertise was an important requirement for a successful partnership outcome. This requires that the mentee develop and articulate specific actionable goals for the partnership and that she focus the agenda for each interaction on some aspect of goal attainment. Mentees are asked to document development goals in their on-line profile and do discuss these with Menttium staff. In the three partnerships rated as highly effective, mentees had clearly defined goals and regularly worked on these goals with their mentor. Examples included 'Learn how to promote myself and my accomplishments when my leadership network is not co-located with me' or 'Develop my influencing and negotiating skills to get support for my proposals'. Mentees frequently shared samples of their work and their leadership assessment profiles with their mentor so interactions were focused on mentee's developmental needs. This is in contrast to situation in the partnership rated as moderately effective by partners. In this instance, the mentee was unclear as to why she was selected for the program and had difficulty understanding how participation would benefit her job performance; "I do not fully understand why I have been nominated for this program and do not understand the aims and application to my daily job." Although she did articulate partnership goals, she did not intentionally prepare for or focus meetings with her mentor on these goals. Rather, she used the time to discuss the most pressing issue of her day which, because she was in sales, dealt with things like motivating and incentivizing her sales team. Although both mentor and mentee rated these discussions as valuable, the mentor believed that the partnership could have benefitted from greater goal clarity even if articulated as a need for impromptu day to day advice.

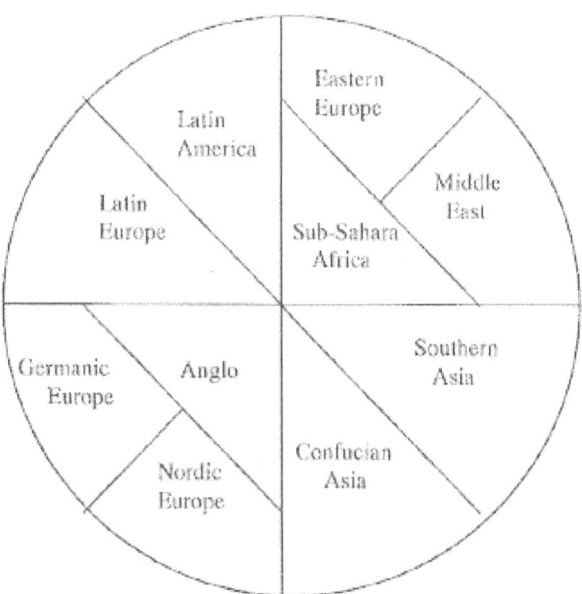

Figure 3. Cultural Distance by Country Cluster [17]

Mentoring Practices and Support
Use of certain mentoring practices and support mechanisms appear to help reduce virtual distance in a partnership. Participation in either a formalized virtual kickoff event or session to agree on terms and logistics of the partnership

can be the first step in developing rapport. Menttium now offers a launch webinar for mentors and mentees to learn about program resources and best practices for successful partnerships. At the conclusion of the formal launch event, mentors and mentees have time to connect with each other via phone or Skype to begin relationship building and to establish logistics of their partnership like methods of communication, frequency of interaction and expectations. Although in only two of the three highly effective rated partnerships, did mentor and mentee participate in a formal kickoff, in the third collaboration, the partners did use their first connection to agree on expectations and terms of the partnership. In the moderately effective partnership, partners did not participate in a formal launch event nor did the mentee take advantage of Menttium support.

Having the ability to meet face-to-face at some point during the partnership was mentioned as beneficial to the formal partnership and continuation of a long term relationship. In three highly effective partnerships, mentors and mentees were able to meet at least once face to face. However, partners indicated this was not a necessary condition for an effective partnership and probably contributed more to continuation of the relationship after formal collaboration concluded.

Another mentoring technique that appear to support both formation of a trusting partnership and helping mentees meet their development goals involved collaborating and providing feedback on actual mentee work products. This involved not only reviewing written documents and presentations but also listening in as mentees facilitated virtual meetings with their teams.

Technology Usage
Mentors' and mentees' access and level of comfort using technology also appear to be important factors in reducing virtual distance in e-mentoring collaborations. In the partnerships studied, telephone calls and email were the key communication channels utilized. When these mechanisms were used, those relationships where individuals sent pictures to enable virtual partners to 'see' each other and provide some context about their environment, families and community, were rated higher on development of rapport. Having access to technology outside the office was also important for both mentors and mentees to support connecting across time zones. In the partnership rated as moderately effective, the mentee did not have access to technology at home nor was she able to post photos on line. The entire time of the partnership, she and her mentor spoke without even knowing what each other looked like. In one of the partnerships rated as highly effective, Skype was used regularly. This tool proved to be an excellent enabler for developing rapport particularly as its technical reliability improved over the partnership.

SUMMARY AND RECOMMENDATIONS
Participant observation and pilot survey and interview data highlight several challenges inherent in diminishing virtual distance between a mentor and mentee so that a trusting, comfortable partnership can develop. This trust is postulated to be a necessary condition for an effective partnership. In addition to the physical distance of geography, time zones and organizations, the partnership must bridge contextual differences related to business conditions, national cultures and often the complexities of organizational cultures and sub-cultures related to gender and ethnicity. How effectively this bridge occurs often makes the difference between a successful and unsuccessful e-mentoring partnership. Several enablers were suggested from the preliminary data:

- Use a mentee-mentor matching process that first attempts to minimize functional and affinity distance by aligning development goals and personal and family interests.
- Ensure mentee development goals are clearly articulated and documented.
- Use the virtual distance model to anticipate mentor-mentee virtual distance. Prior global business and personal travel experience and language proficiency should be comprehended in assessing mentor and mentee cultural intelligence. When one partner's cultural intelligence is limited, every effort should be made to better match the language proficiency of partners.
- Partners should be better advised on the need for access of technology at home. Support to increase partners' comfort with technologies like Skype would help relationship development. Skype could be demonstrated in a formal kickoff meeting to ensure partners know how to access and use this media rich tool.
- At least one face-to-face meeting is desirable; however, use of Skype and other video conferencing tools can be employed to reduce affinity distance when a face to face meeting is not feasible.
- Provide mentors and mentees with a tool kit of mentoring techniques and best practices including ways for mentors to 'virtually' observe mentee's job performance.
- Plan for partnership support check-ins periodically throughout the process as well as formal surveys – Menttium's process appears to be a best practice
- Document case studies in the literature of successful intercultural collaborations so that others may learn how to develop successful global e-mentoring partnerships.

NEXT STEPS
Participant observation and pilot survey and interview data from four global e-mentoring partnerships suggests that virtual distance can be a useful construct for understanding the effectiveness of these types of intercultural

collaborations. The ability to identify, measure and reduce virtual distance could positively impact the success of global e-mentoring partnerships through appropriate intervention. Four such interventions are proposed as potential reducers of virtual distance in the conceptual model put forth in this paper: 1) the mentor-mentee matching process, 2) partnership goal clarity, 3) a robust tool kit of mentoring techniques, and 4) access to and comfort with technology. A mixed quantitative and qualitative research study will be fielded later this year to validate an adapted virtual distance construct for global e-mentoring partnerships. Mentors and mentees involved in global e-mentoring partnerships facilitated by Menttium will be surveyed using virtual distance measures initially developed by Sobel Lojeski [29] in her work with virtual teams but adapted to e-mentoring collaboration. Additionally, the cultural intelligence construct developed by Ang et al [1] will be utilized to better represent affinity distance as part of the virtual distance construct. Furthermore, additional partnership effectiveness measures will be incorporated beyond subjective assessment of partners. A subset of participants will be interviewed to further enrich data collected from survey.

This research focuses on relevant academic and business needs drawing on the literature as well as theory and methods from business, anthropology and engineering. It is intended to address gaps in the literature by proposing and validating a construct for anticipating, measuring and reducing virtual distance for improved intercultural e-mentoring effectiveness. It will also provide business practitioners with insight on how to more effectively deploy e-mentoring for global talent development. This issue is critical given the current shortage of cross cultural executive talent [22] and the need to fill the pipeline with a more diverse set of candidates. Virtual distance also has ramifications beyond e-mentoring since effective virtual one-on-one communication is an important competency of e-leadership.

ACKNOWLEDGMENTS
We thank Dr. Pam Dixon, Director of Research and Assessment at Menttium, Dr. Karen Sobel Lojeski, professor at Stony Brook University and founder of Virtual Distance International and Dr. Sheri Perelli and Dr. Toni Somers from Wayne State University School of Business for their support on both this paper and our future research study.

REFERENCES
1. Ang, S., Van Dyne, L., Koh, C., Yee Ng, K., Templer, K.J., Tay, C. & Chandraseker, N.A. Cultural intelligence: Its measurement and effects on cultural judgment and decision making, cultural adaption and task performance. *Management & Organization Review 3*, 3 (2007), 335-371.
2. Belasco, J., Foreward in M. Goldsmith, L. Lyons & A. Freas (eds.) *Coaching for Leadership: How World's Greatest Coaches Help Leaders Learn.* Jossey-Bass/Pfieffer, San Francisco, CA, 2000.
3. Bierema, L.L. & Hill, J.R. Virtual mentoring and HRD. *Advances in Developing Human Resources 7*, 4 (2005), 556-568.
4. Bierema, L.L. & Merriam, S. E-mentoring: Using computer mediated communications to enhance the mentoring process. *Innovative Higher Education 26,* (2002), 211-227.
5. Boyle Single, P. & Muller, C.B. When email and mentoring unite: The implementation of a nationwide mentoring program, in *Creating Mentoring and Coaching Programs*, L.K. Stromei (ed.), American Society for Training and Development, 2001, 107-122.
6. Crocitto, M., Sullivan, S.E. & Carraher, S.M. Global mentoring as a means of career development and knowledge creation: A learning-based framework and agenda for future research. *Career Development International 10,* 6/7 (2005), 522-535.
7. Day, D. Leadership development: A review in context. *Leadership Quarterly 11,* 4 (2000), 581-613.
8. Earley, P. & Ang, S. *Cultural Intelligence: Individual Interactions across Cultures.* Stanford University Press, Stanford, CA, 2003.
9. Ensher, E.A., Heun, C. & Blanchard, A. On-line mentoring and computer-mediated communication. *Journal of Vocational Behavior 63,* (2003), 264-288.
10. Gluesing, J., Alcordo, T., Baba, M. et al., The development of global virtual teams. In *Virtual Teams That Work: Creating Conditions for Virtual Team Effectiveness,* Gibson, C. & Cohen, S.G. (eds.), Jossey-Bass, San Francisco, CA, 2003, 353-380.
11. Gluesing, J. & Gibson, C. Designing and forming global teams. In *Handbook of Research on International Organizing and Managing,* Maznevski, M., Lane, H., Mendenhall, M. & McNett, J. (eds.), Blackwell, Oxford, England, 2004, 199-226.
12. Giber, D., Carter, L. & Goldsmith, M. (eds.) *Linkage Inc.'s Best Practices in Leadership Development Handbook.* Linkage Press, Lexington, MA, 1999.
13. Groves, K.S. Integrating leadership development and succession planning best practices. *Journal of Management Development 26,* 3 (2007), 239-260.
14. Headlam-Wells, J. E-mentoring for aspiring women managers. *Gender in Management 19*, 4 (2004), 212-218.
15. Headlam-Wells, J., Gosland, J & Craig, J. There's magic in the web: E-mentoring for women's career development. *Career Development International 10,* 6/7 (2005), 444-459.
16. Hegstad, C. & Wentling, R. The development and maintenance of exemplary and formal mentoring

programs in Fortune 500 companies. *Human Resource Development Quarterly 15,* 4 (2004), 421-448.

17. House, R., Hanges, P., Javidan, M., Dorfman, P. & Gupta, V. *Culture, Leadership and Organizations: The GLOBE Study of 62 Societies.* Sage Publications, Inc., Thousand Oaks, CA, 2004.

18. Hunt, K. E-mentoring: Solving the issues of mentoring across distances. *Development and Learning in Organizations 19,* 5 (2005), 7-10.

19. Hunt, D.M. & Michael, C. Mentorship: A career training and development tool. *Academy of Management Review 8,* 3 (1983), 475-485.

20. Kram, K.E. *Mentoring at Work.* Scott Foresman & Co., Glenview, IL, 1985.

21. Li, C. *Open Leadership: How Social Technology Can Transform the Way You Lead,* Jossey-Bass, San Francisco, CA, 2010.

22. Lublin, J.S. Hunt is on for fresh talent – Cultural flexibility in demand. *Wall Street Journal,* April 11, 2010.

23. Moodian, M. (ed.) *Contemporary Leadership and Intercultural Competence: Exploring the Cross-Cultural Dynamics within Organizations.* Sage Publications, Inc., Thousand Oaks, CA, 2009.

24. Mueller, S. Electronic mentoring as an example for the use of information and communication technology in engineering education. *European Journal of Engineering Education 29,* 1 (2004), 53-63.

25. O'Neill, D.K., Wagner, R. & Gomez, L.M. On-line mentors: Experimenting in science class. *Educational Leadership 54,* 3 (1996), 39-42.

26. Rosser, M.H. & Egan, T.M. The experiences of CEOs in mentoring relationships: A qualitative study. *Proc AHRD,* 2005.

27. Scandura, T.A. Membership and career mobility: An empirical investigation. *Journal of Organizational Behavior 13,* (1992), 169-174.

28. Sobel Lojeski, K. & Reilly, R. *Uniting the Virtual Workforce: Transforming Leadership and Innovation in the Globally Integrated Enterprise.* John Wiley & Sons, Inc., Hoboken, NJ, 2008.

29. Sobel Lojeski, K. *Leading the Virtual Workforce.* John Wiley & Sons, Inc, Hoboken, NJ, 2010.

30. Stead, V. Mentoring: A model for leadership development? *International Journal of Training and Development 9,* 3 (2005), 170-184.

31. Thomas, D. & Inkson, K. *People Skills for Global Business: Cultural Intelligence.* Berrett-Koehler Publishers, Inc., San Francisco, CA, 2003.

32. Vinnicombe, S. & Singh, V. Locks and keys to the boardroom. *Women in Management Review 18,* 6 (2003), 325-333.

33. Zey, M.G. *The Mentor Connection.* Dow Jones-Irwin, Homewood, IL, 1984.

Building a Mexican Startup Culture Over the Weekend

Ruy Cervantes and Bonnie Nardi

Department of Informatics
University of California, Irvine
{ruy, nardi}@ics.uci.edu

ABSTRACT

In Mexico, a grass-roots community of entrepreneurs is working to transform the Internet industry from one that merely provides low value-added services to one that is innovation-based. To do so, it must create a culture that promotes innovation and startup companies. In countries such as China, Taiwan, and Israel a multitude of skilled returnees from Silicon Valley have established a community of startups. But in Mexico, entrepreneurs leverage those few relationships they have with Silicon Valley, and are learning from social media and foreign travels to recreate innovation practices at home. In this paper, we examine how this community of entrepreneurs used the Startup Weekend events to introduce new innovation practices in Mexico. At these events, participants shared their Internet product ideas and formed multidisciplinary teams that raced to create functional prototypes within the weekend. Startup Weekend worked as a catalyst for building a culture of innovation, strengthening the startup community, and in some cases forming startup companies. Participants primed themselves with business and technical knowledge. Entrepreneur communities formed in previous face-to-face events and through social media, served to create an environment of trust and sharing during and after each Startup Weekend event.

ACM Classification Keywords
K.4 COMPUTERS AND SOCIETY; K.4.3 Organizational Impacts

Author Keywords
Entrepreneurship; technological innovation; collaboration; globalization; cultural change; Mexico; Internet industry

General Terms
Human Factors; Management

Permission to make digital or hard copies of all or part of this work for personal or classroom use is granted without fee provided that copies are not made or distributed for profit or commercial advantage and that copies bear this notice and the full citation on the first page. To copy otherwise, or republish, to post on servers or to redistribute to lists, requires prior specific permission and/or a fee.
ICIC'12, March 21–23, 2012, Bengaluru, India.
Copyright 2012 ACM 978-1-4503-0818-2/12/03...$10.00.

INTRODUCTION

Middle-income countries[1] such as China, India, Indonesia, Colombia, Mexico, and Brazil are upgrading their economies from low value-added manufacturing and services to innovation-based economies. Although the majority of the IT and software industry in these countries delivers low value-added services, there is a push to create startup companies that build innovative software products with global impact. Startup companies require a set of practices and skills different from those in service-oriented companies. Developers, designers, marketers, and managers of these companies need to learn how to develop new technology that addresses the needs and sensibilities of global consumers. They must create innovative business models to sell products in global markets, and create scalable organizations to achieve high growth. Local and global networks of innovation are crucial for startups for recruiting people, acquiring specific technical knowledge, and finding potential investors, clients, and partners.

To create an environment where these startup companies can flourish, it is necessary to build an ecology of economic, social, cultural, and material resources that make innovation possible [19]. The startup industries in India and China have benefited from "brain circulation" [14]: large numbers of engineers and managers have returned home to create startups after having worked in Silicon Valley. These returnees transmit the innovation practices learned in the US. They bring home their global connections to develop networks of clients, partners, and investors. But many other middle-income countries such as Indonesia and Mexico lack a substantial diaspora of qualified engineers and managers, and must follow alternative paths to build the conditions needed for high-tech industries.

A community of Internet entrepreneurs in Mexico is building a startup culture, even if it entails transforming the local business culture, by amplifying the few connections they have with Silicon Valley. This community is purposefully introducing innovation practices created in Silicon Valley and elsewhere into the Mexican context. However, innovation practices generated in Silicon Valley do not translate directly to other locations. While globalization links places and allows innovation practices to travel, local actors need to undertake efforts to adapt practices to local contexts [17].

---

[1] World Bank, "How we Classify Countries," accessed Oct/30/2010 http://data.worldbank.org/about/country-classifications

In this paper, we analyze the introduction of Startup Weekend events in Mexico, where aspiring entrepreneurs form teams, build products, and launch startups over a weekend. Introducing Startup Weekends is an emblematic example of the efforts to build a startup culture in Mexico. Initially, a few Mexican entrepreneurs experienced these events in their travels to the United States. These Mexicans realized the potential Startup Weekends had to catalyze a startup culture at home. To organize the first events in Mexico, these entrepreneurs mobilized their local networks. They also used the support of a US-based organization that seeks to promote Startup Weekend across the world. During Startup Weekends participants created entire startups during the weekend. Participants also built a network of like-minded entrepreneurs, and improved their skills. After each event more entrepreneurs committed themselves to develop a startup culture in other Mexican cities. Startup Weekends were quickly reproduced across the country. During Startup Weekends, people experienced deep learning that could only be afforded by being physically present. For entrepreneurs acquiring new innovation practices, face-to-face interaction was crucial to enable the ease of collaboration needed to create startups.

The case we present here was for many Mexicans their first encounter with Silicon Valley's innovation culture and practices. Startup Weekends were designed to allow more Mexicans to very quickly be exposed to the ways of Silicon Valley. During these encounters participants were empowered by the potential of these practices to create new innovations. Leveraging the intensity of face-to-face interactions, the event provided an experience where participants realized the potential these foreign practices had to transform Mexico's Internet industry.

We first describe how Startup Weekend arrived in Mexico. We then analyze the work done in appropriating the practice in the local context. We discuss the impact of the Startup Weekend in the creation of a startup culture in Mexico, such as building a stronger startup community and introducing new ways of collaboration to the entrepreneurs.

Figure 1. Pitching an idea to the audience during the first hours of Startup Weekend Guadalajara.

STARTUP WEEKEND BACKGROUND

The original concept of Startup Weekend was created as a for-profit company in 2007. In 2009 Startup Weekend was transformed into a non-profit organization based in Seattle, US, to "provide the world's premier experiential education for entrepreneurs" [14]. More than 400 events, in close to 200 cities across five continents, had been organized by 2011 [14]. This non-profit organization supports local organizers to create these events globally by getting a trained facilitator for each event and by providing a large network of contacts and IT infrastructure for the event. The Startup Weekend non-profit ensures uniformity of quality of all events, typically with twenty to a hundred participants, and a balanced number of participants with complementary skills: designers, developers, and people with a business profile, including marketing, finance, public relations, and business development. On the first day of the event participants present their business ideas in the form of one-minute pitches in an open microphone session (see Figure 1). The public votes for their favorite ideas. The top ideas are selected, and teams of between three to seven people are formed to work on them. On the second day of the event, teams work to build a product and test its market acceptance. Work is intense and highly collocated. Usually all teammates sit together at the same table (see Figure 2). Many teams work through the night. Business and technical mentors are available throughout the weekend to help the teams (see Figure 3). On the last day, teams present their product pitches to a panel of judges who evaluate the execution, innovation, and market viability of the product. Small, in-kind prizes are often given to winning teams.

Startup Weekend comes to Mexico

Involvement of the existing startup community was crucial for Startup Weekends to become viable in Mexico. The first Startup Weekend in Mexico took place in Chihuahua in November of 2010, but as this effort was isolated from the larger startup community it only had local impact. A few months later Santiago experienced Startup Weekend in Silicon Valley. Santiago was a key leader of the startup community of Mexico, and also a partner at a recently created US venture capital firm focused on Mexican startups. In that Silicon Valley event Santiago teamed up with three Mexican entrepreneurs. This team soon realized the strong potential of Startup Weekend to allow more Mexicans to learn about building a startup in practice. During the spring of 2011, Santiago sent an e-mail to several members of the startup community, recruiting volunteers to organize Startup Weekend events in Mexico City and Guadalajara. Seven people volunteered for Guadalajara and five for Mexico City. Startup Weekends in Mexico were organized with a degree of autonomy from Startup Weekend USA. At the events we observed only three of the organizers and four of the mentors had experienced Startup Weekend in the USA. Mexico City's Startup Weekend facilitator was from the USA. All subsequent events we observed were facilitated by Santiago, who was trained by the US organization to become an official facilitator. The community was able to organize the events independently, leveraging their experience in organizing technical and entrepreneurship events, and the support they had from the rest of the startup community.

While Mexican organizers were able to carry most of the activities, having the backup of Startup Weekend in the US was key to validating the quality of the event in the eyes of participants, local investors invited to the event, and local sponsors. Also, having the facilitators trained by the US organization ensured that there was a consistency between the events in Mexico and those realized in other countries. Participants knew that what they were taking part in was very similar to an event in any other country.

After the initial events in Mexico City and Guadalajara, Startup Weekend expanded across Mexico. Several participants of the first events organized Startup Weekends in their cities of origin including Monterrey, Hermosillo, and Puebla. A follow-up event was organized in Chihuahua. In all events, the entire startup community in Mexico was highly supportive, helping with the diffusion of the events across the country, and attending as judges, mentors, and participants.

RESOURCES TO BUILD STARTUPS IN MEXICO

A series of technologies have accelerated the speed of Internet product development so entire startups can be created over a weekend. Ries [10] developed the concept of "lean startup" to encompass all of these technologies and techniques developed around the world, but especially in Silicon Valley. According to Ries, the rapid creation of startups is possible due to the low cost and high productivity of modern web development frameworks, "cloud" platforms that provide infrastructure to deploy scalable web applications with very little capital investment, Agile software development methodologies [2] that allow the creation of software in rapid iterations, and finally customer-centric processes [4] that make it possible to iteratively discover and develop the market for a new product. A movement within the Internet industry worldwide advocates the use of these techniques for startups to grow faster. Most organizers and participants of Startup Weekend adhere to this lean startup movement.

Aspirational, social, and financial factors have also contributed to making it more attractive and feasible to create a startup in Mexico. First, there is more motivation to build startups because an educated workforce of engineers, programmers, and designers has been exposed to the stories of entrepreneurs who made it big in Silicon Valley, igniting their ambition and imagination to become entrepreneurs in Mexico. These stories travel via the Internet or the movies, or in some cases when Mexicans themselves travel and work at global centers of innovation. Second, there is a network of entrepreneurship and technical communities in Mexico that is building conditions under which creating a startup in Mexico has become more feasible now than it was four or five years ago. These entrepreneurs are creating networks of innovation that are helping individual companies and the entire industry to grow faster. Entrepreneurs in Mexico can find a series of resources in these networks. Technical and entrepreneurship communities allow entrepreneurs to learn more about startups and network with other like-minded professionals. "Hackerspaces" and "coworking spaces" provide low-cost working locations for startups and freelancers and a place for community gatherings. Learning trips to Silicon Valley enable entrepreneurs to soak up the culture of that advanced center of innovation. In online forums entrepreneurs share knowledge and cooperate to get work done. Entrepreneurs are also connected using Twitter and Facebook, discussing the latest news and gossip of the Internet industry. A series of formal and informal events have been crucial resources for building a strong startup community in Mexico. At such events (Startup Weekend among them) entrepreneurs meet face-to-face and new innovation practices are shared. Also, formal organizations such as TechBA (http://techba.org) are supporting high-tech entrepreneurs' entry into international markets by giving them consulting and training. Finally, a new series of venture capital and seed stage funds specializing in the Mexican Internet industry started operations in 2011, including Alta Ventures (http://altaventures.com/), Mexican.vc (http://mexican.vc/), Startup Factory (http://www.startupfactory.com.mx/), and Wayra (http://wayra.org), making it possible for more entrepreneurs to finance their startup company. All of these factors have made it more feasible in recent times for Mexican entrepreneurs to create a startup.

REVIEW OF THE LITERATURE

We situate our work in studies of innovation [5,11,13,14,17,19]. We contribute to this literature by analyzing how the Mexican Internet industry is appropriating a series of global innovation practices. Studies on Silicon Valley carried out by Saxenian [13] and by Brown and Duguid [5] showed how the capacity of individuals and firms to cooperate was related that region's capacity for innovation. Those studies allowed us to contrast the work needed to achieve a culture of cooperation at our location, with a very different social,

Figure 2. Teams worked at the same table to facilitate collaboration. Startup Weekend Mexico City.

cultural, and economic context than that of Silicon Valley. The studies of global networks of innovation [11,14,17] helped us to understand how entrepreneurs built these networks, and to realize that the work needed to create a context for innovation varied with the local conditions. Within this subset, Takhteyev's [17] study of how locality affects technological innovation in software practice was crucial for contrasting the findings of our location. Using the lens of practice, Takhteyev focused on how to understand what Brazilian software developers did and how their doings interacted with ideas and discourse, and the material elements of their practice. In our study, we also use the lens of practice to understand how innovation practices were acquired and recreated by the Mexican startup community. But our study differs from Takhteyev's in that we investigate how an industry seeks to transform itself, purposefully creating holistic changes in its environment and its culture to become more innovative.

A second strand of literature we draw upon is cultural studies of globalization, making us mindful of how many actions within the local context have to be continuously shaped by global resources and constraints [1,3,7]. Appadurai [1] explained how the global flows of people and media move practices and symbols across locations, and how these practices and symbols are constantly appropriated in the new locations. Irani et al. [6] uncovered the work that goes into adopting practices that accommodate better intercultural collaboration in transnational work, but they also suggest the substantial work needed to recreate these practices locally.

From the CSCW literature on collocation we learned that radical collocation dramatically increases the productivity of teams [8,18], and face-to-face interaction has no substitute to create the strong interpersonal connections that make effective work possible [9,10]. These findings allowed us to clarify the power of the Startup Weekend events to achieve great team productivity, and create meaningful, lasting relationships among participants. It is also important to note that Startup Weekend is greatly influenced by Agile software development methodologies, which advise teams to arrange themselves in highly collocated environments in order to achieve greater productivity [15].

METHODS
This research is part of an ethnography of the Internet industry in Mexico from October 2010 to September 2011, focusing on the innovation practices of companies and communities, using a participant-observer approach. The field researcher conducted extensive observations at a range of startups, from recently formed to matured companies. He conducted extensive observations and participated in the activities of a number of entrepreneurship and technical communities, as both attendee and organizer in some of them. This fieldwork allowed us to gain perspective of the impact of the Startup Weekend in the innovation practices and culture of the Mexican Internet industry.

We were able to follow the case of Startup Weekend in Mexico from its introduction to its adoption. We followed the organization leading up to each event, observed the event itself, and interviewed selected people afterwards. The field researcher fully disclosed his identity on all occasions. He participated in the Mexico City and Monterrey events as a regular attendee. He also worked as an organizer in the Guadalajara event, to have a positive and concrete impact in the community, and gain better access to the site. Our extensive field notes reflect the dynamics of the event, including the interactions among team members, mentors, and organizers. To complement field notes we analyzed photos and videos shot at the event. Interviews were conducted with fifteen participants from the Mexico City and Guadalajara events about their motivations, experiences, and personal outcomes. The interviews also included six organizers from Mexico City, Monterrey, Puebla, Chihuahua, and Hermosillo to learn about their motivations and roles. The field researcher is Mexican and a native Spanish speaker. All interviews in Mexico were conducted in Spanish. Two additional interviews were conducted with members of the US Startup Weekend organization to gain insight on their perspective of the Mexico events: the Chief Operations Officer of that organization, and the Mexico City facilitator. These two interviews were conducted in English. All interviews were transcribed and coded. Pseudonyms are used for all participants.

FINDINGS
Startup Weekend in Mexico was an opportunity to change the culture of the country's Internet industry to become more innovative, inspired by some elements of Silicon Valley's culture. These events presented an opportunity to enact a culture of cooperation and innovation that is typical of Silicon Valley, but uncommon in Mexico. Startup Weekend's participants, mentors, and organizers were eager to learn how to create startups. Following the innovation practices proposed by this event, they created their startups cooperating in teams and among teams. The learning and cooperation experiences of participants during the event compelled more people to integrate into the startup community. The event became a symbol of how the Internet industry in Mexico can be transformed.

Cooperation is normal in Startup Weekend Mexico, not in Mexico
To maintain the productive and stimulating nature of the event, Startup Weekend participants had to cooperate in meaningful ways, by sharing their ideas and working in teams with strangers. Organizers and mentors were volunteers who committed a substantial amount of time to the events. A cooperative culture is needed to organize such events. This culture is common in places such as Silicon Valley, but very unusual in the Mexican context. Mexican business people tend to feel that in general it is hard to cooperate with others. This behavior was characterized as

"cangrejismo" by several of the participants (roughly translatable to English as "crab-ism"), where Mexican business people behave like crabs in a bucket, who will pull each other down if someone tries to escape from the bucket, rather than pull each other up to get out of it.

In contrast, the spirit of cooperation fostered by the Startup Weekend events was remarkable for people who observed the event from outside. Sergio, a former high-ranking official of several government economic agencies, came to observe Startup Weekend Guadalajara for a few hours. Sergio noted that he was surprised by how participants, many of them strangers to each other, could quickly start to cooperate in teams that worked to create a new business. Sergio explained that when he was in the ministry, it was hard to make Mexican businessmen cooperate with each other, even when there were clear business opportunities for all parties. The community spirit in Startup Weekend was evident to Kav, a US-based developer who volunteered as Startup Weekend facilitator and ran the Mexico City event, tweeting from his account just before the event ended,

"Mexico City has one of the most important things for a successful startup community: people who support and lift each other up."

Reflecting on Kav's comments, Cesar and Arturo, two of the organizers, commented how the startup community in Mexico was very different from what was happening "outside," pointing out to the street. Cesar explained that while the problem of "cangrejismo" was present in most Mexican industries, it did not impact the startup community in Mexico. The startup community in Mexico was greatly inspired by the culture of Silicon Valley, aiming to create an environment of cooperation. This same environment was recreated during the Startup Weekend events.

Building a culture that is inspired by, not copied from, Silicon Valley

Several members of the startup community in Mexico identified a set of qualities that were conducive to innovation in the Silicon Valley culture. These qualities included a capacity to learn from their failures, ability to collaborate with each other, and being resourceful using whatever they had at hand. This view on Silicon Valley's culture among Mexicans came from their readings, travels to the area, and connections with some American entrepreneurs. These Mexicans wanted to cultivate these qualities of Silicon Valley into their community. They wanted to move away from the risk-averse, distrustful, and un-collaborative culture that was perceived as being dominant in most Mexican businesses.

For the startup community, Startup Weekend events were a new and effective way to allow wider audiences to experience how learning and collaboration enabled innovation. Many participants cooperated with each other, sharing their knowledge and time without looking for an immediate return or reward. Most mentors were ready to patiently share what they knew with participants of all levels of sophistication. For example, Jorge, an experienced consultant at a business accelerator, spent a great deal of his time explaining basic business concepts to any participant who would ask. We observed how teams experienced important problems, for example, not being able to organize to deliver a prototype by the end of the weekend. Participants also learned from these problems and reflected on factors to change on future occasions.

The startup community was very attentive to and reflective of how Startup Weekend was allowing these qualities to become embedded in the culture of their community. We heard and participated in many conversations among organizers, mentors, and participants about Startup Weekend. In these conversations, the community would discuss the effects of Startup Weekend in introducing innovation practices, and changes in the behavior of the community. The community agreed that while they were seeking to cultivate some aspects of Silicon Valley's culture, it was impossible to replicate this culture in Mexico. Rather, they had to adapt that culture to the Mexican context. For instance, Cesar, a mentor and organizer of the event, observed that in Silicon Valley successful entrepreneurs are the role models for upcoming entrepreneurs in the United States. However, the developing startup community in Mexico lacked successful entrepreneurs and had to seek mentoring in alternative ways. For instance, Cesar observed how Carlos, a talented but young entrepreneur, took on a mentoring role during two Startup Weekend events. In more mature startup communities, such as Silicon Valley, Carlos would have been receiving mentorship rather than giving it. But in the Mexican context, Carlos had plenty of experience to share, being a great asset for Startup Weekend participants. Cesar believed that the startup community in Mexico could not wait for role models to emerge, and instead the community had to "share what they had" and "build [the community and their companies] around those experiences."

Learning from lived experiences

Startup Weekend allowed the startup community to create a learning environment where a greater audience could experience a culture of collaboration and innovation. The participants, most of whom came to openly learn and share what they knew, turned the stimulating environment of the event into a learning experience of building startups in practice. These learning experiences were created as participants worked under pressure to create a real product during the weekend, and interacted with their teams, mentors, and fellow participants.

Participants gained a much deeper understanding of startup concepts, as they worked on real-life cases, leveraging the experience of mentors and fellow participants. For instance Omar explained that he "really learned" about the business canvas model, a diagram used to depict the business model of a startup. While Omar was familiar with the concept, working out a realistic scenario for his startup was "completely different." Lengthy conversations went on among the team members in trying to make sense of how the model could be applied to their business situation. Arturo and Cesar, more experienced entrepreneurs, mentored Omar's team to build a realistic business model.

Working on real projects with real teams allowed participants to understand their capacities as entrepreneurs. The event was a learning experience for everyone, even for those working on projects that were not successful. A participant explained that "even for those whose [project] does not turn out well […] they find out what are their weaknesses, what they do not know and they would like to learn in the future." For instance, Manuel's team failed to deliver a functional prototype by the end of the weekend. Manuel explained that despite the problems his team experienced in building a product, the weekend was "a very enriching experience, beyond my expectations to learn about startups." After the event, Manuel explained that he felt much more motivated and confident to continue exploring his opportunities in entrepreneurship.

Participants learned from the difficulties of teamwork. A team in Mexico City, despite having talented individuals, could not reach an agreement on what to build during the weekend and did not finish their prototype. A participant explained that this difficult experience was a chance to learn how "to deal with people, in very life-like situation. Because the majority of times you cannot choose your team, and still you have to get your work done." Another team member from Mexico City learned his lesson. When he participated in Guadalajara's Startup Weekend, he asked his new team use "roman voting" to avoid taking too long on a single decision. Each teammate would vote with their thumbs upwards if they were for or downwards if they were against, and then the team would move ahead with the most popular decision.

Participants developed a greater appreciation for the value of the work of other team members. This was especially true for participants with little experience with multidisciplinary teams, for whom the event was an "eye opener" in understanding the value of such teams. For instance, Angelica, an accountant and member of the Contabot team, had no experience with web development. Angelica explained that "the most important thing" she learned was about "teamwork," experiencing how to coordinate the work of all the members to create a viable product quickly. Angelica was interested in building an Internet business. At the event she understood the value of working with programmers and designers as a core of the team, rather than as hired external consultants.

Empowering participants to transform ideas into products

Startup Weekend was an empowering opportunity where startups could be built in a very short time. An enthusiastic person with a good idea could easily find a team to transform the idea into reality. Expert help from mentors was readily available. If a mentor was required, teams only needed to ask to one of the mentors who were wandering around the rooms. Teams would also ask for the help of other teams, for instance to solve a technical issue or get a quick input on a design.

Even if the organizers and participants of these events were some of the most sophisticated users of Internet technology, they found the face-to-face environment to be much more convenient and efficient for work and cooperation. Being face-to-face allowed participants to be more committed and inspired to work on their project during the entire weekend. Having people with a diverse set of skills and opinions collocated in the same room encouraged informal conversations and collaborations that accelerated the creation of products.

Startup Weekend was instrumental for creating teams comprising complementary skill sets. This was the case for the Contabot team, who after winning the best-product nomination at the Guadalajara event, continued to work full time to create a successful startup. Vladi and Cris, the team members who pitched the idea, came from out of town and did not know anyone at the event. They needed an accountant and a designer. Vladi and Cris networked among the participants on Friday evening. They found the only accountant among the participants and convinced her to join their team. The event also provided an environment to focus on the project. Everyone on the team was sitting next to each other at a big table. Group discussions were frequent but quick, to allow people to work independently but with a clear direction. Team members encouraged each other to stay focused on their work. The help from mentors was beneficial in clarifying certain aspects of their business model. Talking with other teams about their business during recess breaks also served to validate certain aspects of the business. By the end of the weekend, the Contabot team had validated many aspects of their business model. The team realized that they had a promising product that they felt passionate about. As the team bonded well, they continued to work after Startup Weekend. They launched their beta version a couple of months after the event.

To cooperate, ideas must be shared

A key practice in maintaining the environment of cooperation at Startup Weekend was that ideas, especially

Figure 3. A team in Mexico City reviews the business model with a mentor.

business ideas, were shared liberally. This practice is common among the startup communities of Silicon Valley and elsewhere, and the communities related to the Open Source movement. Those who follow this practice believe that the benefits of sharing ideas, namely receiving feedback and gaining more accountability on the idea, outweigh the risk of having the idea stolen. They also believe that most business ideas have little value in themselves. What is valuable is the capacity of the entrepreneur to implement that idea.

Startup Weekend was an opportunity for spreading the practice of sharing ideas. The event organizers and some participants were convinced of the value of sharing ideas, creating an environment where the rest of the participants who were still worried about sharing their ideas would experience the benefits of the practice. Many became convinced by the practice, such as Cristopher, an Internet entrepreneur new to the startup community and participant of the Guadalajara event. Cristopher explained to us that he had a list of ideas he wanted to work on, but being worried about someone stealing the good ones, he pitched the idea that he thought had the least potential. During the event Cristopher experienced how the feedback that team members, mentors, and people from other teams transformed ideas into something "much more bigger […] something different, even to what you have originally conceived." Cristopher told us that if he was to participate in another Startup Weekend he would pitch his "best" idea.

Organizers, mentors, and participants put great care into maintaining the practice of sharing ideas, as they found that this practice allowed them to keep the community collaborative and innovative. Eduardo, an organizer of the Mexico City event, explained that persons who were overly zealous about their ideas would "slow down" the growth of the startup community. An incident involving a participant of the Mexico City event stressed the importance given to the practice. The participant, who pitched an idea of a social network for cats, complained over Facebook when another person in Guadalajara pitched a similar idea. The organizers of the event rushed to answer the person complaining, explaining that is not possible to protect ideas and that there are plenty of existing social networks for pets, and citing the FAQ document of the official Startup Weekend site [18]. In that document it was explained that it was nearly impossible to protect ideas, and that most ideas have been pitched before. This same document explained that "what truly matters is how well you and your team execute the idea" [18]. After this "frustrating" incident, Eduardo explained that was necessary for the organizers to "build an understanding of how things work" among all Startup Weekend participants, implying that all should understand the practice of sharing.

A catalyst for building the startup ecosystem
The startup community in Mexico was actively trying to build a startup "ecosystem." The positive experiences of the participants during Startup Weekend were a catalyst in bringing in more actors. The startup community uses the term "ecosystem" to refer to the network of people, institutions, and resources needed to build startups. This ecosystem includes entrepreneurs from different backgrounds, skills, and levels of experience, as well as private investors, public and private funding institutions, large companies that create infrastructure, and universities. Organizers made an active effort to reach potential actors of this ecosystem who have not interacted previously with the Mexican startup community. The motive of organizers was very explicit: by putting people with a shared interest in startups into a shared activity they would start "exchanging resources between all of them," and ultimately "create a network of people that builds up the [startup] ecosystem." Organizers reached out to invite entrepreneurs, especially those who did not yet belong to the community, using social media, mailing lists, in-person visits to colleges, and traditional media coverage. Organizers also invited investors and government agencies to observe the event. These promotional efforts were well rewarded. For instance the event in Monterrey was organized at a design school, and many designers interacted with members of the startup community of the city. This facilitated more designers becoming integrated into Monterrey's startup community, which lacked people from that background.

Various actors were able to better understand their role within the ecosystem by coming and participating in the event. Manuel, an aspiring entrepreneur who participated in Mexico City, explained that the event was a "mini-ecosystem" where he could clearly "see" how the work of everyone, including his, fitted together to build startups. Charles, a successful investor in the traditional industry and a professor at a top business school, participated in the Mexico City event as a regular attendee with the purpose of understanding startups from the inside. Charles wanted to help aspiring entrepreneurs grow their businesses from the investment side, not only for the economic rewards but also because of his personal conviction about helping people generate wealth in the country. Charles continued participating in other activities of the startup community, including the advisory board of a newly created seed-stage fund for startups. Charles became a link with the investment community in Mexico to start investing in the Internet industry.

Startup Weekend Mexico as symbol of transformation
Startup Weekend made evident the potential of Mexicans to be creative and innovative. Both participants and observers of the event interpreted the experiences of cooperation and innovation during the weekend as a symbol of how the industry was transforming itself. As participants enacted innovation practices that were not typical in Mexico, they demonstrated how a culture of cooperation and collaboration was possible to achieve in the context of the Mexican Internet industry.

Startup Weekend symbolized how the Internet industry could use the power of cooperation to become innovation-based. Gustavo, a mentor for the Monterrey event, said that he was "stunned" to see how participants were ready to create innovative products, cooperate with each other even if that meant they should change their original business ideas, and continue to learn from everyone else. Gustavo found that this mindset was a stark contrast with the "older," risk-averse software companies he knew in Monterrey, which delivered software services only using pre-packaged software solutions produced by foreign software companies. Gustavo explained that the older companies were not interested in continuous education, never attended the relevant courses organized in the city, and saw their programmers as a commodity rather than potential business partners.

Startup Weekend was a symbol of the creativity of the Mexican startup community, as opposed to the destruction created by drug-related violence in Mexico. Monterrey in particular was hit hard by violence. A week before the event, a brutal incident took many innocent lives. Naturally, the city had a bad image in the media. But in a note from a major international technology blog titled "Why Monterrey needed a Startup Weekend," Vlad, one of the Monterrey organizers, explained that the event showed how "there are still a lot of people [in Monterrey] that build instead of destroy." Startup Weekend participants felt that they were part of a change in the city. A few days later, one of the participants of the Monterrey event wrote on Facebook that he was "wearing my SWMTY [Startup Weekend Monterrey] t-shirt :-D So they can notice there are good things about this city…"

Many participants found these events representative of what they stood for, namely a young and ambitious group of people who are able to transform their reality and create with the support of their community. Cesar, from Mexico City, was candid in his final remarks at the Startup Weekend Monterrey. He explained how he was very afraid to come to Monterrey in the first place, but overcame his fears and went to the event.

"And we are here and we are building new things. The reason why this [Startup Weekend] is important, it is because the greatest manifestation of human beings is the capacity to build, it is the capacity of how you can create new things.

And the reason why entrepreneurship, design, and engineering are so fascinating is because all of them are about creating how things will happen. When you combine those three things, this is when you have the power in reality, not [just] in the rhetoric, to change the situations."

Cesar, along with the rest of the startup community, found their startups to be profoundly meaningful. Monterrey and Mexico were experiencing difficult times. Nevertheless, the startup community believed in their ability to transform the reality of their industry, their country, and the world, using the technologies that they were creating and the wealth that their companies could produce.

Startup Weekend symbolized the creative potential of the Mexican startup community in a global context. A few weeks after the Monterrey event, a blog devoted to Mexican startups compared the projects presented in Startup Weekend Monterrey with the projects presented in Tech Crunch Disrupt—a major event in the US presenting upcoming startups from Silicon Valley and elsewhere. The post explained that while the projects presented in both events were comparable in the creativity and timeliness of their concepts, the projects in the US event were much more "developed." The authors of the post explained that while "we're not that far behind in Mexico (specifically Monterrey) at least in idea…We need to improve on implementation." The appeal that the authors made to the community in Mexico showed their conviction that the talent in Mexico is comparable to the best, but that they need to work with dedication to create successful startups.

DISCUSSION

Taktayev [17] argued that while today many developers and entrepreneurs from around the world emigrate and work in global centers of innovation, those who remain at home and have "global dreams" of creating technology innovations, also must create the conditions for these innovations to become viable. To be successful, these entrepreneurs have a double duty: to excel in building up their products and companies, and at same time create an environment where their companies can flourish. To become competitive in the global context of technological innovation, the Mexican startup community needed to create an environment conducive to innovation by making comprehensive changes in their industry. Towards this end, entrepreneurs used Startup Weekend, a global resource, to change local conditions to enable technological innovation.

A global resource to form local conditions

The Mexican startup community used Startup Weekend to build the capacities of aspiring entrepreneurs. Participants had a learning experience while creating startups in an environment akin to Silicon Valley: using lean startup innovation practices, while working in a culture of cooperation and innovation. Working together to achieve a concrete outcome, namely a new startup, participants formed new, meaningful relationships with people with complementary skill sets. In this environment, it made sense to trust one another, to share ideas, to learn, and to work together. Organizers and participants effectively suspended the culture of the "outside," namely the culture attributed to Mexican businesses where the mistrust and lack of learning resemble "cangrejismo." Thus, during the Startup Weekends it was possible to create in Mexico a new environment of cooperation and innovation like in Silicon Valley. Creating such an environment, suspending the negative influences of the local business culture, was an innovation in itself.

To build such an environment, the local organizers had to mobilize a series of social and material resources. First, organizers had to cultivate the disposition of participants to learn a new practice. Then, organizers used the participating members of the startup community to provide an example of sharing and collaborating to the participants new to the community. Finally, the material resources, which included appropriate venues, food, and other materials made all participants feel comfortable with focusing on their learning experience.

The design of the event encouraged participants to learn and cooperate. The event was advertised as a learning experience, attracting participants who were ready to learn something new. The event required participants to share their business ideas, and collaborate with each other in teams to create their products. The face-to-face, collocated environment of the event made it easy to collaborate with teammates, sustained awareness of what other teams were doing, and encouraged informal interactions with all participants.

The already established status of Startup Weekend as a global practice made it easier for organizers to create an event that was appealing to local participants. The support of Startup Weekend US in sponsoring special guests and generating high-quality sponsors helped in convincing local participants to attend. To create a better event in Mexico, organizers used the experiences of other Startup Weekends, including those of the initial group of Mexican entrepreneurs who participated in the events in the US. Finally, the Startup Weekend organization provided valuable human resources, including the facilitator who traveled from the US to the first event in Mexico City, and provided training to Santiago to certify him as an official facilitator.

Creating symbols of the Mexican startup culture

The outcomes of Startup Weekend became a symbol of how the Internet industry in Mexico could be transformed. The concrete products that participants developed during the event highlighted how they had "the power in reality, not [just] in the rhetoric, to change the situations," as Cesar explained during his final remarks at the Monterrey event. The teams worked in an environment of collaboration and innovation, similar to the environment that many startups live in major centers of innovation. Many participants discovered how their own technical skills, used to deliver uncreative services, could be applied to create high value-added products. And the community realized that collectively they had enough creative potential to compete at a global level.

Startup Weekend provided the community with a model to explain their position within the new industry they were aiming to create. Individuals were able to better understand their specific role within the startup ecosystem, since the event was a "mini-ecosystem" where everyone could see how work fitted together to create a startup. The event also provided a model to understand the position of the new industry against Mexico's national reality. The industry's creative potential and their use of the community as a resource, rather than as a liability, was in stark contrast to the destructive forces, like drug trafficking, that loomed in the country. Finally, the event provided a model to locate the new industry in the landscape of the global high-tech industry. The community realized that they had the creative potential to compete at the world stage, although they had to work hard to increase the quality of the implementations of their projects.

The richness in meanings of Startup Weekend came from the experiences that participants had during the event. During the event, participants created an experience of innovation, cooperation, and empowerment, for themselves and each other. Participants experienced product creation as piecemeal, as they personally built the various pieces under an exhausting schedule, next to their teammates and fellow participants. In this tough process of creation, participants learned the limits and capacities of their individual skills, the power of working with teams, and the importance of learning from failures. Those who observed the event from up close, such as Gustavo the mentor, were "stunned" by the capacity of this group of people to create innovative products. In turn, a new generation of the Internet industry was being formed at Startup Weekend. This was a generation ready to work hard and take bold risks to transform Mexico's Internet industry.

The new rules and practices incorporated in Startup Weekend were key elements to create the context in which people could have these meaningful experiences. Under the rules of the event, people were prompted to share ideas, and form teams with others they did not know previously. The new innovation practices from the lean startup movement empowered people to create rapid results. These new rules and practices, along with the members of the startup community who supported the event, allowed participants to discover the creative potential they had as individuals, as teams, and as a community.

Beyond brain circulation

The Mexican case presents a new way of connecting to global networks of innovation. The structure of the network of Mexico's startup community was fundamentally different from the brain circulation pattern featured in India and China [12]. Instead of massive flows of people circulating, as described in the cases presented by Saxenian, a few Mexican entrepreneurs with global connections amplified their global ties to introduce a new practice to the entire startup community, enabling more Mexicans to understand the practices of Silicon Valley. The community was able to amplify the practice of Startup Weekend because they were a strong network, ready to work together. The community leveraged the strong ties that they had built in their online and face-to-face interactions. Santiago, who was part of the initial group that experienced Startup Weekend abroad, quickly assembled a group from the startup community to organize the first events. A series of factors allowed Santiago create this group. First, he had met them before in events organized by the technical and entrepreneurship communities in Mexico. Second, this group had extensive experience in organizing events and strong support among the startup communities across Mexico. Finally, both organizers and participants of the events were primed to innovation practices, by reading international blogs and news sites, and discussing the practices in forums and on Twitter and Facebook.

In turn, Startup Weekend served to expand and strengthen the network of the startup community. During the event participants created meaningful relationships. The powerful experiences participants shared during the event allowed them to know each other on a deeper level. And while only some teams continued to work on their startups beyond the weekend, many people grew closer to the startup community. Participants from other communities found a clear role within the community. Such was the case of Charles, who gained a better understanding of how he could support startups from his investor role. The event also allowed the startup community to expand to more cities. More participants were willing to replicate these events in other cities, as they experienced the power and richness of Startup Weekend.

CONCLUSION

The Mexican startup community deliberately initiated a process of cultural change to make Mexico a more viable place to innovate by acquiring new practices and connecting to global networks of innovation. We argued that Startup Weekend introduced new innovation practices, akin to Silicon Valley, into the Mexican Internet industry. This allowed entrepreneurs to start creating a more innovative and collaborative business culture in Mexico. During the event participants and organizers created an environment of collaboration and innovation, filtering out the distrustful and conservative qualities of Mexican business culture. Startup Weekend became a symbol of the transformation of the Internet industry, and the capacity of the members of this industry to compete at a global stage. This symbol was used as model for participants to understand their individual role within the startup community, and the position of the Mexican industry within the landscape of global technological innovation. The community played out their strengths to create the Silicon Valley-inspired culture they desired. Even without the advantages of brain circulation, Mexicans capitalized on the startup community's strong internal organization, and the aspirations of their members to innovate. Leveraging global innovation practices, including Startup Weekend and the lean startup techniques, this community was creating the conditions it needed to become a more innovate industry.

ACKNOWLEDGMENTS

We thank UC Mexus-CONACYT and Institute for Research on Labor and Employment for the financial support that made this research possible. We thank Nithya Sambasivan and Yong Ming Kow for their thoughtful comments. We thank the startup community in Mexico for their support for us conducting this research and the inspiration that their work brings us.

REFERENCES

1. Appadurai, A. 1996. *Modernity at Large: Cultural Dimensions of Globalization.* Univ of Minnesota Press, 1996.

2. Beck, K., Beedle, M., Bennekum, A.V., et al. 2001. *Agile Manifesto.*

3. Beck, U. 2000. *What Is Globalization?* Wiley-Blackwell.

4. Blank, S.G. 2005. *The Four Steps to the Epiphany.* Cafepress.com.

5. Brown, J.S. and Duguid, P. 2000. *The Social Life of Information.* Harvard Business Press.

6. Irani, L., Dourish, P., and Mazmanian, M. 2010. Shopping for Sharpies in Seattle: Mundane Infrastructures of Transnational Design. *Proc. ICIC 2010.*

7. Iwabuchi, K. 2002. *Recentering Globalization: Popular Culture and Japanese Transnationalism.* Duke University Press Books.

8. Mark, G. 2002. Extreme Collaboration. *Communications of the ACM 45*, 89–93.

9. Nardi, B. and Whittaker, S. 2002. The Place of Face-to-Face Communication in distributed Work. In P. Hinds and S. Kiesler, eds., *Distributed Work.* MIT Press.

10. Nardi, B. 2005. Beyond Bandwidth: Dimensions of Connection in Interpersonal Communication. *JCSCW 14*, 91–130.

11. O'Riain, S. 2000. Net-Working for a Living: Irish Software Developers in the Global Workplace. In *Global Ethnography: Forces, Connections, and Imaginations in a Postmodern World.* University of California Press.

12. Ries, E. 2011. *The Lean Startup: How Today's Entrepreneurs Use Continuous Innovation to Create Radically Successful Businesses.* Crown Business.

13. Saxenian, A. 1996. *Regional Advantage: Culture and Competition in Silicon Valley and Route 128.* Harvard University Press.

14. Saxenian, A. 2007. *The New Argonauts: Regional Advantage in a Global Economy.* Harvard University Press.

15. Shore, J. and Chromatic. 2007. *The Art of Agile Development.* O'Reilly Media.

16. Startup Weekend. 2011. Annual Report.

17. Takhteyev, Y.V. 2009. *Coding Places: Uneven Globalization of Software Work in Rio de Janeiro, Brazil.*

18. Teasley, S., Covi, L., Krishnan, M.S., and Olson, J.S. 2000. How Does Radical Collocation Help a Team Succeed? *Proc. CSCW 2000.*

19. Tuomi, I. 2006 *Networks of Innovation: Change and Meaning in the Age of the Internet.* Oxford University Press.

20. FAQ - Startup Weekend. http://startupweekend.org/about/faq/.

Sources of Miscommunication: Searching for Contextual information in Communication between Chinese and Danish Collaborators

Renée Korver Michan
IT University of Copenhagen
Rued Langgaards Vej 7, DK-2300 Copenhagen S
email address: renee.korver@gmail.com

Pernille Bjørn
IT University of Copenhagen
Rued Langgaards Vej 7, DK-2300 Copenhagen S
email address: pbra@itu.dk

ABSTRACT

Based on an interpretative case study investigating the communication between Danish and Chinese engineers in a global medical engineering company, we identified four key sources of miscommunication: 1) lack of common communication protocols; 2) exclusion of participants; 3) political motives; and 4) misinterpretation of common terms. This paper posits that all four challenges are related to a lack of contextual information due to geographical dislocation and not, as initially assumed, to cultural differences. This finding is essential when investigating cross-cultural communication, because it suggests that we should not forget to examine ordinary communication issues when researching communication between people from different cultural backgrounds.

Author keywords
Virtual teams; distributed collaboration; intercultural collaboration; global engineering; miscommunication.

ACM classification keywords
H.5.3: [Group and Organization Interfaces]: Computer-supported cooperative work;

INTRODUCTION

Despite extensive collaboration across cultures and geography, cross-cultural communication is difficult and prone to miscommunication, disputes, and misunderstandings between collaborators [1, 2]. Particularly in situations where the collaborators do not share common ground and are located in different organizational and national cultures, the risk of miscommunication causing unintended communication breakdowns is high, and communication is prone to failure [3]. Often the approach to sorting out these complexities comes in the form of guidelines for *not* using particular technologies such as email in specific highly sensitive situations [4] and instead turning to more rich media such as video conferencing. Typically it is suggested that discussions of topics with a high risk of misunderstanding should be conducted in synchronous manner such as face-to-face or telephone conversations. However, when people are collaborating across geographical distances and time zones, asynchronous technologies, such as email, are vital to functional collaboration [5]. Moreover, in many cases people cannot know in advance whether a particular subject might turn out to be political or come to concern a high-risk topic. The initiator of an email discussion may believe that he or she is asking a simple, straightforward question, but that question could easily develop into a more complex matter. Geographically distributed collaborators in global engagement cannot refrain from using asynchronous technologies and will thus likely encounter discussions of high-risk issues in such media at some point. It is therefore crucial that we investigate high-risk issues communicated in asynchronous media. In globally distributed collaboration, people depend on asynchronous communication, and in most cases email is their technology of choice.

When investigating cross-cultural communication, we have a tendency to focus on cultural issues and forget that in some situations, where the participants might be geographically located in culturally disparate countries such as China and Denmark, difficulties might be grounded elsewhere. In this paper we carefully investigate the cross-cultural communication between Chinese and Danish employees within a global medical engineering company to determine what the complexities of this communication are and where the sources of miscommunication emerge. Interestingly, we found that the sources of miscommunication were not grounded in the differences between the participants' cultural backgrounds. Instead they were grounded in "ordinary" coordination and communication issues, with no direct link to the participants' country of residence.

In particular, we will focus on the asynchronous correspondence between engineers located in China and

---

Permission to make digital or hard copies of all or part of this work for personal or classroom use is granted without fee provided that copies are not made or distributed for profit or commercial advantage and that copies bear this notice and the full citation on the first page. To copy otherwise, or republish, to post on servers or to redistribute to lists, requires prior specific permission and/or a fee.
ICIC'12, March 21–23, 2012, Bengaluru, India.
Copyright 2012 ACM 978-1-4503-0818-2/12/03...$10.00.

Denmark. We examine in detail their use of email communication at work and illustrate our point by presenting in-depth analysis of one particular email exchange, which ended problematically. Our research question is: Which sources of miscommunication emerge in asynchronous cross-cultural communication between the Chinese and Danish engineers? We identify four key sources of miscommunication: 1) lack of common communication protocols; 2) exclusion of participants; 3) misinterpretation of key concepts; and 4) political motives. Interestingly, none of these sources were linked to the local culture of the participants, as we had initially thought; instead the possible sources of miscommunication were of a more general collaborative nature. This reminds us that although we are interested in cross-cultural communication, we should not forget that sometimes the source of the problem is more basic.

The paper is structured as follows. First we present the related work, and then we introduce our method and the empirical case. Next is the analysis section, where we present the four key sources of miscommunication identified in the empirical data, exemplified by the incident outlined in the empirical case. We then proceed to discuss these findings and end the paper with a conclusion.

RELATED WORK

Collaboration over geographical distance

Collaboration over geographical and temporal distance is an important topic for research on cross-cultural collaboration. Despite this we are still in the early phases of understanding and conceptualizing global interaction and key concepts, such as what culture means for collaboration [6]. Still, we have certain key concepts that researchers generally agree are important when studying communication. Common ground [2] is important for collaborators to share knowledge and know that they have knowledge in common. When investigating cross-cultural communication, we should carefully examine the diverse perspectives of the participants to determine whether they share mutual knowledge on the subject matter or not. Technology and collaboration readiness [3] point to the fact that we must examine whether the participants are ready for the technology as well as for engaging in the collaborative practice. This guides us to examine the participants' perspective on the collaborative practice and use of technology when we investigate their cross-cultural communication. Trust [7] is the foundation for communication, and it tends to be developed based upon one's experience of other people's actions. This means that when we investigate the communication we should try to figure out how the participants experience each others' actions in terms of trust. Awareness and translucence in communication structures [8] are crucial in making collaboration run smoothly. Awareness is about making the collaboration visually available for others to monitor, and translucence is about making participants accountable in their collaboration by making interactions visually available and knowing that others are aware of these interactions.

Asynchronous communication

Email is the most commonly used form of asynchronous technology. It is used widely by participants not only in geographically dispersed situations, but also between people based in the same location – email transcends physical distance [9]. Non-native English speakers have praised email as a more satisfactory medium of communication because of its reviewability and asynchronous nature, which decreases the time pressure on participants [10]. Email has also been found to have negative consequences on office employees' work practices, as email overload can create stress [5]. Several studies have also investigated the diverse use of email [11], for example, in terms of handling coordination [12] or predicting action [13].

In this paper our interest is not to investigate the different aspects of email use. Instead we focus on how geographically distributed Chinese and Danish collaborators use and make sense of email communication and the complexities involved in the process. Here, common ground becomes essential. Creating common ground is a process of grounding [14]. Grounding is the process by which participants together co-construct the meaning of a particular communication instance through gestures and/or spoken words [14]. Common ground is then established when participants gain a shared understanding of the subject matter and know that they share this understanding. Often the grounding process is accomplished by the participants reacting to each others' utterances until they reach a joined understanding. Here, face-to-face situations allow for immediate reaction while the sentences are being uttered, and as such they support the co-construction process. This extra information, which is crucial for the participants' interpretation of each others' utterances, comprises contextual information supporting the development of common ground. In asynchronous communication, access to contextual information is limited. The asynchronous nature of email and low exchange rate of responses further increases the risk of miscommunication.

METHOD

Our investigation of asynchronous communication took form as a larger workplace study [15] in a medical engineering company (MedEng), which has branches all over the world. The workplace approach allowed for in-depth observations combined with detailed interviews of the particular work practices with a focus on collaborative practices and the use of artifacts [16]. Different data material was created in this study, including observation notes, interviews, and a collection of documents. We have chosen to emphasize one particular incident that we observed to illustrate how asynchronous technology can lead to miscommunication. However, it is important to note that the larger empirical study played an essential role in our analysis and interpretation of the data. We will also bring empirical observations from other sources into the analysis.

Table 1: Overview data sources

Data type	Denmark	China
Period	30.08.2010 – 03.11.2010 (in China during 17.10.2010 – 30.10.2010)	
Observation	155 hours (3 days a week for 7 weeks)	80 hours (5 days a week for 2 weeks)
Attended meetings	4 meetings	4 meetings
Formal interviews	8 engineers	5 engineers
Shadowing	-	1 team member, 8 hours
Background research	-	1-day visit to medical factory at InduCH industrial site
Email documentation	Access to copies of email strands where communication breakdowns emerged, selected by participants	

Empirical case: Medical Engineering

Medical Engineering (MedEng) is one of the world's leading consulting and engineering companies within the field of pharma and biotech. With nearly 1700 employees, offices in 12 countries, and a mission to be *"a global company, delivering the best of all worlds to [its] customers"*, MedEng is grounded in collaboration across time zones, geography, and culture. MedEng supports its customers by designing and constructing manufacturing facilities for medical equipment and medical drugs. In this way MedEng does not run manufacturing facilities for itself; instead it provides knowhow and support to its clients' medication manufacturing. Project groups perform the work for clients. Some groups are collocated; others are geographically dispersed. Operating with distributed project teams allows for a pooling of competencies but makes coordinating the efforts and availability of the employees a complex process. MedEng has specialized in designing and adjusting computer systems that support the manufacturing process in factories. The IT developers involved in this work are organized in several departments and at different locations. Two such departments are Optimization and Automation, and they are both geographically dispersed between Denmark and China.

Data sources

Fieldwork was conducted in the Optimization and Automation departments in both Denmark and China. The first author spent in total three days a week over a period of seven weeks at the Danish office and five days a week over a period of two weeks at the Chinese office. She was given access to a large amount of information, which came in the form of emails, internal documents, flyers, folders, the company's intranet, and its official website. Moreover, visiting the Danish office as well as the Chinese office provided the first author with hands-on experience and interactions with the participants. Data was constructed through observation activities and interviews with employees. Extensive field notes were written throughout the whole period.

Data analysis

The data analysis was inspired by the grounded theory approach [17]. Both during and after the empirical study the first author wrote several memos and descriptions of occurrences from the rich data material. This work helped us to reach a data saturation stage, where the first author had a clear, present, and vital understanding of the many complexities of collaborative work practices that had emerged during the empirical study. Through this process we decided to focus on the miscommunications, which occurred during the asynchronous use of email related to project team coordination. While the participants engaged in several email exchanges, we decided to focus on one email strand. In this way the empirical study provided us with an analytical perspective to grasp the tacit, taken-for-granted background assumptions, which emerge in geographically and culturally diverse communication. More precisely, it provided us with a platform, which allowed us to link the different important empirical observations into one coherent entity.

RESULTS: SOURCES OF MISCOMMUNICATION

MedEng has various communication tools available within the organization, which employees use in several different ways. Often-used technologies are a teleconference system, IP phone, and email. Of these, email is the preferred communication technology, especially when coordinating information between several parties. When asked, MedEng employees explained that email was important for their communication because of its asynchronous nature. They had experienced that it was difficult to gather people together at the same time for a synchronous video conference meeting due to the time difference between Denmark and China and people's busy schedules.[1] Moreover, the bad Internet connection in both countries often made it impossible to conduct a video conference meeting.[2] Additionally, the MedEng office in China only had three IP phones (for about 40 employees), and no formal booking system in place which made obtaining them difficult. In addition, the IP phones overtaxed the network, leading to Internet problems for the employees.[3]

---

[1] 20-10-2010 Interview Chinese MedEng engineer

[2] 08-10-2010 Transcription debriefing Danish MedEng project manager, 20-10-2010 Notes meeting Light project

[3] 21-10-2010 Shadowing Chinese MedEng engineer

Email was clearly the preferred communication choice in many cases. Examining the cross-culture email use between the two offices, we found one incident involving Danish managers and Chinese project managers particularly revealing. The following section will describe this incident in more detail. We should reassert that although the focus of the analysis will be on this email incident, other empirical data obtained from MedEng have been included to support, explain, and provide background information essential to interpreting what occurred during this incident.

The correspondence in question comprises a total of 12 emails, which were exchanged between various actors at MedEng from September 30 until October 26, 2010. The incident was initiated by a request from a project manager in Denmark, which at first seemed like a simple yes/no question but soon developed into a frustrating experience for participants. We have detected several sources of miscommunication that caused this frustration.

First challenge: Lack of common communication protocol
Tim is a project manager for the Optimization department in Denmark. He is located at MedEng's office in Denmark but is currently managing a project at a remote industrial site in China (InduCH), where his project team is working in a customer's factory. In other words his team is not geographically located at MedEng's local Chinese office, but rather at the client's factory (InduCH).

Over the last couple of months the project workload has increased, and Tim has experienced a lack of manpower to solve the tasks at hand. On September 30 Tim sends an email to Luna (manager of the Automation department in China) to inquire after extra manpower for his project, to be located at InduCH, for the following three months. Receiving no response from Luna, Tim revisits the topic in a new email one week later, on Wednesday, October 6. Here he inquires after a response to his previous email, and makes it clear that he expects an answer before the weekend. On October 7, Tim receives the following email from Luna:

Hi [Tim]

The reason I didn't reply was I have no 'ready to use' resources, as they are for the moment distributed in projects. (from email correspondence, email 3)

What we see here is that Tim and Luna have different expectations about how to respond to emails. Tim was expecting to receive an answer from Luna, no matter the type of response. Luna, however, interprets that she is not required to respond if she cannot respond positively to the request. This incident might be understood in terms of a difference in culture, that Asian participants typically refrain from giving a negative response and thus might prefer to say "yes," rather than lose face. However, it is important to note that Luna is a Chinese MedEng employee, who has worked under a Danish department manager (living in China) and with Danish colleagues in Denmark for several years, has visited the office in Denmark several times, and even speaks a little Danish.[4] We found that this miscommunication was more grounded in the different expectations from Tim and Luna as individuals, with respect to protocol on how to use email. Tim and Luna expect different types of behaviour in their email communication; they do not share a common communication protocol for email, and MedEng does not have a formal policy on the use of email. Luna might be Chinese and living in China, whereas Tim is Danish; however, these cultural distinctions are not related to their actions. What we see here is a lack of common communication protocol with regard to email, which turned out to be a key source of miscommunication.

Second challenge: Excluding participants After receiving Luna's response Tim is still missing manpower for his project. Luna, however, suggests a solution to the problem in her next email:

I have talked with [Lee], he has a resource who can do the work, depending on the work load and your requirement. Could you talk to him? (from email correspondence, email 3)

Luna explains that she talked directly to Lee (the department manager for the Optimization department in China) and that they had discussed Tim's manpower problem in a face-to-face interaction. Luna and Lee are collocated at the MedEng office in China[5]; thus face-to-face interaction for them is fairly obstruction-free. From Luna's email we also see that she is unclear about the type of competencies and number of hours Tim is requesting. The conditions surrounding Lee's potential spare manpower are not discussed further.

Tim has been excluded from the face-to-face interaction between Lee and Luna, and the result is that he has not had a chance to discuss his manpower requirements directly with Lee. Lee and Tim have not had an opportunity to co-construct a shared meaning about the exact conditions and requirements of the project. This would have resolved the emerging problematic situation, but unfortunately the issue is not resolved at this time.

At the time of the email communication, the resource Lee suggests (Anna) is working full time on another project at the office in China. The resource Tim needs would have to work full time at a remote industrial site in China (InduCH); therefore Anna does not actually meet Tim's requirements. This information could have been exchanged during the face-to-face meeting between Luna and Lee had Tim been included, but because Tim was absent from this meeting, it was not brought up.

---

[4] 15-11-2010 Field notes

[5] 15-11-2010 Field notes

Since Luna and Lee have spoken in person about this subject, they now possess additional contextual information that has not been made available to Tim. It is much easier for people to co-create knowledge when they are collocated. However, because not all the participants in this email communication are collocated, there is a greater need for information to be shared among all parties, so they can use that information and make sense of the messages being exchanged. Sharing all information between all participants is exactly what Lee and Luna remove from the email communication by continuing the discussion off-line and excluding Tim. Since this challenge concerns a change of communication media and therefore a difference in what information is available to the participants involved in the communication, we do not consider this to be a culturally related challenge.

Third challenge: Political motives

After Luna's suggestion, Tim sends Lee an email (copying Greg, manager of the Automation department in Denmark, in the message), inquiring after the possibility of using one of the resources from his department:

Hi [Lee]

[-] we need a PC guy that can do what we first believed [employee at MedEng China] should do – maybe slightly more hands on. [-]

Please let me know my options - but note the work-place is [InduCH] best regards

[Tim] (from email correspondence, email 4)

Instead of emailing Tim an answer to his question, Lee does something that confuses Tim. Lee sends an email to Greg and copies Tim:

Hi Dear [Greg],
Do you have full time resource now from [Optimization IT department] China to help [Tim]?
Old question again, whether we need an extra resource to cover the local needs.
Br. [Lee] (from email correspondence, email 5)

When Tim receives no further answer from Lee, he writes Lee another email three days later and asks him the following:
Hi[Lee],
Not quite sure if I understand you – do you have a free resource[...]? (from email correspondence, email 6)
Tim does not understand why Lee reacts to his request for more manpower by sending an email to Greg in Denmark. Tim therefore sends Lee an email saying that he is "Not quite sure" if he understands Lee, then rephrases and repeats his question to Lee: Does Lee have a free resource available to come to the InduCH site to help him?

Further along in the email strand, Lee revisits the topic. By now Anna has been reallocated to help Tim with his project at the InduCH site. Peter, the Danish project manager to whose project Anna was assigned to on a full-time basis before she was moved to Tim's project, does not agree with Anna's reallocation and complains to his superior, Eric. Eric in turn reacts to Peter's email by sending Lee an email to ask for an explanation for the reallocation. Lee responds to this email as follows:

Hi Dear [Eric],
I was instructed by [Lee's direct superior and Eric's direct superior] that [Greg] is my main contact person regarding the [Optimization IT] off-shoring project, I should follow his order about the [Optimization IT] CN.
Please check the attached email instruction from [Greg], I was following his order.
But, you are right about the situation, I think the only way out to handle the resource conflict is to hire more qualified developers for [Optimization IT] CN.
Br. [Lee] (from email correspondence, email 12)

Lee has attached emails 1 through 8 to prove that he has only done what Greg has told him to do and indicates again that, according to him, more resources should be hired to solve the problem of having more work than manpower.

Looking at the situation from Lee's standpoint, we can find a possible explanation for his reaction to Tim's, and later Eric's email to him and therefore the nature of the miscommunication that has taken place. Optimization as an area of work is still relatively new, and the Optimization department in China was not created until very recently, namely in February 2010. The department started with two employees and later expanded to four employees, and at the time Tim wrote his email requesting an extra resource, the Optimization department was so overworked that that they could have actually used more people themselves. Department manager Lee has foreseen this but cannot hire more people without the approval of his (Danish) superiors. Over the course of several weeks he has used email, IM, and meetings to try and indicate his need, but despite this he has not received approval to hire additional resources.[6]

During an informal conversation he confesses that he is at his wit's end trying to solve the shortage of resources in his Optimization department:

I don't know what to do, [Lee] says. I only have four people. (from Notes 15-19-2010, Field notes)
From Lee's standpoint he has been trying through several channels to draw attention to his concern that the Optimization department is understaffed and that more resources should be hired. Meanwhile Lee's (Danish) colleagues see the lack of resources in a different light.

---

[6] Email correspondence: "weekly news for MIT off-shoring project in the week 40 of 2010", "weekly news for MIT off-shoring project in the week 41 of 2010", "weekly news for MIT off-shoring project in the week 42 of 2010"; 15-11-2010 Field notes.

They are aware that there is enough work now for more people at the Optimization department in China, but what will happen when current projects end?

Right now we have a good manning profile [at the Optimization department in China]. The four employees we have are booked [for projects] until summer next year. We do have a bottleneck in that we could possibly use one, two, three more employees, but that would mean there would be seven people this summer. Will there then be enough projects for those seven men this summer? We do not know, and if we do not have enough work, as it looks now, Optimization IT in Denmark will have to bear that expense [...] Another thing is, will this be the solution that will be suggested every time they [Optimization IT in China] are faced with a milestone, to hire more people.... Will that happen every time? Will that be the solution that is chosen every time? That is not good enough[...]. (from 17-11-2010 Interview with Danish MedEng project manager)

Lee's Danish colleagues would rather not hire more resources because they are uncertain if that would benefit MedEng financially. The whole department is built on having people work on projects for external customers as much as possible. Hours spent on projects for customers are paid by the customer, whereas hours in between projects are paid by MedEng. This has created an unwillingness to hire new employees when there is no certainty of future projects. The department managers in Denmark do not want to be responsible for hiring more resources now if that means those extra people will not have new projects to work on when the current projects end. It is a financial risk that they quite simply are not willing to take.

It now becomes clear why Lee responds to a question from Tim by emailing Greg, the manager for the Automation department and person in charge of off-shoring activities between China and Denmark, with a request to hire more resources. Lee sees Tim's request as a possibility to strengthen his previous requests for permission to hire more people for the department. He uses Tim's request as "evidence" in his case to get permission to hire. Tim, who is not aware of Lee's intentions, is confused by the request, which does not seem relevant to his question, and assumes that Lee must have misunderstood him. When Eric sends his email to Lee asking him for an explanation as to why Anna was reallocated, Lee again uses the occasion to stress the perceived need to hire more people at the Optimization department in China. While some parties are aware of what Lee is trying to accomplish, others are not. This adds confusion to an already confusing communication.

Fourth challenge: Misinterpretation of common terms

The entire incident described above revolves around the allocation of extra manpower for a project at the InduCH site (the client site) in China. Throughout the communication, before and after Anna's reallocation to Tim's project, different terms or concepts are used to refer to the requested manpower, such as: *a guy that could help,* *'ready to used' resource, full time resource, free resource,* and *resource* (from email correspondence, emails 1 through 12). These terms are all used to describe the concept of manpower or resources, but the meaning behind the word "resource" turns out not to be shared among the participants.

When Peter loses his full-time employee Anna to Tim's project, he complains about this to his superior, Eric, who in turn writes to Lee in China:

Dear [Lee]
I have received below message from [Peter], who is surprised to hear that 'his' resources for the [-] project ha[ve] been allocated for other tasks. I presume this is due to a misunderstanding, as the resources have been booked for the [-] project. (from email correspondence, email 11)

In this email Eric indicates what he understands the term resource to mean in the context of project allocation. He does this twice. The first time is when he states that Peter has been very surprised that "his" resource has been reallocated. By using the possessive pronoun "his," he indicates that the resource in question (Anna), was actually considered an employee belonging to Peter's project, and could therefore not be moved. Another indicator for the meaning of the term is given when Eric writes that he assumes the reallocation must be a mistake, as the resource (Anna) has been booked for Peter's project. Again he uses a word indicating a form of possession. By saying that Anna was already "booked" for Peter's project, he indicates that Anna should not have been considered a resource who was available for reassignment to another project.

Anna is the possible resource to be transferred to Tim's project to whom Lee has been referring to in emails. This indicates that he considered her a resource who was suitable for reallocation. From Eric's email, we see that Eric does not agree with this meaning of a resource. This dispute in meaning becomes even clearer when an emergency phone meeting is called between Greg, Lee, and Peter to resolve the issue of Anna's reallocation to Tim's project:

[Peter]: 'Why did [Anna] need to be moved?'
[Lee]: 'I followed [Greg's] instructions.'
[Greg]: 'But I did not specify that it should be [Anna].'
[Lee]: 'With those qualifications it could only be [Anna].'
[Greg]: 'But [Anna] was already assigned to [another] project.' (from 26-10-2010 Meeting resource allocation 2 projects)

Greg, like Eric, indicates that because the resource who was reassigned was already working on another project, she could not be termed a "free resource" and was therefore not available for reallocation. Lee's statements show that he does not share the same meaning of the term "resource." In Lee's understanding Anna did not stop being a resource when she joined Peter's project, and as such she could be reassigned to Tim's project.

A factor that makes creating a shared understanding of common terms even more challenging – and the possibility of certain terms being understood differently by different parties more likely – is that the parties communicating in this collaboration are doing so in a language that is not their mother tongue. During an interview, one of the employees from MedEng's Optimization department in Denmark voices this concern:

[employee MedEng]: then there is I think there is the language of course. When they explain technical issue, there are gaps between how you express and how people understand. So if you don't express in the way they understand, they are lost.
[interviewer]: Are you talking about Danish or Chinese?
[employee MedEng]: English.
[interviewer]: Yeah, but is that true for both the Danes and Chinese?
[employee MedEng]: Well its like if the Dane talk to Chinese he will have to use English. And the way he express English of course will be biased a little bit from Danish. And when the Chinese receive the words, they will have another interpretation. The ideas behind the language will not be 100% transformed if they do this two way translation. (from 11-10-2010 Interview Chinese MedEng intermediate)

As this employee explains, having to communicate using common terms in a language that is not one's own is a complex process. You first must translate the term, then use it and hope that the person you are communicating with will translate the term back to his or her language and end up with about the same concept as the one you started with – and that is only when the term is discussed explicitly. If a common term is used and its meaning has not been discussed explicitly, each party involved in the communication will interpret that term according to his own perception of what it might mean. As we saw in the empirical example, small differences in the interpretation of common terms can have negative consequences for the success of geographically distributed collaboration.

DISCUSSION

We have identified four sources of miscommunication: 1) lack of common communication protocols; 2) exclusion of participants; 3) political motives; and 4) misinterpretation of key concepts. In the following section we will look into the consequences of these issues.

Lack of common communication protocol

The difference in individual communication protocols is often difficult to detect in situations where there are no explicit guidelines from the organizations involved. Still, even if common communication protocols were established formally, there is no guarantee that people would follow them. In the empirical example we saw how Luna and Tim interpreted Luna's inactivity differently. Our example basically illustrates the difficulties in interpreting the meaning of silence [2]. Research has shown that when no explanation is given for a sudden delay in, or lack of response to emails, individuals construe an explanation themselves from what they consider plausible. Yet this explanation is not necessarily correct and could lead to misunderstandings and, in some cases, conflicts. Related to cross-cultural communication, it is important to note that the problem termed as the "meaning of silence" is not grounded in the cultural differences between Asians and Scandinavians, but is instead an example of ordinary collaborative challenges.

Consequences
In the empirical case, a lack of common communication protocol was, unfortunately, never addressed explicitly. The experiences from this incident might influence the manner in which these participants collaborate in the future. The lack of common communication protocol was found to be the first possible source of miscommunication in the asynchronous correspondence between Danish and Chinese engineers in MedEng.

Misinterpretation of a key term

Misunderstanding of key terms in textual asynchronous communication is another possible challenge. The empirical case shows that the effects of this misunderstanding can be substantial, especially when the communicating parties are unaware that they do not share the same understanding. When parties communicate using a term that is commonly used within the organization (for example the term "free resource"), they assume that they all understand that term in the same way. What they fail to take into account is that this term might be used slightly differently depending on the following factors: the position of the employee within the company (project manager vs. department manager), the department he or she works in (Optimization IT vs. Automation), or the office and/or country he or she works and lives in (Denmark vs. China). Schmidt and Bannon [18] argue a similar point, namely that collaborating parties will often each have a different understanding of key terms of communication, which must then be negotiated to create a shared base of knowledge. However, while Schmidt and Bannon talk about a shared knowledge base, our example shows how even the most basic word can create confusion.

Consequences
In misunderstanding a common term, communication partners erroneously assume that they share mutual knowledge. When communicating parties are dispersed, and thus do not regularly work closely together, those parties are much more likely to bring different understandings of terms into the communication. This would suggest that more effort is needed in distributed settings to create mutual knowledge, which in turn will allow communicative parties to collaborate more effectively. This seems to be supported by Cramton [19], who found that distributed collaborators are more likely to differ in cultural, organizational, and contextual backgrounds and thus need to communicate

more about these differences, though they are not skilled at identifying and discussing precisely these issues.

Political motives and excluding participants

While excluding participants and political motives are two separate sources for miscommunication, they are both based upon the complexity that not all parties share the same and equal information. We will first look at these two concepts separately and then discuss how they are connected.

Political motives

The challenge in involving political motivations is related to the challenge concerned with excluding participants. By adding a sentence to the original question (*Old question again, whether we need an extra resource to cover the local needs*), an alternative, political meaning for the message is created, because it is now connected to an "old question": the discussion surrounding the employment of extra resources. The problem with the political strategy in this case is that not all parties are aware of the contextual information needed to make sense of this adjusted version of the message. For Lee the issue of hiring more employees has been something he has been trying to stress to his colleagues for quite some time. Since project manager Tim does not possess this contextual message, he understandably grows confused and tries to re-ground what he meant by his initial request by rephrasing and repeating it [14]. While both Irrmann [20] and Ngwenyama and Lee [21] identified politics as a strategy used in organizations, Schmidt and Bannon [18] found that information to which political issues have been added complicated the meaning-making process for parties involved in the communication. This confirms the findings of this paper that political motives can be a source of miscommunication in email correspondence between Danish and Chinese engineers at MedEng.

Excluding participants

While all participants in our empirical example collectively shared the information written in the email, not all parties were involved in the face-to-face conversation that took place between Lee and Luna. Cramton [2] describes this issue as a "failure of information exchange," which occurs when collaborating parties somehow end up with different information about the issue being discussed. The reason some parties switched to different communication channels is based upon the fact that some of the participants were collocated and the subject matter was possibly not considered suitable for the communication technology including all participants (email) [14]. However, the shift in media excluded certain participants, which created problems.

On the one hand, communication would be most effective if the participants share the same information – and know that they share it – thereby creating a base of mutual knowledge. If, on the other hand, it is more convenient to use another medium, or an issue concerning the communication is not deemed suitable for the medium that is being used, some parties might be tempted to have "outside" communication, either through what they consider to be another, more suitable technology, or face-to-face. Since it is not always possible or convenient to involve all parties in such instances of outside communication, some will automatically no longer share the same information on the communication subject. This is not to say that this source of miscommunication does not occur in collocated situations, but it is more salient in distributed situations because parties do not have many opportunities to (re-)establish mutual knowledge effectively as they do not have the option of meeting spontaneously.

Different but the same

Both of the above challenges are grounded in the issue that not all parties involved in the communication share all the information. The use of a different medium adds *new information* to the communication that is not available for all parties. Involving a political issue in the communication also causes some participants to not have access to the information, but instead of adding new information, one of the participants (in this case Lee) draws *existing information* into the communication. The manpower issue from Tim was linked to the larger discussion of manpower in Automation. Because Lee indicated that the two are related, more background information is now needed to create meaning from the message.

Consequences

Email is a reviewable medium because the messages are recorded in words and can therefore be read over and over again [14]. The reviewability of emails has certain affordances in cross-cultural communication; however, when linked with a face-to-face conversation between some but not all participants on the subject matter, the record of the conversation is lost. The same is true for involving political information in the emails; when Lee does this, he is asking participants to draw on a source of information that is not available to all of them. In effect, these two challenges mean that the information recorded in the emails is no longer enough to decode the messages completely. The entire email conversation loses its reviewability, which in turn has a negative impact on the participants' ability to successfully ground the message that is being conveyed. This seems supported by previous findings [2, 8], which argue that when parties were not included in all information exchanged over email, they were likely to draw wrong or different conclusions from later messages. Thus, creating translucence in communication structure is pertinent for resolving communication breakdowns. In conclusion, both the exclusion of participants and the involvement of political motives were found to be sources of miscommunication.

CONCLUSION

When investigating cross-cultural communication, we have a tendency to focus only on cultural issues and forget that in situations where the participants are geographically located in culturally disparate countries, such as China and Denmark, communication difficulties might be grounded in other types of issues. Initially we asked which sources of miscommunication emerge in asynchronous cross-cultural communication between the Chinese and Danish engineers. Based on the empirical case outlined above we identified the following sources of miscommunication:

1. Lack of common communication protocol
2. Exclusion of participants
3. Involvement of political motives
4. Misinterpretation of a common term

When there was a difference in the common communication protocols of the communicating parties, those parties lacked knowledge of each other's individual communication protocols regarding email. Protocols are formed by the working environment; thus the contextual information related to that environment, which is needed to better align these protocols, might have been available if parties had been collocated. While common terms used in the MedEng offices might be spelled the same, we have seen from the analysis that they are not necessarily used in the same manner across all the offices. A small yet vital difference in how a particular common term was understood caused miscommunication. Again, the source of miscommunication is related to a lack of contextual information, in this case information on the difference between the local uses of a common term (free resource). Using different communication media and involving political motivations in the communication have caused some parties to have access to more information than others, leading those excluded parties to create meaning from different contextual information on the subject.

The problem with lacking contextual information is that this information is often crucial to correctly decode meaning from messages that are communicated between parties. Obtaining this information might be easier if parties are collocated. Parties can walk by and have a discussion at the coffee machine and in doing so readjust the information they share. As one of the Chinese engineers from MedEng describes

They are in Denmark, they are close to the customer, they are close to the project manager, they always got first-hand information. That's kind of the reason when they do something we do not quite understand we assume they have more information than us. That's kind of a problem when we are working. I know they [project managers in Denmark] have a weekly meeting with the client. When [a project manager] talks to the client he posted what happened, but that was first time. Before that, we don't get minute meetings.... maybe [team member in Denmark] cannot get any minutes from [project manager] but maybe they would drop by the coffee machine and talk a few minutes and then they got information. We [team members in China] cannot get that information. The only thing we can do is guess, from their actions, maybe they know something. (from 29-10-2010 Interview with Chinese MedEng engineer)

This quote was made in direct connection with a lack of contextual information, which several of the Chinese employees located in China experience. When parties communicate, they either assume they share the same background knowledge on the subject under discussion, or they create that background from the most plausible of possibilities for that particular context. As we have seen from the challenges discussed in this paper, a lack of contextual information can cause a number of hindrances to the success of communication between geographically distributed parties.

A surprising factor in the outcome of the data collected through our fieldwork was not the fact that distributed communication was prone to miscommunication, but that the source of this miscommunication was not necessarily based on cultural differences. From several interviews and observations, it became clear that even the employees of MedEng did not feel cultural differences were crucial to communicative problems. This is not to say that culture did not play any role whatsoever, but rather it played a much smaller role than these researchers had expected at the outset of this study.

This paper paves the way for future research investigating cross-cultural communication and new technologies that could support such endeavours beneficially. This research could focus on how to communicate contextual information. It may give new insight into contextual information sharing, and from there strategies may be developed to help improve current practices in globally distributed collaborative practices across geographical, temporal, and cultural boundaries.

ACKNOWLEDGeMENTS

Thanks should be given to MedEng for participating in this study and in particular to all the employees at both the Danish and the Chinese offices, who were very kind and open about their challenges in collaborating across cultures and geographical distance.

REFERENCES

1. Jarvenpaa, S.L. and D.E. Leidner, *Communication and Trust in Global Virtual Teams*. Organization Science, 1999. **10**(6): p. 791-815.

2. Cramton, C.D., *The Mutual Knowledge Problem and its Consequences for Dispersed Collaboration*. Organization Science, 2001. **12**(3): p. 346-371.

3. Olson, G.M. and J.S. Olson, *Distance Matters*. Human-Computer Interaction, 2000. **15**: p. 139-178.

4. Duarte, D. and N. Snyder, *Mastering virtual teams: Strategies, tools, and technoques that succeed* 2006, San Francisco, California: John Wiles & Sons Inc.

5. Dabbish, L. and R. Kraut, *Email overload at work: An analysis of factors associated with email strain*, in *CSCW* 2006, ACM: Banff, Alberta, Canada. p. 431-440.

6. Hinds, P., et al., *What's up with culture?*, in *Panel at CSCW* 2010: Savannah, Georgia, USA.

7. Jarvenpaa, S.L., K. Knoll, and D.E. Leidner, *Is Anybody out there? Antecedents of Trust in Global Virtual Teams.* Journal of Management Information Systems, 1998. **14**(4): p. 29-64.

8. Bjørn, P. and O. Ngwenyama, *Virtual Team Collaboration: Building Shared Meaning, Resolving Breakdowns and Creating Translucence.* Information Systems Journal, 2009. **19**(3): p. 227-253.

9. Hollan, J. and S. Stornetta, *Beyond being there*, in *CHI* 1992, ACM. p. 119-125.

10. Ishii, H., *Cross-cultural communication and CSCW*, in *Global networks: Computers and international communication*, L. Harasim, Editor 1993, MIT Press. p. 143-152.

11. Mackay, W., *Diversity in the use of electronic mail: A preliminary inquiry.* ACM Transactions on Information Systems, 1988. **6**(4): p. 308-397.

12. Bellotti, V., et al., *Quality versus quantity: Email-centrix task management and its relation with overload.* Human computer interaction, 2005. **20**: p. 89-138.

13. Dabbish, L., et al., *Understanding email use: Predicting action on message*, in *Computer human interaction (CHI)* 2005, ACM: Portland, Oregon, USA.

14. Clark, H. and S. Brennan, *Grounding in Communication*, in *Perspectives on Social Shared Cognition*, L. Resnick, J. Levine, and S. Teasley, Editors. 1991, American Psychological Association: Washington DC. p. 127-149.

15. Randall, D., R. Harper, and M. Rouncefield, *Fieldwork for design: Theory and practice* 2007, London: Springer.

16. Luff, P., J. Hindmarch, and C. Heath, eds. *Workplace studies: Recovering work practice and informing system design.* 2000, Cambridge University Press: Cambridge. 283.

17. Glaser, B.G. and A.L. Strauss, *The Discovery of Grounded Theory: Strategies for Qualitative Research* 1967, New York: Aldine De Gruyter.

18. Schmidt, K. and L. Bannon, *Taking CSCW Seriously: Supporting Articulation Work.* Computer Supported Cooperative Work (CSCW): An International Journal, 1992. **1**(1-2): p. 7-40.

19. Cramton, C.D. and P. Hinds, *Subgroup dynamics in internationally distributed teams: Ethnocentrism or cross-national learning.* Research in Organizational Behavior, 2005. **26**: p. 233-265.

20. Irrmann, O., *Culture as communication: A theory of perception and dissonance in intercultural interaction*, in *International conference on Intercultural communication (ICIC)* 2010, ACM: Copenhagen. p. 87-92.

21. Ngwenyama, O.K. and A.S. Lee, *Communication Richness in Electronic Mail: Critical Social Theory and the Contextuality of Meaning.* MIS Quarterly, 1997. **21**(2): p. 145-167.

Bridging Cultures via an Online Business Simulation over Different Time Zones

Iris Fischlmayr
Johannes Kepler University
Altenbergerstrasse 69
4040 Linz, Austria
Iris.fischlmayr@jku.at
+43/732/2468/9125

ABSTRACT

The handling of culture in virtual multicultural teams is crucial for successful collaboration. As little is known about the different kinds and ways of its occurrence, individual participant reflections analyzed with Grounded Theory reveals its multifaceted influence directly in the field. The article introduces the online business simulation VIBu RealGame™, which helps to overcome cultural differences as well as to acquire skills required for virtual multicultural teamwork. This form of experiential learning is unique in a way that it provides the opportunity to undergo the challenges of time zone coordination, virtual communication and collaboration, and furthermore allows applying and reflecting about the acquired skills immediately.

Author Keywords
Online business simulation; time zones; multicultural virtual teams; cultural differences; experiential learning

ACM Classification Keywords
H.5.m Information interfaces and presentation (e.g., HCI): Miscellaneous.

General Terms
Human Factors; Design; Management.

INTRODUCTION

In the last decades the business world has at the same time become more international and more virtual. Working together over different cultures and time zones with the support of electronic media has turned into a daily issue in globally operating companies. In many cases, virtual teams are established in order to fulfill tasks and projects.

For the purpose of preparing students for their future jobs, business schools incorporate elements in their curricula, which cover issues such as virtual collaboration, multicultural teamwork, online project management etc. Culture resp. cultural differences are often focused in these programs.

This article shall introduce an online business simulation that allows at the same time to become sensitive for virtual multicultural teamwork and its challenges, to gain awareness about the influence of culture on certain aspects and to acquire skills needed in this form of collaboration.

The main aims in this article are to highlight the **occurrence of culture in virtual collaboration.** Furthermore, it shall be shown **how the business simulation VIBu RealGame™ supports bridging cultures and time zones** rather than focusing on differences. This serves for a better understanding about the role of culture in virtual multicultural teams and provides a concrete approach how to create cultural synergy.

THE ROLE OF CULTURE IN VIRTUAL MULTICULTURAL COLLABORATION

The fact that culture plays a role in teams with multicultural composition has been issue of many studies (e.g. [32], [6]). The same if true for teams acting virtually (e.g. [2], [30], [23]). Results vary in the opinion of whether culture has a weakening [32] or accelerating [26], [8], [2] influence on team performance. Bachmann [2] rather speaks about diversity than cultural differences and comprises – besides culture – also aspects such as gender, age, organizational or professional background etc. This diversity is at the same time a great potential for qualitative results and innovative problem solutions as well as a huge challenge, especially concerning cultural differences [2].

But how can these potentials be supported, provoked and increased, how can synergy be created instead of focusing on hindrances, differences and process losses?

In order to answer this question, we need to have a closer look at the role and influence of culture in virtual collaboration. Although the overall influence of the construct "culture" (or diversity) is observed in many studies related to virtual collaboration, it is limited to single aspects such as trust [16], [28], group cohesion [2], communication and collaboration [17] and similar ones, but is not dealt with from a holistic point of view.

But in which form does culture occur? In which way is it perceived? Does it have a direct or rather indirect influence? Or is it even unconscious?

The following qualitative study brings some light into the field by finding out more about the role and influence of culture in virtual collaboration.

METHOD

Individual reflections reporting the experiences, learning, critical incidents etc. of international students´ virtual team projects (Rem.: the virtual project in question, namely VIBu RealGame™ will be described later on in the article) have been used for qualitative research. 218 of those essays have been analyzed with the help of Grounded Theory. This method is especially appropriate for complex social phenomena where little is known about. Thus, it rather looks at primary data "directly in the field" instead of formulating and testing hypotheses based on existing assumptions [9].

The central characteristic of Grounded Theory is constant comparison. For the "inventors" of that method [9], this means as a first step, finding out key words and crucial topics in the broad qualitative material (that should be collected as "unguided" as possible, thus without direct and concrete questions). This is done by line-by-line analysis in most of the cases. "Codes" (key words) that are related to each other and occur under the notion of one and the same topic, are subsumed under one category (broader issue). The aim is to find relationships between those concepts and categories in order to know more about reasons, consequences or factors having influence on that particular topic. Reading one text after the next means adding new codes and categories all the time and at the same time comparing them to the already existing ones. As soon as no new codes are emerging and no more changes are being carried out, so-called "theoretical saturation" (as required by Grounded Theory) is reached [10]. With the help of that procedure a systematic development of theory and empirical data can be guaranteed [10], [22]. Thus, Grounded Theory is especially applicable when little is known about complex social phenomena. The resulting theory might later on serve as a basis for further studies in the field.

But what could be found in particular in the essays cultural aspects?

RESULTS

Culture as such

Culture as such was seldom mentioned in the reflective essays but in some cases, students reported about different working styles of team members with different cultural backgrounds (e.g. relationship oriented cultures did some small talk beforehand in order to establish trust; highly task oriented cultures such as the US or Germany divided tasks into clear packages, set deadlines and did not lose a single minute for personal conversations), about their idea of the purpose of team meetings (is it for work or relationship building and team cohesion?), or about different ways of communication (e.g. lots of small talk; very direct and clear sentences; e-mails without any personal line, etc.). Especially students having had courses on cultural sensitivity or cross-cultural management before referred to particular cultural dimensions (e.g. [11], [14], [31]) or expressions stemming from culture-related knowledge (e.g. *"I see myself as polychromic and US students as monochromic "* or „*Maybe they did not want me to lose face"*). In single cases, statements about culture ended up in pure stereotyping such as *"The Americans are so pushy."*, *"The Spaniards talk and talk and only care about relationships."* or *"Typically, the French always have to be the leaders."* In contrast, some explicitly mentioned the non-influence of culture, *"Culture is no issue; in virtual [...] teams it is **never** an issue"*.

Generally, participants showed the tendency to ascribe differences or difficulties to cultural aspects than to personality of single team members. This is especially astonishing with regards to attribution theory: in the perception of persons we tend to make quick and secure attributions about these persons, the more obvious some personal characteristics are. When it comes to our own person, we rather try to find reasons for our behavior or for the results of our behavior in the environment (e.g. bad luck, unfair boss, etc.) but we ascribe it to their personal characteristics and personality when it comes about perceiving others [20]. Nevertheless, some students have also mentioned personality as a reason for the specific behavior of a person in the project. Maybe Hardin et al.´s [12] findings give an explanation in their study by linking performance in virtual teams to both culture and efficacy. They have found that when referred to individuals and their performance in virtual teams, members from individualistic cultures show more self-efficacy (i.e. confidence in one´s ability) than members from collectivistic cultures. In contrast, as soon as the team is the point of reference, people from collectivistic cultures showed more efficacy (in that case efficacy means believing in the ability of the team) than the ones from the individualistic cultures.

Hidden influence of culture

In even more essays, culture was not mentioned per se but its influence came out in a hidden form between the lines, e.g. in behavior, communication, attitudes etc.

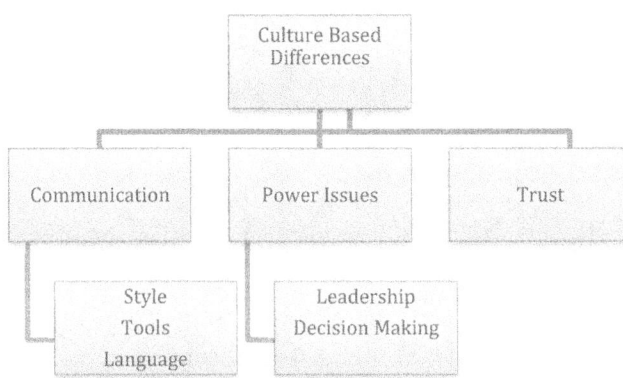

Figure 1: Culture-based differences

First and foremost, the topic of **communication** turned out to be culture-based. There, (1) the different communication styles *"They did not want to make small talk but they only wanted to talk about business and the work we had to do."*, (2) the preference for certain communication tools *"We tried Skype but the Finns were not interested. Thus, we had to communicate with them by e-mail, it was much more difficult."*, and (3) language skills, i.e. natives versus non-natives *"I think there was some in participation in our group as some members spoke English better than the others."* were mentioned. Communication during the game took place via Skype, (Skype) chat and e-mail. Interestingly, culture-based preferences on the use of different communication media could be stated: the Finnish participants, for example showed a clear priority on e-mail or chat in comparison to Skype. Their argument based on having more time for reflection and thinking before reacting. In one of the student's essays the following statement about the Finns could be found: *"The Finnish are supposed not to like talking – email is a good alternative where they do not have to talk."* Even bargaining and negotiating was done via Skype chat or e-mail. The Austrians, the Americans, the Australians, and several others, on the contrary, relied on Skype, talked a lot, showed enthusiasm and were happy to use ICT in a university course officially. An explanation might be the concept of Finnish quietude: Berry et al. [3] dig deeper into the stereotype of the silent Finns and have come to the conclusion that while in Western cultures basically a "preoccupation with talk [is] presumed", it is the "preoccupation with quietude" in Finland [3, p. 272]. Thus, two different approaches clash: the "absence of silence" versus the "absence of speech" [3, p. 272] – a fact that is majorly not known.

Literature supports the influence of culture on communication in virtual teams as for example in Kayworth & Leidner's [17] study more than 50% of their virtual team members in question reported an enormous influence of cultural differences on both communication and collaboration. Reasons for that observation are that communication is the key element for relationship building, information exchange and trust development [33]. Team members even see cultural and in particular culture-related communication and language differences as resulting in miscommunication. Consequently, this leads to risky trust levels, lower team cohesion and decreased team identity [29]. Especially the "slower pace of nonnative speakers´ communication, in particular when using synchronous communication channels" [29, p. 681] was seen as most critical. For Chen et al. [5] language is even stated to influence the team success and performance significantly.

As a further culture-based difference, **power issues** were found, amongst them leadership resp. the need and wish to have a leader. Here, some cultures have clear preferences for strong, autocratic leaders (such as France, US, Spain) „*The only thing why I participated was that we had an autocratic leader.*" or *"A leader is important for projects that need to be structured. One person has to be responsible for the decisions. It is impossible to make group decisions with very big teams."* Others (such as Sweden) made a clear decision against a leader and did not see any need for having one *"There has not been any leader because of our equal knowledge about the matter and small size of the group."*

The wish for having a leader can be regarded as highly culture-specific. Hofstede´s power distance [14], for example, can be seen as influencing the need for a strong authority, especially in high power distance cultures such as the US, France or Spain, referring to the observations from the essays. At the same time, members from those cultures did not want to have power on their own. Kirkman et al. [18] who support this relation, add that societies which emphasize status (resp. power) differences and show at the same time great respect for older members of the society, view strong, autocratic leaders necessary for the performance of a team.

Decision-making was another topic where cultural differences occurred. While some cultures such as Sweden are striving for consensus and democratic decisions, it was stated by the students, that „*Western cultures decide quickly, easily and in cooperation, the Eastern European countries have difficulty in using their skills even if they have a good education.*", or *"The US students decided quickly, the French analyzed much."*

The influence of culture on decision-making is clearly supported by the literature although not many researchers have put their emphasis on that issue. The above stated tendencies might be related to both the concept of task- versus relationship-orientation [1] or the disposition to take risks as reflected in Hofstede´s [14] uncertainty avoidance.

Last but not least, **trust** is highly culture-based. Here, only the accumulation of all the essays paired with certain line-by-line reading allowed finding patterns. Neither was trust mentioned explicitly very often, nor was there any reference to cultural differences. But statements such as *"After we had played a while we started to make decisions independently."* Or *"I personally like to know the people who I negotiate with."* gave more information about the trust topic.

When it comes to literature about cultural differences and trust, authors seldom link culture or cultural dimensions per se to this topic. If they do, (e.g. [16], [7]), the concept of individualism and collectivism is often taken as a point of reference: while there is a positive relationship between trust and collectivistic cultures, there is a negative one in individualistic ones. The reason, in particular in the first case, is the high belief in collective interests, and common values and beliefs. Hofstede [15] who has originally defined these concepts, sees a collectivistic orientation in a group as enough to serve as basis for high trust levels as in those groups, the moral involvement is said to be higher than in individualistic ones.

AN ONLINE BUSINESS SIMULATION TO UNITE DIFFERENT CULTURES AND TIME ZONES?

The knowledge about the occurrence and influence of culture in virtual collaboration provided a basis for developing a training concept around an online business simulation, which addresses these topics and tries at the same time to enhance building bridges between cultures rather than to focus on cultural differences. The following paragraphs give an overview on the simulation:

VIBu RealGame™

VIBu – Virtual International Business – is the name of a training concept, which aims at making participants familiar with collaborating in a virtual environment from wherever they are located. Based on the online business simulation RealGame™, participants are assigned to multicultural virtual teams (at a minimum 6 persons in size) in order to represent a company. Before the first session, the single teams receive the task to organize their team´s time shifts, as the simulation runs over 18 hours and as the participants typically come from different time zones. Information about RealGame™ is only given about the main scope of the companies and the basics about the production they conduct (e.g. components needed for their products, dependencies from other companies etc.). Given the complexity of the simulation, the lack of information and the uncertainty that go hand in hand, shall enforce communication and collaboration amongst the team members. As the different companies are either competing with or depending on each other in typical business processes of an internationally operating production company, interaction and negotiation is required throughout the whole simulation. All communication is taking place via ICT, mainly Skype and Skype chat.

During the simulation, the participants have to make decisions continuously and on a real-time basis. They are informed about their business results regularly. Additionally, they receive information on potential reasons and backgrounds for their business figures. Based on that knowledge, they are asked to reflect about the simulation, their learning, conflicts, critical incidents etc. individually after the simulation. In form of a reflective essay, each participant has to write three to five pages on his/her own experience from the game as well as observed group processes. After the first session, each team has to analyze the team processes and the performance of their company in form of two SWOT (strengths, weaknesses, opportunities, threats) analyses, one about the team collaboration, and the second one about the company´s performance. One more part of the assignment is to formulate strategies for the next session. One or two weeks later, a second 18-hour-simulation takes place in the same setting than the first one. This allows participants to use and reflect about their acquired knowledge and skills immediately. Again, individual reflective essays after the second session support their learning. The focus there is also on a linkage between theoretical concepts learnt in class and the simulation as well as on their individual learning experience. Depending on the course format VIBu is part of, students might have another face-to-face class at each location, where in a detailed debriefing session, individual and collaborative learning is discussed intensively.

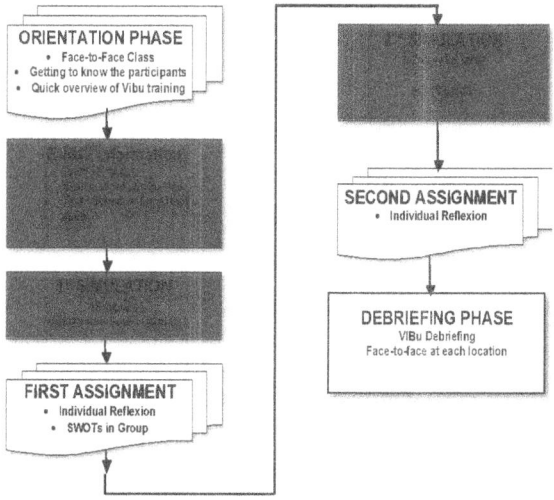

Figure 2: Structure of the Online Simulation Training VIBu

A particular strength of VIBu RealGame™ is its flexible use in different types of classes, as it is for example implemented in courses on cross cultural management, international negotiations, multicultural team work, virtual collaboration or international business. It differs from similar business simulations as the real-time basis forces the participants to make continuous decisions under an extremely stressful and time-urgent environment. The clock speed accelerates parallel to increasing experience in playing the game. This setting allows having insight into the very complex business processes of an internationally operating production company.

VIBu RealGame™ in Action

Typically, after receiving the names and e-mails of their internationally distributed teammates, the single teams (8-10 participants) have to make their shift plans for an 18-hour simulation as a first task. The only requirement given is that each participant has to be online resp. has to actively participate in the simulation for 6 hours, either in one or in distributed blocks. Scheduling the virtual shifts over the time zones is a major challenge for most of the students. Almost all of them totally underestimate the complexity of that collaborative task. Here, they also have to overcome different approaches due to cultural backgrounds for the first time as especially relationship-oriented cultures are first and foremost not schedule or task driven and often do not respond or do not take their shift hours seriously. They rather have a tendency to remain flexible and participate "whenever there is time".

The same is true for the change in shifts during the game: acquired knowledge and recommendations for handling the simulation has to be transferred to the next shift (i.e. in most cases also to the next time zone) in any form. Besides simple shift overlaps, many teams usually find creative and innovative ways ensuring a smooth flow of information, e.g. by documenting decisions and agreements via Google-Docs or by applying online project management tools. Here again, task-oriented cultures show more structured and organized approaches than relationship oriented ones which sometimes fail in handing over their shifts to the next time zone resp. subteam.

During the simulation, students face challenges concerning different topics inherent to virtual team collaboration, such as trust, technical problems, team process hindrances, language barriers, cultural differences, communication problems and misunderstandings, leadership issues etc. These topics are also reflected in the essays afterwards. Students mostly provide an honest and critical point of view about the simulation and the team processes. The reflections help them to become aware of factors influencing virtual teamwork, to acquire sensitivity for one´s own behavior and reactions in the virtual environment, and to get a feeling for the team members coming from different cultural backgrounds.

On a group level, the students evaluate the SWOTs resp. the collaboration in between the two sessions positively. The reflection on the teams resp. companies and the processes going on there help them to create an awareness of the topic "virtual team collaboration" as well. Furthermore, these considerations support strategy building for the second simulation round.

The second round is more or less trying out different strategies in order to gain competitive advantages. As the rules of the simulation and the environment are known by then, trying out different strategies is typically the main topic. But still, obstacles in the team processes might occur, new challenges often come up and students are sometimes fighting with unknown problems in the simulation (Remark: the tutors do add some challenges to the game in the second round). The reflective essays after the second round typically support that idea.

Pedagogical Approach

In VIBu RealGame™ the participants are trained to cope with demands regarding cultural differences, virtual and multicultural communication, coordination amongst different cultures and time zones, team processes etc. Particularly these topics have been found to be highly relevant in virtual teams resp. virtual team training by different researchers [4], [13], [27]. Specifically cultural sensitivity is said to play a crucial role in virtual multicultural teams. Besides acquiring theoretical knowledge about those topics, the participants should be confronted with the challenges related to them in practice. By involving them in a rather intense, stressful simulation, they are likely to experience most of those topics. A sort of competitive situation as well as a mid-term perspective (i.e. by continuing the simulation in a second round) forces them in a certain way to find solutions for upcoming problems as well. The feelings, emotions and stressful situations they experience during these hours make them aware of "real" issues in virtual collaboration. Not only do they acquire awareness but also strategies how to cope with those challenges in practice. Experiencing these challenges with personal involvement allows being aware of one´s own behavior better and ensuring learning.

VIBu RealGame™ bases on an experiential learning approach, which goes back to Jung, Rogers, Lewin and other psychologists. In his holistic learning model he sees learning as a cycle where concrete experience is followed by data collection and participant observation related to that experience. The analysis of these data is given as feedback to the participants in order to be taken into account in their behavior. The approach follows these main paradigms [19]:

1. Learning is a process, not a result: students must be involved in a process which accelerates their learning
2. Learning is re-learning: a topic that has been touched once, is reflected, tested, repeated etc.
3. Learning is a holistic process for a better adaptation to the world: thinking, feeling, perceiving, behaving
4. Learning needs conflicts, difficulties, differences
5. Learning is a result of transactions between persons and their environment
6. Learning is gaining knowledge with acquiring social knowledge as a besides-product. It is not the transfer of stable ideas.

Thus, learning is a process where knowledge is generated by transforming experiences.

Especially intercultural competence requires all three levels of learning: cognitive, behavioral and emotional. As intercultural situations are often linked to emotions (positive or negative ones), learning is encouraged.

Involving participants from different contexts such as different universities can enforce the quality and intensity of cultural learning as cultural aspects are easier to recognize – in particular when they are not expected. On the other hand, conflict is also capable of making people conscious of something. As diversity is likely to produce conflicts, learning as also enhanced.

From the above description of the VIBu RealGame™ it can easily be seen, that the simulation covers all the above-mentioned points. It provides a great learning base for holistic experiential learning. The challenges and conflicts during the simulation make people conscious about factors playing a role in virtual collaboration and involve emotions. The common aim, the collaboration as well as the coordination regarding shifts or knowledge transfer serve as bridges between the different cultures.

Summarized, the educational aims are manifold:

- Participants shall acquire a holistic perspective on an internationally operating production company resp. an integrated corporate thinking by experiencing topics such as stock keeping, inventory calculation, delivery problems of ordered goods, time lags in international trade and their consequences on company performance.
- By being confronted with challenges from cultural aspects, geographical dispersion and time zone differences, team members shall learn how to cope with the importance for communication, cooperation, coordination and teamwork in virtual multicultural settings.
- Awareness about several topics resp. potentially occurring challenges is raised. Students shall get a feeling of what is or might be playing a role in virtual collaboration. Additionally, they should create an understanding on how the influence of culture differs in virtual and face-to-face teams.
- Participants acquire a feeling of how ICT might support the bridging between cultures, put the challenge of cultural differences and create an environment where common goals, commitment and coherence count more than divergence.

Learning from and with VIBu RealGame™

But still the question remains whether students have really acquired skills and competences useful for virtual collaboration? And how can learning be made obvious? Does the simulation serve the purpose to build a bridge between cultures?

An in-depth reflection of the simulation is a main part of the simulation and supports learning. The reflection is done step-wise in order to ensure intense considerations on all levels:

1. Individual reflection in form of written essays
2. Group reflection in form of SWOT analysis in the teams
3. Individual reflection in form of written essays
4. Classroom reflection in form of discussion, exchange of experiences and directed questions by the moderator/teacher

The different levels allow enlarging the insights in each step: individual experiences are broadened by reports from different group members. On a group level, discussions from and with all groups help to learn from each other as well.

First of all, the self-assessment in the reflective essays provides a first insight about the participants' own estimation of their learning. Reading and analyzing the texts line-by-line also allows getting an idea about how deep the reflection is done by each individual, to which extent critical incidents or challenges are reflected and commented, or how far certain understanding is generated. The same is true for the group level: from the single points that are seen as strengths, weaknesses, opportunities or threats one can easily guess the level of reflection as well as the level of consciousness about different influential topics. In the second simulation round, observations and the analysis of Skype chats provide valuable insights.

Above all, the learning can be seen in changed patterns in terms of planning resp. strategy, communication, role distribution, communication and coordination. Most probably, the intense reflections are the reason for these changes. Reading the essays after the second simulation round, it becomes clear in the majority of cases that students have profited from the experience and have incorporated the learning. This can be seen by direct statements referring to the learning, for example *"In the beginning I was a bit skeptical about it but it was really fun and a nice and fruitful experience. Compared to other "normal" courses at university I would say that one profits the most for the real business life from such simulations. Of course I would have been happier if we could have been able to reach a better result, but as the tutors told us and we all know, it is not really about the result but about the experience everyone gains from this."* Or by reading that in between the lines, *"In session two, our online and phone communication was very goal oriented. Even if the actions decided didn't actually lead to an achievement of those goals. Everyone had the chance and was invited to speak his or her mind. Members not present at meetings were updated individually and 'one on one' sessions on 'how to deal with time zones' were established."*

Additionally, the simple business result of the companies reflected in operating figures such as profit, cash flow development, costs per unit, inventory costs, EBIT – earnings before interests and taxes, etc. might also be used as an indicator for learning. Generally, the more experience the participants gain, the better they understand the idea of the simulation, the more insight they get about the consequences of various activities and actions in the simulation and the better the team collaborated, the better the business figures.

VIBu RealGame™ as a Cultural Bridge

The largest ever-online VIBu training was conducted with 165 participants (mainly business students on the master level) from 8 universities in 6 different time zones (ranging from Australia, Indonesia, over Austria, Denmark, Sweden, Finland, the US East Coast to Columbia) in October 2011.

Although there are cultural differences in the approaches to several issues occurring in virtual teams and although it has revealed that culture does play a role in virtual teams, the analysis of the essays as well as the observations show that these differences did not lead to huge difficulties. Moreover, one might even conclude that the involvement in the simulation, the communication via ICT, the common goal as well as the enthusiasm to be part of a worldwide project with different time zones and cultures as well as universities involved, served as a bridge over the different cultures.

"It is always nice to work when you know that all of the other team members are also willing to contribute and reach a better result. Therefore it was no need to influence some team members or try to steer them in the right direction in order to show more presence, because everything was fine as it was and in my opinion everyone was giving his/her best. I would also say that everyone in the team had equal power and responsibilities. I could not figure out any leader and we also were not designating anyone from the beginning. As I already said everyone had the same rights, responsibilities, power and possibilities to contribute (with new ideas)."

Virtuality thus brings certain equalization into multicultural teamwork. In a different context, as for example leadership in virtual multicultural teams, similar findings have been made [21], by observing spontaneously shared leadership in self-managed virtual teams. The underlying concept of shared leadership [24] is that power is shifting in the team and every member is or might be leader at one and the same time. It bases on social relations and networks as well as a discourse between the actors. In a highly dynamic process, team members are their own leaders and accept each other due to existing equality.

These assumptions do for sure require further research, in particular in comparison to face-to-face teams.

LIMITATIONS

VIBu RealGame™ is said to serve as a training tool for students, which prepares them for their future jobs. One might argue that there are many similarities between those two groups, but there are differences as well. In the business world, for example, resources, official functions, hierarchies or department belonging play a huge role. Therefore, running the simulation with people from one company is strongly influenced by those factors. Furthermore diversity in culture, age and gender as well as team or organizational histories might have a much bigger impact than in student teams. While in the latter, students work in self-managed teams where roles and leadership might evolve, they are mostly predefined in management teams. Despite of those differences, the insights and learning for the students is much bigger and more valuable for their future business lives than the barriers. The given design allows to getting a realistic picture of an international business setting, of time pressure (as it is the case in the fast played RealGame™) as well as financial restrictions. And without any doubt: the skills, experiences and abilities acquired will serve their future jobs. Moreover, in particular behavioural aspects (which are emphasized in the training as well) have been found to be similar and comparable between students and managers in previous studies [25].

The Future of VIBu RealGame™

The tremendous interest in participating at VIBu RealGame™ by many highly ranked universities worldwide speaks for its educational value. As stated above, it might be incorporated into different kinds of classes as a variety of issues might be addressed and focused on, depending on the particular purpose of the class. Furthermore, globally operating companies use VIBu RealGame™ as a training platform for their virtual teams and in order to deal with topics critical in their companies (e.g. team leadership, virtual communication, team coherence, and above all cultural influences on their international collaboration). Exactly this broad interest requires and guarantees a further development of the setting. Together with the advancements in technology, a modern, research-based, holistic training tool can be ensured with VIBu RealGame™.

Remark

Parts of this paper have been subject to prior, unpublished conference papers.

References

1. Apfelthaler, G. *Interkulturelles Management*, Manz Schulbuch GmbH, Vienna, Austria, 1999.
2. Bachmann, A.S. Melting Pot or Tossed Salad? Implications for Designing Effective Multicultural Workgroups. *Management International Review 46*, 6 (2006), 721-747.
3. Berry, M, Carbaugh, D. and Nurmikari-Berry, M. Communicating Finnish Quietude: A Pedagogical Prosess for Discovering Implicit Cultural Meanings in

Languages. *Language and Intercultural Communication 4*, 4 (2004), 261-280.
4. Blackburn, R., Furst, S. and Rosen, B. Building a Winning Virtual Team. In: Gibson, C. B. & Cohen, S. G. (Eds.) *Virtual Teams that Work* (pp. 95-120). San Francisco: Jossey-Bass, 2003.
5. Chen, S., Gleuykens, R. and Choi, C.J. The Importance of Language in Global Teams: a Linguistic Perspective. *Management International Review 46*, 6 (2006), 679-695.
6. DiStefano, J. J. and Maznevski, M. L. Creating Value with Diverse Teams in Global Management. *Organizational Dynamics 29,* 1 (2000), 45-63.
7. Doney, P.M., Cannon, J.P. and Mullen, M.R. Understanding the influence of national culture and the development of trust. *Academy of Management Review 23,* 3 (1998), 601-620.
8. Driver, M. Diversity and Learning in Groups. *The Learning Organization 10*, 3 (2003), 149-166.
9. Glaser, B.G. and Strauss, A.L. *The discovery of grounded theory: strategies for qualitative research.* New York: Aldine, 1967.
10. Goulding, C. *Grounded theory*. Sage Publications, London, UK, 2002.
11. Hall, E.T. *Beyond culture*. Anchor Books, New York, USA, 1976.
12. Hardin, A.M., Fuller, M.A. and Davidson, R.M. I Know I Can, But Can We? Culture and Efficacy Beliefs in Global Virtual Teams. *Small Group Research 38,* 1 (2007), 130-155.
13. Hertel, D.A. Managing Virtual Teams: A Review of Current Empirical Research. *Human Resource Management Review* 15 (2005), 69-95.
14. Hofstede, G. *Culture's Consequences*. Sage Publications, London, UK, 1980.
15. Hofstede, G. *Culture's Consequences: Comparing Values, Behaviours, Institutions and Organizations across Nations* (2nd ed.). Sage, Beverly Hills, USA. 2001.
16. Huff, L. and Kelley, L. Is Collectivism a Liability? The Impact of Culture on Organizational Trust and Customer Orientation: A Seven-Nation Study. *Journal of Business Research 58,* 1 (2005), 96-102.
17. Kayworth, T. and Leidner, D. The Global Virtual Manager. A Prescription for Success. *European Management Journal 18,* 2 (2000), 183-194
18. Kirkman, B.L., Gibson, C.B. and Shapiro, D.L. "Exporting Teams": Enhancing the Implementation and Effectiveness of Work Teams in Global Affiliates. *Organizational Dynamics 30,* 1 (2001), 12-29.
19. Kolb, D.A. *Experiential Learning*. Prentice Hall Inc., New Jerysey, USA, 1984.
20. Krech, D. and Crutschfield, R., et al. *Grundlagen der Psychologie.* Vol. 7, Sozialpsychologie. Beltz Verlag, Weinheim and Basel, Germany, 1985.
21. Lähteenmaki, S., Fischlmayr, I. and Saarinen, E. Spontaneous Sharing of Leadership in Virtual Teams – A Breakthrough for the New Leadership Paradigm? Paper presented at the *Academy of Management*, Chicago, USA, August 2009.
22. Lamnek, S. *Qualitative Sozialforschung.* 3rd ed., Beltz Psychologie Verlags Union, Weinheim, Germany,1995.
23. Maznevski, M. and Chudoba, K. Bridging Space Over Time. Global Virtual Team Dynamics and Effectiveness. *Organization Science 11*, 5 (2000), 473-492.
24. Pearce, C.L. and Conger J.A. *Shared Leadership*. Sage Publications, Inc., Thousand Oaks, CA, USA, 2002.
25. Reber, G. and Berry, M. A Role of Social and Intercultural Communication Competence in International Human Resource Development. In: S. Lähteenmäki, L. Holden and I. Roberts (Eds.), *HRM and the Learning Organisation* (pp. 313-343). Publications of the Turku School of Economics and Business Administration, Series A-2, 1999.
26. Richard, O. C. Racial Diversity, Business Strategy, and Firm Performance: A Resource-Based View. *Academy of Management Journal 43*, 2 (2000), 164-177.
27. Rosen, B., Furst, S. and Blackburn, R. Training for Virtual Teams: An Investigation of Current Practices and Future Needs. *Human Resource Management, 45,* 2 (2006), 229-247.
28. Schoorman, F.D., Mayer, R.C. and Davis, J.H. An Integrative Model of Organizational Trust: Past, Present and Future. *Academy of Management Review 32*, 2 (2007), 344-354.
29. Shachaf, P. Cultural Diversity and Information and Communication technology Impacts on Global Virtual Teams. An Exploratory Study. *Information & Management* (2008), 131-142.
30. Staples, D. S. and Zhao, L. The Effects of Cultural Diversity in Virtual Teams Versus Face-to-Face Teams.*Group Decisino and Negotiation 15*, 4 (2006), 389-406.
31. Trompenaars, F. *Riding the Waves of Culture*. N. Brealey, London, UK, 1993.
32. Watson, W. E., Kumar, K. and Michaelsen, L. K. Cultural Diversity's Impact on Interaction Process and Performance: Comparing Homogeneous and Diverse Task Groups. *Academy of Management Journal 36,* (1993), 590-602.
33. Webber, S.S. Development of Cognitive and Affective Trust in Teams. A Longitudinal Study. *Small Group Research 39,* 6 (2008), 746-769.

Using Social Networks for Multicultural Creative Collaboration

Foad Hamidi
Department of Computer
Science and Engineering
York University, Toronto,
Ontario, Canada M3J 1P3
fhamidi@cse.yorku.ca

Melanie Baljko
Department of Computer
Science and Engineering
York University, Toronto,
Ontario, Canada M3J 1P3
mb@cse.yorku.ca

ABSTRACT
Social networks can facilitate creative dialogue between participants whose geographical, cultural and social circumstances normally does not allow for such exchanges. In this paper, we present a case study of a collaborative process in which 19 participants from around the world created the multimedia, multi-language poem, "Our Digital Tapestry", on the Facebook social network. We identify and discuss the affordances of this platform with respect to *support for play, control, diversity, inclusion of hypertext and multimedia, communication* and *relationship exploration*. We also identify several restrictions of the medium that affected the project.

Author Keywords
Collaboration; social networks; poetry; creativity; empathy; Facebook

ACM Classification Keywords
J.5 [Arts and Humanities]: Literature - Hypertext;

General Terms
Collaboration, social networks, poetry, creativity, empathy, Facebook

INTRODUCTION
Social networking sites have reached unprecedented heights in recent years. Such public interactive systems (where "system" is understood as a constellation of multiple artifacts) provide arenas of experience to which the trichotomy of *user, spectator*, and *system* can be brought to bear as a tool of analysis [4]. Facebook, the most prominent of the social network sites, is the second most visited website on the Internet and currently has more than "300 million users, making it the fourth largest 'nation' on the planet by population" [1, 11]. Membership in these networks provides the user with many possibilities for social engagement. Maintaining an active membership can increase both social capital [8] and sources of technical support and knowledge [27].

Participation in these networks also blurs one's roles: that of the *user* of an interactive system and that of the *performer*. The distinction of the latter role from the former, recently discussed Reeves et al. [22], centers on the results of one's *manipulations* (i.e., actions carried out by the user) achieving the stance of being *effects* (i.e., becoming results that are observable by others).

Previous research has identified many characteristics of social networks that can support creative collaboration. These networks provide members with control over content and timing, ease of communication over a wide geographical area and the possibility of engaging with a diverse group of people with minimal cost, effort and risk [24, 27]. Furthermore, many social networks support sharing of various media such as images, video and audio, making collaboration on multimedia projects possible. Recently, novel uses of social networks have emerged that capitalize on these characteristics to create information networks at times of crisis [23].

In this work, we use the multimedia poetry project, "Our Digital Tapestry", as a case study to investigate the effects of these factors on the Facebook social network website. This collaborative and participatory poem was mediated by the Facebook social network website; we will discuss its affordances as they pertain to the creative output. A key motivation behind this work was to examine the possibility of engaging people from different cultures and background in a common creative project. We wanted to find out to what extent the affordances of the social network, access to an international audience and an open forum, allowed non-professional poets to transcend cultural and language barriers and engage in a meaningful conversation? Furthermore, how the medium affected the interaction and what were the main factors that stood out as having an important influence? In this work, we focus on the characteristics of the social network as a medium and content creation tool and leave the literary analysis of the poem to a future study.

Prior research has established the value of insights gained by the artist-researcher in revealing the emotional, psychological and intellectual aspects of the impact of the use of digital tools on artistic practice [26]; in this study the primary author assumed this role in the project. By collaborating with fellow artists and engaging in the creative process firsthand, it is possible to reveal issues that are difficult to detect using other inquiry techniques [15]. In addition to using empathy, we use autoethnography to examine and understand the factors that were encountered in the creative process by the artist-researcher [7]. This method involves reporting from a personal perspective including reporting one's personal experiences and observations. In prior research, autoethnography is shown as an effective method for understanding the affordances of using weblogs for the development of research ideas [7].

BACKGROUND

Collaborative and Participatory Poetry

The history of the tradition of collaborative poetry goes back to ancient times. *Renga* is an ancient form of Japanese collaborative poetry in which participants take turn composing and reciting poems in response to each other [16]. In modern times, many artists from Surrealists such as André Breton, Paul Éluard and René Char with their collection *Ralentir Travaux* to Beat Generation poets Jack Kerouac, Allen Ginsberg and Neal Cassidy with their collective poem *Pull my Daisy* have composed collaborative poems. Various methods to facilitate collaboration have been developed. In the Surrealist's *exquisite corpse* method each participant reads only the last written line and adds one line to the developing poem before passing it on to the next person. Charles Henry Ford, an American poet, developed chain poetry in the 1940s, in which the developing poem is mailed to a participant who adds one line to it before mailing it to the next person [6]. These examples demonstrate the process of the poem; that during its construction or co-construction, it is "alive" in a manner that ceases to be once the poem is completed. This is not to say that poems, once completed are fossilized --- clearly this cannot be true since the reader is an active constructor of meaning. However, the collaborative poem, as a poem-in-creation, has a strong element of *performativity* that is integral to its form and materiality.

The advent of digital media has affected literature greatly. Some critics go as far to state "all literature in the twenty-first century is computational," in the sense that "almost all print books are digital files before they become books" [13]. The possibility of using computer's flexibility in arranging various media such as text, video and audio has motivated many poets to explore the expressive potential of participatory multimedia poetry. For example, in his work *The Exquisite Mechanisms of Shivers,* poet and artist Bill Seaman combines text, audio and video into an installation that engages visitors and enables them to collaborate with the artist to create different manifestations of the work [28].

Historically, in different cultures around the world, the form and content of literary works have been affected by the introduction of new media. For example, Persian poetry, a long standing tradition, was greatly affected by the introduction of newspapers and literary magazines which inspired a new generation of poets to challenge and revise traditional poetic forms and start a modern poetry movement [17]. The use of social networks as a tool to create poems and other creative content in a new way is a recent example of this phenomenon.

Using Social Networks for Collaboration and Creative Endeavour

Recent increases in Internet bandwidth and network performance have made sharing large multimedia files easy and accessible. Additionally, new authoring tools make the creation of multimedia content by amateur users easier than ever before [2]. Many recent collaborative projects use digital technology to create content. In "Mopie", participants used cell phones equipped with video cameras and GPS units to capture footage while exploring a city; the footage was then uploaded to a central database and used in a virtual city walking application [14]. "Ototonari" is a pervasive game, implemented using ad-hoc mobile networks, in which participants create music by walking around in a field and interacting with each other [25].

Previous research has identified many characteristics of social networks that can support distributed creative collaboration. By transcending geographical and social boundaries, these networks provide members with the opportunity to socially engage with a diverse group of people with minimal cost and risk. While being involved in a social network creates more possibilities for accessing technical and emotional support, it does not directly impose requirements on the level of involvement for each member and provides them with flexibility in the content and timing of their engagement with other members. Furthermore, the lack of social status cues fosters relationships that transcend offline social barriers [27]. In the current project, we found that many of these characteristics directly affect collaboration on these networks.

Social networks have been used to facilitate collaboration in the business environment [3]. The researchers suggest that sharing personal information with colleagues as well as creating a personal profile with updated information by each member create a sense of intimacy and trust that facilitates better collaboration.

Smith [24] has observed that many artist groups use Facebook to share information about art projects and events and as a place to meet other artists with common interest. While professional artists use this space mainly to provide promotional information about their art, amateur artists are more open to actual artistic collaboration using the medium.

Bardzell [2] has discussed how the interface of an authoring tool and content generation platform can affect the format and ultimately content of a creative piece. In particular, the collaboration was mediated by Facebook, so the process was subject to the structuring mechanisms of that particular site. For instance, contributions from the poets were made under the mantle of a "comment" on the status of the first author and all contributions were made in terms of such units. The contributions were not editable once posted and were highly sequentialized, where the vertical spatial layout corresponds to a timeline. These characteristics affected the content of the work, by making it resembling a poetic dialogue.

OUR DIGITAL TAPESTRY

In this work, 19 participating poets from 5 cities collaborated on a multimedia poem, "Our Digital Tapestry", entirely written using existing Facebook utilities [10]. The poem was written over 4 weeks in two languages, English and Farsi, and included hyperlinks to videos and images. The participants contributed from various geographical locations (Guelph, Ottawa, Tehran, Toronto and Victoria, BC).

The poem along with information about the collaborating poets is online [20]. Each week an original short poem was posted on the researcher's Facebook profile and for the duration of the week, collaborators participated by adding their own poetry or posting links to online multimedia on the page. Thus, the researcher was involved in the project not only as an initiator and collaborator but also as the main social link between all the participants. The participants were all members of the social network of the researcher and their collaboration was solicited through a Facebook message prior to the start of the project.

Figure 1 shows a section of "Our Digital Tapestry". Each contribution is marked by a timestamp as well as a thumbnail of the profile picture of the contributor. As can be seen, two languages were used to write this section of the poem: English and Farsi. The contributions in Farsi made use of two writing systems: the Farsi script and "Pinglish", which is a folk Romanized Persian alphabet (e.g., Farsi written using English letters). In the following sections we examine the characteristics of the social network and their effect on the collaboration.

Transcending Boundaries

A characteristic of social networks that is of particular importance for collaboration is their support for overcoming geographical and cultural boundaries [27]. The effects of this on the current project are striking. Not only were participants from 5 different cities across the world, they were also from diverse cultural backgrounds and used different languages to express themselves. The social network supported *diversity* by not imposing restrictions on the location of its members and by supporting international languages. Figure 1 shows an excerpt from the poem with components written in different languages.

Figure 1. A section of "Our Digital Tapestry"

Thus, it is easy to see the potential of social networks as a platform for the creation of controversial political and social creative content. This is particularly relevant for artists living in political and social circumstances in which offline creative dialogue is difficult or even impossible. A possible consideration is to provide the possibility of anonymous contribution to artists whose safety might be compromised by the interaction as it is obvious that digital commentators are already being prosecuted for their online activities [29]. Before deployment such a system should consider privacy laws in the domains in which it is used to inform and protect its users.

Diversity was not limited to the cultural and geographical backgrounds of the participants. It was also evident in the content of their contribution. This was the effect of another related characteristic of social networks identified previously as their support for transcending social obstacles by lack of physical and societal clues about the hierarchical relationship of members [27]. With respect to encouraging creative self-expression it is important to engage participants in an informal atmosphere that minimizes personal and status risk. In this project, the lack of direct and public judgment provided an informal space where poetic content of varying quality and styles were contributed. Thus, fear of risking one's image by participating was reduced. This in turn supported a sense of playfulness that was conductive to the exploration of the creative space and affected the range of the contents of the poem. Since there were no formal rules about the content, some contributors chose to use unconventional abbreviations:

It's always fascinating to deal w a song thats stuck on replay.

One participant used a special sequence of characters to delimit parts of his contribution:

Good to hear from that ocean blue :: is her journey of shade really true?

The importance of support for *play* in creative collaboration is stressed in previous work [26]. One constraint that in my experience hindered this support was that the format of the status field only supported sequential commenting and it was not possible for authors to select a location other than following the last entry in the poem to place their contribution. In my experience, I would have liked to respond to multiple authors and their specific contributions but the system was not flexible enough to allow this.

Control over Content

Social networks can also support member's *control* over the content and timing of their contribution [27]. In this project, the participants were able to contribute as many times as they wanted and could also delete their work at any time if desired. A few of the participants, including the author, used this control to provide their contribution in short pieces. In my case, it facilitated a more spontaneous creative flow where I was not afraid to post a contribution and add to it or modify it later. However, a shortcoming of the social network was that authors could not edit previously created content in place and had to remove and replace them at the end of the poem.

The participants also had control over the level of their involvement: they could contribute whole sections to the poem, include a quotation, or just vote for the poem by "liking" it. On Facebook, "liking" refers to selecting an option to note that a member likes posted content. The contributions ranged from whole paragraphs to very short sentences.

In previous work, the role of the leader in online creative collaboration is examined [18, 21]. In the absence of formal rules, we defined a moderating role for the leader before the start of the project. Thus, we informed the contributors, at the outset of the project, that the primary researcher reserves the right to modify or delete parts of the contributions. While this right was never exercised in this specific project, it provided a safety mechanism against offensive or inappropriate content. Assuming the role of the "benevolent dictator" is a recognized practice in online content creation platforms [21].

As the primary researcher and project leader and following the autoethnographic process, I made several observations related to prior findings about leadership in online content-creation platforms [18]. One of the themes identified as important is the reputation and experience of the leader. My artistic activities during the past years, including conducting solo and group poetry readings, composing and performing in several musical groups as well as making available various poetry translations was known and respected within the community. During private conversations four of the contributors expressed confidence in my leadership and subsequent presentation of the work. I also contributed to the poem regularly which strengthened another important theme in leadership, namely that of dedication and communication. In accordance to what was reported previously, the theme of planning and structure was not as important a factor as it would have been in the case of an open-source software development project [18]. In fact, I decided to keep the format open to invite more contributions. This is, of course, a choice specific to this project in which the priority was to make available a space for poetic self-expression to new poets rather than strive for structured quality poetry. Additionally, as an artist I felt imposing too much structure or planning I would unnecessarily challenge the artistic authority of the contributors.

Figure 2a. "Our Digital Tapestry" excerpt. Currently, multimedia are included as hyperlinks.

The social network supported embedding hyperlinks in contributions which made referencing other material on the Internet possible. For example, links could point the reader to a book or encyclopedia entry. This also made including multimedia content possible, thus extending the expressive power of the medium. For example, when the poem's topic revolved around the subject of human unity and sharing experiences, one participant included a link to an offsite video on neuroscience. There were also links to original images that became part of the poem (Figure 2a). As a poet, I find mixing words and images expressive and often do it during poetry readings and embed them in other poetry projects so I found this support for the *inclusion of hypertext and multimedia* important for creative collaboration. That two other participants also used this feature to link images and video to the poem shows the importance of this feature.

Figure 2b. An alternative design sketch where in-place multimedia links are allowed

A shortcoming of the medium was that in place image or video embedding was not supported. As can be seen in Figure 2a, in its current form the user has to navigate away from the poem by clicking on the hyperlink to see the multimedia content. This affects the appearance of the poem and is disruptive. Thus, a design, for example similar to the one suggested in Figure 2b, is desirable.

Communicating with Contributors

As can be seen from Figure 1, each time a participant added a contribution to the poem, their name and a thumbnail of their profile picture, directly linked to the profile page, was placed next to their entry. This provided ready access to updated personal and contact information for each participant and supported *communication* between collaborators. In previous research, it is emphasized that having access to information about a collaborator creates a sense of intimacy and trust that can facilitate the creative process [3].

From the audience's point of view, this ability to readily access personal information about an author directly from a text demonstrates how using hypertext can enrich a reading experience. This supports new ways of reading in which personal information about the creator of a work can mingle with the actual creative output. Furthermore, the thumbnail images are automatically updated each time a user changes their profile picture and this adds a "live" quality to the work: while the text remains static, the author lives and changes over time and this change is reflected in the work by updated profile pictures. The profile picture is an image representation of a member. While typically this picture is of the member, it is not uncommon for members to choose symbolic pictures that they feel somehow represent them. Thus, placing this picture next to an author's contribution links a self-representation of their identity on the network to their contribution. This quality was, of course, lost once the poem was taken off Facebook and archived in another online space once the project was finished.

This way of attributing a contribution to a participant also supports the important issue of *authorship*. As shown in previous work, supporting for authorship is one of the important challenges of platforms that allow collaborative work [5]. In our case, the issue is dealt with by the platform's automatic attribution of each piece of collaboration to its author.

Other Aspects

While many of the participants did not know their fellow poets, they knew that they shared at least one social dimension with them, i.e. familiarity with the researcher. This was stressed because the poem was "published" on the researcher's profile page. This familiarity can create trust and empathy that are important factors in facilitating creative collaboration [26]. Furthermore, it was possible for the participants to explore their relationship with another participant by visiting their profile page and viewing information such as common friends and common interests. The support for *exploring relationships* is an important part of social networks and can enrich the experience.

During the project, we observed that the poem often took the form of a dialogue between different participating poets. This resembled, in form, the messages regularly sent in Facebook via the "status" field. The main difference was in the language used. By consciously engaging in a poetry project, the users were expressing themselves in a poetic form on a public space. Since the researcher was also the initiator and a collaborating poet in the project, many of the submitted poems were written in response to his original posts.

Previous research has shown that Facebook users rate activities that have public performance aspects as the most memorable experiences [12]. In this project, collaborator's input was made public as soon as it was posted by a contributor. Thus, collaboration was performative and by posting a poem each participant shared his or her work not only with fellow collaborators but also with visitors to the researcher's profile. In my case, I was greatly motivated by the prospect of presenting my poem to an audience. After each submission I anticipated responses and felt inspired by the number of people responding to and reading my contributions. This public nature of the contribution affects how users experience their interaction with the system; they do so with the knowledge that they are (potentially) putting on a performance for spectators. Not only are they being-a-performer-for-others, but also being-aware-that-one-is-being-a–performer-for-others [4]. The communication by and to contributors has a necessary element of self-awareness of its own public nature. Similar to how the contributors tailored their own representative thumbnail images; engaged in a process of identity creation, so were their contributions tailored. In this regard, the social network supported the *performative* aspects of the collaboration and made presenting the art immediately to an audience possible. While this aspect of the collaboration can be beneficial for engaging and motivating some participants to make contributions, it might cause concerns of privacy and authorship for some artists.

CONCLUSION AND FUTURE WORK

In this work, we have used an empathic method to identify and examine the characteristics of social networks that support creative collaboration. These factors are *play, control, diversity, inclusion of hypertext and multimedia, communication* and *exploring relationships*. We also identified support for the *performative* aspect of the collaboration as a factor that should be taken into account by designers of collaborative projects. We have examined these factors in relation to a collaborative poem, "Our Digital Tapestry", written on the Facebook social network.

In future, we plan to revise and rewrite several "remixed" versions of the poem and explore strategies to deal with issues of authorship and presentation. Another future project involves conducting a live collaborative session in which the poem is displayed on a screen while authors, either in the same room or remotely, log on to the social network and contribute to the poem. This will allow an observation of interactions occurring offline in the shared physical space as well as possible technical issues such as synchronization.

REFERENCES

1. Alexa.com. 2010. Top 500 Global Sites. Accessed 14 February, 2010 <http://www.alexa.com/topsites>.
2. Bardzell, J. 2007. Creativity in amateur multimedia: Popular culture, critical theory, and HCI. *Human Technology*, 3, 1, 12-33.
3. Cohen, T. and Clemens, B. 2005. Social networks for creative collaboration. In *Proceedings of the 5th Conference on Creativity & Cognition* (C&C '05), 252-255.
4. Darlgaard, P. and Hansen, L. K. 2008. Performing perception - staging aesthetics of interaction. *ACM Transactions on Computer-Human Interaction*, 15, 3, 1-33.
5. Diakopoulos, N., Luther, K., Medynskiy, Y., and Essa, I. 2007. The evolution of authorship in a remix society. In *Proceedings of the Eighteenth Conference on Hypertext and Hypermedia* (HT '07), 133-136.
6. Duhamel, D., Seaton, M., Trinidad, D. (Eds.) 2007. *Saints of Hysteria: A Half-Century of Collaborative American Poetry*. Soft Skull Press, Brooklyn.
7. Efimova, L. 2009. Weblog as a personal thinking space. In *Proceedings of HyperText'09,* 289-298.
8. Ellison, N.B., C. Steinfield, and C. Lampe. 2007. The benefits of Facebook "friends": Social capital and college students' use of online social network sites. *Journal of Computer-Mediated Communication,* 12, 4, 1143-1168.
9. Goolsby, R. 2010. Social media as crisis platform: The future of community maps/crisis maps. *ACM Transactions on Intelligent Systems Technology,* 1, 1, October 2010, Article 7.
10. Hamidi, F. and Baljko, M. 2010. Collaborative poetry on the Facebook social network. In *Proceedings of the International Conference on Supporting Group Work* (GROUP '10). 305-306.
11. Harrison, C. 2009. Introduction: Metamorphosis. *ACM Crossroads,* 16, 2, 2.
12. Hart, J., Ridley, C., Taher, F., Sas, C., and Dix, A. 2008. Exploring the Facebook experience: A new approach to usability. In *Proceedings of the 5th Nordic Conference on Human-Computer interaction: Building Bridges* (NordiCHI '08), 358, 471-474.
13. Hayles, N. Katherine. 2008. *Electronic Literature: New Horizons for the Literary*. University of Notre Dame Press, Notre Dame.
14. Inakage, M. 2007. Collective creativity: Toward a new paradigm for creative culture. In *Proceedings of the 2nd International Conference on Digital interactive Media in Entertainment and Arts* (DIMEA '07), 274, 8.
15. Johanasson, M. and Linde, P. 2005. Playful collaborative exploration: New research practice in participatory design. *Journal of Research Practice* 1, 1, Article M5.
16. Keene, D. 1995. *Japanese Literature: An Introduction for Western Readers*. Grove Press, New York, NY.
17. Kianush, D. 1996. *Modern Persian Poetry*. The Rockingham Press, Ware, UK.
18. Luther, K. and Bruckman, A. 2008. Leadership in online creative collaboration. In *Proceedings of Computer Supported Cooperative Work* (CSCW '08). 343-352.
19. Okolloh, O. 2009. Ushahidi, or 'Testimony': Web 2.0 Tools for Crowdsourcing Crisis Information. *Participatory Learning and Action,* 59, 1, 65-70.
20. Our Digital Tapestry. <http://www.cse.yorku.ca/~fhamidi/tapestry.html>.

21. Reagle, Jr. J. M. 2007. Do as I do: Authorial leadership in Wikipedia. In *Proceedings of WikiSym '07*, 143-156.
22. Reeves, S., Benford, S., O'Malley, C., and Fraser, M. 2005. Designing the spectator experience. In *Proceedings of Human Factors in Computing Systems* (CHI '05), 741-750.
23. Shapiro, S. 2010. Revolution, Facebook-style. *New York Times*. January 2009, MM34, accessed on February 1st 2011: <http://www.nytimes.com/2009/01/25/magazine/25bloggers-t.html>.
24. Smith, S. 2009. The creative uses of Facebook as a tool for artistic collaboration. In *Proceedings of the Electronic Visualization and the Arts* (EVA '09), 181-191.
25. Tokuhisa, S., Iguchi, K., Okubo, S., Niwa, Y., Nezu and Inakage, M. 2006. OTOTONARI: Mobile ad hoc pervasive game that develops a regional difference. In *Proceedings of the 2006 International Conference on Game Research and Development* (CyberGames '06), 155-162.
26. Treadaway, C. 2007. Using empathy to research creativity: collaborative investigations into distributed digital textile art and design practice. In *Proceedings of the 6th ACM SIGCHI Conference on Creativity & Cognition* (C&C '07), 63-72.
27. Wellman, B. 1996. For a social network analysis of computer networks: a sociological perspective on collaborative work and virtual community. In *Proceedings of the 1996 ACM SIGCPR/SIGMIS Conference on Computer Personnel Research* (SIGCPR '96), 1-11.
28. Wilson, S. 2001. *Information Arts: Intersection of Art, Science, and Technology*. MIT Press, Cambridge.
29. Yong, W. 2001. Political skullduggery suspected in Iranian doctor's death. *New York Times,* September 2010, A8, accessed on February 1st 2011: <http://www.nytimes.com/2010/09/29/world/middleeast/29iran.html>

Supporting Collaboration in Wikipedia Between Language Communities

Ranjitha Gurunath Kulkarni
Carnegie Mellon University
5000 Forbes Ave
Pittsburgh, Pennsylvania 15213
ranjithagk@gmail.com

Gaurav Trivedi
National Institute of Technology
Karnataka, Surathkal
Srinivasnagar, DK, Karnataka,
India 575025
gtrivedi@nitk.ac.in

Tushar Suresh
National Institute of Technology
Karnataka, Surathkal
Srinivasnagar, DK, Karnataka,
India 575025
iamtushar@gmail.com

Miaomiao Wen
Carnegie Mellon University
5000 Forbes Ave
Pittsburgh, Pennsylvania 15213
mwen@cs.cmu.edu

Zeyu Zheng
Carnegie Mellon University
5000 Forbes Ave
Pittsburgh, Pennsylvania 15213
zeyuz@cs.cmu.edu

Carolyn Rose
Carnegie Mellon University
5000 Forbes Ave
Pittsburgh, Pennsylvania 15213
cprose@cs.cmu.edu

ABSTRACT

This paper describes an application of machine translation technology for supporting collaboration in Wikipedia. Wikipedia hosts separate language Wikipedias for hundreds of different languages. While some content is specific to these different versions of Wikipedia, some topics have pages within multiple different Wikipedias. Similarly, while some users participate only in one Wikipedia, we find users who play a bridging role between these sub-communities and participate in the process of maintaining similar pages in different Wikipedias. Since these are not the majority of users, a support tool that allows stretching the effort of these specialized users further by indicating where their effort is needed could be a tremendous benefit to the community. An evaluation of the proposed approach demonstrates promise that such a tool could substantially reduce the effort involved in playing this bridging role on Wikipedia.

Author Keywords
Wikipedia; Computer Supported Cooperative work; Cross-lingual Document Similarity.

ACM Classification Keywords
H.5.2; I.2.7

General Terms
Human Factors

INTRODUCTION

In this paper we present a tool for supporting inter-cultural collaboration in Wikipedia. Wikipedia is valued worldwide as a repository for knowledge, with pages in over 280 languages. In 39 of these languages, it has over 100,000 pages, and at least 10,000 in 65 more languages. Not only does it provide a valuable resource for the individual cultures that possess their own language specific Wikipedia, it also provides a context in which a meaningful inter-cultural exchange can take place online. In particular, for many topics, similar pages exist in the Wikipedia of multiple languages, and some editors who possess the requisite language skills contribute towards maintaining different versions of the same page in two or more language specific Wikipedias.

For example, one of the most popular pages for September 27, 2011 on the English Wikipedia was a page about Wangari Maathai, who was Kenya's first woman to have earned a Nobel peace prize. Not surprisingly, there is a corresponding page about her in the kiSwahili Wikipedia. Some of the editors are shared between the two versions of the page. For example, on September 27, 2011, a user with username Lucas-bot made an edit to the English version of the page. And on the same day, the same user made two edits to the kiSwahili version of the page. Despite valuable bridge people between language specific Wikipedia communities, the multiple versions of the same page within different language Wikipedias are not kept equally up to date. For example, the kiSwahili version of the Wangari Maathai page is very short and mainly discusses the Nobel Peace Prize that she won, while the English version of the page is much more elaborate, giving much more detail about her life, travels, and educational experiences abroad in the US and in Germany, personal information about her private life, and in depth discussion of her political views.

Keeping content up-to-date in all of the language specific versions of the same page is challenging. Not all contributors to Wikipedia are capable of maintaining similar pages in multiple languages. Thus, in order to use human resources most efficiently, a solution that identifies those places where the contributors who possess this specialize knowledge are needed to perform this valuable community service would facilitate this inter-cultural exchange and thus benefit the international Wikipedia community as a whole. In this paper we present a technical solution for identifying these opportunities by employing machine translation technology to translate content from source pages into English, and then compare content in English to identify the extent to which inconsistencies exist. Due to the limitations of web accessible machine translation techniques, it is challenging to find similarities in text written in different languages. Along with directly comparing the text on English and corresponding translated non-English page, our approach takes into consideration, other language-properties like homophones and synonyms.

We focus on content included in the Wikipedia Info Boxes. Much prior work in the Machine Translation community has already targeted the problem of aligning texts from multiple languages [22, 23, 24] Semi-structured knowledge, such as is found in Info Boxes, presents different challenges. The terse nature makes it less amenable to existing text similarity measures [25, 26, 27], and the decontextualized nature of the encoded knowledge makes it less amenable to typical alignment techniques. Thus, our evaluation provides knew knowledge that contributes to a longer term effort to support inter-cultural collaboration in the Wikipedia community.

In the remainder of the paper, we first review some related work. Then we offer and overview of the proposed multi-stage technical approach. Next, as a proof of concept we present an ablation study in which we evaluate the contribution of each separate level towards the accuracy we achieve on a parallel English-Hindi corpus, with 50 pages represented both in the English and the Hindi Wikipedias. Next, we present a larger evaluation on all pairs of English, Chinese, and German on a parallel corpus of 100 pages represented in the English, Chinese, and German Wikipedias. We conclude with a discussion of our continued research.

PREVIOUS WORK
Several studies on Wikipedia highlighting the cross-cultural differences have been done in the past. Findings from such work show that there is a significant difference in various language wikipedias [17]. They support the view that Wikipedia is a diverse community where cultural differences that exist in the world external to the online Wikipedia world also exist within that online world.

Within this context, Wikipedia bots have proven to be a very useful resource to increase contributions from members [19]. This line of work builds on prior social psychology work on feeling of responsibility that demonstrates that people feel less responsible when they know responsibility is shared rather than specific to them [18]. Users who are able to contribute to multiple language specific Wikipedias are a valuable resource. While their abilities are not unique, they are unusual. Thus, the problem we target in this paper would fall within the scope of applicability of these findings. Thus, for our application, if it were possible to create a bot that could identify opportunities where these bridge people were needed to address mismatches in content, it could apply findings from this work by emphasizing the specialized knowledge that user had with respect to this identified maintenance need.

Studies on the pattern of growth in contribution to communities like Wikipedia [20] illustrate a trajectory in which novice users begin their editing experience by correcting minor mistakes in articles. As they move from peripheral participation into more core participation, they shift their concern from these relatively insignificant details to the maintenance of the integrity and overall quality of Wikipedia. Shifts in the nature of edits to Wikipedia pages over time may indicate movement along this trajectory and may provide useful information in identifying users to target with update requests. Furthermore, core Wikipedia community members may value tools that assist them with their goal of maintaining the integrity of Wikipedia by directing their effort where it is most needed. Such tools may be viewed as belonging to the set of affordances of the kind of socio-technological infrastructure that helps in maintaining the quality of Wikipedia [21].

Our work focuses on the problem of identifying the mismatches in content. This task requires comparing content across similar pages in different language specific Wikipedias. Existing techniques for document similarity [25, 26, 27] leverage patterns of word co-occurrence and word order regularities. In case of cross-lingual document similarity, assumptions such as these must be relaxed since, among other concerns, we know languages differ systematically in terms of word order. Automatic translation services that are freely or cheaply available today are weak in addressing such issues. Since our work leverages these weak translators, we must consider that the results we get as part of our process may be noisy and unreliable. Furthermore, we aim to evaluate how far we can push a simple and fast approach that can readily be applied to relatively low resource languages that nevertheless have web-based translation services available.

Prior work on cross-lingual document similarity compensates for some of these issues using carefully constructed multi-lingual thesauri, which are unfortunately only available in certain languages [2]. Relying on a resource like this would limit the generality of our approach to low resource languages such as Indian and African languages. In contrast, our proposed technique places only limited constraints of the choice of language. Specifically, any language for which there is an automatic translation service available on the web is fair game. Google translate, as an example, provides a translation service for 63 languages to English at the time of writing this paper.

While our task is unusual, it is not completely unique. Information arbitrage across multilingual Wikipedia [16] is another related effort that has so far been demonstrated with four European languages, namely English, Spanish, French, and German. However, this prior work does not demonstrate any generality to languages outside of Germanic and Romance languages, which share a relatively similar language structure; whereas we have demonstrated generality of approach to Hindi and Chinese, which have a far more different structure from English.

TECHNICAL APPROACH

We describe an approach to checking the consistency of information contained in info boxes on pairs of pages devoted to the same topic but in different language Wikipedias. We first give an overview of the process and then describe the technical details of the most complex portions of the process in greater depth.

Overview

The example in Figure 1 illustrates an example where the information contained on corresponding pages in two Wikipedias is very inconsistent, and both could benefit from including information contained on the alternate page. Specifically, we see the info box from the Barclays Bank page on the English and French Wikipedias respectively. The English version focuses on the history, assets, services, and trade related information. The French page, in contrast, contains information necessary to make international bank transfers, such as the BIC and IBAN.

Figure 1. Example of Info boxes extracted from the Barclays Bank page on the English Wikipedia (left) and the French Wikipedia (right).

An overview of the proposed translation and matching process can be found in Figure 2. One goal of the approach is to apply to as wide range of language pairs as possible. Thus, we choose English as an intermediate representation. Regardless of the source language of a page, we first extract attribute value pairs from all of its info boxes. For pages in source languages other than English, these attribute value pairs are then translated into English using an online automatic translation service, specifically the Google Translate API. These translation services are known to produce errorful translations. However, part of the contribution of the work presented in this paper is a demonstration that nevertheless, we can use the output from these online translation engines usefully in our process.

The English attribute value pairs from both pages are then passed into an Attribute Name Pairwise Matching module that identifies potential matches between attribute names on the two pages. This is nontrivial since in addition to potential errors introduced at the translation stage, the translation may result in attribute names from the two pages having the same meaning but expressed through different words. When a potential match is identified, then the attribute values must be matched to determine whether the information contained within the corresponding info box entries is consistent across the two pages. This matching process is challenging for similar reasons to those just enumerated for the attribute name matching stage.

Attribute-name matching

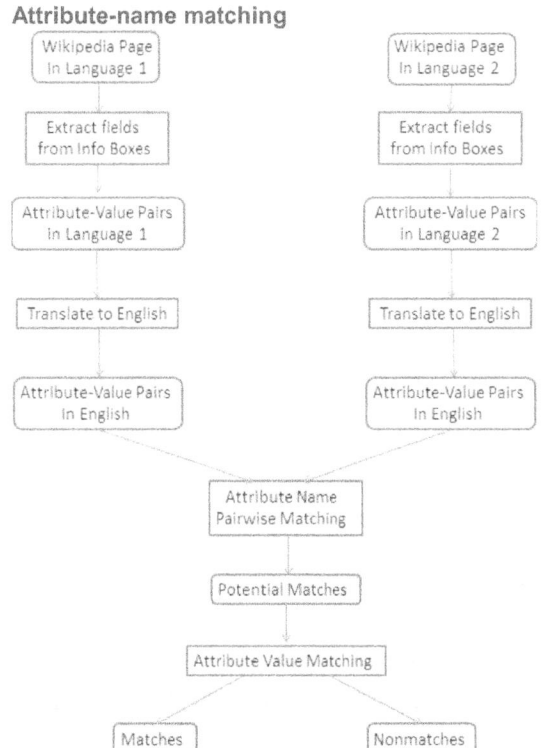

Figure 2. Overview of translation and matching process

The attribute-names comparison is done in two levels. An initial very conservative comparison is done by computing the percentage similarity between the two strings (or sets of strings) using the similar-text function provided by the standard PHP library [9, 10]. The pairs of attribute-names (e.g., of English and Hindi) are marked as a match if their percentage similarity is greater than a threshold. In this case, we set the threshold to 95% so as to mark only those pairs which match to a very high extent. At this stage, most of the matching attribute names are identical or nearly identical.

The attribute names from either page that did not find a match in the first stage are then fed into a second, less conservative matching process. To overcome some of the challenges and limitations of the automatic machine translation, we introduce sense matching into our approach. For each word in the attribute name, sets of synonyms called synsets are obtained from a language resources called WordNet[12]. Using the synsets obtained from WordNet, we can compute the percentage of overlap between the synsets extracted for every pair of attribute-names. A normalized score is obtained for each attribute-name pair (A, B) using the following formula:

$$\text{Score (A, B)} = \frac{(\text{Words with matching sense})^2}{(\text{words in } A) * (\text{words in } B)}$$

All those pairs with a score greater than a threshold are marked in the comparison matrix just as in the previous stage. In case of more than one match for a given attribute-name, the one with the highest match score is selected. Examples of attribute names that match include things like *Altitude* and *Height* or *Ruler_position* and *Leader_title*.

Attribute-value matching

Once matching attribute names are found across pages, the associated values must then be checked for consistency. To obtain a similarity assessment between attribute values, as mentioned above, the first step is a direct comparison where the set of letters and their ordering is considered. As most of the times the attribute values are either nouns or names, there is a high possibility that the translator may get the spelling wrong. Therefore the next step is to check if the two values are homophones. We first identified nouns using a Parts Of Speech tagger [15]. We then generated metaphone codes [13][14] for each of the identified nouns, and then checked for equality. If the metaphone codes match, then the pair of values was considered as homophones and a match was declared. An example of metaphones declared as a match is "*bayaluseeme*" and "*bayalusime*". Every comparison of attribute value pairs is associated with a normalized score. All attribute pairs evaluated with a score less than the threshold are reported to be inconsistent. Additionally, attributes that are missing on either of the articles are flagged as inconsistent. Examples of inconsistences are values of "5th" and "3rd" for population rank or "*siddaiah, ias*" and "*dr. r. subrahmany*" for leader name.

EVALUATION

We conducted two separate evaluations of our approach. The first evaluation was designed to evaluate the contribution of each stage in the process separately, in order to motivate the design of the approach. The second evaluation was conducted on a larger set of examples, but only examines the final result rather than evaluating the output at each stage in the pipeline. We consider the first evaluation to be a proof of concept, and the second to be a larger scale, fully fledged system evaluation. Both evaluations demonstrate that the pipeline is well motivated and that the approach, though simple, holds promise for assisting in keeping the variety of existing language Wikipedias consistent with one another.

Datasets

We constructed a dataset for each evaluation by finding corresponding pages represented within 2 or 3 language Wikipedias where the pages within the resulting set all contained info boxes.

Data set 1

The first set comprised a collection 50 English and corresponding Hindi Wikipedia articles on the cities of India. We observed that pages within this scope had a lot of inconsistencies between their corresponding articles in different languages. The 50 cities were selected randomly from the set of page pairs that met the criteria just mentioned.

Data set 2

The second set comprised 100 Wikipedia articles each in English, German and Chinese on US based companies. These articles were chosen based on the availability of infoboxes in all the three language Wikipedias.

In both evaluations the same pipeline illustrated in figure 2 was applied to identify inconsistencies between all pairs of languages. Thus, for the second evaluation, 3 pairwise comparisons were made, specifically English-German, English-Chinese, and Chinese-German.

Evaluation 1: Proof of Concept

As mentioned, the first evaluation was meant as a proof of concept that demonstrates the contribution of each stage within the pipeline introduced earlier in the paper. The infoboxes of the collected dataset were compared using that pipeline, and inconsistencies were identified and noted using this fully automatic approach. We then calculated the following performance metrics: Accuracy, Precision, Recall and F-measure. These are standard metrics that allow us to assess the quality of automatic matching our approach achieves. These metrics were computed by comparing the automatic analysis to a gold standard analysis created by native speakers of the languages involved. This gold standard was constructed as follows.

First the judges examined the full set of attribute value pairs from the two pages. Each one was then assigned to one of the following two categories:

E1: Attributes that are classified as present and similar

E2: Attributes that are either missing or dissimilar

For each attribute, we can also obtain a classification into E1 or E2 based on the system's assessment of match or non-match on attribute names, and then consistent versus inconsistent on the values of the matching attributes.

Gold Standard: Manual classification of attributes.

		Condition as determined by the *Gold standard*	
		true	false
Obtained classification	E1	tp (true positive)	fp (false positive)
	E2	tn (true negative)	fn (false negative)

Figure 3. Confusion matrix used to compute precision, recall and f-measure from the gold standard and automatically assigned E1 and E2 codes.

Precision, recall, and f-measure of result was computed for three versions of the system. First, a Baseline system simply evaluated exact match on attribute names and values. This is the most conservative and simple approach. Next, a Level 1 system included Wordnet based synset matching, but not homophone matching. A final Level 2 system included also the homophone matching.

	Accuracy	Recall	F-measure
Baseline	0.76	0.29	0.45
Level 1	0.79	0.38	0.54
Level 2	0.85	0.58	0.72

Table 1. Results of Evaluation part 1

Because even the Level 2 system was very conservative in identifying matches, there were never false positives in this evaluation, and thus the Precision is always 1. For the reported metrics in Table 1 we see consistent increases in performance as we move from the most conservative baseline system to the least conservative system.

The increase in recall at every level was due to the decrease in the number of false negatives. From baseline to level 1, the number of attribute names which were wrongly declared as unmatched were now being matched. Ex: Consider the attribute-name-value pair,

Area = Bayalusime (Hindi)

Region = Bayaluseeme (English)

Here, the term Area if translated back to the native language Hindi, actually refers to Region. But due to translation errors, this attribute-name pair comes out as a mismatch in the baseline system. Whereas, after the synset matching is introduced in level 1, such errors are minimized and hence the above argument of increase in recall.

Similarly in case of level 1 to level 2, some attribute names that were previously labeled as unmatched were found to match. This can be seen in the above example, where the noun "*Bayaluseeme*" has different spellings but sound the same. Such attribute values get matched at level 2 which checks for homophones. Hence the further increase in recall.

In order to interpret what the performance values mean in terms of human effort, we developed an additional performance metric, which we have termed "Reduced human effort". This metric computes the amount of work saved by humans by the system's work in flagging the inconsistencies. This metric is defined as follows:

$$Reduced\ Human\ effort = \left\langle \frac{X}{Y} \right\rangle$$

Here, X is the number of inconsistencies found on a page, while Y denotes total attributes present on the page. The reduced human effort calculated showed us that on an average, around 55% of the set of attributes were either missing or inconsistent on either of the two infoboxes. By flagging these, a human user who is capable of fixing the info boxes on the page pairs could save time by focusing attention on the subset that was identified automatically rather than checking everything manually.

In future work we may experiment with lowering the threshold values to make the process less conservative. In that case, we expect that recall will increase and precision will decrease. Currently, however, we find it more advantageous to maintain the conservative stance since it eliminates the problem of false positives. We are more interested in those attributes that are wrongly classified as a mismatch and will be moved to their right classes after application of our approach.

Evaluation 2: A Larger Multi-Lingual Evaluation

As the second dataset comprised of 3 languages, evaluation was done on 3 pairs of languages namely, English- German, Chinese- German and English- Chinese.

They were evaluated at two levels:

Level 1: In this analysis, only the matching of Attribute-name pairs across languages is evaluated. Consider that there are X attributes on the first page and Y attributes on the second page. Each of the X attributes on the first page can be matched with any of the Y attributes on the second page. Furthermore, each attribute on one page has the possibility of not being matched to anything on the other page. Thus, the total number of pairwise decisions that need to be made about matches is $(X+1)*(Y+1)-1$. Out of those, some subset M should be marked as a match based on an expert judge's gold standard analysis. Some subset N was marked as a match by the system. Thus, Precision is computed as the cardinality of the intersection between M and N divided by the cardinality of N. And Recall is the cardinality of the intersection of M and N divided by the cardinality of M.

Level 2: In this analysis, the number of Attribute-value pairs that matched is evaluated (given the number of attribute-name matches in level 1). Thus, we began with the pairs that were identified as matches in the Level 1 analysis regardless of whether it was correct. There were several cases to consider:

- If an attribute from one page was correctly identified as not matching any attribute from the other page, it was counted as a true negative.
- Attribute pairs that should have been identified as matching but were not were counted as false negatives.
- If an attribute pair was incorrectly matched, it was counted as a false positive in this analysis.
- If an attribute pair was correctly matched and the values were correctly identified as a match, it was counted as a true positive.
- If an attribute pair was correctly matched and the values were correctly identified as not matching it counted as a true negative.
- If an attribute pair was correctly matched but the values were incorrectly identified as not matching it was counted as a false negative.
- If the attributes were correctly matched and the values were incorrectly identified as matching it was counted as a false positive.

Precision, Recall and F-measure were calculated and the following results were obtained:

	Precision	Recall	F-Measure
Level 1	0.63	0.55	0.57
Level 2	0.86	0.63	0.70

Table 2. Results for English-German pair

	Precision	Recall	F-Measure
Level 1	0.95	0.77	0.84
Level 2	0.74	0.62	0.64

Table 3. Results for English-Chinese pair

	Precision	Recall	F-Measure
Level 1	0.72	0.45	0.54
Level 2	0.74	0.69	0.69

Table 4. Results for German-Chinese pair

The results obtained in the second stage of evaluation record high values of Precision, Recall and F-measure (at level 1) for the Chinese - English language pair when compared to the other two pairs. This can be accounted by the fact that both Chinese and English Wikipedia infoboxes have very similar attribute names even before translation (template given in English) unlike German infoboxes (as illustrated in following figures 2, 3, and 4).

```
{{Infobox dot-com company
| company_name    = Amazon.com, Inc.
| company_logo    = [[File:Amazon.com-Logo.svg|250px]]
| company_type    = [[Public company|Public]]
| traded_as       = {{Nasdaq|AMZN}}<br>[[NASDAQ-100|NASDAQ-100 Component]]
| foundation      = 1994
| founder         = [[Jeff Bezos]]
| location        = [[Seattle]], [[Washington (state)|Washington]], U.S.
| area_served     = [[World]]wide
| key_people      = [[Jeff Bezos]]<br><small>([[Chairman]], [[President]])
```

Figure 3. Infobox Template of an English article (screenshot from Wikipedia edit page)

```
{{Infobox Company
| company_name   = 亚马逊公司
| company_logo   = [[File:Amazon.com logo.svg|225px]]
| company_type   = [[上市公司]] {{nasdaq|AMZN}}
| company_slogan = "...and you're done"
| foundation     = 1994
| founder        = [[:en:Jeff Bezos|Jeffrey P. Bezos]]
| location       = {{flagicon|USA}} [[西雅图]]
| area_served    = [[全球]]
| key_people     = [[:en:Jeff Bezos|Jeffrey P. Bezos]]<br /><small>([[主席]])
```

Figure 4. Infobox Template of a Chinese Article (screenshot from Wikipedia edit page)

```
{{DISPLAYTITLE:amazon.com}}
{{Dieser Artikel|behandelt das Unternehmen ''Amazon''. Zu anderen Verwendungen
{{Infobox Unternehmen
| Name            = Amazon.com, Inc.
| Logo            = [[Datei:Amazon.com-Logo.svg|130px|Logo]]
| Unternehmensform = [[Gesellschaftsrecht der Vereinigten Staaten#Corporation|
| ISIN            = US0231351067
| Gründungsdatum  = 1994
| Sitz            = [[Seattle]], [[Vereinigte Staaten]] {{USA|#}}
```

Figure 5. Infobox Template of a German Article (screenshot from Wikipedia edit page)

Hence when German infoboxes are compared, the attribute names are translated into English, which introduces a large number of translation errors. For example, "*Sitz*" in German refers to "*Location*" in English/Chinese articles. But it gets translated as "*Seat*" which even after comparing synsets will not match with "*Location*".

The values of evaluation metrics increase from level 1 to level 2 in case of German-English and German-Chinese pairs. This is because the comparisons to be made after the attribute names match mainly include numbers and nouns. Hence only the conservative text comparison and homophones matching are needed to give us these results. But there are some errors as explained in the next section, which if avoided might lead to better results.

The decrease in the values in case of the Chinese-English pair is because of translation errors getting introduced at this level. The attribute values in Chinese articles are all in Chinese though their attribute name were in English in the template.

Errors that contribute to the system can be divided into two main categories: 1. Syntactic errors. 2. Semantic errors.

Syntactic errors refer to the errors introduced in the system due to errors in the way the text is represented:

For example, attribute names that are represented as a single token in English may be represented as a phrase after translation from German, and that phrase may have a nontrivial match with the corresponding English tag. This occurred at least once in approximately 20% of the pages.

Semantic errors are more common compared to the syntactic errors. Here are a few of them,

1. Attribute-values in one language article being a single word description for their corresponding set of words in another language.

Ex:

*industry=graphics card, motherboard, power supply, desktop computer and pc accessory manufacturing (*German*)*
*industry=computer hardware (*English*)*

2. There might be composite attributes (one attribute in one language article may be a combination of two or more attributes in another language article.)

Ex:

"*Foundation*" in some articles in Chinese gives us information about both "*date*" when the company was founded and its "*location*". Whereas English has different attributes for "*date*" and "*location*".

3. Sense disambiguation errors because of bugs in translator. This is the most common type of error seen. Average number of such cases seen was 2-3 per article of 9-10 attributes in case of German to other language comparisons. This error is not evident in English – Chinese comparison as the attribute-names do not undergo translation.

```
English   Spanish   French
{{Infobox_Unternehmen
| Name           = Autodesk, Inc
| Logo           = [[Datei:Autodesk logo.svg|200px|Logo von Autodesk]]
| Unternehmensform =
[[Gesellschaftsrecht_der_Vereinigten_Staaten#Corporation|Incorporated]]
| ISIN           = US0527691069
| Gründungsdatum = 1982
| Sitz           = [[San Rafael (Kalifornien)|San Rafael]], [[Vereinigte Staaten|USA]]
| Leitung        = [[John Walker (Programmierer)|John Walker]], Gründer<br /> [[Carl
Bass]], [[Chief Executive Officer|CEO]] und Präsident
| Mitarbeiterzahl = > 6.800
| Branche        = Softwarehersteller
| Umsatz         = $ 1.952 Milliarden [[US-Dollar|USD]] (FY2011) <ref>
[http://www.wikinvest.com/stock/Autodesk_(ADSK)/Data/Income_Statement#Income_St
atement Umsatz]</ref>
| Homepage       = [http://www.autodesk.com/ www.autodesk.com]
}}
```

```
English   Spanish   Arabic
{{Infobox_Unternehmen
| Name = Autodesk, Inc.
| Logo = [[File: Autodesk logo.svg | 200px | Logo Autodesk]]
| Corporate form = [[# Gesellschaftsrecht_der_Vereinigten_Staaten Corporation |
Incorporated]]
| ISIN US0527691069 =
| Founded = 1982
| Seat = [[San Rafael (California) | San Rafael]], [[United States | USA]]
| Line = [[John Walker (programmer) | John Walker]], founder <br /> [[Carl Bass]], [[Chief
executive officer | CEO]] and President
| = Number of employees> 6.800
| Industry = Software Vendor
| Revenue = $ 1.952 billion [[USD | USD]] (FY2011) <ref>
[http://www.wikinvest.com/stock/Autodesk_ (ADSK) / Data / Income_Statement #
Income_Statement Sales] </ref>
| Homepage = [http://www. autodesk.com/ www.autodesk.com]
}}
```

Figure 6. Illustrating Errors due to Translation from German to English (screenshot from http://translate.google.com)

CONCLUSION

In this paper, we present an approach to automatically point out differences between two articles written in different languages. We proposed an approach that uses the concepts of homophones and synonyms in addition to direct comparison. Our evaluation showed that there was a significant increase in recall after the concepts of homophones and synonyms were applied in addition to the direct text comparison.

Two evaluations on two different language sets that cumulatively include English, German, Chinese, and Hindi, which have very different language structures, demonstrates that the proposed approach has some generality across languages. It can also be seen that the two domains considered namely Cities of India and Companies based in the United States were not similar and hence our method also has some generality across domains where the corresponding pages in Wikipedia include info boxes.

The high number of inconsistent and missing attributes suggests that there is need for such automation and a bot that could leverage such analysis might be a useful tool to support inter-cultural collaboration in the Wikipedia community.

Nevertheless, weaknesses in the results suggest that the simplistic approach taken here may be substantially improved using more sophisticated language analysis techniques. Our approach currently depends on the lexical database "WordNet" for synonyms. We anticipate that stronger lexical databases would improve the effectiveness, potentially substantially increasing the recall. The current method does not address some common types of translation errors namely phrase translations. When phrases that are translated from one language to another are compared with single words giving the same meaning as the phrase, our system fails to recognize the match. One reason is that WordNet does not provide any information about how words may be paraphrased into a short phrase. Also, abbreviations, units conversion and geographic location matching is not handled by the current system.

To address the above mentioned errors, there are a few solutions we are focusing on, namely: for geographic location matching, the use of Gazetteer databases might help in providing information about different names and formats in which a given region is referred to. The abbreviations issue can be handled by introducing domain specific dictionaries for abbreviations. The template issues mentioned earlier in the paper need special attention as well. Thus we plan on improving the system by addressing all of these issues one by one.

In the long term, our goal is to expand on this work and produce a Wikipedia bot that can be used to support the work of bridge editors between similar pages on separate language Wikipedias. The bot would highlight those parts of the page that need attention. In case, there is missing information, the bot would prompt them on that particular page. Also the bot would give information about which language version has the most updated information. Before this vision can be realized, however, the work presented in this paper must be integrated with approaches to text similarity [25, 26, 27] that would allow the technique to be generalized from info boxes to the main text of the article.

In reference to the scenario described at the beginning of the paper, the resulting bot would point out to a user seen as an editor both of English and KiSwahili pages that there is a lot of information missing in the Kiswahili version of Wangari Maathai page and that the user can refer to the English page to update it. Specific pointers both to the info boxes as well as the main text would be given. The targeted pointers would facilitate efficient intervention of the contacted user.

ACKNOWLEDGMENTS

This work was funded in part by National Science Foundation Grant SBE 0836012.

REFERENCES

1. Christof M ller and Iryna Gurevych. 2009. Using Wikipedia and Wiktionary in Domain-Specific Information Retrieval Evaluating Systems for Multilingual and Multimodal Information Access, Springer Berlin /Heidelberg, pp. 219-226.

2. Steinberger, Ralf and Pouliquen, Bruno and Hagman, Johan 2002. Cross-Lingual Document Similarity Calculation Using the Multilingual Thesaurus EUROVOC EProceedings of the Third International Conference on Computational Linguistics and Intelligent Text Processing, pp. 415-424.

3. Aminul Islam and Diana Inkpen. 2008, Jul. Semantic Text Similarity Using Corpus-Based Word Similarity and String Similarity ACM Transaction on Knowledge Discovery from Data, Vol. 2, No. 2, Article 10.

4. Wikipedia Infoboxes Help. (2010, Dec.) [Online].Available:
http://en.wikipedia.org/wiki/Help:Infobox

5. Wikipedia Infoboxes Categories. (2010, Dec.)[Online].Available
http://en.wikipedia.org/wiki/Category:Infobox templates

6. MediaWiki API Documentation. (2010, Dec.) [Online]. Available: http://www.mediawiki.org/wiki/APIox

7. GoogleTranslate API, developer's guide (v2): Using REST. (2010, Dec.) [Online]. Available: http://code.google.com/apis/language/translate/v2/using rest.html

8. Libcurl - C API documentation. (2010, Dec.) [Online]. Available: http://curl.haxx.se/libcurl/c/

9. PHP similar text function documentation (2010, Dec.) [Online]. Available: http://php.net/manual/en/function.similar-text.php
10. Jonathan J. Oliver. 2008, Jul. Decision Graphs - An Extension of Decision Trees. Available: http://www.cs.monash.edu.au/ jono/TechReports/TR173.dgraph.ps
11. Metzler, Donald and Dumais, Susan and Meek, Christopher 2007. Similarity Measures for Short Segments of Text Advances in Information Retrieval Vol. 4425,Springer Berlin / Heidelberg, pp. 16-27.
12. C. Fellbaum. 1998. WordNet: An Electronical Lexical Database. The MIT Press, Cambridge, MA.
13. PHP metaphone code generation function by Lawrence Philips. (2010, Dec.) [Online]. Available:http://php.net/manual/en/function.metaphone.php
14. Binstock & Rex. 1995. Practical Algorithms for Programmers Addison Wesley.
15. Parts Of Speech Tagging, PHP/ir, Information Retrieval and other interesting topics. (2010, Dec.) [Online].Available: http://phpir.com/part-of-speech-tagging
16. Adar, Skinner and Weld 2009, Information Arbitrage Across Multi-lingual Wikipedia WSDM'09, Barcelona, Spain
17. Ulrike Pfeil, Panayiotis Zaphiris, Chee Siang Ang 2006, Cultural Differences in Collaborative Authoring of Wikipedia.
18. B. Latane, K. Williams, and S. Harkins. Many hands make light the work: The causes and consequences of social loafing. J. Pers. Soc. Psych., 37:822–832, 1979.
19. D Cosley, D Frankowski, L Terveen… - 2007, SuggestBot: Using Intelligent Task Routing to Help People Find Work in Wikipedia.
20. SL Bryant, A Forte… - 2005, Becoming Wikipedian: Transformation of Participation in a Collaborative Online Encyclopedia
21. Slattery, S. P. (2009). "Edit this page": the socio-technological infrastructure of a Wikipedia article. In *Proc. of the 27th ACM international conference on Design of communication* (pp. 289-296). Bloomington, Indiana, USA: ACM.
22. Liu, Y., Liu, Q., & Lin, S. (2006). Tree-to-string alignment template for statistical machine translation, *Proceedings of the 44th Annual Meeting of the Association for Computational Linguistics*
23. Gildea, D. (2003). Loosely tree-based alignment for machine translation, *Proceedings of the 41st Annual Meeting of the Association for Computational Linguistics*
24. Och, F. & Ney, H. (2000). Improved statistical alignment models, *Proceedings of the 28th Annual Meeting of the Association for Computational Linguistics.*
25. Mohler. M. & and Mihalcea, R. (2009). Text-to-text Semantic Similarity for Automatic Short Answer Grading, in *Proceedings of the European Chapter of the Association for Computational Linguistics (EACL 2009),* Athens, Greece
26. Gbrilovich, E. & Markovitch, S. (2009). Wikipedia-based semantic interpretation for natural language processing, *Journal of Artificial Intelligence Research* 34(1).
27. Metzler, D., Dumais, S., & Meek, C. (2007). Similarity Measures for Short Segments of Text, *Advances in Information Retrieval,* Volume 4425, pp 16-27.

Analysis of Discussion Contributions in Translated Wikipedia Articles

Ari Hautasaari	Toru Ishida
Department of Social Informatics	Department of Social Informatics
Kyoto University	Kyoto University
Yoshida-Honmachi, Sakyo-Ku,	Yoshida-Honmachi, Sakyo-Ku,
Kyoto-Shi, 606-8225, Japan	Kyoto-Shi, 606-8225, Japan
arihau@ai.soc.i.kyoto-u.ac.jp	ishida@i.kyoto-u.ac.jp

ABSTRACT
Translation of articles in Wikipedia is one of the most prominent methods for increasing the quality of different language Wikipedias. Discussion pages in Wikipedia contribute to a large portion of the online encyclopedia, and are used by Wikipedia contributors for communication and collaboration. Although the discussion pages are the main channel between Wikipedia contributors all over the world, there have been relatively few in-depth studies conducted on communication in Wikipedia, especially regarding translation activities. This paper reports the results of an analysis of discussions about translated articles in the Finnish, French and Japanese Wikipedias. The results highlight the main problems in Wikipedia translation requiring interaction with the community. Unlike in previous work, community interaction in Wikipedia translation activities focuses on solving problems in the translation of proper nouns, transliteration and citing sources in articles rather than mechanical translation of words and sentences. Based on these findings we propose directions for designing supporting tools for Wikipedia translators.

Author Keywords
Wikipedia; translation; discussion;

ACM Classification Keywords
H.5.3. Group and Organization Interfaces: Web-based interaction.

General Terms
Human Factors; Design; Languages.

INTRODUCTION
Wikipedia is the largest collaboratively edited online encyclopedia available. Currently there are close to 19 million articles in 280 languages, and 29 million registered users in the multilingual Wikipedia. The English Wikipedia is currently the largest in terms of the amount of articles (3,6 million) and active users (145,000) followed by the German and French Wikipedias [23].

The overall growth of the English Wikipedia has slowed down in recent years due to problems in coordination, growing resistance to new content and tools available for editors and administrators [17]. However, coordination of activities in the non-encyclopedic pages, such as the Wikipedia article discussion pages, has continued to increase [12].

Consequently, one of the biggest issues in Wikipedia is making information available in all languages. The English Wikipedia is often used as the source language for translation activities aimed to enhance the quality of the multilingual Wikipedia. Translation activities in Wikipedia may be aimed at creating new articles in the target language Wikipedia, or increasing the quality of existing articles.

Few supporting tools tailored for Wikipedia translators exist today. For example, the Language Grid is an online infrastructure, which provides tools and resources for supporting Wikipedia translation activities [5, 6]. The language services, such as machine translators and multilingual dictionaries, available through the Language Grid are used for multilingual discussion support as well as for article translation with the aim of improving the quality of the multilingual Wikipedia and making information available in all languages.

Discussion in Wikipedia
Wikipedia discussions have a clear goal - reaching consensus within the community, and improving the Wikipedia article quality. Every Wikipedia page includes a "discussion" (or "talk") page for the purposes of interaction between Wikipedia contributors. In case of popular or controversial articles, the discussion pages may grow considerably in size, even exceeding the related article in terms of number of edits and length [18]. Where the article specific discussion pages include discussions mostly related to the corresponding article, discussions about policies and coordination of activities can span to various non-encyclopedic pages in the multilingual Wikipedia. For example, policies and guidelines in Wikipedia are created by the community members, and discussions about specific

policies can include hundreds of contributions in the corresponding discussion pages[1].

Contributors outside the immediate working group of a particular article also use the discussion pages as a means of asking orienting information, and offering assistance for the article development [16]. For example, controversial articles often receive interest from casual editors (e.g. domain experts who edit articles anonymously). In the case of controversial articles, the anonymous contributions on discussion pages have been shown to increase animosities among the discussants, but anonymous article edits often have a positive effect on the article quality [10]. This suggests that problem and conflict resolution in Wikipedia discussions requires a vastly different set of strategies compared to other domains.

Besides the discussion pages related to articles, communication in Wikipedia is also conducted through specific WikiProjects and personal pages of registered users. The WikiProject pages include discussions ranging over multiple topics and activities, not necessarily related to particular articles, but often act as hubs for contributors interested in the same domain. For example, WikiProject:Japan[2] aims to improve the quality of articles related to Japan and Japanese culture in the English Wikipedia. In popular WikiProject pages, discussion contributions may often also be in foreign languages (e.g. Korean discussion contributions in the English language WikiProject), making it hard for users without the sufficient language ability to participate in the discussion.

In this study, we observe the communication and collaboration between Wikipedia contributors in relation to collaborative article translation in the Finnish, French and Japanese Wikipedia discussion pages. The aim of this paper is to identify the type of community interaction needed for successfully creating or amending an article via Wikipedia translation activities. Furthermore, we discuss the type of community interaction in relation to the different stages of a translated article. Based on these findings we propose directions for designing supporting tools for Wikipedia translators.

RELATED WORK

Previous research on communication in Wikipedia has focused on the correlation between discussion contributions and article quality [9, 10], but also on the analysis of content [15, 16, 18] and the structure of discussion pages [12]. Even though the content and interaction patterns have been observed in previous research, there are few studies available in the multilingual context. Especially considering the slowing growth of the English Wikipedia, translation activities in other language Wikipedias should be given more attention in order to support activities aiming to increase the quality of the multilingual Wikipedia.

Previous studies on Wikipedia translation have focused on supporting multilingual discussions between Wikipedia translators with machine translation tools [2, 3], creating a conversation control system developed from collaborative Wikipedia translation protocol [7], and supporting collaborative translation and editing of wiki-content with machine translation [1]. However, to best of our knowledge, there have not been studies focusing on the type of community interaction, mono- or multilingual, needed to solve problems specifically in Wikipedia translation activities.

HYPOTHESES

The main research questions in this paper are:

RQ1: What are the main tasks and problems requiring community interaction in Wikipedia article translation?

RQ2: Are there differences in collaborative translation and editing practices in different stages of the article evolution?

Firstly, we expected the majority of discussions to be about coordination between contributors related to editing the article and the article content [15]. Furthermore, we expected to find a high frequency of discussion contributions regarding the content of the partly or completely translated articles [18].

H1: Discussions about editing a translated article have a high frequency of contributions regarding the content of the article.

Secondly, we expected to find discussions about translation specific activities, such as help requests on how to translate certain words or sentences. More specifically, we expected a high frequency of help requests directed at domain experts regarding specific words and expressions in the translated articles [1].

H2: Discussions about translating an article have a high frequency of contributions regarding translation of specific words and expressions.

H3: Differences in the distribution of discussion contributions exist between the different stages of article evolution.

Differences in collaborative editing practices from a cultural point of view are discussed in [13]. Based on this work, we expected to find differences in the collaborative work practices in Wikipedia translation requiring community interaction in the three language Wikipedias.

---

[1] Policies and Guidelines project page in the English Wikipedia
http://en.wikipedia.org/wiki/Wikipedia:Policies_and_guidelines

[2] WikiProject:Japan in the English Wikipedia
http://en.wikipedia.org/wiki/Wikipedia_talk:WikiProject_Japan

H4: There are differences in the type of community interaction conducted in discussion pages between Finnish, French and Japanese Wikipedias

DATA COLLECTION

In previous work, content analysis on the Wikipedia discussion pages has been done mostly in the English Wikipedia, focusing on a selected sample of general article pages [12, 15]. The data for this study was collected from the Finnish, French, and Japanese Wikipedias. The Finnish Wikipedia and the Japanese Wikipedia both represent a language group, which is dominant only in one country, whereas the French Wikipedia represents a language group ranging to multiple countries and cultures. Translations in the target Wikipedias are often conducted from the English Wikipedia due to the availability of new information [1].

For this study, we chose a data set from the categories listing partly or completely translated articles in each language [20, 21, 22]. The categories do not include all translated articles, but are a representative set of partly or completely translated articles in the target Wikipedias. Each identified category was mined for articles with contributions in the related discussion pages. We limited the discussion pages to be added in the data set to the articles in the categories of partly or completely translated articles, excluding related project and user pages.

We extracted 228 discussions pages with 720 discussion contributions from the Finnish Wikipedia, 93 discussion pages with 644 discussion contributions from the French Wikipedia, and 94 discussion pages with 330 discussion contributions from the Japanese Wikipedia (N = 1694).

ACTIVITY, CONTEXT AND ACTION IN WIKIPEDIA DISCUSSIONS ABOUT TRANSLATION

The individual contributions in the discussion pages were each categorized in three dimensions (activity, context and action) in order to identify the types of community interaction related to translating Wikipedia articles. The categorization used in this study was created after carefully reading the contributions once and definitions clarified before actual annotation.

In terms of article evolution in Wikipedia, it is important to identify the different stages of a translated article. More precisely, articles may be translated partly, completely or extended through translation activities. Partly translated articles can be further edited using target language sources. Thus, it is reasonable to differentiate between the discussion contributions related to these specific activities.

In the analysis of the discussion pages, two main *activity* categories emerged, where the discussion was either about *editing* a translated article (with no regard to the original source article), or about *translating* an article. As mentioned above, the activities of the Wikipedia contributors in different stages of the article evolution are distinctive, including the community interaction aspect. Furthermore, discussion pages, where the general topic is about translation, tend to focus only on translation. Similarly, discussion pages about editing a translated article focus on editing activities. Hence, every discussion contribution was categorized as part of an *editing* activity or a *translation* activity.

Categories for Message Context and Action for Discussion Contributions

Six categories for the *context* of the discussion contributions were identified, answering the question *"What is he/she talking about?"* The following categories indicate the main context of individual discussion contributions in relation to the corresponding article:

- Content: Discussion about the content of the article.
- Layout: Discussion about the layout of the article, including links, figures, templates, ect...
- Sources: Discussion about citing sources in the article.
- Naming: Discussion about naming of the article, sections and sub-sections, use of names and proper nouns, and transliteration in the article.
- Significance: Discussion about the significance of the article, section or sub-section.
- Wording: Discussion about how words, phrases and grammar are used in the article.

In this categorization, *naming* and *wording* are the two identified, mutually exclusive, topics of discussion about the use of language in the translated articles. *Wording* indicates, for example, a discussion about grammatical errors in sentences. *Naming*, on the other hand, includes discussions about article titles, or how to correctly refer to well known events (e.g. Watergate scandal).

As Wikipedia can be edited by anyone, *significance* of Wikipedia content is a common topic. A number of policies and guidelines have been established on whether content is notable enough to be included in Wikipedia (e.g. guidelines for notability of web content[3]). In this categorization, *significance* indicates discussion contributions about whether an article, or specific part of the content, is considered significant enough to be included in Wikipedia, or in the corresponding article.

In addition to the message context, the main intended *action* of a discussion contribution was coded, answering the question *"What does he/she do, or want others to do?"* Seven categories for *action* were identified:

- Help request: User asks for help directly or indirectly.

---

[3] http://en.wikipedia.org/wiki/Wikipedia:Notability_(web)

- Help provide: User provides help spontaneously or by request.
- Edit request: User requests for an edit on a specified topic, or for the whole article.
- Edit notice: User notifies that an edit has been conducted on a specified topic, or on the whole article.
- Critique: User provides critique regarding the article without directly prompting for action.
- Coordination: User coordinates actions with other users.
- Policy: User refers to an established Wikipedia policy calling for action, or calls for creation or modification of a local policy.

In cases where no clear categorization could be established for a discussion contribution, category "Other" was used. This category includes mostly personal insults and spam, which are not regarded as part of the discussion about article translation, and thus excluded from the analysis set.

Each discussion contribution was carefully read and categorized in three dimensions based on the main *activity, context* and *action*. In some cases discussion contributions could be very long and elaborate including multiple contributions in one. The coders would in these cases choose the most appropriate categorization representing the main intended contribution.

Inter-annotator agreement was tested with a reliability set of 90 items by two additional reliability coders in each language. The reliability coders were trained with a training set of 30 items in the target language not included in the reliability set. Fleiss' kappa was calculated for each language set for *activity, context* and *action*. The inter-annotator agreement in all languages is reported in Table 1. As the *kappa* may be unproportionally low with higher amount of categories, the overall agreement percentage is also reported in all languages.

Language	Kappa			
	Activity	Context	Action	Total
Finnish	0.74	0.82	0.65	84%
French	0.88	0.75	0.68	89%
Japanese	0.64	0.69	0.56	78%

Table 1. Inter-annotator agreement for activity, context and action in each language.

Examples of Discussion Contribution Categorization

Example 1 - activity is *editing*, context is *content* and action is *critique* without explicitly requesting an edit:

"Limiting imaginary line. What is that supposed to mean?" (Translation from Finnish by author)

Example 2 - activity is *editing*, context is *layout* and action is *edit notice*:

"The links were directing only to a template, so there is no need for modification. If the author approves, it is OK to request a removal, but since it is fine to leave them here I will make them redirect." (Translation from Japanese by author)

Example 3 - where activity is *translation*, context is *sources*, and action is *critique* without explicitly requesting an edit:

"I cannot support this request for fear that it imposes a non-neutral image in the article. I read the German article and its main concern is to criticize the basic supporters of the initiative in assuming a breach of international law and so on. So I'm sure we can find better sources." (Translation from French by author)

Example 4 - activity is *translation*, context is *layout*, and action is *policy*:

"[…] I added the translation template after the translation. […] If adding the template after the translation is done is not allowed, it can be removed." (Translation from Finnish by author)

Example 5 - activity is *translation*, context is *content*, and action is *edit notice*:

"I added the English version. I will probably redirect it to the summer and winter [articles] [...]." (Translation from Japanese by author)

DISCUSSION ABOUT EDITING A PARTLY OR COMPLETELY TRANSLATED ARTICLE

The results in the *editing* activities were similar to previous studies on the discussion page contributions in terms of the frequency of discussions about content and coordination [15, 18]. In discussions about *editing* activities, the majority of contributions were about the *content* and the *layout* of the related Wikipedia article in all three languages. Figure 1 represents the distribution of discussion contributions in the three language Wikipedias regarding *editing* activities. In the Finnish Wikipedia (N = 404), discussions about *content* and *layout* each comprised 25.25% of the discussion contributions (50.50% in total). Similarly, in the French (N = 405) and the Japanese (N = 112) Wikipedias the majority of discussion contributions were about *content* and *layout* (72.09% and 68.75%, respectively). In this data set, the Japanese Wikipedia was the only one with more discussion contributions about *layout* than *content* when the discussion was about *editing* activities (40.18%).

The French Wikipedia had the highest frequency of contributions regarding *content* (58.02%). This can be partly explained by the amount of active contributors and articles, as well as the relative age of the French Wikipedia. The results are also similar to the English Wikipedia discussion contributions reported in [11]. In the older, or larger, Wikipedias, practices and policies are likely to be better established than in the younger, or smaller,

Wikipedias leading to a lower frequency of discussions about *layout*. Currently, the French Wikipedia ranks the third in number of articles and active users after the English and German Wikipedias [23].

Discussions about citing sources were relatively common in the Finnish and French Wikipedias (18.81% and 12.35%, respectively). In the Japanese Wikipedia, sources were less common with 7.14% of all discussion contributions regarding *editing* activities.

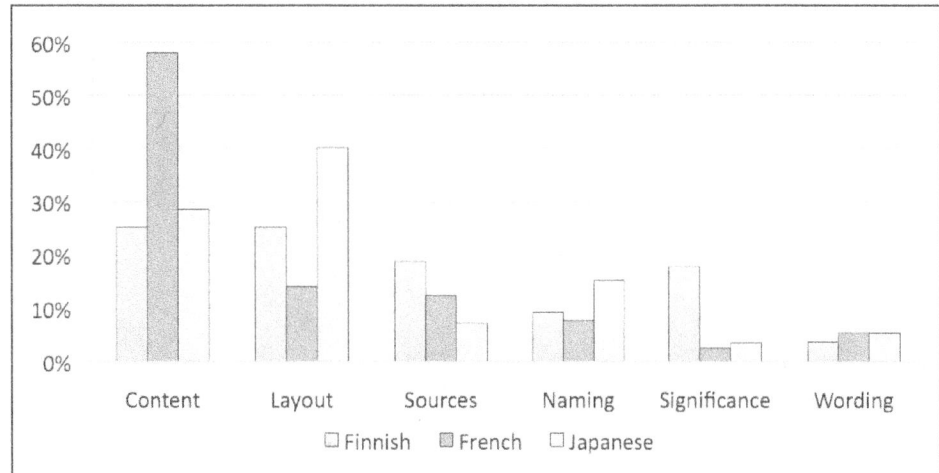

Figure 1. Distribution of *context* in discussion contributions related to *editing* activities in Finnish (N = 404), French (N = 405) and Japanese (N = 112).

DISCUSSION ABOUT TRANSLATING AN ARTICLE

In discussions about *translation* activities, the majority of discussion contributions were about *naming*. As described above, *naming* here refers to resolving the proper form for the title of the article, section or sub-section, names or proper nouns, and transliteration in the corresponding article. The context of these contributions is notably different from *wording*, as the category does not include phrasing or resolving proper translation of individual words or expressions.

Figure 2 represents the distribution of discussion contributions in the three Wikipedias regarding *translation* activities. In the Finnish Wikipedia (N = 302), *naming* is most common by 53.97%, whereas only 12.91% of contributions are about *wording*. Similarly, the French (N = 190) and Japanese (N = 217) discussion contributions are mainly about *naming* (54.21% and 49.31%, respectively), with only a small portion of contributions regarding *wording* (11.05% and 12.44%, respectively).

The results were unexpected as we assumed a high frequency of discussion contributions regarding *wording* (*H2*). The hypothesis was based on the assumption that Wikipedia translators would ask for help from domain experts regarding domain specific words [1] and article content [18]. However, in *translation* activities community interaction was required most frequently when resolving problems in *naming* based on other language Wikipedias and external sources, such as target language media.

Compared to discussions about *editing* activities, discussions about *translation* activities include far less contributions regarding *sources*. The tendency was consistent across all languages, with 12.6% in the Finnish discussions, 6.8% in the French and 1.4% in the Japanese discussions.

Example 6 is a typical case of discussion about a *translation* activity. The discussion contributor makes a direct reference to the translation of the article name. Example 6 also illustrates a recurring phenomenon in discussions about *naming*. The reference for using the version in a Finnish language newspaper or other media is often associated with *naming* practices. This is related to the policy stating that Wikipedia contributors do not create content, be it the name of an incident or transliteration, but use outside resources for accurate encyclopedic articles.

Example 6 - activity is *translation*, context is *naming*, and action is *edit request*:

"*I think the article name is fairly bad. Presumably, 'Norwegian*

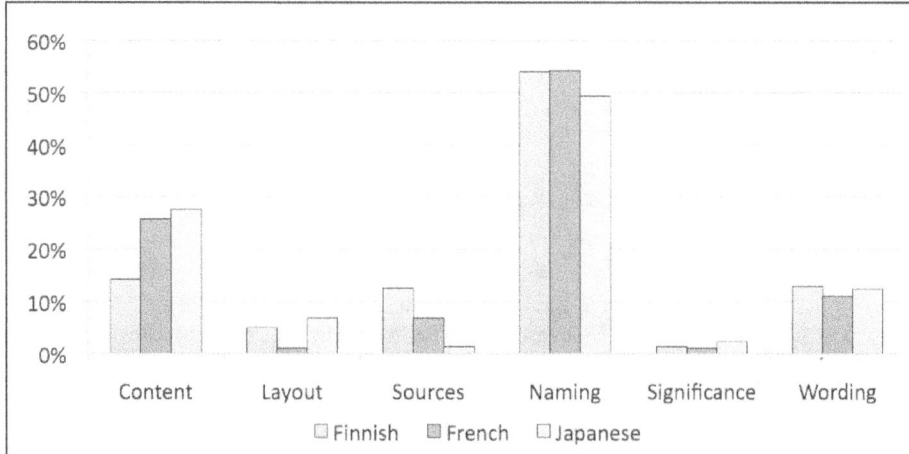

Figure 2. Distribution of *context* in discussion contributions related to *translation* activities in Finnish (N = 302), French (N = 190) and Japanese (N = 217).

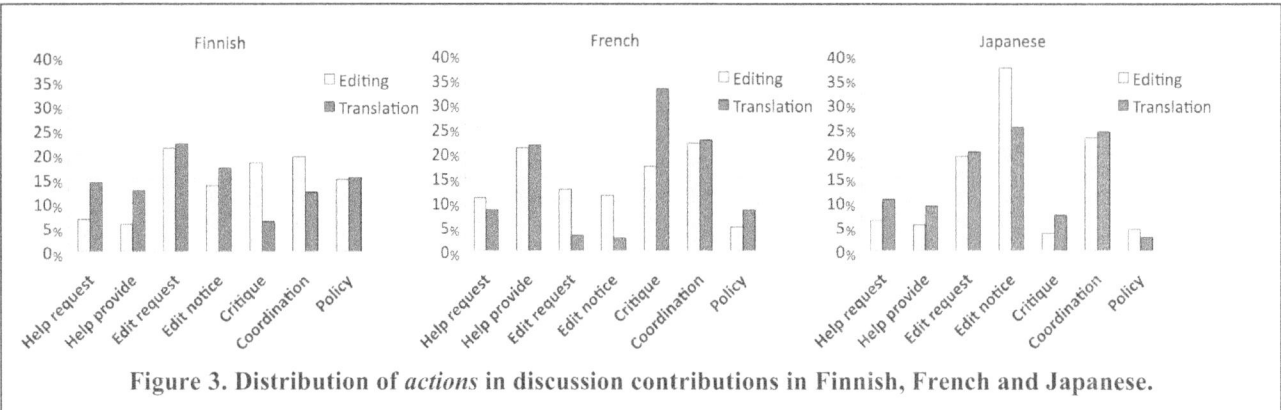

Figure 3. Distribution of *actions* in discussion contributions in Finnish, French and Japanese.

Rocket Incident' is a direct translation from the English Wikipedia, but [the title] *has not been used anywhere. It would be better to find what the incident is called in the* [Finnish language] *newspapers."* (Translation from Finnish by author)

ACTIONS IN DISCUSSION CONTRIBUTIONS

The distribution of *actions* in each language regarding both *editing* and *translation* activities is illustrated in Figure 3. The frequency of discussion contributions in the French Wikipedia were slightly higher in the *help provide* (21.18%) and *critique* (22.35%) categories compared to Finnish and Japanese Wikipedias. On the other hand, the frequency of *edit requests* (21.67% and 20.06%) and *edit notices* (15.16% and 29.48%) were slightly higher in the Finnish and Japanese Wikipedias, respectively.

The discrepancies between the types of *actions* can be explained by slightly different practices expressed in the discussion contributions. While it was common in the French Wikipedia to provide help unsolicited, the contributors' aim would be to increase the quality of the article. Similarly, the Finnish and Japanese contributors' intention was to increase the article quality by asking for a revision or an edit on a particular subject, which would prompt an *edit notice* from other contributors. The trend was also consistent between *editing* and *translation* activities in each language (Figure 3).

The age and size of a given Wikipedia may be a factor in the type of behavior expressed in discussion contributions. The Finnish Wikipedia, being the smallest in terms of number of contributors, and youngest in terms of number of articles, may not have as well established practices within the community as in the French and Japanese Wikipedias. This is also observable in the frequency of discussion about *policy* (15.01%) as opposed to the French (6.0%) and Japanese (3.3%) Wikipedias.

RESULTS

Regarding *editing* activities in the translated articles, our results were consistent with previous research, with a high frequency of discussion contributions about *content* and *layout* (*H1*). However, the trend did not persist in discussions about *translation* activities. Our hypothesis was that there would be high amount of discussions about how to translate certain domain specific words and expressions. In other words, we expected a high amount of *help requests* regarding *wording* (*H2*).

The majority of discussion contributions regarding *translation* activities were about *naming*; transliteration, translation of names and proper nouns and resolving article, section and sub-section titles based on various language sources. *Help requests* on *wording*, translation of words and expressions, were observed, but not nearly as frequently as discussions about *naming*. The mechanical translation practices of Wikipedia contributors were not in the scope of this study, but based on these results we can conclude that the tasks or problems requiring community interaction are more often related to *naming* rather than mechanical translation of words and phrases.

One reason for the large amount of discussions about *naming* is the diversity in naming practices of events between different language sources, such as mass media. Especially in the Finnish Wikipedia, discussion about *sources* was common (16.15%). These two topics are loosely related, as direct translations of the names of well-known events are often not acceptable in the target language Wikipedia. In other words, if an event has had some media coverage, the commonly used name should be adopted also in the same language Wikipedia. The following example illustrates this observed behavior.

Example 7 includes a discussion about a *naming* of an article, where the community members dispute the article name choice based on the unavailability of target language references. The first discussion contributor has translated the article from English and chosen the title based on his translation, but it has been changed by another contributor (Example 7.2). In Example 7.1, the original translator notifies that he reverted the change. The second editor disputes the translated article name and implies an edit request referring to lack of sources. The conversation ends when the original translator is not able to produce a source

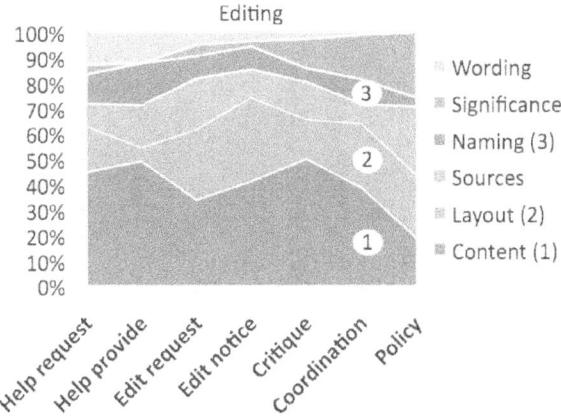

Figure 4. Distribution of discussion contributions related to *editing* activities in all three languages.

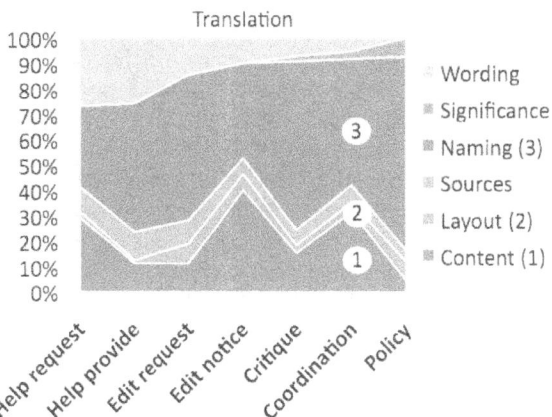

Figure 5. Distribution of discussion contributions related to *translation* activities in all three languages.

in the target language that includes a reference to the disputed article name (Example 7.3).

Example 7.1 – activity is *translation*, context is *naming* and action is *edit notice*:

"*I know that* [name of article] *is its own separate concept. I just translated it from the English Wikipedia.*" (Translation from Finnish by author)

Example 7.2 – activity is *translation*, context is *sources* and action is *edit request*:

"*Could you present a source example where the Finnish concepts have the difference in meaning.*" (Translation from Finnish by author)

Example 7.3 – activity is *translation*, context is *naming* and action is *coordination*:

"*A book called* [reference]. *However it talks about* [unrelated subject]. […] *I have nothing against changing the name to* [original article name]" (Translation from Finnish by author)

Our results imply that the current approaches for supporting Wikipedia translation are not necessarily solving the main problems in Wikipedia translation. For example, a system introduced in [11] supports mechanical article translation with machine translation support, but does not address two key problems identified in this paper – target language *sources* and *naming*.

Effect of Activity Type

As predicted in *H3*, the type of *activity* related to the discussion contributions has an effect on the distribution of the messages in terms of *context*. In other words, when participants discussed about *translating* an article the distribution of discussion contributions was significantly different than when discussing about *editing* an article ($\chi^2 = 54.4$, $p < .05$).

As illustrated in Figure 4 and Figure 5, the frequency of discussions about *content* (1) and *layout* (2) is much lower in discussions about translation. Furthermore, frequency of *naming* (3) is considerably higher when translating an article compared to editing activities. The shift in the distribution of discussion *context* between activities illustrates the most common types of collaborative work practices of the Wikipedia translators in different stages of the article evolution:

- Translating an article – Resolving translation of article title, subsection titles, names, proper nouns and transliteration. Resolving problems in translation of words and expressions. Finding target language sources.

- Editing a translated article – Discussing editing activities and resolving disputes regarding the article content. Citing sources in target language. Resolving problems in article layout.

Differences in the Distribution of Context and Action of Discussion Contributions Between Finnish, French and Japanese Wikipedias

As predicted in *H4*, differences in the distribution of *context* were found between the Finnish and French Wikipedias ($\chi^2 = 16.7$, $p < .016$). In the distribution of *action*, there were differences between all languages (Fi-Fr: $\chi^2 = 23.0$, $p < .016$, Fi-Ja: $\chi^2 = 18.5$, $p < .016$, and Fr-Ja: $\chi^2 = 41.8$, $p < .016$). However, the results here are not straightforward (i.e. clear cultural differences cannot be indicated). Firstly, it is not reasonable to generalize the results to a cultural level for a number of reasons. The results indicate that community interaction is indeed different in the different language groups in some aspects, but considering the scope of the data set, we cannot say if the differences rise from the group composition itself (i.e. Wikipedia contributors), language, culture or some other factors.

Secondly, there are observable similarities within the data set. For example, the distribution of *naming* and *wording* in discussions regarding *translation* of an article is consistent between the three languages (Table 2). This suggests that problems in mechanical translation of words and expressions, as well as translation of names and proper nouns are equally common between different language and different size Wikipedias. From a user point of view, the two translation problems require equal amount of community interaction regardless the target language of the translated article.

	Naming	Wording
Finnish	53.97%	12.91%
French	54.21%	11.05%
Japanese	49.31%	12.44%

Table 2. Frequency of naming and wording in discussions related to translation activities.

Thirdly, although there were some discrepancies between the different language Wikipedias regarding the distribution of *actions*, the results cannot be generalized. As we discussed above, the different behavioral aspects in discussion contributions all have the same goal – improving the quality of the related article. Furthermore, the French Wikipedia represents a language group that spans over multiple countries and regions. Hence, it is unreasonable to draw a generalization about the cultural aspects of the Wikipedia contributors based on this data set, but rather use the results as an indication of behavioral tendencies in discussions about translation in different language Wikipedias in future studies.

OPPORTUNITIES FOR DESIGN

The MediaWiki software, originally designed to run Wikipedia, has been constantly updated in terms of features, but the basic functionalities have stayed the same. A number of open source developers have created a vast variety of extensions for the software to increase its functionality in Wikipedia as well as in other sites. Based on our results, we propose directions for designing supporting tools for Wikipedia translation, especially through open source development of MediaWiki extensions[4].

Support for Consistent Translation of Names and Proper Nouns

The emergent problem identified in this study is the consistent translation of proper nouns and names, as well as transliteration. Firstly, the problem stems from the translators' inability to properly notate the given proper noun or name in the target language. Currently there are many solutions to overcome the problem of transliteration. For example, foreign names can be automatically

---

[4] http://www.mediawiki.org/wiki/Manual:Extensions

transliterated to Japanese katakana characters, but in many cases there may not be a direct equivalent available, especially for more complex names [14]. Reversely, names written in kanji characters (e.g. Chinese) can be transliterated to English using machine translation techniques [19].

However, a more complex problem emerges when translating a name of a current event. In general, names of events have an established form, such as "Watergate scandal", but in the case of a very recent event, it might be difficult to determine the proper name. Especially in the case of Wikipedia, the naming of an article is important because of search engines; if an article is named improperly, users do not find the information with the common search words.

In case of breaking news events, such as major natural disasters, online communities engage in diverse forms of collective action to share the rapidly changing information [8]. However, if there is no established method to translate keywords in the disaster information, such as the common name of the event and location, it can be difficult for translators to make use of the emerging information in a timely fashion. Furthermore, it can be very hard for different language speakers to find information through search engines until the keywords included in the information, such as article topics, have a well established form.

To ensure that translation of names, proper nouns and transliteration is consistent over multiple translated articles, the following design aspects should be considered:

- Accessibility to a user editable multilingual dictionary resource (e.g. multilingual domain specific naming dictionary) for referencing established translations of names and proper nouns in the target language Wikipedia.
- Dictionaries and dictionary entries should be arranged according to the domain of the translated article (or sentence) to avoid mistranslations in unrelated articles (see e.g. [4]). In other words, when multiple entries exist, the domain of the translated article is used to resolve the disambiguation.
- Ability for users to browse/search the dictionary entries in Wikipedia as well as combine available dictionaries with other language resources.
- Ability for contributors to coordinate through discussion pages directly related to a specific dictionary or dictionary entry in order to resolve inconsistencies in a centralized repository.

There are still open questions on the use of dictionaries in translation, namely on how to decide which of multiple entries is the correct translation. Especially in the case of specialized words and expressions, interaction with domain experts is essential to avoid word-sense disambiguation in user-edited domain specific dictionaries. A multi-language discussion platform developed for supporting communication between Wikipedia translators and domain experts in such tasks is introduced in [2].

Support for Citing Sources in Translated Articles

As discussed above, source citing in translated articles is another prominent problem. In general, the consensus in Wikipedia communities is to "*always cite sources in the target language*". However, finding the right sources in the target language can be a time consuming effort, especially in cases where the translator is not familiar with the topic (i.e. not a domain expert). Further, a source containing the particular information may not exist in the target language.

We propose two approaches for supporting Wikipedia translators in terms of source citing:

- Automated search for a translated source material in the target language available in online archives (e.g. with cross-referencing standard book numbering, closest match of machine translated title/author name, mining available web resources, ect.)
- Development of crowdsourcing translation tool for open content sources not available in the target language using machine translation as a supporting tool.

The problems in translation found in this study are likely also present in other translation domains. For example, crowdsourcing translation is becoming increasingly popular for cheap translation of large amounts of text. However, the problems in *naming* may be increasingly difficult in crowd translation services, if no communication channel between collaborators is available.

CONCLUSION

Translation activities in Wikipedia aim to improve the quality of the multilingual Wikipedia by making information available in all languages. Numerous communities and WikiProjects are working towards improving the articles in their domain of choice via article translation. Discussion pages are the main communication channel between Wikipedia contributors for organization and coordination of activities in the corresponding article, user pages and other non-encyclopedic Wikipedia pages.

In this paper, we observed the discussion contributions in three language Wikipedias, focusing on discussions about partly or completely translated articles. We identified two types of activities, *editing* and *translation*, reflected in the discussion contributions. This showed that Wikipedia article translation is a two-fold process, where an article is first partly or completely translated to the target language and edited by Wikipedia contributors as a separate activity, or an existing article is improved via translation activities.

The discussion contributions were further divided in to six categories based on the *context*, and seven categories based on the intended *action*. *Context* reflects the general topic of a discussion contribution and *actions* reflect the action requested or provided by the message contributor. In combination, these dimensions provided a distribution of discussion contributions, which revealed collaborative tasks and problems requiring community interaction specific to Wikipedia translation.

Our results were consistent with previous research in terms of type of discussions about *editing* a translated article, with high frequency of contributions regarding the *content* and *layout* of the related Wikipedia article. However, in all three Wikipedias, discussions about *translation* activities were most frequently about proper *naming* of articles, sections and sub-sections, transliteration, proper nouns and names. Our results show that community interaction is needed most frequently when translating or transliterating names and proper nouns based on target language sources, in all observed languages.

Our results imply that current approaches to Wikipedia translation may not answer the most pressing questions in the quality of translated articles in Wikipedia. For example, current machine translation tools available for Wikipedia translation do not accommodate adequate and consistent translation of names and proper nouns across several related articles. Furthermore, as seen in this paper, resolving the proper *naming* practices often requires community interaction centralized in one particular article's discussion page making consistent *naming* difficult in related articles.

Although we only found few multilingual discussion contributions in the data set, it is apparent that given the right tools, Wikipedia translators would greatly benefit from access to domain experts and contributors in other language Wikipedias. Our approach for overcoming inconsistencies especially regarding *naming* practices in multiple related articles is to implement a multilingual collaboratively edited domain specific dictionary as a supporting tool for Wikipedia translation. By providing a domain specific multilingual dictionary, discrepancies in *naming* could be lowered significantly without affecting articles outside the given domain. The concept was first introduced in [4], and an existing infrastructure for distributing language services, such as user created domain specific dictionaries, is described in [5, 6].

FUTURE WORK

This study focused on Wikipedia discussions in three language Wikipedias, which is more than most studies thus far have included. Even though the English Wikipedia is the largest, and moreover the best resource for data, there are cultural aspects in Wikipedia communities in different language Wikipedias, which are not observable in the English Wikipedia. Hence, a follow-up study including a wider variety of languages is needed.

A temporal study on the evolution of a translated Wikipedia article in relation to the community interaction including the mechanical aspects of Wikipedia translation will be reported in a future paper. We are aiming to support translation of Wikipedia articles to multiple languages, as well as supporting multilingual discussions between translators and domain experts with different language abilities using machine translation tools.

ACKNOWLEDGMENTS

This research was partially supported by Kyoto University Global COE Program: Informatics Education and Research Center for Knowledge-Circulating Society, and Strategic Information, and Communications R&D Promotion Programme (SCOPE) from Ministry of Internal Affairs and Communications of Japan.

REFERENCES

1. Desilets, A., Gonzalez, S., Paquet S., and Stojanovic, M. Translation the Wiki Way. In *Proc. of the 2006 International Symposium on Wikis,* ACM Press (2006), 19–32.
2. Hautasaari, A., Ishimatsu, M., Xia, L., and Ishida, T. Supporting Multilingual Discussion of Wikipedia Translation with the Language Grid Toolbox. *IEICE technical report. Natural language understanding and models of communication 109(390)* (2010), 67-72.
3. Hautasaari, A., Takasaki, T., Nakaguchi, T., Koyama, J., Murakami, Y., and Ishida, T. Multi-Language Discussion Platform for Wikipedia Translation. In *Ishida, T. (ed.). The Language Grid - Service-Oriented Collective Intelligence for Language Resource Interoperability*, Springer (2011), 231-244.
4. Hautasaari, A., and Ishida, T. Semantic Web Approach to Support Wiki-to-Wiki Translation Communities. In *Proc. JAWS 2009*, 483-488.
5. Ishida, T. *The Language Grid - Service-Oriented Collective Intelligence for Language Resource Interoperability*. Springer, 2011.
6. Ishida, T. Language Grid: An Infrastructure for Intercultural Collaboration. *IEEE/IPSJ Symposium on Applications and the Internet,* IEEE Computer Society (2006), 96-100.
7. Ishimatsu, M., Murakami, Y., Hautasaari, A., and Ishida, T. Supporting Wikipedia Translations Based on Protocol Analysis. *IEICE technical report 110(428)* (2011), 63-68. (In Japanese)
8. Keegan, B., Gergle, D., and Contractor, N. Hot off the wiki: dynamics, practices, and structures in Wikipedia's coverage of the Tōhoku catastrophes. In *Proc. WikiSym '11*, ACM (2011), 105-113.
9. Kittur, A., and Kraut, R.E. Harnessing the wisdom of crowds in Wikipedia: quality through coordination. In *Proc. CSCW'08*, ACM (2008), 37-46.
10. Kittur, A., Suh, B., Pendleton, B., and Chi, E. He says, she says: Conflict and coordination in Wikipedia. In *Proc. CHI'07,* ACM Press (2007), 453-462.
11. Kumaran, A., Saravanan, K., Datha, N., Ashok, B., and Dendi, V. Wikibabel: A wiki-style platform for creation of parallel data. In *Proc. of the ACL-IJCNLP 2009 Software Demonstrations,* ACL (2009), 29–32.
12. Laniado, D., Tasso, R., Volkovich, Y., and Kaltenbrunner, A. When the Wikipedians talk: network and tree structure of Wikipedia discussion pages. In *Proc. ICWSM*, AAAI Press (2011), 177-184.
13. Pfeil, U., Zaphiris P., and Ang, C.S. Cultural Differences in Collaborative Authoring of Wikipedia. *Journal of Computer-Mediated Communication, Volume 12, Issue 1* (2006), Blackwell Publishing Inc, 88–113.
14. Qu, Y., Grefenstette, G., and Evans, D.A. Automatic transliteration for Japanese-to-English text retrieval. In *Proc. SIGIR '03,* ACM (2003), 353-360.
15. Schneider, J., Passant, A., and Breslin, J.G. Understanding and Improving Wikipedia Article Discussion Spaces. In *Proc. SAC'11*, ACM (2011), 808-813.
16. Stvilia, B., Twidale, M.B., Smith, L.C., and Gasser, L. Information quality work organization in Wikipedia. *JASIST,* 56(6) (2008), 983-1001.
17. Suh B., Convertino, G., Chi, E., and Pirolli, P. The singularity is not near: slowing growth of Wikipedia. In *Proc. WikiSym '09,* ACM (2009), 1-10.
18. Viegas, F.B., Wattenberg, M., Kriss, J., and van Ham, F. Talk before you type: Coordination in Wikipedia. In *Proc. HICSS'07,* IEEE Computer Society (2007), 1-10.
19. Virga, P., and Khudanpur, S. Transliteration of proper names in cross-lingual information retrieval. In *Proc. of the ACL 2003 workshop on Multilingual and Mixed-Language Named Entity Recognition*, ACL (2003), 57-64.
20. Wikipedia - Finnish Wikipedia (Referred: April 2011): http://fi.wikipedia.org/wiki/Luokka:Käännetyt_lähteettömät_artikkelit/.
21. Wikipedia - French Wikipedia (Referred: April 2011): http://fr.wikipedia.org/wiki/Catégorie:Projet:Traduction:Articles_liés/.
22. Wikipedia - Japanese Wikipedia (Referred: April 2011): http://ja.wikipedia.org/wiki/Category:%E7%BF%BB%E8%A8%B3%E4%B8%AD%E9%80%94/.
23. Wikipedia - List of Wikipedias (Referred: 30.5.2011): http://meta.wikimedia.org/wiki/List_of_Wikipedias/.

Computational Representation of Discourse Practices Across Populations in Task-based Dialogue

Elijah Mayfield, David Adamson, Alexander I. Rudnicky, and Carolyn Penstein Rosé
Carnegie Mellon University
Language Technologies Institute
5000 Forbes Avenue, Pittsburgh, PA 15213
{emayfiel, dadamson, air, cprose}@cs.cmu.edu

ABSTRACT
In this work, we employ quantitative methods to describe the discourse practices observed in a direction giving task. We place a special emphasis on comparing differences in strategies between two separate populations and between successful and unsuccessful groups. We isolate differences in these strategies through several novel representations of discourse practices. We find that information sharing, instruction giving, and social feedback strategies are distinct between subpopulations in empirically identifiable ways.

Author Keywords
task-based dialogue; discourse practices; information sharing; intercultural collaboration

ACM Classification Keywords
I.2.7 Artificial Intelligence: Natural Language Processing—*Discourse*;

INTRODUCTION
A critical task in natural language processing is understanding how dialogue is structured and information is shared between speakers. This structure is not captured well with surface-level features such as word distributions, and varies drastically based on who is speaking to whom. In the systemic functional linguistics literature, it has frequently been argued that making discourse practices associated with social interpretations explicit is an important step towards resolution of social problems related to positioning within an interaction or within a community more broadly [24].

In this paper we illustrate the usage of a machine learning methodology for identifying cultural differences in discourse practices between communities. We demonstrate through corpus based experimentation the important connection between the representation of the data and the nature of the differences that can be identified using such a methodology. We present multiple novel representations of discourse practices, all driven by structured dialogue annotation based on sociolinguistic theory. We also present analysis of the impact of these strategies on task success, and discuss implications for design of culturally aware interactive systems.

Advances in internet based collaboration technology have enabled industry and academia to create distributed, multi-disciplinary teams that can address complex problems on an unprecedented scale. The Boeing Dreamliner and the Airbus A380, each a project on the order of 10 billion USD, involved tens of thousands of workers in hundreds of companies around the world [19]. Such global teams have the advantage of providing a diverse set of disciplinary and cultural perspectives on a topic, but at the same time mismatches in disciplinary and cultural conventions, work styles, power relationships and conversational norms. Such mismatches can lead to misunderstandings that negatively affect the interaction, relationships among team members, and ultimately, the quality of group work.

Building on our previous work, in this paper we explore the use of a different conversational construct that has both task and social relevance. Specifically, we use the Negotiation coding scheme, which operationalizes the authoritativeness of stance taken by participants within an interaction in relation to one another. This work has its roots in the systemic functional linguistics literature [24] and was first formalized in our prior work, where we not only define the coding scheme but show that it can be automatically applied in real time with high accuracy [26]. The conversational moves within this framework become the building blocks with which we represent differences in communication practices between cultures.

The result of our analysis in this paper is a description the relationship between speakers in terms of authority over information; an empirical model of the trajectory of a conversation as speakers take on more or less authoritative roles; and an understanding of the way that these behaviors are impacted by the influence of culture and group success.

This paper is divided into three overarching sections:

1. We give a brief overview of related work, our data, and a qualitative and quantitative overview of observations motivating our exploratory analysis.

2. We introduce three detailed methodologies for describing interactions between speakers:

(a) Extracting frequent patterns of interaction over multiple turns in sequence.

  (b) Building transition matrices of adjacent turns and examining differences in edge weights.

  (c) Plotting authority over time, given a definition of authority based in our coding schemes.

3. We then use these frameworks to describe empirical findings on two problems:

  (a) Identifying differences in discourse practices between cultures.

  (b) Identifying behaviors that lead to task success.

RELATED WORK

This work is certainly not the first attempt to represent information sharing in interaction. In addition to the approaches we describe below, work in collaborative learning especially has studied the transfer of information in groups, through the use of statistical discourse analysis [10] or uptake graph analysis [35]. This prior work is more focused specifically on the process of group problem-solving in collaborative learning and is less generalizable to other domains, but has been shown to be particularly useful for the study of intercultural collaboration [36], a key goal of our work.

Studies suggest that problems do indeed arise when people from different cultural backgrounds converse face to face or via the Internet [13]. For example, an individual from a task-oriented culture such as the United States may focus exclusively on achieving an external goal, overlooking the social niceties expected by a teammate from a relationship-focused, high power distance culture such as China or Japan. Similarly, an individual from a culture that relies primarily on verbal language may miss subtleties of facial expressions or tone of voice that can modify or contribute to the meaning of the verbal language in other cultures. Gao (2000) describes differences in communication styles of Chinese students in Australia and of native English-speaking Australians (e.g., fewer politeness markers, more indirectness, and different uses of nonverbal behaviors on the part of the Chinese) that can lead to erroneous inferences about a speaker (e.g., an English-speaking Australians may perceive a Chinese speaker as rude) [15]. Recent work on large scale machine learning analysis of regional dialect differences in Twitter has revealed differences in term distributions associated with specific regions in the US [14]. However, interpretation of the implications of some of these linguistic differences in light of issues like trust and effective communication is unclear. Many of the differences between cultural groups that have been measured have failed to reliably predict the lower levels of trust and understanding that have been measured in inter-cultural groups in comparison with homogeneous groups [29, 33].

On the other hand, some prior work in the intercultural communication literature suggests that stylistic differences in communication that have tangible implications for collaboration may exist at a deeper level [13, 33]. For example, Chen (1995) compared dyadic conversations between Americans vs. Americans and Americans vs. East Asians and found

Figure 1. Example pair of maps from the MapTask corpus.

that the topics of messages in the American dyads were more likely to overlap [9], suggesting that members of culturally homogeneous pairs were more likely to engage in what is referred to as transactive conversational behavior, where interlocutors orient their contributions towards the contributions of their partners [6]. Similarly, Li (1999) found more problems in information exchange when a nonnative speaker was talking to a native English speaker than vice versa [22]. She suggests that nonnative speakers may not realize they do not understand and thus fail to ask for needed clarification, which may also be indicative of low transactivity. Transactivity has been noted to be associated with trust and intimacy between conversational partners [4]. These differences reflect aspects of conversations that have both task relevance and social relevance, since rich constructs like transactivity represent the process of building consensus within groups and also reflect a level of multual respect between group members. Machine learning work measuring transactivity from text [30, 2], as well as speech [17] illustrate the importance of rich representations of text and speech in addition to powerful machine learning algorithms.

THE COLLABORATIVE TASK

In this work, we analyze the MapTask direction-giving setting. In this task, pairs of participants are each given a map. Each map has approximately twelve landmarks distributed across the map. One participant, hereafter referred to as the "Instruction Giver", has a start and finish point, with a path drawn between them, on their map. The other participant, who we refer to as the "Instruction Follower", has only the start point marked. The task is for the Giver to instruct the Follower to reproduce the path to the finish point as closely as possible, navigating the landmarks over the course of the dialogue.

A complication for the participants is that the maps are similar but not identical. Half of the landmarks on each pair of maps are identical; however, the other half of the landmarks are altered. These alterations include different names (e.g. *Ancient Ruins* instead of *Ruined City*), swapped landmarks (different landmarks occupying the same space on each map), invisible landmarks (only marked on one participant's map), or duplicated landmarks (appearing once in the same place on each participant's map, and a second time in a different location on one of the two maps).

Our data for this study comes from two previously collected corpora. The original HCRC MapTask corpus [3] was collected from 64 participants in Scotland, totalling 128 dialogues. The DCIEM MapTask corpus [5], collected later in Canada, reproduced the same study to examine the effects of sleep deprivation on military personnel. 66 dialogues were completed under normal conditions, and 150 additional dialogues were recorded in various impaired conditions.

In this work we sample 28 dialogues from the HCRC corpus and 33 conversations from the control condition of the DCIEM corpus (where there is no sleep deprivation or drug use). This corpus is a superset of the 20 used for analysis in [26]. In total, these 61 conversations make up 14,720 lines of dialogue. From this point forward, we consistently refer to the two subpopulations as the Scottish Civilian or Canadian Military groups.

BASELINE ANALYSIS WITH WORD DISTRIBUTIONS

The state-of-the-art in modeling regional dialect variation within the language technologies community starts with a representation of text referred to as a "bag of words" model [14]. In this paradigm, a text is represented as a binary vector with n dimensions, where n is the vocabulary size, and each dimension maps to a single word. For each instance in a data set, a given dimension receives a value of 1 if its word appears at any point in the text, and value 0 if it does not appear. While this representation is simple, it has proven to be surprisingly robust as in a wide range of language modeling tasks where content is the focus. However, it poses challenges with respect to generalizability of trained models where style rather than content is the focus.

Here we illustrate a different issue, namely that the regional dialect differences that are discovered may not be task relevant. To illustrate this, we begin by building a linear support vector machine (SVM) classifier that takes this "bag of words" representation of dialogues, and predicts the subpopulation, namely Scottish versus Canadian. Such a model is 100% accurate in cross validation - given an entire dialogue worth of text, it can predict with virtual certainty which corpus a dialogue has come from.

By standards of success typically adopted within the language technologies community for classification tasks, this would be considered a success. However, by observing the weights assigned to each feature, we are left with quite a different impression. The most predictive pair of words is "round" (weighted heavily towards Scottish civilians) and "around" (weighted heavily towards Canadian military). In context, these words are used for direction giving - speakers of Scottish dialects will instruct the follower to *"go round... [the landmark]"*, while speakers of Canadian dialects will say *"go around..."*. Similar examples exist for "little" and "wee", "anyway" and "anyways", region-specific measurements such as "inches" and "centimetres", or region-specific terms like "aye". While these differences are arguably indexical of culture, and lexical differences such as these can be important playing cards in interactions where cultural dialect differences are associated with differences in status, we will see that the differences we are able to detect using richer representations of the language operate at a level that is more task relevant, whereas these word level differences are not.

Some distinctions across word distributions would arguably be task relevant. For example, we find when we examine the corpora a difference in use of cardinal directions, with 71.8% of words such as "north", "east", "southeast", etc. occurring in Canadian dialogues, and relative terms occurring more frequently in Scottish dialogues ("over" and "under", for instance, occur 63.4% of the time in Scottish conversations). While these differences are potentially interesting, they are given very little weight by any machine learning model as they are not as predictive as dialect specific but task-irrelevant keywords.

Instead of modelling conversations based on word choices, then, we wish to study how a discourse is structured, and the high-level ways in which groups go about completing a task.

ANNOTATION WITH THE NEGOTIATION FRAMEWORK

The relationship between sharing information and task success has been repeatedly examined in a variety of contexts. Issues such as shared visibility and common grounding of objects [18], recognizing understanding or comprehension in the partner you are speaking to [11], and the use of physical action to communicate intent or understanding [16] have all been shown to have a major impact on the efficiency of communication. The issue of how communication differs between groups is particularly important to any research on interactive systems where cultural styles of interaction are relevant. Prior work has shown that subpopulations react to and interact with systems very differently [1]. Other work has also shown the utility of dialogue systems in military applications, such as soldier training [28]. Designing systems for specific groups of users should take into account the specific interaction patterns common among those users.

To represent information about communication and information sharing at a level near that described above, we base our analysis on the Negotiation framework, developed in the systemic functional linguistics (SFL) community [24]. Annotation with the Negotiation framework gives us the building blocks with which to study interaction. Annotation is only an initial step, however. Counts or even distributions of these annotations are not informative enough from our perspective. What lends the most insight into styles of interaction and footing between participants are sequences of annotations.

The Negotiation framework attempts to describe how speakers use their role as a source of knowledge or action to position themselves relative to others in a discourse [24]. The Negotiation framework is primarily made up of four main codes, K1, K2, A1, and A2. The four main codes are divided on two axes, illustrated in Figure 2. First, is the utterance related to exchanging information, or to exchanging services and actions? If the former, then it is a K move (knowledge); if the

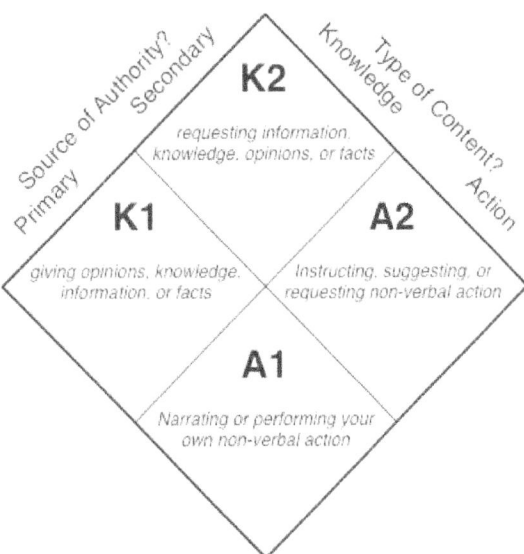

Figure 2. The main codes of the Negotiation framework.

latter, then an A move (action). Second, is the speaker acting as a primary or secondary source of action or knowledge? In the case of knowledge, this often corresponds to the difference between assertions (K1) and queries (K2). For instance, a statement of fact or opinion is a K1:

    g   K1   *well i've got a great viewpoint here just below the east lake*

By contrast, asking for someone else's knowledge or opinion is coded as a K2:

    g   K2   *what have you got underneath the east lake*
    f   K1   *a tourist attraction*

In the case of action, the codes usually correspond to narrating action (A1) and giving instructions (A2), as below:

    g   A2   *go almost to the edge of the lake*
    f   A1   *yeah okay*

Four additional categories are used for all other moves. These categories were selected from a larger set available in the systemic functional linguistics literature, and are the most common codes to appear repeatedly in different authors' analyses.

- Followup (f) moves are marked when a K1 or A1 move is being directly acknowledged as understood, without contributing additional new content to the discourse (such as backchanneling).

- Challenge (ch) moves are marked when a move directly undermines some assumption of the previous line, as in the example below:

    g   A2   *come directly down below the stone circle and we come up*
    f   ch   *I don't have a stone circle*
    g   o   *you don't have a stone circle*

- Tracking moves (tr) indicate a restatement or request for restatement, and are simply marking a failure to hear or understand what was said because of poor emphasis or pronunciation.

- Finally, all other moves are classified as o. This includes floor-grabbing moves, false starts, preparatory moves, and any other non-contentful contributions.

Agreement between annotators for this scheme is high both for distinguishing our four core codes and a collapsed "other" category ($\kappa = .74$) and for labelling all codes ($\kappa = .66$).

A final layer of complexity in the Negotiation annotation scheme is that labels are not assigned independently. Instead, there is a notion of a sequence - a connected series of moves, similar to the concept of adjacency pairs in conversation analysis. This notion states that a series of turns must follow some consistent structure, based around a primary move. A sequence is defined as a primary move (K1 or A1) and the context around that move, be it a secondary move (K2 or A2) that requested the move, o moves representing false starts or floor grabbers, and responses to the primary move in the form of followup or challenge moves. This structure was defined as a set of formal constraints in the first publication of this framework [26].

Analysis Details

Throughout our analysis, we use a consistent set of labels. We mark, for each turn, which of the eight possible codes from the Negotiation framework the line was annotated with, crossed with the speaker of the label. Therefore, a turn from the instruction giver which was labelled as a K2 receives the label "gK2". This gives sixteen possible labels for our analysis, and allows us to study the interacting effects of both speaker roles and turn-by-turn behavior. In this work, these labels were applied by hand; however, they have been shown to be reproducible with high reliability [26], meaning that these analyses could be incorporated into real-time systems.

In the next section we describe multiple representations of conversation which circumvent these dialect-specific keywords by relying solely on coded labels from the Negotiation framework. We show that coding schemes can be represented in meaningful ways to describe sequential events, without overfitting to dialect or topic, and instead highlighting the ways in which information sharing and instruction giving differ across subpopulations. This analysis allows us access to the next level of analysis, determining which practices have an impact on what results are achieved, and which are culturally specific but do not impact a group's ability to collaborate.

REPRESENTING INTERACTION IN DIALOGUE

Numerous disparate communities have informative and distinct methodologies for studying sequential conversational data. We believe that these approaches are complementary, and as such we draw inspiration from three distinct fields for our data analysis: transition graph analysis; stretchy interaction patterns; and trajectories of authority.

Transition Matrix Analysis

Exploratory sequential data analysis (ESDA) has been used as a phrase to describe a large number of different approaches to data mining [32]. Here, we use the term to describe a specific style of analysis where sequences of moves are analyzed for frequently co-occurring activities. This analysis usually involves deriving a transition probability matrix based on observed moves and interpreting the resulting transition graphs. This has been successfully applied to infer subtasks based on closely co-occurring moves [37], the impact of gender or argument style on group interactions in message boards [21, 20] and studying collaborative problem solving in student groups [34, 8].

The primary unit of analysis for ESDA is an interaction graph. These graphs represent transitions between adjacent labels in some sequential data, and are in theory a complete graph. First, a transition matrix T is built, with cell $t_{x,y}$ counting the number of times label x occurred immediately before label y. Then, a complete graph can be built giving the probability that for any utterance u, label y will occur after label x for any possible combinations of x and y.

These graphs are difficult to interpret in their complete form, as the number of edges grows polynomially. However, comparisons between two subsets of a data set can be made by building two graphs, one from each subset, and comparing the differences in probabilities between graphs. In our visualizations, only the transitions that we are interested in describing qualitatively will be displayed, to make graphs readable; other connections were not significant or are not relevant to our conclusions.

Stretchy Interaction Patterns

Prior work has introduced the notion of a "stretchy pattern" [25]. These patterns display the sequence of categories of behavior that occur, based on a coding scheme. A limitation of transition matrices is that they limit the observations of interactions between annotations to adjacent turns. Stretchy patterns overcome this by allowing longer interactions to be captured, if they are frequent and informative enough. The resulting patterns cannot be comprehensively listed in a matrix; hwoever, the advantage they give in expressive power allows them to be analyzed in more detail individually.

A pattern is comprised of a series of tokens which can be drawn from a small number of classes. These tokens also encode the speaker of an utterance. A token may also be a gap, which is allowed to consume up to some number of concrete tokens; or a shift in sequence, either to the next sequence (marked by →) or shifting back to a previous sequence that was unfinished (marked by ←). In our case, we set the range of allowed pattern sizes to be 3 − 6 tokens, with gaps (marked by □) allowed to consume from 1 − 3 tokens. Location of gaps is fixed at particular points and thus mirrors and extends the concept of lags in sequential data analysis [31].

Authority Trajectories

We may also consider a conversation based on two constantly adjusting metrics: the flow of information between speakers (Information authority), and the flow of directions for action between speakers (Action authority). At each utterance, we define these measures based on the Negotiation codes that have occurred up to that point. In our representation, a K1 move from the instruction giver represents a shift of +1, while a K2 move from the instruction giver represents a shift of -1; similarly, a K1 move from the instruction follower is a shift of -1 and a K2 move from the follower is a shift of +1. The same formula can be used for Action authority, but the polarity is reversed; an A2 move represents an authoritative move, thus an instruction giver A2 move is marked as +1, and so on.

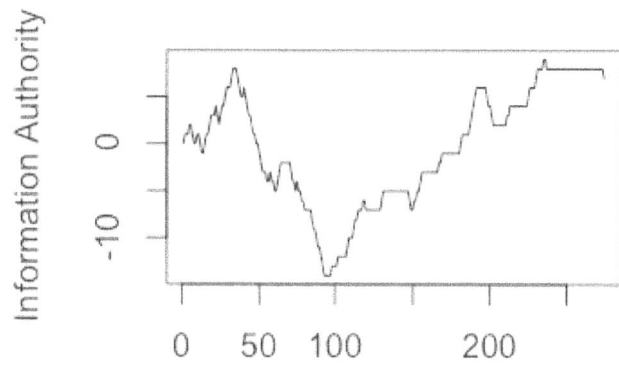

Figure 3. Example K-authority trajectory over a single conversation.

An example of the resulting trajectory is given in Figure 3, showing only information authority. In that dialogue, authority shifts towards the instruction giver early, before drastically shifting towards the instruction follower as a series of questions are asked by the giver about the follower's map, followed by a gradual shift back to the instruction giver for the rest of the dialogue.

Trajectories as described above give a quick visual depiction of the flow of information and instructions between speakers over the course of a conversation. To understand similarities between these trajectories across multiple conversations, we want to empirically group similar conversations together. To do this, we use time series clustering based on dynamic time warping [7], a standard method for measuring similarity between time series data with different lengths. From this, we can build a similarity matrix between each conversation. Conversations are then grouped together through hierarchical agglomerative clustering [23], a standard clustering algorithm. The resulting output is a progressively more refined taxonomy of conversations, which can be simplified to arbitrary levels of granularity.

An advantage of the trajectory formulation is that it can be used for any span of utterances, not just the spans from first to last utterance of a conversation. In our experiments, we consider both this whole-conversation case, and a second case which parallels the segmentations from the other representations of our data - only utterances within sequences for a given landmark are analyzed to produce the trajectory for the mentions of a given landmark can be considered.

The final stage of this trajectory analysis is to cluster trajectories. Using hierarchical agglomerative clustering, we group similar trajectories. We cluster whole conversations twice, once by Action authority and once by Information authority. This results in a dendrogram of relatedness which can be grouped at arbitrarily refined subsets. We produce clusters such that each cluster contains at least four conversations. This results (coincidentally) in eight clusters for both Action authority and Information authority.

TASK: IDENTIFYING A DYAD'S SUBPOPULATION

We first consider the problem of identifying, based on a transcribed and annotated conversation, whether that interaction comes from the Canadian Military subpopulation, or the Scottish Civilian subpopulation. Later, we will come back to these same patterns and identify which are relevant to success at completing a task, and which may cause misunderstandings between culture but do not have an impact on performance.

We divide our data based on landmarks, from the first time a landmark is mentioned to the last. The notion of sequences, introduced when defining our framework, is key to this analysis - if any utterance in a sequence contains a reference to a given landmark, the whole sequence of turns is included in the interaction on that landmark. Because landmarks often overlap, the same sequence of turns may occur multiple times in our data set, once in the context of each landmark that sequence references.

Transition Matrix Analysis

The single most common interaction in the MapTask domain is instruction giving. Therefore, the way in which this interaction is structured is worth especially detailed study.

Figure 4 gives a detailed breakdown of the instruction-giving process from our ESDA analysis, and the variations in how instruction is given and received between subpopulations. We see that the standard interaction is as expected - the instruction giver begins with an A2 move, followed by an A1 move from the instruction follower, and a followup move from the giver to show that the narration was noticed.

A pattern for A2 instructions and responses is clear in both subpopulations. Differences exist between subpopulations. Most notably, the feedback from the instruction giver is more common in the Canadian military population; over half of all actions from the instruction follower are met with an acknowledgement, compared to roughly one third among Scottish civilians. We also see more non-contentful o moves from the instruction follower at the end of an instruction in the Scottish civilian population. The Canadian military population, by contrast, is much more likely to shift immediately to the next instruction.

An explanation of this that emerges from examining the graph in Figure 4 is based on the formulaic nature that seems to emerge most strongly in Canadian military dialogues. The **gA2-fA1-gf** pattern is very strongly emphasized, and deviations from that cycle are unusual. In the Scottish civilian cycle of instructions, however, there is more noise. Fewer moves from the instruction follower are explicitly acknowledged, more time is filled with non-contentful moves, and a

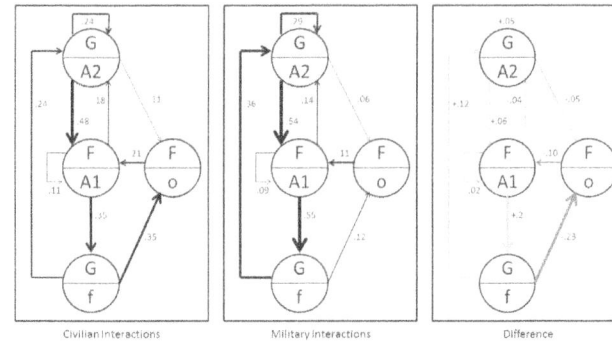

Figure 4. Variation in standard instruction sequences between subpopulations. In our diagrams, line thickness corresponds to probability, and color in the final graph denotes direction of difference - blue lines represent a transition more common in the left-hand graph, orange lines are more common in the right-hand graph.

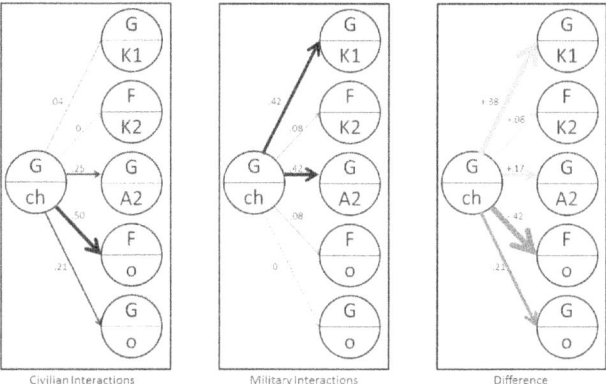

Figure 5. Differences in responses elicited from a challenge move from the giver between subpopulations.

return to the gA2 label for the next instruction is much weaker (indicating divergences to other parts of the graph not shown).

Challenge moves and the breakdown of common ground

Challenge moves are relatively rare in our data set (1.1% of utterances in total), but they are in fact critical points in a discourse. From qualitative analysis, we know that challenges are made when assumptions about shared information clash. An A2 move about a landmark you cannot see may prompt a challenge, for instance, as the instruction is undermined.

Responses to challenge moves are distinctly different between conditions in our data set. Figure 5 shows the difference in subpopulations when an instruction giver makes a challenge. The Scottish civilian response is usually contentless - a backchannel or acknowledgement before any response is made. In the Canadian military subpopulation, however, the follower very rarely responds directly to a challenge move; instead, the instruction giver follows immediately with a contentful move (A2 or K1). This suggests that, as we have observed a much more formulaic structure to the interactions in the Canadian Military subpopulation, a challenge move may prompt the instruction follower to stay silent until the dialogue resumes its formulaic structure.

Stretchy Patterns Analysis

Examples from within the top 25 stretchy patterns for each population are shown in Table 1. While the ESDA analysis highlighted the tightly-knit structure of instruction based interactions, the stretchy pattern analysis finds a stronger signal in the information based sequences, where interruptions, false starts, and other more minor moves are more common and transition matrices (which observe only immediate transitions) are less likely to find a signal.

In the Canadian military population, many of the dominant patterns highlight part or all of an information exchange. **gf** moves are shown to frequently follow immediately after or within a few tokens of **fK1**. Among the most distinctively Scottish-civilian patterns, most deal with action exchanges. The top Scottish pattern **fA1** → □ → □ → also illustrates that a succession of short turns, starting with an **fA1** action-completed move, is indicative of this population. We also see a number of strong Scottish patterns that begin with moves labelled **go**. In particular, we see patterns along the lines of **go gA2** - this represents the instruction-giver grabbing the floor before requesting an action.

Authority Trajectory Analysis

Trajectories of Action authority highlight differences in the ordering of information sharing. Figure 6 shows information authority clusters, for a visual understanding of the difference in trajectories; each graph represents the average trajectory of the dialogues in that cluster, normalized for length. We also show the distribution of subpopulations in each cluster. In some conversations, exclusively Canadian, the Action authority trajectory is flat for the first third or half of the conversation. These groups were clustered together in our unsupervised algorithm. This pattern highlights a strategy of delayed instruction giving; initial communication is almost entirely building a shared knowledge base, going over the entire map, and clarifying differences.

We see that this two-phase process is not always well-explained even within a pair. For instance, the instruction giver sometimes is forced to clarify that their explanations are not instructions, but attempts to build common ground:

g	K1	*bottom line of the green bay would be between the word haystack and the actual haystack*
g	K1	*and it starts about uh an inch and a half to the right of the haystack*
f	K2	*so i go over the top of the haystack or underneath*
g	A2	*you're not drawing any line yet*

We find that Action authority almost uniformly climbs towards the instruction giver, as expected. The remaining difference in Action authority clusters seems highly dependent on the slope; that is, the total number of instructions given. These slope differences do not discriminate between subpopulations.

Differences in Information authority are more starkly different, and show patterns of information sharing that are specific to subpopulations. The most starkly different is cluster

Pattern	Predicts	Kappa
fK1 □ gf →	Canadian	0.424
gK2 □ fK2 □ gf →	Canadian	0.415
fK1 gf □ → □ gA2	Canadian	0.310
fA1 → □ → □ →	Scottish	0.179
go □ gA2 □ →	Scottish	0.143
go □ fK2	Scottish	0.134

Table 1. Highlighted patterns predictive of the source subpopulation of an interaction.

3. Conversations grouped in this cluster gave almost no information about the instruction giver's map, and instead focused entirely on building common ground from the instruction follower's perspective, describing locations on their map. This behavior is exclusively existent in the Canadian military subpopulation.

Other clusters showed clearer splits between authority of the two speakers. Clusters 4 and 7 are related in that for the first half of the conversation, information is given mostly by a single speaker, and incremental information is then fixed by the opposite speaker in the second half of the dialogue; however, the roles are reversed between clusters, and these clusters correspond to subpopulations. Groups giving the instruction follower precedence are exclusively Canadian military, while groups beginning from the instruction giver's perspective are more likely to be Scottish civilian.

The remaining clusters show a more balanced approach to information giving, with both instruction giver and instruction follower trading roles of information authority as needed. In some cases, information sharing stops almost entirely at a certain point, shifting entirely to instruction giving (potentially when a group feels a sense of "hitting a stride").

Synthesis of findings

Interactions in the Canadian Military subpopulation are distinctly more orderly and predictable, compared to the Scottish civilian subpopulation. This emerges in all phases of interaction, from question-answer pairs, to instruction giving, to the response to challenges and problematic points within an interaction. Also, two distinct strategies for building common ground emerge - one where participants spend a large amount of time at the beginning of an interaction to collaboratively build a shared representation of the map, and a second where information is shared on an as-needed basis, immediately jumping to instruction giving. The first strategy appears only in Canadian military interactions, while the second occurs in both populations.

TASK: PREDICTING GROUP SUCCESS

Differences in discourse practices between subpopulations can be identified with our analysis techniques. We now shift to a related question: are these practices related to the end success of a group at completing a task?

Work on task success in the MapTask corpus has usually been based on absolute error between drawn paths and source paths

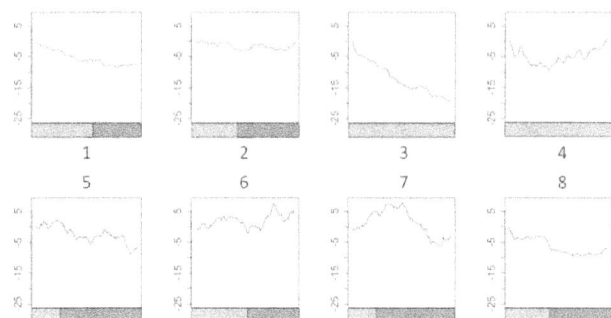

Figure 6. Averaged trajectories of Information Authority across clusters, normalized for time. For each cluster, the distribution is shown for Canadian military (orange) and Scottish civilian (blue) conversations.

[25, 27]. This error, measured in cm^2, is useful as an aggregate comparison between groups. However, we wish to understand successful interactions at a much more fine grained level, specifically at the level of an individual landmark. In order to achieve this, we first divide our conversations based on the spans of utterance that a landmark is referenced in. These segments will serve as the unit of analysis for the following section.

Aggregate analysis

Our first analysis is to test the predictive values of participant metadata on success. In our analysis, we use Visibility as a moderating variable. Since some landmarks are more challenging than others, we also use Landmark as a moderating variable.

We associate each landmark segment with a success metric, which we refer to as the Grade, using the Incorrect Entity Score metric first used in [12]. This measure marks, for each landmark, whether the drawn path reproduces the source path for that particular landmark. In each conversation, each landmark is marked as perfect, "good" miss (for a path that is too close or too far from a landmark, but passes it on the correct side or corner), "bad" miss (for a path that passes a landmark on the wrong side or goes through the landmark), or no attempt (for a path that never comes close to a landmark). The HCRC MapTask corpus (Scottish Civilian) was already annotated with these landmark references; we reproduce that annotation for the DCIEM MapTask corpus.

The first question we must address is whether there is any main effect of cultural subpopulation on task success. We do this using a χ^2 analysis where Subpopulation is the Independent variable, Grade is the Dependent variable, and Landmark and Visibility are moderating variables. When we examine the Likelihood ratio tests we find that Landmark ($p < .0001$) and Visibility ($p < .05$) are significant predictors of Grade. Subpopulation is not significant, nor is there an interaction between Subpopulation and Visibility.

Transition Matrix Analysis

An ESDA analysis of task success highlights the importance of the **ch** move. Differences in responses to challenges exist for both giver and follower challenges, though the response is distinctly different. Giver challenges in successful interactions are usually responded to with a backchannel from the follower; however, in unsuccessful interactions, those challenges are immediately followed up with an A2 move from the instruction giver.

For follower challenges, a similar pattern emerges; in successful interactions, the next turn is usually an acknowledgement from the instruction giver, while in unsuccessful interactions, the follower is much more likely to continue the conversation, whether with a K1 or K2 move. An acknowledging o move from the other speaker, in both cases, is more likely in successful interactions. On the other hand, when no vocal acknowledgement is made in response to the challenged assumption, future moves may not be as likely to shift to compensate.

Authority Trajectory Analysis

Earlier in this work we clustered conversations based on their authority trajectories. We did this for both action-based authority trajectories (A-clustering) and knowledge authority trajectories (K-clusters). We now test to see whether these same clusters are predictive of task success.

Using a χ^2 test, we confirmed that these clusters represent significant distributions of the Canadian and Scottish subpopulations, however most are not solely dominated by one subpopulation or another. Task relevance to the behavior patterns represented by the clusters then are consistent with the nature of cultural differences between populations. These clusters do not predict cultural subpopulation, but some are more strongly associated with particular subpopulations.

To assess the task relevance of these differences, we again conduct a χ^2 analysis with Grade as the Dependent variable and Landmark and Visibility as moderating variables. This time the Independent variable is alternately the K-clustering or the A-clustering.

In the A-clustering analysis, we find a marginal main effect of A-clustering ($p = .1$), and a significant interaction between A-clustering and Visibility such that Visibility only has a significant effect for certain patterns of behavior. The effect of K-clustering is only a trend ($p = .16$) and there is no significant interaction with Visibility.

The result trends in favor of the marked pattern of delayed instruction giving in the Canadian subpopulation, until common ground is achieved. It is notable that the evidence of task relevance is relatively weak; in particular, weaker than one would expect given how strongly individuals may cling to cultural practices. Despite the extensive differences in trajectories of authority and the rate and distribution of moves for reaching common ground, there was no main effect on task success related to these differences. Patterns extracted from just the successful interactions (and likewise from just the unsuccessful instances) for each cultural group were nearly identical to those extracted from the whole dataset. We do not consider these results to indicate a failure on the part of the analysis technique. Rather, they suggest that cultural differences are not the driver of task success.

Synthesis of findings

Our findings highlight the difficulty of attributing success to any one indicator of group composition. We highlight the importance of challenges indicates a breakdown of communication, where shifts in shared common ground may depend on appropriate acknowledgement of disagreements. However, our main finding is that those differences which separate out cultures are only weak predictors of group success. This affirms the findings of prior work, which has focused on improving communication between diverse groups, rather than coercing participants into culture-specific behaviors stereotyped as more or less effective.

CONCLUSIONS

This work presents a thorough discussion of the issue of information sharing and instruction giving in dialogue. We began by showing that a simple surface representation of dialogue is insufficient for answering questions about information sharing and building of common ground. Three more complex representations for sequential data analysis were highlighted: transition matrices, interaction patterns, and authority trajectories.

A general factor which repeatedly arises in our results is the relative orderliness of the Canadian military interactions. The structure of instruction giving, followed by narration, and then acknowledgement ($gA2 \rightarrow fA1 \rightarrow gf$) is much more consistent in that subpopulation. Similarly, challenge moves are responded to with contentful moves G far more often than acknowledgements, which are more common in the Scottish civilian subpopulation. We also observe a difference in information sharing strategies over the course of an entire conversation. Scottish civilians gave information almost entirely on an as-needed basis, not planning past the next landmark. Canadian military pairs split between an this as-needed strategy and a strategy of building common ground to start a conversation, before giving any instructions.

These findings show that our methodology for describing interactions is effective both at the turn-by-turn level, describing frequent sequences of interaction multiple turns long, and over the course of a dialogue, describing the shift in roles over time. This means that similar techniques can be used both in real-time systems, which rely on a short window of previous turns, and in post hoc analyses of interactions, which can take advantage of full transcripts.

Most importantly, though, our work suggests that the most significant barrier to effective intercultural collaboration is not the adoption of strategies specific to one culture or another. The relatively stronger impact of subpopulation on behavior, rather than task success, suggests that the development of methodology and technology that improves on mutual understanding of cultural practices is needed, and is likely to make the largest contribution to intercultural collaboration moving forward. Incorporating these elements in a real-time system is a non-trivial task, but is promising given that prior work has already shown that automatic annotation of these labels is highly accurate [26].

This automated process will motivate continued research on this topic. One issue that we have not yet studied is the problem of threading. In a single dialogue, multiple issues may be relevant at any given moment. Speakers may refer to both on-task and off-task information, and even as information relates to a task, speakers may be attempting to resolve multiple issues concurrently. This problem is only exacerbated as we extend our analysis to domains with more than two speakers. Resolving these issues of threading and proper attribution of authority to topics is a major thrust of our continuing work.

Acknowledgements

The research reported here was supported by National Science Foundation grant IIS-0968485, and in part by the Pittsburgh Science of Learning Center, which is funded by the National Science Foundation grant SBE-0836012.

REFERENCES

1. H. Ai, A. Raux, D. Bohus, M. Eskenazi, and D. Litman. Comparing spoken dialog corpora collected with recruited subjects versus real users. In *Proceedings of the ACM SIG on Discourse and Dialogue*, 2007.

2. H. Ai, M. Sionti, Y.-C. Wang, and C. P. Rosé. Finding transactive contributions in whole group classroom discussions. In *Proceedings of the International Conference of the Learning Sciences*, 2010.

3. A. Anderson, M. Bader, E. Bard, E. Boyle, G. Doherty, S. Garrod, S. Isard, J. Kowtko, J. McAllister, J. Miller, C. Sotillo, H. Thompson, and R. Weinert. The hcrc map task corpus. In *Language and Speech*, 1991.

4. M. Azimitia and R. Montgomery. Friendship, transactive dialogues, and the development of scientific reasoning. In *Social Development*, 1993.

5. E. Bard, C. Sotillo, A. Anderson, and M. M. Taylor. The dciem map task corpus: Spontaneous dialogue under sleep deprivation and drug treatment. In *ESCA-NATO Tutorial and Workshop on Speech under Stress*, pages 25–28, 1995.

6. M. Berkowitz and J. Gibbs. Measuring the developmental features of moral discussion. In *Merrill-Palmer Quarterly*, 1983.

7. D. Berndt and J. Clifford. Using dynamic time warping to find patterns in time series. In *AAAI Workshop on Knowledge Discovery in Databases*, 1994.

8. M. Cakir, F. Xhafa, N. Zou, and G. Stahl. Thread-based analysis of patterns of collaborative interaction in chat. In *Proceedings of AI in Education*, 2005.

9. L. Chen. Interaction involvement and patterns of topical talk: A comparison of intercultural and intracultural dyads. In *International journal of Intercultural Relations*, 1995.

10. M. M. Chiu. Group problem-solving processes: Social interactions and individual actions. In *Theory of Social Behavior*, 2000.

11. H. Clark and M. Krych. Speaking while monitoring addressees for understanding. In *Memory and Language*, 2004.

12. B. Davies. Principles we talk by: Testing dialogue principles in task-oriented dialogues. In *Pragmatics*, 2010.

13. E. Diamant, S. Fussell, and F.-L. Lo. Collaborating across cultural and technological boundaries: Team culture and information use in a map navigation task. In *International Workshop on Intercultural Collaboration*, 2009.

14. J. Eisenstein, N. A. Smith, and E. P. Xing. Discovering sociolinguistic associations with structured sparsity. In *Proceedings of the Annual Meeting of the Association for Computational Linguistics*, 2011.

15. M. Gao. Influence of native culture and language on intercultural communication: The case of prc student immigrants in australia. 2000.

16. D. Gergle. *The Value of Shared Visual Information for Task-Oriented Collaboration*. PhD thesis, 2006.

17. G. Gweon, P. Agarwal, M. Udani, B. Raj, and C. P. Rosé. The automatic assessmnet of knowledge integration processes in project teams. In *Proceedings of Computer Supported Collaborative Learning*, 2011.

18. J. E. Hanna, M. K. Tanenhaus, and J. C. Trueswell. The effects of common ground and perspective on domains of referential interpretation. In *Memory and Language*, 2003.

19. A. Hellemans. Manufacturing mayday. In *IEEE Spectrum*, 2007.

20. A. Jeong. The sequential analysis of group interaction and critical thinking in online threaded discussions. In *American Journal of Distance Education*, 2003.

21. A. Jeong and G. Davidson-Shivers. The effects of gender interaction patterns on student participation in computer-supported collaborative argumentation. In *Educational Technology, Research, and Development*, 2006.

22. H. Li. Grounding and information communication in intercultural and intracultural dyadic discourse. In *Discourse Processes*, 1999.

23. C. Manning, P. Raghavan, and H. Schutze. *Introduction to Information Retrieval*. 2008.

24. J. Martin and D. Rose. *Working with Discourse: Meaning Beyond the Clause*. 2003.

25. E. Mayfield, M. Garbus, D. Adamson, and C. P. Rosé. Data-driven interaction patterns: Authority and information sharing in dialogue. In *Proceedings of AAAI Fall Symposium on Building Common Ground with Intelligent Agents*, 2011.

26. E. Mayfield and C. P. Rosé. Recognizing authority in dialogue with an integer linear programming constrained model. In *Proceedings of Association for Computational Linguistics*, 2011.

27. D. Reitter and J. Moore. Predicting success in dialogue. In *Proceedings of ACL*, 2007.

28. A. Roque, A. Leuski, V. Rangajaran, S. Robinson, A. Vaswani, S. Narayanan, and D. Traum. Radiobot-cff: A spoken dialogue system for military training. In *Proceedings of Interspeech*, 2006.

29. C. P. Rosé and S. Fussell. Towards measuring group affect in computer-mediated communication. In *ACM SIG-CHI Workshop on Measuring Affect in HCI: Going Beyond the Individual*, 2008.

30. C. P. Rosé, Y.-C. Wang, Y. Cui, J. Arguello, K. Stegmann, A. Weinberger, and F. Fischer. Analyzing collaborative learning processes automatically: Exploiting the advances of computational linguistics in computer-supported collaborative learning. In *International Journal of Computer Supported Collaborative Learning*, 2008.

31. G. Sackett. The lag sequential analysis of contingency and cyclicity in behavioral interaction research. In *Handbook of Infant Development*. 1979.

32. P. M. Sanderson and C. Fisher. Exploratory sequential data analysis: foundations. In *Human-Computer Interaction*, 1994.

33. L. Setlock, S. Fussell, and C. Neuwirth. Taking it out of context: Collaborating within and across cultures in face-to-face settings and via instant messaging. In *Proceedings of the Conference on Computer-Supported Cooperative Work*, 2004.

34. G. Stahl. *Group Cognition: Computer Support for Collaborative Knowledge Building*. 2005.

35. D. Suthers, N. Dwyer, R. Medina, and R. Vatrapu. A framework for eclectic analysis of collaborative interaction. In *International Conference on Computer-Supported Collaborative Learning*, 2007.

36. R. Vatrapu and D. D. Suthers. Cultural influences in collaborative information sharing and organization. In *International Conference on Intercultural Collaboration*, 2010.

37. O. Vortac and M. B. Edwards. Sequences of actions for individual and teams of air traffic controllers. In *Human-Computer Interaction*, 1994.

Studying the Influence of Culture in Global Software Engineering: Thinking in Terms of Cultural Models

Hina Shah	Nancy J. Nersessian	Mary Jean Harrold	Wendy Newstetter
College of Computing	College of Computing	College of Computing	Department of Biomedical Engineering
Georgia Institute of Technology	Georgia Institute of Technology	Georgia Institute of Technology	Georgia Institute of Technology
hinashah@cc.gatech.edu	nancyn@cc.gatech.edu	harrold@cc.gatech.edu	wendy@bme.gatech.edu

ABSTRACT
Culture appears to have a greater influence on software-engineering practice than originally envisioned. Many recent studies have reported that cultural factors greatly impact global software-engineering (GSE) practice. However, many of these studies characterize culture as a set of dimensions (e.g., Hofstede's), which significantly limits the meaning of culture. In this paper, we discuss the limitations of such a dimensional approach to studying culture by highlighting the aspects of culture that such dimensions fail to capture. Next, we present the idea of thinking of culture in terms of cultural models (inspired by Shore's work), and illustrate this idea by presenting cultural models adopted by the software-engineering domain. Then, based on this idea of cultural models, we present a conceptual reference framework for studying the influence of culture in the global software-engineering setting. Finally, we present some examples that use this framework, which illustrates the benefits of such a framework for studying culture's influence on GSE practice.

Author Keywords
Culture; cultural dimensions; cultural models; software engineering; software testing; qualitative study; ethnography

ACM Classification Keywords
D.2.m [Software Engineering]: Miscellaneous;

1. INTRODUCTION
Global software engineering (GSE), and particularly offshored software development, is a large industry [4], and it is expected to continue to grow rapidly [4]. The perceived benefits of this offshoring and outsourcing practice are reduction in costs, access to skilled resources, effective time-zone utilization, and improved quality of the work. However, studies have indicated that 69% of all outsourcing projects fail, completely or partially; the studies report that the main reason for these failures is the cultural incompatibilities between clients and vendors and poor relationship management [2]. Casey reports that cultural differences negatively impact global software teams [8]. A recent Accenture[1] study reports that "mis-communication and a lack of cross-cultural understanding can hinder the effectiveness of global sourcing" [1]. Studies have shown that culture also impacts the functioning of specific GSE activities, such as offshored software testing [3, 8]. Thus, GSE practice is increasingly growing but the quality of work and productivity may be suffering because of cultural incompatibilities [1, 30]. Understanding how cultural incompatibilities may be affecting software-development activities is crucial [28]. Thus, it is important to study GSE from the cultural perspective.

Like any discipline, software engineering possesses its own culture. This culture has emerged over time and across nations, and is influenced by and embedded in other cultures (e.g., national and organizational). For example, according to Fendler, the design and practice of software engineering as a discipline is highly influenced by western culture [11].[2] Additionally, with the increased practice of offshoring and outsourcing in the software industry, both national culture and site-specific organizational culture play significant roles in shaping the software-engineering practice at a site. Software-engineering literature recognizes and discusses the existences of these cultures and their differences. Many recent GSE-related studies have reported that cultural factors greatly impact the global software practice (e.g., [5, 6, 8, 19, 31]).

However, most of these studies have directly applied frameworks, such as Hofstede's five cultural dimensions (i.e., power distance, uncertainty avoidance, individualism versus collectivism, masculinity versus feminity, long-term versus short-term orientation) [14] and Trompenaars and Hampdeen-Turner's seven layers of culture (i.e., universalism/particularism, individualism/communitarianism, specific/diffuse, affective/neutral, achievement/ascription, sequential/synchronic, internal/external control), to show culture's influence on the GSE practice [29]. Although these dimensions help GSE researchers show that culture has an impact on GSE practice, the dimensions send a message that culture's impact is restricted to these dimensions, which is not the case in reality. Moreover, these dimensions do not describe how practice in specific settings is informed by and imbued by culture, and they make it difficult to explain the implications of cultural impact on GSE practice [5, 9, 27]. Additionally, the meaning of culture is significantly limited by these dimensions [16, 21, 27]. Given that culture plays an important role in GSE practice, it is necessary to conduct appropriate research studies (e.g., ethnographic studies) to understand culture's role in this practice [5, 9, 17].

---
[1] Accenture is one of the top global technology service and outsourcing service provider companies.

[2] Fendler observed the difficulty of fitting the recommended western software-engineering practice into African culture in Namibia [11].

To facilitate such studies, in this paper, we present the idea of thinking in terms of cultural models—"patterns that govern conventional behaviors"—inspired by Shore's work on Culture in Mind [27, p. 6]. A major advantage of this approach is that the nature of cultural models are not pre-determined. The assumption is that all humans, as cognitive and sociocultural beings, create and enact cultural models. Our argument is that determining these models through detailed in situ studies (ethnographic, narrative [12]), will help to better understand how and why culture affects the GSE practice. Such studies will also provide a rich understanding of the supports and barriers of this practice so that culturally-aware solutions can be designed to improve the practice. In this paper, we also present a reference framework for conducting cultural studies in GSE practice, such as the offshored setup. Furthermore, we explain this framework with examples from field studies done in the offshored software-testing domain.

The main contributions of this paper are
- a description of the current understanding of culture in the GSE field and its limitations
- a discussion of a novel reference framework for studying culture based on thinking of culture through models
- an illustration of culture through models using examples of cultural models derived from GSE field studies

2. CULTURE AS DIMENSIONS PERSPECTIVE

Culture is defined in many ways in the literature (e.g., Kroeber and Kluckhohn have compiled a list of different definitions of culture [20]). Although, culture is difficult to define, many researchers have tried to simplify the definition of culture by reducing it to a succinct set of dimensions. In the GSE literature, the most common way in which culture is perceived is as sets of dimensions as described by researchers such as Hofstede [14], Trompaneer and Hampdeen-Turner [29], and Hall [13]. In this section, we discuss these commonly-used conceptions of culture in the GSE.

Hofstede's dimensions
According to Hofstede, culture is defined along five dimensions. First, *power distance* relates to the extent to which members of the society accept and expect unequal distribution of power. Second, *uncertainty avoidance* relates to the extent to which culture governs the feeling of comfort or discomfort among members of the society in uncertain situations and to the degree to which the society tries to control the uncontrollable situations. Third, *individualism vs. collectivism* relates to the degree to which members of the society hold an individualistic approach or a collective approach where they coexist in unified groups, such as family. Fourth, *masculinity vs. femininity* relates to the emotional role distributions between the genders. Fifth, *long-term vs. short-term orientation* relates to the extent to which a culture governs its members to orient towards long-term prospects vs. short-term prospects.

Trompenaar's and Hampden-Turner's dimensions
Trompenaar and Hampden-Turner describe culture using three layers [29]. The outermost layer, called *explicit culture*, is the observable reality in the form of artifacts and products. The middle layer, called *norms and values*, relates to the mutual sense of right and wrong and of good and bad. The innermost layer, called the *assumption about existence*, relates to core levels of human existence and survival. Furthermore, Trompenaar and Hampden-Turner define seven fundamental dimensions of culture. First, *universalism vs. particularism* distinguishes cultures based on whether they hold an objective or subjective approach to factors such as correctness. Second, *individualism vs. communitarianism* relates to the degree to which the culture is individualistic vs. collectivist (i.e., Hofstede's third dimension). Third, *neutral vs. emotional* relates to the degree to which emotions are allowed to influence interactions. Fourth, *specific vs. diffuse* relates to the degree to which relationships have the personal vs. professional element. Fifth, *achievement vs. ascription* relates to the manner in which the society judges its members; cultures that exhibit the achievement dimension tend to judge their members based on recent accomplishments, whereas cultures that exhibit the ascription dimension tend to attribute status to their members based on factors such as kinship, gender, and age. Sixth, *attitudes to time* refers to the way in which societies perceive time—sequential or synchronic. Seventh, *attitudes to the environment* relates to the way members of the society view the control to/by the environment.

Hall's dimensions
For Hall, culture is communication, which consists of verbal expression (words), power and status expression (material things), and feeling expression (behavior) [13]. Furthermore, he identifies key cultural dimensions that are classified based on time and communication patterns. Based on *time*, he classifies culture as monochronic cultures that perceive time linearly performing one activity at a time and polychronic cultures that perceive time more flexibly by allowing activities to be performed simultaneously. Based on *communication patterns*, he classifies cultures as high-context cultures, in which importance is given to the context rather than the content, and low-context cultures, in which importance is given to the content (information is exchanged through explicit and clear messages giving more data to reduce misunderstandings).

3. LIMITATIONS OF CULTURE AS DIMENSIONS

The culture-as-dimensions conception of culture has several limitations [21], especially when applied to GSE. In this section, we discuss these limitations.

Dimensions not embodied in the practice
The culture-as-dimensions approach is being used in the global software-development community by applying the predetermined dimensions to the settings (or the situations being studied) and then comparing the results across settings (or situations). Using this approach, the dimensions do not emerge from the practice, and are thus, not embodied in the practice. Instead, the dimensions are applied externally to the practice. The problem with applying a predetermined list of factors to a particular practice is that there is a significant risk that cultural facets or features particular to that setting and that practice will be missed. To capture these features requires the use of qualitative and interpretive methods for examining the culture "from within." As Boden and colleagues argue, it is important to address these missing factors:

> The predominance of GSE [Global Software Engineering] studies that apply survey-type instruments utilizing forms of Hofstede's dimensions of cultural variation is problematic for the field, as it tends to over shadow the value of other, more interpretive approaches to understanding the myriad ways in which communication and coordination [and other cultural aspects] across globally distributed software teams is affected by local, organizational and professional 'cultures' [5].

Thus, to better understand culture's impact on GSE, it is crucial to capture the cultural factors embodied in the practice, which the dimensional approach currently fails to achieve, through the use of more qualitative and interpretive methods.

Dimension pose risk of stereotyping

As discussed above, researchers (practitioners) in GSE typically apply Hofstede-like dimensions externally to the practice to draw culture-based conclusions about their experiences in interacting with different cultures. However, there is strong argument against using such dimensional approaches to study culture because there is a risk of stereotyping [24]. Although, the use of such dimensions may help to gain a different perspective about the situations, it may cause the researchers (practitioners) to generalize their conclusions by stereotyping. Such stereotyping is clearly described in the expatriate story discussed by Gertsen and Søderberg, in which one of the expatriates uses Hofstede's theoretical concept of power distance to justify why he feels at ease with the Americans [12]. Based on this story, the authors report

> What is interesting, though, is that the interviewee's use of one of Hofstede's concepts to explain his own affinity for the US leads him to talk about a colleague's difficulties in China, where he himself has never been, as a counterexample. The quote illustrates how a theoretical concept of a cultural dimension may be used discursively in different manners—to explain one's attitude based on presumed cultural similarity, but also to stereotype a culture with which one has not yet had any contact. [12, p. 254]

Meaning of culture significantly limited

Because culture is difficult to define, it is not surprising that there is inadequate understanding of culture in the first place, particularly in the GSE culture-based research community. In addition, dimensional frameworks' representation of culture tends to misdirect many researchers into believing that culture revolves around these predetermined dimensions. Thus, researchers are inclined to explain any situation or behavior by fitting these dimensions to the situation or behavior, rather than attempting to determine other potential cultural facets that emerge from those specific data. Because of the manner in which these dimensions are being used to understand culture in the GSE domain, culture's meaning is being significantly limited. An understanding that culture encompasses facets beyond these dimensions appears to be missing. Imposing beforehand a set of dimensions along which to view culture in a particular situation or practice hinders the discovery of nuances specific to that culture that might be highly significant for understanding the problematic factors of that situation. This approach results in incomplete description of culture's influence on the global software practice.

Culture viewed as static

With the use of the culture-as-dimensions approach, culture is being viewed as a static and rigid entity that is represented by a set of characteristics embedded in these dimensions. Cognitive anthropologists, such as Shore and Hutchins, argue that culture is a process that is ongoing and is continuously influencing and being influenced by the environment and individuals in the environment [16, 27]. However, culture, in the form of numerical values of Hofstede's dimensions,[3] has not changed over time, which indicates that the culture-as-dimensions approach misses the gradually evolving and transforming nature of culture. Thus, viewing culture in the form of such dimensions misses the important aspects of culture as being dynamic and as gradually transforming in nature.

Culture described as national only

These Hofstede-like dimensional views of culture describe culture solely in terms of national characteristics. However, many researchers have argued against culture being restricted to purely national, especially the way it has been portrayed by these dimensional views of culture [18, 17]. Moreover, such a national culture-based perspective imposes serious limitations for studying culture, particularly in GSE. Global software practice has observed an increased migration of people around the world. For instance, Silicon Valley has many companies with the majority of employees being non-U.S. citizens. Thus, people from different nationalities work together at one location and are distributed across different locations. Directly applying these cultural dimensions to such settings without appreciating the heterogeneity of the cultural backgrounds of the people may result in distorted findings.

4. CULTURE AS MODELS PERSPECTIVE

A more promising school of thought views culture as a process that creates and uses models. The idea of cultural models stems from a perspective that sees culture and cognition as mutually constitutive. The cultural models idea argues that people both understand the world in terms of models and enact models in cultural behavior. The nature of a specific culture's models cannot be predetermined, but can be uncovered only through studying that culture and its practices. Shore defines culture as a dynamic, on-going process that produces models (not amenable to list-like formulations), which are organized structures of thought and action that represent tacit shared knowledge that people acquire and use to interpret experiences and generate social behavior [27]. Hutchins also argues that "culture is a process, and 'things' that appear on list-like definitions of culture are residua of the process" [16]. Under this view, cultural dimensions are *products* of culture not culture itself. Hutchins adds that culture is an adaptive process that gathers partial solutions of frequently occurring problems.

The notion of cultural models provides an analytical tool for interpreting cultural behavior to be used in a way that parallels the use of the notion of kinship. Anthropologists assume that human societies have kinship relations, but what the specific relationships are can be determined only by studying the specific culture. So too, we assume humans are model-making beings but the nature of the cultural models can be determined only by studying that specific culture.

---

[3] Hofstede associates numerical values to his cultural dimensions for many countries (e.g., India's power distance index value is 77)

In the next section, we describe the idea of culture as models (Section 4.1), and then we illustrate this idea with examples from the software-engineering discipline (Section 4.2).[4]

4.1 Describing Cultural Models

In *Cultural Models in Language and Thought*, the authors argue that culture is organized in the form of cultural models [15]. These models are "presupposed, taken-for-granted models of the world that are widely shared by the members of a society and that play an enormous role in their understanding of that world and their behavior in it [15]."

Building on this idea of cultural models, Shore further describes these models and their topology. According to Shore, these models may be individual (resides in the mind) or public (resides in the world), and they are constantly changing and are changed by the individuals and the environment around them. From this perspective, culture can be viewed as a heterogeneous (and large) collection of models wherein each model is a set of patterns that governs the "conventional behaviors" of an individual in a cultural community [27].

Models are classified into categories based on various aspects. The first classification is based on where the model resides—"in the mind" (internal) or "in the world" (external).

- Internal models, also known as *cognitive mental models*, reside in the minds of the individuals. These internal models are further divided into two categories. The first category is *personal mental models*, which are idiosyncratic models created based on individuals' personal experiences and they are not shared in great detail with other members of the community (e.g., using my own mental map to remember directions to a place). The second category is *conventional mental models*, which are models that are internalized and transformed based on an individual's experience with the external social world and that form a part of the shared cognitive resources of the community (e.g., conventional gesture of Japanese head bow).

- External models, also known as *instituted models*, reside in the social world. Instituted models are the externalization of experiences in the social world. These models are recognized as being instituted models when they are "objectified as publicly available forms" (e.g., house structures and public spaces in the U.S. versus Europe) [27, p. 51]. This process of objectification of models as publicly available forms is known as *institutionalization*.

The instituted models are *internalized* to construct and transform the conventional mental models. The conventional mental models and the instituted models together form the cultural models, with the former residing in the mind and the latter residing in the social world.

The second classification is based on whether the models represent specific purpose models or more abstract schemas. Cultural models may be identified as *foundational schemas*, if they depict more general, abstract, and global representation than specific and concrete instantiations (i.e., models). However, this distinction is relative rather than absolute, and is useful in cases in which a set of cultural models share some common general characteristics.

The third classification is based on the perspective that the cultural models imply. Shore discusses two perspectives. The model created based on the actor's perspective (the *actor's model*) organizes the actor's experiences of the action in which she is engaged. The model created based on the observer's perspective (the *observer's model*) organizes the observer's experiences from a more neutral, outsider perspective.

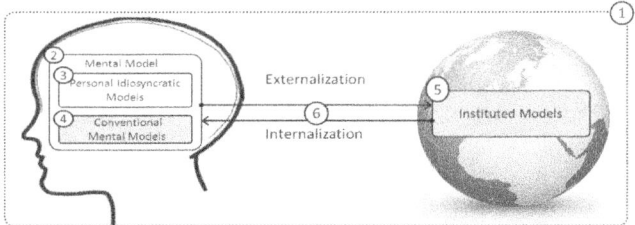

Figure 1. Culture as a set of models with respect to an environment.

Figure 1 shows our conceptualization of the cultural models based on the classification of where the models reside. The models in the shaded boxes represent the cultural models. The numbers in the figure represent the different aspects:

1. Environment or cultural community boundaries
2. Cognitive mental models of the individual in that community (i.e., the internal model of the individual)
3. Personal idiosyncratic models created by the individual
4. Conventional mental models created in the mind through internalization of experiences in external social world
5. Instituted models that represent experiences externalized in the social world
6. Internalization and externalization activities between the two cultural models—conventional mental models and instituted social models

4.2 Illustrating Cultural Models

In this section, we explain the idea of cultural models by presenting an example that we (1) derived from the literature on software engineering (Section 4.2.1) and (2) developed from our own studies (Section 4.2.2) [26].

4.2.1 Software Engineering: A Modularized Culture

We present this example to illustrate the abstract notion of cultural models that we have been discussing. From the literature on software engineering, modularization appears to be a cultural model widely adopted in the software-engineering community. In *Software Engineering: A Practitioner's Approach*, Pressman (an American) discusses different software-process models that guide the software-development life cycle. These process models possess a modular nature where modularity may be defined as a strategy of breaking complex wholes into elementary units that can be recombined to form different patterns [27]. The modular nature of the

---

[4]Note that the cultural models discussed in these examples are still developing because the research study is ongoing. The purpose of discussing these examples here is to give readers a flavor of this rich concept of cultural models by explaining the concept in terms of a more familiar context of software engineering.

process models is distinctly evident in the way they are divided into smaller units (i.e., framework activities, software-engineering actions, and task sets) [23, p. 78]. Any process model, such as waterfall, is divided into modules of activities (or phases): requirements gathering, design, development, and testing. Each activity can be divided further. For example, similar to the software-development life cycle there is software-testing life cycle, which divides the software-testing life cycle into phases (e.g., requirements elicitation, test planning, test development, test execution, test reporting, and project sign-off).

Not only is this modularity evident in the software-engineering processes, it is also evident in other aspects of software engineering, such as software-development programming paradigms. For example, the object-oriented paradigm adopts the idea of thinking in terms of modular units of objects and classes that are contained in packages and that contain methods. These modular units can be rearranged and reused easily in other contexts. Thus, modularity appears to be a tacitly-assumed design strategy that is adopted by this community. Hence, modularity may be viewed as one of the cultural models that exist in this discipline.

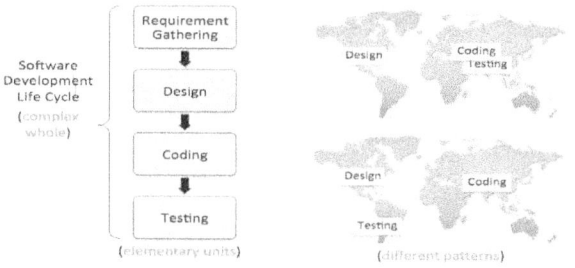

Figure 2. Modular nature of the global software-engineering setting. The figure shows the software-development life cycle divided into elementary phases (left) that are globally distributed to form two different patterns in the GSE setting (right).

This modularized cultural model may provide insights into the reasons for rapid adoption and promotion of the idea of GSE. As Figure 2 shows, the complex whole of the software-development life cycle is modularized as elementary independent units (phases). In the GSE setting, these units are rearranged to form various globally-distributed team patterns. Thus, this taken-for-granted modular cultural model appears to promote the perception of a complex software-development activity as a set of elementary reconfigurable units that form various GSE settings. Researchers have argued that software-engineering culture is greatly influenced by western culture [11]. In fact, Shore has also shown that a modularity model is a powerful and pervasive cultural model in many modern American institutions (e.g., shopping malls, corporate modules, and educational systems) [27]. He argues that this modular cultural schema underlies the great successes of manufacturing production lines in America: "American industrial genius was for breaking down production processes into their primitive constituents and then maximally rationalizing production by conceiving of labor and time as module entities subject to manipulation" [27, p. 131]. Software-engineering globalization is thought to be an extension of the manufacturing globalization practice. Thus, it is conceivable that the modularity cultural model in GSE could derive from a more pervasive cultural model of modularity in manufacturing, wherein processes (in this case software development) are broken into primitive constituents (i.e., phases), and manipulated so as to obtain maximal production. The existence of this tacit cultural model may be the reason that the U.S. is the leader in adopting the GSE practice.

4.2.2 Software Testing as a "Second Standard" Field

We extracted the examples presented next and in Section 5.2 by reanalyzing the data collected in the field studies that we conducted at two multinational vendor organizations in India [25, 26]. The organizations are involved in GSE (particularly offshoring and outsourcing) service. Three teams from each organization participated in the studies. We interacted with 54 participants in total across six teams in the two organizations. The study focused on understanding the offshored software-testing[5] practice. Thus, we selected the teams so that all team members were working on software-testing related activities. We collected the data primarily using qualitative open-ended interviews, with occasional observations. For data analysis, we used the thematic-analysis framework [7]. The examples presented in this paper emerged from our reflections on several research questions: (1) How are global software-engineering activities perceived by the participants at each organization? (2) Are these perceptions in line with what is being observed in the environment? (3) What is the cultural knowledge that is taken-for-granted in these GSE settings?

We now provide an illustration of the cultural models extracted from our data. This "software testing as 'second standard' field" cultural model can be seen as playing a role in the cultural transformation process. The model also highlights the struggles associated with this transformation that one of our participants—a software test engineer at one of the organizations we studied—underwent. This example is representative of many similar experiences shared by other participants involved in our study. In this example, we discuss a portion of the interview with the participant. During the interview, the researcher asks the participant about her experience as a software test engineer. In her response, she exposes the cultural model of software testing. In her own words

> If you go out in the market...there is a rumor that testing is not a very good field. Testing is considered as a second-standard [class] field... When you are a fresher [novice software engineer], when you enter [join] the industry, you do not want to make a career in testing, you want to start with development.

This conversation shows the taken-for-granted cultural model of software testing in the community is that it is not a desirable field. The conversation clearly shows the reluctance that novice software engineers have to joining the industry as software test engineers mainly because of this strong cultural knowledge in the community that testing is not a very good

---

[5]Software testing is a phase in the software development life cycle that focuses on ensuring that high quality software is being build.

field. Furthermore, she expresses the inclination of these novice software engineers towards a software-development job profile and reluctance towards a software-testing job profile because of the preconceptions formed based on this tacit cultural knowledge: "Initially when I was into testing, I seriously did not like it because I was [had] more of a development mindset." However, the participant mentioned that her organization's work customs are such that the employees do not get to select the job profile that interests them. Instead, employees are randomly assigned job profiles and, consequently, she was forced to work as a software-test engineer: "[the company] has a random pattern that anybody is assigned any technology or any expertise (i.e., job profile)."

Interestingly, after the participant began working as a software-test engineer, she started appreciating this job profile:

> So when I went into testing, I learned the practices—they are totally different. A developer's mindset is totally opposite to a tester's mindset. We have to actually break the code and they have to actually create the code. So initially, it was challenging to me because I was not very familiar with the practices, processes that are involved, but slowly I developed interest... testing is actually challenging, because you are always pressurized [pressured] due to deadlines. A developer might take 20 days to develop a code but you have to test it within the time line and within the given deadline. You cannot break [miss] it. [The] developer can break [miss] the deadline, you cannot break [miss] the deadline. That is the major challenge as a tester.

This conversation exhibits the gradual transformation of the participant's cultural model of software-testing practice. Her internal model of this practice now is a departure from the instituted external cultural model of this practice. She expresses her inclination towards this new profile. Nonetheless, she admitted that, earlier, she had conceived the same instituted cultural model of testing as being "second standard:"

> I was of the same mindset, but I broke that box [internalized a new meaning of software-testing profile] and finally I developed interest in testing because actually it was not possible for you to switch the expertise...if you have been assigned testing, you actually make your career, you build up your profile in that particular expertise only. So slowly and steadily by getting to know about it, knowing various processes, I finally developed interest, and finally I like testing, I can say.

What is interesting here is that her discussion implies a need to justify why she started liking testing. Such a justification echoes her internal conflict because she has now started internalizing the software-testing-practice model differently from the presumed cultural model in the society. Eventually, she gives up on this conflict of clashing models ("broke that box and finally I developed interest in testing") and accepts her inclination towards this profile.

However, inclination towards testing may invite its own new cultural struggles particularly because of the strong cultural model of software testing as a "second standard" field in the community. These challenges are evident in the way a software engineer, who is a software tester for a prolong period of time, is perceived in some communities. For instance, one of the participant managers mentioned that, in the western countries (e.g., he had worked with a client in U.S.), people may prefer to be testers for many years. He had met someone who was a tester in a software organization for the last 30 years: "however, in India, if you are a tester for such a long time, then you are perceived to be not capable to do other roles [e.g., managing or leading a team] so you are a tester."

Consequently, there seems to be a struggle to change this popular cultural model of testing as being "second standard." In our earlier work, we reported a manager's effort to change this cultural perception by reorganizing some organizational strategies around testing activities [25]. Discussion with another manager shows the transformation process towards the perception of the testing profile that he underwent:

> I feel positive about it [software testing]... if you look at any project, 40% of the cost of the project is given to testing. So it's a whole lot of responsibility, and good amount of importance is given to it nowadays. That was not the case 6-7 years before. Earlier, it was seen as a wasteful exercise. When I started my career... it was seen as mandatory evil, like you need to have it. So since the last 5 1/2 years I have been with [the company], it seems like big companies have different notions. Since then I have seen testing in a better light, and it is considered a very essential part.

These examples illustrate the gradually evolving and transforming nature of culture (i.e., culture of software testing). The question remains, however, of why software testing is considered as "second standard"? Is it because software testing is the last phase in the software-development life cycle? Would it have made any difference if it were first in the phase? Is that the reason why design and development profiles are considered as higher-status job profiles in the community? Does the order of phases in the software development life cycle have such deep cultural implications in the software-engineering communities? Such questions need further investigation to better understand the implications of culture and to direct the changes in the communities in the right direction.

5. THINKING THROUGH MODELS

We speculate that one reason the culture-as-dimensions approach (e.g., Hofstede's dimensions) has gained such popularity among disciplines, such as software engineering, is because it provides a framework for cultural analysis in the form of dimensions. Such dimensions can facilitate quick identification of cultural factors that are influential in a setting by providing pointers that guide the researcher in the direction of what to look for in the setting. However, as we discussed in Section 3, there are several limitations to using such a dimensional approach for studying culture. In this section, we propose a reference framework for studying culture through cultural-models analysis based on Shore's idea of thinking in terms of cultural models.

5.1 Describing a Cultural-Models Framework for GSE

Figure 3 shows a conceptual framework of the cultural models and their connections in a GSE setup. The solid (black) lines show the interactions that occur between the models, whereas the dashed (red) lines show the interpretations and comparisons that can occur. The models and connections in the figure are numbered and described as

1. Environment (community) boundaries of the client team
2. Cognitive mental models of the client team member in the client community (i.e., the individual's internal model)
3. Personal idiosyncratic models of the client team member
4. Conventional mental models of the client team member through internalization of experiences in social world

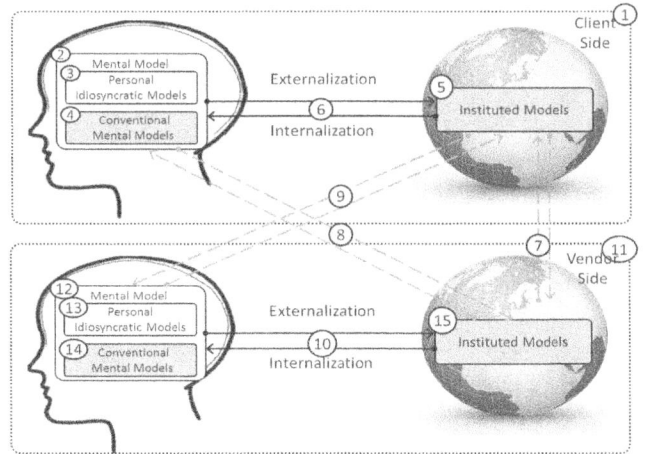

Figure 3. Reference framework for cultural models and their connections in a GSE setting.

5. Instituted models that represent experiences of the client team member, externalized in the social world
6. Internalization and externalization activities between the two cultural models—conventional mental models and instituted social models—of the client team member
7. Comparison of the instituted models of the two communities—client and vendor
8. Interpretations of the instituted cultural models of the vendor teams, as internalized by the client team member
9. Interpretations of the instituted cultural models of the client teams, as internalized by the vendor team member
10. Internalization and externalization activities between the two cultural models—conventional mental models and instituted social models—of the vendor team member
11. Environment (community) boundaries of the vendor team.
12. Cognitive mental models of the vendor team member, (i.e., the internal model of that individual)
13. Personal idiosyncratic models of the vendor team member.
14. Conventional mental models of the vendor team member through internalization of experiences in social world
15. Instituted mental models that represent experiences of the vendor teams, as externalized in the social world

To understand culture's influence on GSE, a researcher may use the framework described above as a reference for his study. The researcher may conduct in-depth studies (e.g., ethnographic studies) of client and vendor teams to gather information for building the models shown in the figure. In the context of studying culture's influence on GSE that we are addressing in this paper, it is crucial to conduct detailed qualitative studies, such as ethnographically-informed studies, because such methods emphasize understanding insider perspectives. Moreover, the methods facilitate the capture of conventional mental models of the individuals being studied. Additionally, to obtain a holistic understanding of culture's influence on any specific aspect of GSE, it is important to construct at least the instituted models and the conventional mental models of both the client and the vendor teams (4, 5, 14, and 15 in Figure 3). Comparison of the two instituted models will provide insights into the different perceptions held in the client and vendor communities. This comparison can contribute greatly towards reasoning about differences in behavior patterns of the client and vendor organizations' perspectives on certain ideas (e.g., Section 5.2).

Moreover, culture is the process of externalization and internalization in which individuals and environment influence and are influenced by each others' models (connections 6, 8, 9, and 10). Externalization involves the process in which individuals influence the environment, and internalization involves the process in which individuals internalize the external instituted model. A researcher can construct and compare the mental and instituted models at the client organization to study internalization and externalization processes within the client organization (e.g., connection 6) for understanding the influence that the organization has on the individual's activities and vice versa (i.e., studying internal organizational culture at a company). In addition, the researcher can construct and compare client teams' conventional mental models with vendor teams' instituted mental models and vice versa (connections 8 and 9). Such comparisons may facilitate understanding of potential misunderstandings among client and vendor teams by providing insights into the expected and observed behaviorial patterns of the team members.

Using a reference framework like the one we illustrate can be beneficial in several ways. First, such a reference framework can help the researcher compare and contrast different models, which will help in understanding the similarities and differences among different cultures. For instance, a researcher can focus the study to create instituted models of software-test engineers job profiles at the client side and the vendor side. The client's instituted models may view testing jobs as highly-valued and prestigious (e.g., Japanese culture [32]), whereas the vendor's instituted models may view testing jobs as secondary, less-privileged (e.g., Indian culture [25]). Comparing these instituted models will help researchers understand cultural differences between the two communities, and subsequently reason about the consequences of differences in their behaviors. Such comparisons can benefit understanding of which and how cultural issues need to be addressed so as to foster the relationships between client and vendor teams for better quality and productivity of work.

In addition, such a reference framework can provide a road map for identifying aspects that need to be studied further before drawing any conclusions about culture, and thus, avoiding the mistake of blaming culture for other issues (Damian and Zowghi report that sometimes blame was attributed to cultural differences to explain issues that were actually managerial [10]). Based on the framework and the research goals, the researcher may choose to perform an exhaustive study of a GSE setting by studying all aspects (all 14 aspects in Figure 3) or specific aspects (i.e., a subset of the aspects). For instance, continuing with our previous example of software testing, a researcher might choose to study the mental models of the communities because, according to Myers, software testing "involves some important considerations of economic and human psychology" and the mental models contribute towards understanding human cognitive psychology [22].

Moreover, such a framework can help in accommodating the cultural transformations due to acculturation, because the differences between the conventional models and the instituted models of the individuals being studied will provide insights into the acculturation-related transformations.

5.2 Illustrating Cultural Models in GSE

We extracted examples from the study we discussed earlier (Section 4.2.2) [26]. These examples illustrate how the GSE framework can help to capture cultural models salient in the GSE practice. Such a framework may motivate researchers to use the cultural-models approach, instead of using the dimensional approach, to study culture's influence on GSE.

5.2.1 Unproductive productivity

This example illustrates the differences in cultural models of productivity for client and vendor teams [26]. Because the field studies were conducted only at the vendor organizations, based on the available data we constructed two specific cultural models of productivity. The first is the actors' model of productivity, which represents the productivity cultural model as perceived by the vendor participants. The second is the observers' model of productivity, which represents the productivity cultural model of the clients as observed by the vendor participants. From what the vendor-team members mentioned, productivity was measured in numbers (e.g., number of test cases created/tested over a given period of time) by their clients. This productivity measure is evident in the participant discussions:

> So...the onshore manager, what they basically want was numbers; their main focus was numbers. So, we were completing four scripts per day...they are least bothered about complexity, and that was the challenge that we had to manage.

To show that the vendor team members were productive each day, participants said that they were expected to send status reports indicating the number of tasks they completed.

For the vendor teams, productivity seems to be measured in the extent to which tasks requested by their clients were completed. This productivity measure is evident in the discussion between the researcher and one of the test-engineer participants. As discussed in Reference [26], the participant was narrating an incident wherein he was expected to write 100 test cases for a given module. However, he strongly believed that there was no need to write 100 test cases:

> So for five to six cases if I am going to write 100 some test cases ... this number will look good but you know its not logical work. I mean to say it won't be smarter work. Instead of having 100 test cases, why don't you have 5-6 test cases...

Further in the discussion, the researcher asked whether the participant tried to convey this issue to his superiors or the clients. He replied that he had tried discussing this with his manager, but also added that:

> Why should I talk? Because you know, she [on-site coordinator] has provided everything to the client. If I go and reduce this estimation hour to 20 [which translates to the reduction in the number of test cases], everything goes wrong for [on-site] coordinator, lead, and they will be bouncing back on me only [laughs]...they can have so many reasons to defend [themselves].

His choice of words indicate that, although he believed there were better ways of performing the testing activity, he was not willing to put extra effort to make things efficient. This conversation also reflects an attitude that, as far as he is concerned, he has to complete the assigned tasks so that he shows he has been productive. This action seems to result in experiences of *unproductive productivity* wherein "vendor-team members were productive because they produced the results that the clients wanted despite their belief that they had been unproductive in producing those results" [26].

The reason for this unproductive-productivity experience may be explained by highlighting the existence of two different cultural models of productivity—numerical and completion. A productivity cultural model may be defined as a specific cultural model that orients people towards a common productivity goal. Additionally, there may be specific cultural models that function under the productivity model. Based on the example, the client's cultural model appears to be *numerical productivity model*—where clients focus heavily on numbers to measure productivity; whereas, the vendor's cultural model may be *completion-productivity model*—where vendors focus heavily on completing the tasks given by the clients.

5.2.2 Hesitant to always say yes

In much of the literature on culture and global software engineering, researchers have reported that some cultures possess the cultural model of *always saying yes* [8, 31]. Based on Hofstede's dimensions, some researchers explain this behavior by stating that these cultures are "collectivist" where maintaining harmony is important and confrontations are not encouraged (e.g., [8, p. 137]). Based on our reference framework (Figure 3), this behavior may represent the client's conventional mental model of the instituted cultural model of the vendors as internalized by the clients (connection 8 in Figure 3). Also, the completion-productivity model, discussed above, appears to align with this cultural model.

However, the above example also appears to expose an alternative conflicting model that is opposing the always-say-yes model. The clashing behavior generated from the conflicting model is highlighted in the sentence: "but you know it's not logical work. I mean to say it won't be smarter work." Other participants also expressed similar hesitance against this cultural practice of always saying yes. One participant discussed an incident in which she was expected to meet an infeasible deadline only because the clients were promised it earlier. She clearly expresses her disappointment

> Whether the clients are like that or the managers, we don't know. It's also like we don't know where the things are getting masked ... it's not like we are not reaching [meeting] the deadlines or we lack the information, skills, or we are not punctual. It's like we have practical concerns and we are not understanding why the client is not understanding these practical things.

Her repeated questioning indicates her urge to explain the infeasibility to the clients (which means saying no to the clients or negotiating with them for doing a certain tasks), and shows the glimpse of the conflicting model.

Although, we were unable to capture these alternative conflicting models in detail (because of time constraints), the clashing behaviors hint that the vendor's cultural model is gradually transforming such that the always-say-yes practice is now being questioned. Thus, these examples illustrate the evolving and transforming nature of culture. The question remains, however, of why the completion-productivity (cultural) models continue to dominate the behaviors of the participants, while the other conflicting models exist, despite their experiences such as unproductive productivity situations. For answering such questions, it is important to build the vendor's instituted models of response to client's request and the client's mental models, and compare these models. We believe that by gaining a better understanding of the differences in these cultural models, efforts could be redirected to implementing better GSE strategies. At the very least, exposing such differences will lead to (1) more productivity and less boredom for the vendor teams and (2) cost savings for the client teams by avoiding the execution of unproductive tasks.

5.2.3 Owning rather than modularizing

In Section 4.2, we presented the discussion of the modularized culture of software engineering. We also illustrated the modularization of the testing phases into different units of activities—requirements elicitation, test planning, test development, test execution, test reporting, and project sign off. However, based on what the study participants described, they seem to have internalized a slightly different model than the well-known modularized model. Their model of the testing phases is structured around three high-level phases: preparation, execution, and client management. The *preparation phase* begins when the teams receive the functional requirements and ends when the developers deploy the code. The *execution phase* begins as soon as the development team deploys the software. The *client-management phase* begins when the testing team, based on satisfactory test results, approves the product by signing it off.

Thus, instead of these phases being divided into atomic modules (as might be popular in the software-engineering literature), the participants seem to have internalized these phases based on who currently "owns" the code. During the preparation phase, the developers own the code (i.e., the developers create the code); during the execution phase, the test engineers own the code; and during the client-management phase, the clients own the code once it is deployed and shipped to them. Moreover, this specific cultural model of ownership is more of the conventional mental model instead of personal idiosyncratic model because it seems to be commonly, but implicitly, shared among these test engineers. Such a model that describes the phases as perceived by the practitioners helps in better understanding the practice.

5.3 Advantages of Thinking of Culture as Models

The culture-as-models perspective addresses the limitations of the culture-as-dimensions perspective discussed in Section 3 in several ways. First, the culture-as-models perspective defines culture as a collection of cultural models that are embodied in the practice because they emerge within it. Second, this definition does not limit culture's meaning to predetermined dimensions. Instead, it facilitates the identification of hidden cultural facets, providing richer descriptions of culture's influence on practice. Moreover, it provides a flexible way to capture a range of cultural facets, from specific cultural models to generic foundational schemas. Third, this perspective reduces the risk of stereotyping because it emphasizes the discovery of models that are embedded in the practice rather than externally applying predetermined dimensions. Fourth, it views culture as a process. Thus, it captures the dynamically evolving and transforming nature of culture. Finally, it does not restrict culture's definition to national. Instead, it is easily extendable to capture acculturation.

In addition to the above-mentioned advantages, the cultural-models perspective offers other benefits. Culture, when based on dimensions, omits crucial characteristics that the culture-as-models view enables researchers to capture. In most current studies of culture and GSE, the focus is largely on cultural models from the external models' perspective (e.g., national culture). This focus fails to consider that cultural models are also internalized (i.e., conventional mental models), and affect a person's thinking as well as their actions. Furthermore, following Shore's thinking, different countries are likely to be institutionalizing both external cultural models—organizational and occupational—differently [14]. Thus, each individual is likely to be internalizing these cultural models differently to produce different personal and conventional mental models. The culture-as-models perspective facilitates capturing the "'twice born character' of cultural forms"— mental models in the mind and instituted models in the world—on the GSE practice.

Unless culture's influence on GSE has been studied from both these perspectives—what Shore calls inside-out and outside-in—the study findings may result in a distorted understanding of culture's influence on the GSE practice. This distorted understanding may make it difficult to ensure that client and vendor teams have the same understanding of the meaning and expectation of software-development activities so that both clients and vendors get what they want. Moreover, it is important to understand the influence of both the cultural forms on GSE practice because, although the instituted models will help in understanding aspects of the external configurations in the practice, the mental model will help in understanding each individual software engineer's orientation towards the practice. For example, a software-test engineer might perform testing activities in a certain way because of the institutionalized culture of the organization's configuration of software-testing processes. However, her strategies might differ from others, resulting in her performing better than her colleagues, because she may have internalized a different mental model of best practices.

Studying the cultural models in GSE practice will help in gaining an understanding of the culturally-embodied meaning of software-engineering practice from both client and vendor perspectives. This understanding will, in turn, help to (1) identify differences in the understanding of the meanings, (2) explicate them to the organizations, and (3) build culturally-aware solutions (e.g., through cross-cultural training and developing culture-aware communication models) to address these differences. Moreover, given that culture plays an important role in GSE practice, it is necessary to conduct such studies to provide a rich understanding of the strengths and weaknesses of this practice so that recommendations can be made to improve it.

6. CONCLUSION AND FUTURE WORK

Culture plays an important role in global software engineering (GSE). However, the majority of studies on culture and GSE seem to use a culture-as-dimensions (e.g., Hofstede's dimensions [14]) approach to define culture. In this paper, we make three main contributions. First, we illustrate the disadvantages of using dimensional approaches by explicating cultural facets that such dimensional approaches fail to capture. Second, we discuss a new perspective—culture-as-models—based on the idea of cultural models inspired by Shore's work on *Culture in the Mind* [27]. To explain this idea, we present examples of cultural models that exist in the software-engineering discipline. Third, we describe a reference framework for capturing cultural models in the GSE domain and provide examples to illustrate the benefits of such a framework. Such a framework can easily be extended to other disciplines and settings for studying culture's influence.

Through such a framework and the underlying culture-as-models perspective, we attempt to provoke thinking and conceptualizing culture in GSE in ways that are newer than the culture-as-dimensions perspective. Although, we do not claim that this perspective is the only way to conceptualize culture, we do believe that this perspective is promising based on our findings. However, our findings are currently limited to studies conducted mainly at vendor organizations. Hence, we are in the process of designing ethnographically-informed studies using our framework to study both sides—the client and the vendor—involved in GSE practice to better understand the two cultural experiences.

7. ACKNOWLEDGMENTS

This research was supported in part by NSF CCF-0541048, CCF-0725202, and CCF-1116210, and IBM Software Quality Innovation Award to Georgia Tech. The vendor organizations allowed us to perform the study, and the participants gave us their valuable time and feedback to collect the data. The reviewers provided many helpful suggestions that improved the paper's presentation.

8. REFERENCES

1. Improved cross-cultural communication increases global sourcing productivity. http://newsroom.accenture.com/article_display.cfm?article_id=4376, Jul 2006.
2. Overcome cultural differences in the outsourcing process. http://www.osf-global.com/, Apr 2009.
3. L. R. Abraham. Cultural differences in software engineering. In *Proc. ISEC*, pages 95–100, 2009.
4. W. Aspray, F. Mayadas, and M. Y. Vardi. Globalization and Offshoring of Software: A Report of the ACM Job Migration Task Force. http://www.acm.org/globalizationreport/pdf/fullfinal.pdf, 2006.
5. A. Boden, G. Avram, L. Bannon, and V. Wulf. Knowledge sharing practices and the impact of cultural factors: reflections on two case studies of offshoring in sme. *Journal of Software Maintenance and Evolution: Research and Practice*, 2010.
6. G. Borchers. The software engineering impacts of cultural factors on multi-cultural software development teams. In *Proc. ICSE*, pages 540–545, 2003.
7. V. Braun and V. Clarke. Using thematic analysis in psychology. *Qualitative Research in Psychology*, 3:77–101, 2006.
8. V. Casey. *Software Testing and Global Industry: Future Paradigms*. Cambridge Scholars Publishing, United Kingdom, 2009.
9. A. Cater-Steel and M. Toleman. The impact of national culture on software engineering practices. *International Journal of Technology, Policy and Management*, 8(1):76–90, 2008.
10. D. E. Damian and D. Zowghi. An insight into the interplay between culture, conflict and distance in globally distributed requirements negotiations. In *Proc. HICSS*, 2003.
11. J. Fendler and H. Winschiers-Theophilus. Towards contextualised software engineering education: an african perspective. In *Proc. ICSE*, pages 599–607, 2010.
12. M. C. Gertsen and A.-M. Søderberg. Expatriate stories about cultural encounters: A narrative approach to cultural learning processes in multinational companies. *Scandinavian Journal of Management*, 26(3):248–257, 2010.
13. E. T. Hall. *Beyond Culture*. ANCHOR Books, New York, 1976.
14. G. Hofstede. *Culture's Consequences: Comparing Values, Behaviors, Institutions and Organizations Across Nations*. Thousand Oaks CA: Sage Publications, 2001.
15. D. Holland and N. Quinn. *Cultural Models in Language & Thought*. Cambridge University Press, 1992.
16. E. Hutchins. *Cognition in the Wild*, volume 19. MIT press Cambridge, MA, 1995.
17. L. Irani and P. Dourish. Postcolonial interculturality. In *Proc. IWIC*, page 249, 2009.
18. L. Irani, J. Vertesi, P. Dourish, K. Philip, and R. E. Grinter. Postcolonial computing: a lens on design and development. In *Proc. CHI*, pages 1311–1320, 2010.
19. S. Krishna, S. Sahay, and G. Walsham. Managing cross-cultural issues in global software outsourcing. *CACM*, 47:62–66, 2004.
20. A. L. Kroeber and C. Kluckhohn. *Culture: A critical review of concept and definition*. Kraus Reprint Co, 1978.
21. B. McSweeney. Hofstede's model of national cultural differences and their consequences: A triumph of faith - a failure of analysis. *Human Relations*, 55:89–118, 2002.
22. G. J. Myers. *The Art of Software Testing*. John Wiley & Sons, 1979.
23. R. S. Pressman. *Software Engineering: A Practitioners Approach*. McGraw-Hill, sixth edition, 2005.
24. T. Segal and S. Vasilache. Plea against cultural stereotypes. In *Proc. ICIC*, pages 275–278, 2010.
25. H. Shah and M. J. Harrold. Studying human and social aspects of testing in a service-based software company: case study. In *Proc. CHASE*, pages 102–108, 2010.
26. H. Shah, S. Sinha, and M. J. Harrold. Outsourced, offshored software-testing practice: Vendor-side experiences. In *Proc. ICGSE*, 2011.
27. B. Shore. *Culture in mind: Cognition, culture, and the problem of meaning*. Oxford University Press, USA, 1996.
28. D. Smite, C. Wohlin, T. Gorschek, and R. Feldt. Empirical evidence in global software engineering: a systematic review. *Empirical Software Engineering*, 15(1):91–118, 2010.
29. A. Trompenaars and C. Hampden-Turner. *Riding The Waves of Culture: Understanding Diversity in Global Business*. McGraw Hill, 1998.
30. Ventoro. Offshore 2005 Research: Preliminary Findings and Conclusions. http://www.ventoro.com/Offshore2005ResearchFindings.pdf, Jan 2005.
31. J. Winkler, J. Dibbern, and A. Heinzl. The impact of cultural differences on outsourced offshoring. *Information Systems Frontiers*, 10:243–258, 2008.
32. T. Yamaura. Why Johnny can't test [software]. *IEEE Software*, 15(2):113–115, 1998.

"Are You a Trustworthy Partner in a Cross-cultural Virtual Environment?" – Behavioral Cultural Intelligence and Receptivity-based Trust in Virtual Collaboration

Ye Li
Center for Doctoral Studies in Business, University of Mannheim
Schloss 68163, Mannheim, Germany
liye@mail.uni-mannheim.de

Hui Li
Institute of Human Factors and Ergonomics, Department of Industrial Engineering
Tsinghua University, Beijing, 100084, P.R. China
hli.sunshine@gmail.com

Alexander Mädche
Chair of Information Systems IV, University of Mannheim
Schloss 68131, Mannheim, Germany
maedche@eris.uni-mannheim.de

Pei-Luen Patrick Rau
Institute of Human Factors and Ergonomics, Department of Industrial Engineering
Tsinghua University, Beijing, 100084, P.R. China
rpl@tsinghua.edu.cn

ABSTRACT
Globally distributed work has been prevalent in organizations. However, cultural issues in distributed work are still challenging team performance. Cultural intelligence, defined as individuals' capability to perform in cross-cultural settings, has great potential in untangling these issues. The present study examines three individual capabilities (behavioral cultural intelligence, language proficiency and technical skills) and their effects on partners' receptivity-based trust and satisfaction in a cross-cultural virtual environment. We develop a theoretical model based on the extended adaptive structuration theory (EAST) and verify the model in a cross-border experiment. The result suggests that focal members' behavioral cultural intelligence strongly influences their remote partners' receptivity/trust. This effect is moderated by language proficiency; 57% of the variance of partners' satisfaction is predicted by receptivity/trust and the focal members' technical skills.

Author Keywords
Trust; virtual teams; cultural intelligence; receptivity; satisfaction; collaboration

ACM Classification Keywords
H.5.3 [Information Interfaces And Presentation]: Group and Organization Interfaces - Computer-supported Cooperative Work;

Permission to make digital or hard copies of all or part of this work for personal or classroom use is granted without fee provided that copies are not made or distributed for profit or commercial advantage and that copies bear this notice and the full citation on the first page. To copy otherwise, or republish, to post on servers or to redistribute to lists, requires prior specific permission and/or a fee.
ICIC'12, March 21–23, 2012, Bengaluru, India.
Copyright 2012 ACM 978-1-4503-0818-2/12/03...$10.00.

INTRODUCTION
Setting up globally distributed teams to support international business has been prevalent in contemporary organizations. Such teams, also termed global virtual teams (GVT), bring together members with diverse skills, expertise and experience over temporal, functional and national boundaries [43]. They enable organizations to reduce costs of cross-border operations, improve flexibility and agility, and gain competitive advantages in international markets [5, 7]. Along with the obvious advantages and necessity of setting up GVTs, it is also well-known that such teams face additional challenges introduced by the heterogeneous team composition and high dependency on ICT [7, 41], which may impede the development of strong interpersonal relationship [9, 37], and adversely influence teams' affective and performance outcomes [53, 61, 64]. Carried out in industry, Economist Intelligence Unit's survey involving 407 participants from different industries showed that 56% of the respondents did not agree that their virtual teams were well managed and the greatest challenge for virtual team management were misunderstanding due to cultural differences. The survey also suggested that 44% respondents agreed that difficulty in building rapport and trust in virtual teams was one of the primary challenges [66].

In the exploration of critical success factors in GVTs, a considerable amount of scholars have stressed that bridging the national cultural barriers (e.g. different languages, communication styles, perceptions of task-technology fit, senses of timing and value systems) among global dispersed and culturally diverse members is crucial for team performances [25, 38]. In recent years, researchers started to explore which individual characteristics and behaviors impact team process and performance in cross-cultural GVTs, and they found that some individuals consistently performed better than others did. This suggests that good team performance might have been ensured by recruiting right persons with specific criteria (e.g. cross-cultural social skills, cultural sensitivity) [13, 23, 58]. While most of the results are descriptive and qualitative, the question remains: Which capabilities are reliable and effective in predicting individual's behaviors and performance in a cross-cultural virtual environment? Moreover, can these capabilities be reliably assessed during recruitments?

An emergent stream in cross-cultural studies on individual's competence to effectively perform in culturally diverse settings, also defined as cultural intelligence (CQ) [18], has the potential to untangle the above issue. Cultural intelligence has been verified as a reliable predictor of peer trust and team performance in multicultural collocated teams [13, 21, 57]. However, in a virtual working environment when only a constrained set of communication cues can be transmitted (e.g. vocal, visual, symbolic), interaction is highly task-oriented and often short-term and communication quality can be influenced by technical infrastructures and individual's technical skills, whether or not cultural intelligence will still leverage one's performance is unknown.

In the present study, we focus on three individual capabilities, namely CQ, language proficiency and skills of using collaborative technology, and examine their impact in a cross-cultural virtual environment. Our study is guided by the following two questions: 1) How do individual capabilities influence remote partners' trust? 2) How do individual capabilities influence peer satisfaction? 3) How do individual capabilities interact during the work process?

We ground the study on the extended adaptive structuration theory (EAST) for team work [47] and examine the effects in a laboratory experiment to better control the influence of other factors.

CONCEPTUAL FOUNDATIONS
Cultural Intelligence
In culturally diverse situations, it is observable that some individuals can consistently outperform others. To describe this individual difference and predict individual effectiveness in a multicultural setting, a type of intelligence, cultural intelligence (CQ), was introduced by Earley and Ang in 2003 [18]. CQ is formally defined as the capability to function and manage effectively in culturally diverse settings. It is a multidimensional construct, containing four facets: meta-cognitive, cognitive, motivational and behavioral CQ [18]. *Meta-cognitive CQ* reflects one's control over knowledge procurement and comprehension process. People with high meta-cognitive CQ will be aware of the mental models they apply when interacting with other cultural groups and adapt the mental models to others' preferences. *Cognitive CQ* refers to the knowledge about other cultures' social norms, social structures, custom and languages. People with higher cognitive CQ are more knowledgeable and more likely to understand value systems and behaviors in other cultures. *Motivational CQ* refers to individuals' capability to direct and maintain attentions to perform in culturally unfamiliar situations as well as their confidence in performing in such situations. People with higher motivational CQ appear more enjoyable and confident in intercultural. Finally, *behavioral CQ* reflects one's capability to adjust and adapt one's own verbal (e.g. tones, wording) and nonverbal behaviors (e.g. facial expressions, gestures) when interacting with people from other cultures [4]. Therefore, people with higher behavioral CQ are more likely to be understood by and have more common ground with culturally diverse others.

Researchers in the field of psychology and management have been actively applying the concept of cultural intelligence to cultural adaptation in daily life [3], to multicultural team interaction [21, 57] and team performance [6, 63], to performance in cross-cultural assignments (e.g. offshoring, intercultural negotiation) [6, 36], and to expatriate assessment and trainings [1, 19, 60]. Within the scope of multicultural team interaction and team performance, in 2008 Rockstuhl [57] set up an experiment with 623 dyads and found that cultural diversity (e.g. different language, communication styles and non-verbal behaviors) negatively affected trust. Moreover, focal members' cognitive CQ and metacognitive CQ as well as partners' behavioral CQ moderated the negative effect of cultural diversity on trust. Chua, Morris, and Mor's experiment extended the scope of CQ by incorporating joint performance. They found that participants with higher metacognitive CQ are more likely to develop affect-based trust with members from another culture, which consequently facilitated their information sharing and improves joint creative performance [13]. Although prior studies provided fruitful empirical results on the effect of CQ in culturally diverse teams, scarce ones are carried out in a virtual environment. It is arguable whether the effect of CQ can be generalized to virtual settings, since rich contextual cues and nonverbal communication that facilitate intercultural communication and promote the development of interpersonal relationships are largely eliminated in cyberspace. Rather, individuals' behaviors and performance are technology-related. This study aims at verifying the effect of cultural intelligence and its interaction with other individual capabilities on partners' trust and affective reactions in a cross-cultural virtual environment. The findings will thus provide concrete managerial implications for global virtual team recruitments and trainings.

Receptivity Based Trust in Cross-cultural Virtual teams
Trust-based relationships play a central role in maintaining virtual collaboration [46], since control mechanisms based on physical proximity in traditional organizations disappear

in a virtual environment. Prior studies strongly suggest that building trust in virtual teams is crucial for ongoing team process and high performance [50, 55]. Seeing the importance of trust in virtual teams, researchers have been active in analyzing trust development and trust building. Jarvenpaa and Leidner [37] found that in a temporary virtual team, members develop swift trust [44] based on the premise that remote partners will behave as expected and the swift trust can initiates collaborative behaviors; however, such swift trust is very fragile and vulnerable to social and functional communication. Therefore, trust during or after a certain period of interaction in virtual teams is normally considered as a social emotional state emergent during team process and shaped by members' communication [14].

Due to the interlinking relationship between communication and trust, we adopt a relational communication perspective of trust [31] and focus on trust emergent from communication partners' receptivity--the degree to which interest and concern or lack of interest and disregard are expressed [31]. This type of trust is of particular interest in a virtual environment, where communication is largely verbal or text based. Lack of receptivity can be perceived as irresponsibility or lack of commitment in collaborative tasks, which leads to low trust and satisfaction [58]. Studies in virtual settings have indicated that receptivity can manipulate trust through frequent and concurrent communication [23, 54] and one-to-one rather than team-level communication [51]. In collocated cross-cultural communication, researchers also found that responsive and clear communication predicts success in intercultural communication [62]. However, we found little empirical evidence that demonstrates influence of individual capabilities on receptivity in a cross-cultural virtual environment. We consider individuals can manifest their capabilities in behaving receptively in a cross-cultural communication. This receptivity will lead to high trust and consequently results in high peer satisfaction.

Cross-cultural Communication

A wealth of research on cross-cultural communication has found that cultural barriers exist in cross-cultural communication. Individuals with different cultural values communicate in different styles and they have different preference and perception on communication partners' communication styles [17, 39, 48, 65]; they also differ in conversational content and interest [27, 28]. Various cultural values and frameworks have been found manifested in communication. Hall's high- and low-context cultural dimension suggested that cultures are different in terms of to which extend information is communicated through explicit codes [32]. In high-context cultures (e.g. China, India), a large amount of information is transmitted through nonverbal communication or contextual cues, whereas in low-context cultures (e.g. Germany, United States) information is largely communicated through verbal communication. Hofstede's individualism-collectivism cultural dimension also has explanatory power for cross-cultural differences in communication [35]. It is found in individualistic cultures (e.g. Germany) that individuals' needs, values, and goals are seen as superior to groups' needs, values, and goals whereas in collectivist cultures people have reversed priority [26]. Besides, cultures also differ in levels of uncertainty avoidance [35] and time perceptions in nonverbal communication (e.g. punctuality, willingness to wait, perception of silence, speed of speech) [33].

Being aware of these cultural differences in communication and being culturally adaptive, virtual team members are able to establish a shared communication pattern and reduce misunderstanding and communication breakdowns. As suggested by cultural intelligence, it is an individual capability to adapt to other cultures in intercultural communication [4]. In a cross-cultural virtual environment, we expect verbal-based cultural adaptation will overcome the cultural barriers, facilitate intercultural communication, and lead to high peer trust and satisfaction.

RESEARCH FRAMEWORK AND HYPOTHESES

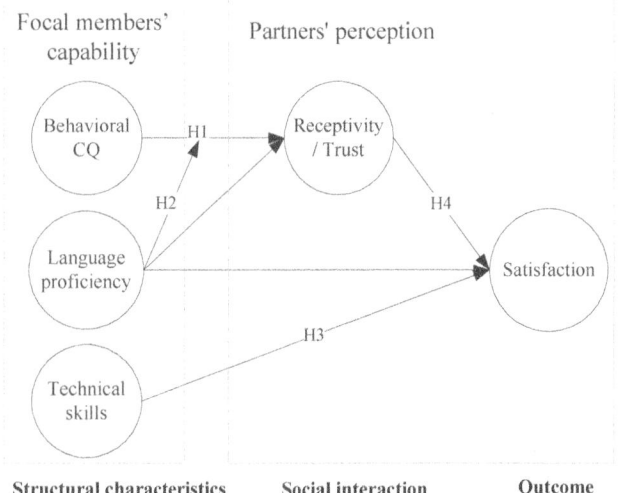

Figure 1 Research framework

According to Schiller and Mandviwalla's review on virtual team theories, adaptive structuration theory (AST) stands out to be a valid theory to explain the interplay between technology and social processes [15, 59]. Naik and Kim [47] developed the extended adaptive structuration theory (EAST) by combing AST with the input-process-outcome model (IPO) [29, 40], which is widely applied in analyzing group work as well as virtual teams [42]. The advantages of EAST are it adapts AST to the virtual team context and provides a clear view of five dimensions of structural characteristics (i.e. organizational, task, technology, team, and individual dimension) and indicate their impacts on team process and outcomes. In the present study, we focus on the individual dimension. Qualitatively we examine how individual capabilities affect their usage of technology and interaction with remote partners; quantitatively we analyze impacts of individual capabilities on receptivity-based trust during social interaction and peer satisfaction as an affective outcome. The theoretical model is shown in Figure 1 (only quantitatively examined constructs are presented in the structural model).

We test this theoretical model at the dyadic level in a cross-cultural virtual environment. We label two members in one dyad as "focal member" and "partner", respectively, according to their sequence in one paragraph. According to the previous conceptual foundations, we develop four hypotheses as follows.

Behavioral CQ measures one's capability of verbal or nonverbal cultural adaptation in cross-cultural settings; people with high behavioral CQ are more capable of adjusting their verbal communication (e.g. wording, transmission of contextual information) or paralanguage communication (e.g. pause and silence, speed of speech, tone) if a cross-cultural situation requires. In a cross-cultural virtual environment, such cultural adaption can overcome the cultural barriers in communication, facilitate information transmission and behave more receptively to others' messages, which leads to high peer trust.

H1: A focal member's behavioral CQ positively affects the remote partner's receptivity-based trust

In a virtual setting, verbal-based (e.g. telephone, web conferencing, voice chatting tools) or text-based (e.g. emails, instant messaging, online discussion forums) communication tools are most widely adopted [66]. If communicators are from different cultures without sharing the same mother languages, they have to agree on a common language to enable the communication. In this case, at least one communicator has to speak in a foreign language, in which his/her proficiency in the chosen language plays a central role in determining to which extent a smooth communication can be carried out. Therefore, the effect of cultural adaptation during communication is also affected by one's language proficiency. When one's language proficiency is high, high frequency of intercultural communication can be carried out, which is sufficient to a perception of high receptivity and trust, and the relationship between behavioral CQ and receptivity/trust tends to be weak. In contrast, when one's language proficiency is low, low frequency of intercultural communication will be carried out, and people are more sensitive to others' paralanguage reactions. In this situation, the impact of behavioral CQ is more likely to be explicit and the relationship between behavioral CQ and receptivity/trust is high.

H2: A focal member's language proficiency moderates the effect of behavioral CQ on a remote partner's receptivity-based trust in the direction that low language proficiency leads to weak relationship between behavioral CQ and receptivity/trust

In a virtual setting, all communication and collaboration is technology supported and technology adaption is highly important to team performance and affective outcomes [8]. Individuals' knowledge and experience in information communication and collaborative tools can affect their behaviors in technology adaptation (e.g. ways of using technology). Individuals with low technical skills may use collaborative technology in an inefficient or wrong way, which disturbs virtual communication or even leads to failures in collaborative tasks. Such inefficiency or failures will consequently reduce peer satisfaction.

H3: The focal member's technical skills positively influence a remote partner's satisfaction with him/her

Receptivity-based trust is developed through communicators' receptive behaviors (e.g. willing to listen, express interest, open to others' concerns). The trust is an indication of the communicators' integrity and openness, which is theoretically predictive to satisfaction with the communicator.

H4: A partner's receptivity-based trust predicts his/her satisfaction with the focal member

METHODOLOGY

Laboratory experiment is chosen as the research method, since virtual team process and outcomes are vulnerably to various factors (e.g. task, interaction duration, technology adoption, organizational culture, regulations)[55] and in a laboratory setting, we can minimize the influences of uninterested factors and draw causal relationships between focal members' capabilities and partners' perception.

Participants

Seventy-two students (36 Chinese and 36 Germans) at both undergraduate and graduate levels were recruited in a public Chinese university and a public German university. They were randomly assigned to 36 cross-cultural dyads. Chinese participants took part in the experiment as a course-related practice while most German participants were recruited through flyers distributed in classes or via public mailing lists. All participants had citizenship in the targeted country (i.e. German citizens in Germany, Chinese citizens in China) or had stayed in the country for at least 10 years. As a reward for the participation, Chinese participants received an assessment report on their performance in culturally diverse settings one month after the experiment while German participants could choose either an assessment report or €7 paid after the experiment. Seven among the 36 German participants chose cash as the reward.

Platform Setup

Three types of collaboration tools were used in the experiment: a text-based chat tool (Google Talk), a voice communication tool (Google Talk), and a synchronous shared editor (Google Docs). According to Mittleman et al's classification of collaboration technology, text-based conversation tools and shared editors belong to the jointly authored pages, a single window to which collaborators could contribute, often simultaneously; voice communication tools belong to streaming technologies that provide a continuous feed of changing data [45]. We established our experimental platform on Google Apps, which enables easy multiple accounts management and incorporates the required collaborative tools. Every participant was instructed and constrained to communicate and collaborate with his or her partner only. All text-based chat logs, verbal conversations, document revision histories were recorded.

Task

A proposal-writing task named "Social Media for Business" was developed for this study. Participants were described as employees in a medium-sized international company who were responsible to write a proposal for the managerial board about adopting social media for business purpose. The writing task contained three subtasks: brainstorming (creative task), justification (reasoning task) and analysis (analytical task). In the brainstorming task, each dyad was required to generate at least eight ideas about how to use social media to benefit the company. In the justification task, they were asked to select three ideas among the generated ideas and provide reasons for the selection. In the analytical task, they need to analyze risks and benefits of using social media for business. The three subtasks required different team processes in terms of information exchange and work division, and they had the potential to trigger non-routine interpersonal interactions and capture a multi-faceted interaction process in the experiment. A proposal template was prepared in Google Docs and participants were given 30 minutes to complete the task.

Procedure

The study was carried out by one research team in China and one research team in Germany simultaneously. It consisted of a pre-experiment survey and a laboratory experiment. Before participants came to the laboratories, they completed an online pre-experiment survey assessing individual characteristics (i.e. demographic information, CQ, language proficiency and international experience). On experimental dates, participants in both countries came to the labs, provided information on their experience and knowledge about the experimental task and with the collaborative tools, read task instructions, watched a training video and practiced in Google Docs for about five minutes. At a prescheduled time point, they started an audio call with their cross-border partners vie Google Talk and completed the collaborative writing task in Google Docs within 30 minutes. The participants were asked to communicate in English. Finally, participants filled out a post-task questionnaire about their trust on their partners, perceived involvement (as manipulation check) in the teamwork, satisfaction on the partners, and the intention to collaborate with the partners in the future. The complete experiment lasted about one hour. All written instructions, training videos and questionnaires were given in English.

Measurements

Individual Capabilities

We assessed participants' behavioral CQ with the subscale in Cultural Intelligence Scale (CQS) developed by Ang et al. [4]. By eliminating non-verbal related items (e.g. I alter my facial expressions when a cross-cultural interaction requires it), we adapted the scale to a virtual environment where only verbal communication and text-based communication is feasible. The final scale contained 3 items, and the internal consistency was $\alpha = 0.66$. The behavioral CQ was positively correlated with participants' cross-cultural team self-efficacy (CCTSE) (adapted from [34]) (Pearson correlation=.364, $p< .01$), metacognitive CQ (Pearson correlation=.511, $p< .01$), cognitive CQ (Pearson correlation=.388, $p< .01$) and motivation CQ (Pearson correlation=.539, $p< .01$), which indicated good convergent validity.

Language proficiency was self-assessed with the Common European Framework of Reference for Languages on a 6-point scale (A1=elementary, C2=proficiency). After the experiment, the first author randomly sampled 50% of the dyads' communication records during the experiment and assessed participants' language proficiency with the same assessment framework. Then the external ratings were compared with the self-assessed ratings, resulting in an inter-rater reliability as high as 0.887. Therefore, the self-assessed language proficiency was considered reliable and taken as the participants' language proficiency for all participants.

Technical skill was formatively constructed by two items: participants' previous experience and familiarity with instant messaging tools (e.g. Google Talk, skype) and with collaborative writing tools (e.g. Google Docs, Zoho Writer). All items were measured on a 7-point Likert scale (1=not at all, 7= extremely).

Receptivity/Trust

In the post-task questionnaire, participants reported their trust on their partners with the receptivity/trust subscale in the relational communication scale [31]. This scale contained six items (e.g. he/she was open to my ideas; he/she was sincere in communicating with me) and each item was rated on a 7-point Likert scale (1=strongly disagree, 7= strongly agree). It was particularly constructed to measure perceived receptivity and sincerity of conversational partners during interpersonal communication, which is suitable for a verbal-based virtual communication.

Affective Outcomes

We adapted one scale of group outcome perceptions from Hardin et al. [34] to measure participants' satisfaction on their partner in general (e.g. I was pleased with the way my partner and I worked together) with 3 items. Three questions were added to the peer satisfaction scale asking about participants' satisfaction with the partner's contribution, communication and collaboration specifically (e.g. I was satisfied with my partner's contribution in the teamwork), resulting in a six-item peer satisfaction scale.

Manipulation Check

As a manipulation check, participants reported their involvement in the virtual team work with Zaichkowsky [67] Personal Involvement Inventory. This instrument was originally developed to measure consumers' involvement with products, but also adapted to measure team members' involvement in team work [11]. It contains 20 bipolar pairs (e.g. important/unimportant, interesting/uninteresting) rated on a 7-point Likert scale. The calculated internal consistency was high (α_{CH}=0.94; α_{DE}=0.93). The average involvement was 5.42 (SD=0.91) and 5.64 (SD=0.68) for the Chinese and the German sample, respectively, which indicated a high degree of involvement in the experiment.

RESULTS

Descriptive Statistics of Member Characteristics

Table 1 presents the comparisons of means of member characteristics between the Chinese and the German cultural group. In the present study, English was the common language for the two cultural groups. The Chinese sample had significantly lower English proficiency than the German sample. This difference might be due to different degree of language similarities, different language education systems and different opportunities for foreign exposures. We consider the difference in the samples' English proficiency is representative of prevailing conditions when comparing Chinese and German universities.

	Chinese		German		t (70)
	M	SD	M	SD	
Behavioral CQ	4.48	0.83	4.77	0.74	-1.56
IM experience	4.97	1.42	5.39	1.10	-1.39
CW tool experience	2.28	1.03	2.78	1.59	-1.59
Language proficiency	3.33	1.22	5.33	0.68	-8.61**
Task experience	3.58	1.54	4.14	1.55	-1.53
Intl. experience	14.25	58.24	24.78	47.22	-0.84
Age	21.39	0.84	21.50	2.49	-0.25
Gender†	1.44	0.50	1.58	0.50	-1.17

Note: **p< .01 (2-tailed). N_{CH}=36, N_{DE}= 36. CI=95%. † 1=male, 2=female

Table 1 Descriptive statistics and comparisons of means on member characteristics

Testing of Hypotheses

Partial least square (PLS) was selected to test the hypotheses for two reasons. First, it is capable of handling small sample sizes [22]. Second, it is appropriate for causal predictive analysis in the early stage of theory development [22]. Since this study is an early attempt at developing a theoretical model to predict effects of individual capabilities on cross-cultural virtual collaboration and the sample size is relatively small, PLS was suitable for the data analysis. In this study, SmartPLS [56] was adopted.

PLS Measurement Model

We assessed all constructs in the PLS measurement model with discriminant validity and additionally assessed constructs with reflective measurements with reliability and convergent validity [30]. For constructs with reflective measures, constructs' internal consistency, composite reliability and average variance extracted (AVE) by constructs were calculated in SmartPLS [22]. As shown in Table 2, both the composite reliabilities are above 0.8 [49] and the internal consistencies are above 0.7 [30], indicating good reliability. The calculated AVE is above the recommended level 0.5 [22], which indicated adequate convergent validity. Discriminant validity was assessed through cross loading in SmartPLS and all measurements loaded more highly on the intended construct than on other constructs, which indicated adequate discriminant validity (see Table 2) [24].

Scale	AVE	Composite reliability	Cronbach's α
Behavioral CQ	0.80	0.89	0.76
Receptivity/Trust	0.52	0.87	0.82
Satisfaction	0.76	0.95	0.94

Table 2 Reliability and convergent validity of the measurement model

PLS Structural Model

PLS as a variance-based approach of structural equation modeling tends to overestimate indicator loadings in the measurement model and to underestimate path coefficients in the structural model [12]. This bias can be eliminated effectively by using a sample size at least ten times as large as the largest number of independent constructs influencing a dependent variable. In our case, the largest number of independent constructs for one dependent construct was three, and the sample size (72) was large enough to overcome this issue.

With the adequate measurement model, we tested hypotheses by analyzing the structural models and evaluated the explanatory power of the structural model with R^2 value (variance accounted for). As shown in Figure 2, the model explained 18% of the variance of receptivity-based trust and 57% of the variance of peer satisfaction. These values exceeded 10%, which indicated substantive explanatory power according to Falk and Miller's recommendation [20].

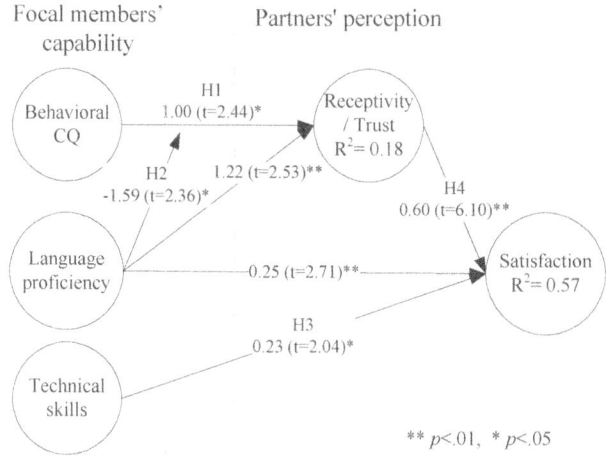

Figure 2 PLS Structural Model

We used bootstrapping to resample 5000 samples in SmartPLS to calculate t-values for all paths. As shown in Figure 2, all hypotheses were supported. The result indicated that a focal member's behavioral CQ significantly influences his/her partner's receptivity-based trust in him/her (H1, t=2.44, p=.02). However, this relationship was moderated by the focal member's language proficiency (H2, t=2.36, p=.02); when the focal member's language proficiency is low, the positive relationship between the focal member's behavioral CQ and the partner's trust was stronger than when the focal member's language proficiency is high. Besides, the focal member's experience and knowledge with collaborative tools significantly affects the partner's satisfaction on him/her (H3, t=2.04, p=.04). The partner's receptivity-based trust also significantly predicted his/her satisfaction on the focal member (H4, t=6.10, p<.01).

DISCUSSION

The results clearly demonstrate that individuals' behavioral CQ impacts partners' trust in a cross-cultural virtual environment. Our findings are in line with Chang, Chuang, and Chao's proposition, in which they suggested that individual's cultural adaptation was positively related to communication quality and trust [10]. Our study confirmed this effect by assessing cultural adaptation with cultural intelligence and testing causal relationships using an experiment setting analyzed within the PLS structural equation framework. The findings showed that in a virtual environment, when visual information and behavioral communication is largely constrained, cross-cultural verbal adaptation still functions in facilitating communication and improving partners' receptivity-based trust. Such trust strongly predicts peer satisfaction, which is an indication of team cohesion and wellness.

While the importance of language proficiency in cross-cultural virtual collaboration has long been identified [52, 58], our finding seems to provide a prescription for those who suffer from language barriers in global virtual collaborations. If one cannot speak the cross-cultural remote partners' language very well, at least he/she can be verbally adaptive to their ways of talking, use the pause and silence accordingly, vary the rate of speech and change the tone and accent to fit into the cross-cultural conversations. In being behavioral cultural intelligent, virtual team members have a good chance to sound receptive and win their remote partners' trust. The qualitative analysis of communication records in the experiment also supports the above findings. For example, in team 4, where the German partner spoke very fluent English but had relatively low behavioral CQ, she was unable to adapt to the relatively long pause between consecutive conversations in Chinese culture, and the result was that she kept interrupting the Chinese partner's speech or spoke at the same time as the Chinese partner did. The Chinese partner rated the German partner as low receptivity/trust in the post-task questionnaire. In contrast, we observed in multiple dyads that the Chinese partner had relatively low English proficiency and high behavioral CQ. He/she adapted to the German partner's high uncertainty avoidance and low context communication by providing agree or disagree responses frequently with simple words (e.g. "Yes" "I see" "I agree") and communicating with explicit codes (e.g. "I am talking about the second line in the third point.") In these dyads, the German partners generally provided high evaluation on their Chinese counterpart's receptivity/trust.

Knowledge and skills of using information and communication tools is also important for a cross-cultural virtual collaboration. Low competence in using communication tools may interrupt the ongoing communications and leads to communication breakdowns; inefficient usage of task-related tools (e.g. search engine, shared editor) may result in underperformance and failures in tasks. These effects are observable and sensible for the remote partners, which will consequently lower their satisfaction.

According to the extended adaptive structuration theory [16, 47], technology, tasks and team characteristics are mutually influential and shaping one another during the complete team life. In our study, we also found qualitative evidence to describe these interactions. For example, some participants in China encountered internet connection issues during the tasks, and thus they could not open the Google Docs or see what their partners were typing. In teams where at least one member had high technical skills, they could solve this problem quickly by stating that "Ok, you (the Chinese partner) can tell your ideas to me (through the audio communication tool). I will type (in Google Docs)." "I (the Chinese partner) can send my ideas to you in Gtalk (through the instant messaging tool)". In teams where both members had low technical skills, the solutions were not quickly brought up. They chose to cease the online collaboration temporally and waited until the internet connection recovered by stating, "I (the Chinese partner) will try again later. Maybe you can write your ideas down first". In this case, collaboration is interrupted, which leads to unbalanced contribution, broken down communication and reduced peer satisfaction. It is evidential that individual's capability will change one's way of using technology, which adjust the work process and consequently affect social interaction and outcomes.

On the other hand, the functionality of technology will also affect the effect of individual capability. In the virtual environment, if technology cannot transmit visual or verbal information, positive effects of certain individual capabilities (e.g. behavioral adaptation, language proficiency) will be substantially suppressed, which can adversely affect team interaction and outcomes.

CONCLUSIONS

This study investigated the impact of behavioral CQ, language proficiency and technical skills on peer trust and satisfaction in a cross-cultural virtual collaboration. It supports that a focal member's behavioral cultural intelligence can improve remote partners' receptivity-based trust; when the focal member's language proficiency is low, such effect is stronger.

The receptivity-based trust and the focal member's technical skills jointly predict the remote partner's satisfaction. The study is an early attempt to apply the extended adaptive structuration theory [47] in analyzing cross-cultural virtual collaboration empirically. Future studies should explore the power of EAST and be aware of the interlinking relationships among technology, team and task structures. This is especially true for virtual team studies, in which team interaction is highly technology dependent [8].

The findings have clear implications for virtual team management: in a virtual environment, technical skill is important for team wellness; in a cross-cultural virtual environment, language proficiency and behavioral CQ is crucial for cross-cultural communication and peer trust. Therefore, the combination of the three capabilities should be a major criterion when recruiting members into cross-cultural virtual teams. Since behavioral CQ is a capability that can be improved through trainings [2], organizations adopting global distributed work should also provide corresponding trainings to improve employees' behavioral CQ and technical skills to fit into the dynamic virtual working environment.

Information technology developers should be aware of the new requirements in the virtual environment and seek to develop culturally intelligent toolkits to support the cross-cultural virtual work. For example, cross-cultural communication tools can monitor interaction process, provide instant feedbacks on the compatibility and coherence of the communication patterns between culturally diverse members. Information technology can also support the cultural adaption by providing trainings based on simulated cross-cultural scenarios. We expect that innovative cultural bridging toolkits will be an emerging stream in the near future.

REFERENCES

1. Alon, I. and Higgins, J.M. Global leadership success through emotional and cultural intelligences. Business Horizons, 48 (6). 501-512.

2. Ang, S. and Van Dyne, L. Handbook of cultural intelligence: Theory, measurement, and applications. ME Sharpe Inc, 2008.

3. Ang, S., Van Dyne, L., Koh, C. and Ng, K. The measurement of cultural intelligence Academy of Management Meetings Symposium on Cultural Intelligence in the 21th Century, New Orleans, LA., 2004.

4. Ang, S., Van Dyne, L., Koh, C., Ng, K.Y., Templer, K.J., Tay, C. and Chandrasekar, N.A. Cultural intelligence: Its measurement and effects on cultural judgment and decision making, cultural adaptation and task performance. Management and Organization Review, 3 (3). 335-371.

5. Araujo, A. Implementing global virtual teams to enhance cross-border transfer of knowledge in multinational enterprises: a resource-based view. International Journal of Networking and Virtual Organisations, 6 (2). 161-176.

6. Beck, R., Gregory, R. and Prifling, M. Cultural Intelligence and Project Management Interplay in IT Offshore Outsourcing Projects ICIS 2008 Proceedings, 2008, Paper 44.

7. Bergiel, B., Bergiel, E. and Balsmeier, P. Nature of virtual teams: a summary of their advantages and disadvantages. Management Research News, 31 (2). 99-110.

8. Bjørn, P. and Ngwenyama, O. Technology Alignment: A New Area in Virtual Team Research. IEEE Transactions on Professional Communication, 53 (4). 382-400.

9. Cascio, W.F. Managing a virtual workplace. The Academy of Management Executive, 14 (3). 81-90.

10. Chang, H.H., Chuang, S.S. and Chao, S.H. Determinants of cultural adaptation, communication quality, and trust in virtual teams' performance. Total Quality Management & Business Excellence, 22 (3). 305-329.

11. Chin, W., Salisbury, W., Pearson, A. and Stollak, M. Perceived cohesion in small groups: Adapting and testing the Perceived Cohesion Scale in a small-group setting. Small Group Research, 30 (6). 751-766.

12. Chin, W.W. The partial least squares approach for structural equation modeling. in Marcoulides, G.A. ed. Modern Methods for Business Research, Lawrence Erlbaum Associates Publishers, Mahwah, NJ, US, 1998, 295-336.

13. Chua, R., Morris, M. and Mor, S. Collaborating Across Cultures: Cultural Metacognition & Affect-Based Trust in Creative Collaboration. Harvard Business School Organizational Behavior Unit Working Paper 11 (127).

14. Cur and scedil, P.L. Emergent states in virtual teams: a complex adaptive systems perspective. Journal of Information Technology, 21 (4). 249-261.

15. Desanctis, G. and Monge, P. Communication processes for virtual organizations. Journal of Computer Mediated Communication, 3 (4). 0-0.

16. DeSanctis, G. and Poole, M.S. Capturing the complexity in advanced technology use: Adaptive structuration theory. Organization Science, 5 (2). 121-147.

17. Dunkerley, K. and Robinson, W. Similarities and Differences in Perceptions and Evaluations of the Communication Styles of American and British Mangers. Journal of Language and Social Psychology, 21 (4). 393.

18. Earley, P. and Ang, S. Cultural Intelligence: Individual Interactions across Cultures. Stanford Business Books, 2003.

19. Earley, P.C. and Peterson, R.S. The elusive cultural chameleon: Cultural intelligence as a new approach to intercultural training for the global manager. Academy of Management Learning & Education, 3 (1). 100-115.

20. Falk, R.F. and Miller, N.B. A Primer for Soft Modeling. University of Akron Press, 1992.

21. Flaherty, J.E. The effects of cultural intelligence on team member acceptance and integration of multinational teams. in Ang, S. and Dyne, L.V. eds. Handbook of cultural intelligence: Theory, measurement, and applications, M.E. Sharpe, Inc., New York, 2008, 192-205.

22. Fornell, C. and Bookstein, F.L. Two structural equation models: LISREL and PLS applied to consumer exit-voice theory. Journal of Marketing Research, 19 (4). 440-452.

23. Garrison, G., Wakefield, R.L., Xu, X. and Kim, S.H. Globally distributed teams: the effect of diversity on trust, cohesion and individual performance. Database for Advances in Information Systems, 41 (3). 27-48.

24. Gefen, D., Straub, D. and Boudreau, M.C. Structural equation modeling and regression: Guidelines for research practice. Communications of the Association for Information Systems, 4 (1). 7.

25. Goodbody, J. Critical success factors for global virtual teams. Strategic Communication Management, 9 (2). 18-21.

26. Gudykunst, W. and Bond, M. Intergroup relations across cultures. in Berry, J.W., Segall, M.H. and Kagitcibasi, C. eds. Handbook of Cross-cultural Psychology: Social Behavior and Applications, Allyn and Bacon, Boston, 1997, 119-161.

27. Gudykunst, W.B. Issues in cross-cultural communication research. in Gudykunst, W.B. ed. Cross-cultural and Intercultural Communication, SAGE Publications, Inc, 2003, 149-161.

28. Gudykunst, W.B. and Matsumoto, Y. Cross-cultural variability of communication in personal relationships. in Gudykunst, W.B., Ting-Toomey, S. and Nishida, T. eds. Communication in Personal Relationships across Cultures, SAGE Publications, Inc, 1996, 19-56.

29. Hackman, J.R. The design of work teams. in Lorsch, J. ed. Handbook of Organizational Behavior, Prentice-Hall, Englewood Cliffs, NJ, 1987, 315-342.

30. Hair, J.F., Black, W., Babin, B. and Anderson, R.E. Multivariate Data Analysis. Prentice Hall, Upper Saddle River, NJ, 2009.

31. Hale, J., Burgoon, J. and Householder, B. The relational communication scale. in Manusov, V. ed. The Sourcebook of Nonverbal Measures: Going Beyond Words, Lawrence Erlbaum Associates, Inc., London, 2005, 127.

32. Hall, E.T. Beyond Culture. Doubleday, New York, 1976.

33. Hall, E.T. and Hall, M.R. Understanding Cultural Differences: Germans, French and Americans. Intercultural Press, 1990.

34. Hardin, A.M., Fuller, M.A. and Davison, R.M. I Know I Can, But Can We? Small Group Research, 38 (1). 130.

35. Hofstede, G. Motivation, leadership, and organization: do American theories apply abroad? Organizational Dynamics, 9 (1). 42-63.

36. Imai, L. and Gelfand, M. The culturally intelligent negotiator: The impact of cultural intelligence (CQ) on negotiation sequences and outcomes. Organizational Behavior and Human Decision Processes, 112 (2). 83-98.

37. Jarvenpaa, S.L. and Leidner, D.E. Communication and trust in global virtual teams. Journal of Computer Mediated Communication, 3 (4). 0-0.

38. Kayworth, T. and Leidner, D. The global virtual manager: a prescription for success. European Management Journal, 18 (2). 183-194.

39. Kim, M., Hunter, J., Miyahara, A., Horvath, A., Bresnahan, M. and Yoon, H. Individual-vs. culture-level dimensions of individualism and collectivism: Effects on preferred conversational styles. Communication Monographs, 63 (1). 29-49.

40. Kraut, R.E. Applying social psychological theory to the problems of group work. in Carroll, J.M. ed. HCI Models, Theories and Frameworks: Toward a Multidisciplinary Science, Margan Kaufmann Publishers, 2003, 325–356.

41. Martins, L.L., Gilson, L.L. and Maynard, M.T. Virtual teams: What do we know and where do we go from here? Journal of Management, 30 (6). 805.
42. Mathieu, J., Maynard, M.T., Rapp, T. and Gilson, L. Team effectiveness 1997-2007: A review of recent advancements and a glimpse into the future. Journal of Management, 34 (3). 410.
43. Maznevski, M.L. and Chudoba, K.M. Bridging space over time: Global virtual team dynamics and effectiveness. Organization Science, 11 (5). 473-492.
44. Meyerson, D., Weick, K.E. and Kramer, R.M. Swift trust and temporary groups. in Kramer, R.M. and Tyler, T.R. eds. Trust in Organizations: Frontiers of Theory and Research, SAGE, 1996, 166-195.
45. Mittleman, D., Briggs, R., Murphy, J. and Davis, A. Toward a taxonomy of groupware technologies. in Groupware Design Implementation and Use, Springer, Berlin, Heidelberg, 2008, 305-317.
46. Morris, S.A., Marshall, T.E. and Rainer, R. Impact of user satisfaction and trust on virtual team members. Information Resources Management Journal, 15 (2). 22-30.
47. Naik, N. and Kim, D.J. An extended adaptive structuration theory for the determinants and consequences of virtual team success ICIS 2010 Proceedings, Paper 232, 2010.
48. Nelson, G., Batal, M. and Bakary, W. Directness vs. indirectness: Egyptian Arabic and US English communication style. International Journal of Intercultural Relations, 26 (1). 39-57.
49. Nunnally, J.C. and Bernstein, I. Psychometric Theory. McGraw-Hill, New York, 1994.
50. Ocker, R., Zhang, Y., Hiltz, S.R. and Ronson, M.B. Determinants of Partially Distributed Team Performance: A Path Analysis of Socio-Emotional and Behavioral Factors AMCIS 2009 Proceedings, Paper 707, 2009.
51. Ocker, R.J. and Webb, H. Communication Structures in Partially Distributed Teams: The Importance of Inclusiveness AMCIS 2009 Proceedings, Paper 423, 2009.
52. Oshri, I., Kotlarsky, J. and Willcocks, L. Missing links: building critical social ties for global collaborative teamwork. Communications of the ACM, 51 (4). 76-81.
53. Peters, L. and Karren, R.J. An examination of the roles of trust and functional diversity on virtual team performance ratings. Group & Organization Management, 34 (4). 479.
54. Picot, A., Assmann, J.J., Korsgaard, M.A., Welpe, I.M., Gallenkamp, J.V. and Wigand, R.T. A Multi-Level View of the Antecedents and Consequences of Trust in Virtual Leaders AMCIS 2009 Proceedings, Paper 271, 2009.
55. Powell, A., Piccoli, G. and Ives, B. Virtual teams: a review of current literature and directions for future research. ACM SIGMIS Database, 35 (1). 6-36.
56. Ringle, C.M., Wende, S. and Will, A. SmartPLS 2.0, www.smartpls.de, 2005.
57. Rockstuhl, T. and Ng, K. The effects of cultural intelligence on interpersonal trust in multicultural teams. in Ang, S. ed. Handbook on Cultural Intelligence: Theory, Measurement and Applications, M.E. Sharpe, Inc., 2008, 206-220.
58. Sarker, S. and Sahay, S. Implications of space and time for distributed work: an interpretive study of US-Norwegian systems development teams. European Journal of Information Systems, 13 (1). 3-20.
59. Schiller, S.Z. and Mandviwalla, M. Virtual Team Research. Small Group Research, 38 (1). 12.
60. Shaffer, M. and Miller, G. Cultural Intelligence: A Key Success Factor for Expatriates. in Ang, S. ed. Handbook on Cultural Intelligence: Theory, Measurement and Applications, M.E. Sharpe, Inc., 2008, 107-125.
61. Siebdrat, F., Hoegl, M. and Ernst, H. How to manage virtual teams. MIT Sloan Management Review, 50 (4). 63-68.
62. Stahl, G.K., Maznevski, M.L., Voigt, A. and Jonsen, K. Unraveling the effects of cultural diversity in teams: A meta-analysis of research on multicultural work groups. Journal of International Business Studies, 41 (4). 690-709.
63. Templer, K.J., Tay, C. and Chandrasekar, N.A. Motivational cultural intelligence, realistic job preview, realistic living conditions preview, and cross-cultural adjustment. Group & Organization Management, 31 (1). 154.
64. Thompson, L.F. and Coovert, M.D. Teamwork online: The effects of computer conferencing on perceived confusion, satisfaction and postdiscussion accuracy. Group Dynamics: Theory, Research, and Practice, 7 (2). 135.
65. Ting-Toomey, S. Intercultural conflict styles: A face-negotiation theory. Theories in Intercultural Communication, 12. 213-235.
66. Witchalls, C. Managing virtual teams: taking a more strategic approach. Woodley, M. and Watson, J. eds. The Economist, The Economist Intelligence Unit, 2009.
67. Zaichkowsky, J.L. Measuring the involvement construct. The Journal of Consumer Research, 12 (3). 341-352.

Trust and Surprise in Distributed Teams: Towards an Understanding of Expectations and Adaptations

Ban Al-Ani, Erik Trainer, David Redmiles
Department of Informatics
University of California, Irvine
Irvine, CA, 92697-3425, USA
{balani|etrainer|redmiles}@ics.uci.edu

Erik Simmons
Intel Corporation
erik.simmons@intel.com

ABSTRACT
Trust can be defined in terms of one party's expectations of another, and the former's willingness to be vulnerable based on those expectations. Surprise results from a failure to meet expectations, which can influence trust. We conducted an empirical study of surprises stemming from cultural differences in distributed teams and their influence on trust. Our study findings provide two primary contributions. First, we find that trust judgments in culturally diverse teams are made from accumulated experiences that involve a sequence of cultural surprise, attribution, formulation of new expectations, and the application of adaptations in new situations. Second, we document adaptations that individuals develop to avoid future surprises and which ultimately helped them to improve their sense of trust towards others. In general, our findings contribute to the existing body of work by providing evidence of how people attribute specific cultural surprises, the impact on their sense of trust and adaptations.

Author Keywords
Trust; culture; attributions; adaptations; distributed teams.

ACM Classification Keywords
H.5.3 [Information Interfaces and Presentation]: Group and Organization Interfaces – Computer-supported cooperative work.

INTRODUCTION
"Americans are like peaches. We're soft and fuzzy and squishy on the outside until you hit this hard nut and then no one can get inside the pit. Russians are coconuts. Once you break through the outer shell, they're all milk. Some of them let you break through, some of them don't. That's the way they're raised." (P-28)

Collaborations often involve the need to work with people from different cultures, yet many individuals are surprised by the differences in behavior that they encounter [22].

Olson and Olson [22] introduced the term "culture surprise" to refer to such incidents.

Our study was motivated by a need to understand how such surprises influence trust in distributed culturally diverse teams[1]. We conducted our study within distributed development teams at a Fortune 500 organization and found that team members encountered several surprises during their collaboration with others in their team. These surprises were typically attributed to cultural differences, and most often had a negative influence on trust. While these themes provide insights into individuals' perception of culture and their attributions, the adaptations discussed by our participants provide us with a means to understand how these encounters influence their expectations of others in their team.

We began the introduction of this paper with a quotation from one of our study's participants who recited the advice of a colleague (experienced in working with people from Russia). This advice and other experiences she had during her collaborations led her to develop skills for adapting to different situations. Our study not only revealed surprises common across various cultural themes (e.g. regional, professional, etc.), but also the fundamental adaptations which individuals develop to enable more effective intercultural collaborations. The adaptations that we identified extend previous work that has typically focused on technological adaptations e.g. [25] and spoken and written language adaptations e.g. [3]. Our work also addresses questions raised by previous work e.g. [10] regarding adaptations and trust. We found that our participants' adaptations were either conversational, behavioral or a hybrid of both. We discuss these adaptations and their influence on trust in this paper. We emphasize here, however, that our discussions of cultural differences and attributions are presented from the study participants' perspectives rather than from widely accepted definitions of culture and cultural attributes (e.g. Hofstede [11] and Hall [9]). As such, we did not limit our analysis to these accepted yet controversial [20], definitions of culture.

It is the participants' perceptions that shape their adaptations and contribute to our understanding of

---

[1] "Culture surprise" is the verbatim term used by Olson and Olson. For ease of reading, we use the term "cultural surprise" and other variations throughout this paper.

expectations and adaptations in distributed development teams and it is this perception that we discuss in this paper. We also focus on what cultural aspects impact trust and how developers adapt to these cultural attribution, rather than why these cultural attributions are influential. The work presented here is the first step in ultimately understanding how and why differences in culture can affect levels of trust in distributed teams. Our results are more descriptive than analytical at this stage.

CONCEPTUALIZATIONS OF TRUST, CULTURE AND ADAPTATIONS

We base our discussion about the influence of culture on trust, within distributed teams, on surprises typically attributed to a specific culture by our study participants. In this section, we present an overview of the concepts we utilize in our research: *trust*, *culture*, and *adaptations*.

Conceptualizations of trust

Trust is often defined in terms of one individual's expectations of another, and the former's willingness to be vulnerable based on those expectations. Furst et al. [7] conclude that an individual's trust in their team refers to the likelihood that team members will live up to expectations, whereas Sabherwal [27] considers trust a "state involving confident positive expectations about another's motives with respect to oneself in situations entailing risk." These definitions of trust suggest that an instance of surprise can mean that there is a failure to meet expectations. Consequently, a surprise can lead to a breakdown of trust.

Trust is typically classified according to one of two widely accepted categories: cognitive trust and affective trust (e.g. as defined by [13, 14, 19] among others). Cognitive trust refers to the trustor's ability to meet the trustees' expectations of competence and reliability. Affective trust refers to the trustor's ability to meet the trustees' emotional or social expectations. More detailed descriptions of the various dimensions of trust within these two categories and others (swift and fragile trust) have also been discussed [1].

Previous research concluded that trust plays a key role in innovation, efficiency and effectiveness during collaborations, more so in distributed teams where members are unlikely to meet face-to-face [1, 2]. Establishing trust in distributed teams can increase effectiveness as team members will be less likely to spend time cross-checking others' work [4, 13]. Moreover, while distributed teams are typically characterized by cultural diversity that has been found to increase innovation during collaboration, trust must exist for team members to feel they can express innovative ideas to remote team members [12, 26]. Thus we sought to gain a deeper understanding of the influence of culture on trust, a key component of effective collaboration.

Many researchers recognize the relationship between culture and trust. Jarvenpaa and Leidner [13] document the interplay of communication, culture and trust, for example. However, they establish a link between people's cultural attributes and their propensity to trust and do not investigate the impact of cultural diversity on trust and subsequent adaptations.

Conceptualizations of culture

Samovar and Porter define culture as "the deposit of knowledge, experience, beliefs, values, attitudes, meanings, hierarchies, religion, notions of time, roles, spatial relations, concepts of the universe, and material objects and possessions acquired by a group of people in the course of generations through individual and group striving" [28]. This definition illuminates a point crucial to our work: culture implies a shared understanding that is used as a baseline from which expectations are set.

The concept of *cultural surprises* comes from a review of Olson and Olson's work [22]. They found that cultural surprises often appear in work settings where collaborations span geographical boundaries. These differences, they argue, can cause collaborators to be surprised by one another because they are unable to see past their own culture.

Cultural diversity within teams is sometimes discussed within the terms of *faultlines* [16, 8]. For example Lau and Murnighan [16] use the term to discuss the intangible divisions that lead to subgroups forming within the larger team, where faultlines can emerge as a result of demographic and non-demographic team member attributes. Gibbs [8] also uses the term *faultlines* in her discussion of how a person can exhibit behaviors characteristic of many different cultures and that each of these behaviors may emerge or recede depending on the context and environment.

In contrast to existing conceptualizations of culture, we focus on the impact of cultural differences encountered, its influence on an individual's sense of trust and the subsequent adaptations adopted by the individual – if any. We recognize that certain behaviors may be more prevalent in certain regions, as others have proposed, but our investigation is not concerned with examining our participants' attributions nor did we attempt to categorize them in this paper. We refer to others' extensive work in this area for accurate cultural attributions (e.g. [9] and [15]). We present our study participants' attribution only to provide context for the adaptations they describe.

Conceptualizations of adaptations

The term *adaptation* is used to refer to change over time [28]. Researchers have found that an individual's adaptation or "plasticity" is typically in response to pressures that select for or against particular reactions [28]. We propose that such reactions could take the form of changed behavior, conversation or a combination of both.

Our review of Powell et al [25] and other work (e.g. [10] and [3]) led us to several conclusions regarding the different adaptations that individuals in distributed teams may need to adopt in response to during their collaborations. First, we find that there are limited reports of individuals' adaptations to cultural differences when collaborating in distributed development teams. Second, references to adaptations report that members of distributed teams are adept at internalizing external norms thus adapting to changing situations e.g. various technologies introduced to support communication, and team structures. Finally, we found that Powel et al. question whether there are identifiable processes of adaptation that enable distributed teams to overcome the limitations of the distributions. It is this aspect of distributed development that we report within the context of the influence such adaptations have on trust in distributed teams.

METHOD

We studied the practices of distributed systems development teams in AVTO (All Virtual Teams Organization), a pseudonym used to refer to a Fortune 500 organization. We conducted a field study using observations and interviews. A total of 43 individuals volunteered their participation in the study in response to an invitation we sent to a mailing list comprised of approximately 75 subscribers.

A total of 31 participants were interviewed remotely using teleconference and telepresence (high-definition videoconference) technologies. The other 12 participants were interviewed face-to-face, on site. Participants were located in nine different countries, namely: U.S., Costa Rica, Ireland, Israel, Mexico, Poland, China, Taiwan, and Malaysia. The majority of participants (34) were located in the U.S. We interviewed 2 participants from Mexico and 1 participant from each of the other remaining non-US sites. We also found that 7 of our U.S.-based participants spoke a language other than English at home, indicating that they were not necessarily born in the U.S.

The participant pool consisted of 13 female and 30 male employees. Participants had an average of 13 years' experience working in distributed teams and 14 years' experience in the organization. Overall, participants had an average of 25 years of work experience. The participants' roles in the distributed team fell into one of three broad categories: managers: 16 (e.g. project manager), developers: 23 (e.g. tester) and support staff: 4 (e.g. lawyer).

Interviews were conducted over a 6-month period and each interview typically lasted one hour on average. They were recorded, transcribed, and analyzed with a specific focus on surprises, participants' attributions of surprises, and their adaptations to such surprises. We performed open-coding on all 43 transcripts and coded culture along dimensions that emerged from our data, namely: organizational culture, regional culture, and work site culture.

The interview was semi-structured such that it consisted of three main sections. The first section of the interview consisted of questions that focused on gathering information about the participants' background. The second section focused on a single project chosen by the participants. We requested that each participant choose a project where one or more team members were not collocated with the participant and either was an ongoing project or recently completed. Once participants identified a project, we asked them to give an abstract description of the project, the number of team members with whom they collaborated and their locations, duration of project (some were ongoing) in addition to listing dependencies and the tools utilized to communicate during their collaboration

The third and final section of the interview focused on gathering information about the antecedents of trust and the forces that influence trust in distributed teams. Participants were asked questions that required them to reflect on their experiences working in distributed development teams over the years and narrate their experiences of surprises through storytelling.

Storytelling is a technique typically used in interview settings by asking for an account of particular events. Storytelling is often used by social scientists to gather qualitative data e.g. [17, 24]. We chose this approach because it allows researchers to gain insight into both the internal states of the individual at the time of the experience in addition to the context of the experiences and how they collectively influenced the participants. Thus we prompted our participants by asking them to tell us a story of "a time when you were surprised by what a team member said or did". We also asked them what they attributed such encounters to, how they coped with such unexpected situations and how it influenced their sense of trust. It is this portion of the interview that we report on in this paper.

ADAPTATIONS

We use the term *adaptation* to refer to the changes adopted by our study participants in response to their situated collaboration. Participants narrated numerous stories about how they adapted to unexpected situations over the course of their careers as members of distributed teams. Some of these collaborations occurred within AVTO, others took place elsewhere. Most employees stated that they are rarely surprised after years of experience in diverse teams. The following statement by a male participant based in the US- exemplifies the sentiment:

"I think by the time I started working with Malaysia, I'd been around long enough that I wasn't surprised." (P-29)

Whereas another male participant succinctly stated, "*I think it's more just about knowing what to expect*".

We classified adaptations into one of three categories: *behavioral*, *conversational*, and *hybrid*. We identified a *behavioral* adaptation as an adaptation that is neither written nor spoken. Such an adaptation is typically internalized and non-verbal; sometimes leading to changes in actions. For example, a participant who no longer smiles as often as she used to in front of her Russian collaborators made a *behavioral* adaptation. This adaptation is in contrast to a *conversational* adaptation, which is externalized either through speech, writing, or both. For example, a participant who rephrased their spoken sentences several times in order to increase the listener's comprehension made a *conversational* adaptation.

Finally, we consider an adaptation a *hybrid* adaptation when an individual implements change that is both behavioral and conversational. For example, a participant who sent out agendas early with detailed descriptions of talking points made a hybrid adaptation. Sending the agenda early is a *behavioral* change while the agenda, a series of written statements articulating action items, are *conversational*. The participant adopted this *hybrid* adaptation after remote collaborators consistently failed to send out deliverables on time.

We do not link cultural surprise and the adaptation in this paper, as we found no correlation between the type of surprise and the nature of the adaptation. We found that, in general, developers can adapt differently to similar cultural encounters. We will also not discuss the cultural attributions made by our study participants in this report. We recognize that this domain has been studies in-depth by others also found many developers misattributing certain cultural traits in their discussions.

We found that participants often described more than one adaptation to suit their collaboration. In short, we counted 101 adaptations: 28 *behavioral*, 21 *conversational*, and 52 *hybrid*. We present a representative sample of these different types of adaptations in the following sections. For each example in our sample, we briefly summarize participants' expectations, the surprise itself, and to what cause participants attributed the surprise. We then describe the adaptations they adopted.

Behavioral
Many of our participants adopted behavioral adaptations in response to unforeseen situations. In general, the unforeseen circumstances initially had a negative impact on their collaboration and a negative influence on their sense of trust towards their team members. This negative influence decreased as participants adapted their behavior and adjusted their expectations of what they should anticipate from their remote team members. While most reported that they had managed to adapt and adjust their expectations, we did find instances where participants did not adapt to differences and consequently failed to develop a successful collaboration with others in the organization.

One U.S.-based participant did not expect the Israeli team members to be as argumentative as they were. The participant attributed the surprise to the culture of the region:

"In general [Israelis are] a culture that's more debative, and emotional expression and things like that…And I guess I wasn't really expecting that, because we usually weren't as argumentative – openly argumentative, in U.S. meetings." (P-29)

The participant adapted by expecting things to be different when working with individuals from different regions and by *looking* for remote collaborators' subtle physical cues:

"I watch how and when people speak. Right? What their body language is saying. And again, now I just go in expecting to have to figure that out as I'm there, now…."

These statements exemplify the behavioral changes consciously adopted by members of a distributed team who have, through previous interaction, learnt to anticipate differences. This participant is consistently seeking to identify and adapt to these difference by watching others. We observe that this participant, like others in distributed teams, typically only has the opportunity to *watch* their remote team members' speech. He attempts to observe *how* (attitude, tone, etc.) remote team members' speak and *when* they speak (e.g. hierarchy).

While many participants were unable to interact face-to-face with their remote team members, some did. These interactions were also challenging because of the differences in cultures. For example, the participant we quoted early in the paper was also surprised by her Russian team members' lack of friendliness:

"Nobody smiles at you, never… And I couldn't figure it out and one of the guys – Americans, he said, "I was having problems too until I realized what it is." And I said, 'What is it? Help me.'" (P-28)

She attributed this to the culture of the region after talking with a colleague with experience in the region (an excerpt of which is reported in the introduction). Finding herself in this situation, the participant adapted by deliberately changing her behavior:

"When I stopped smiling so much and stopped nodding so much and stopped laughing so much, the temperature of the room warms up… I let [a colleague] approach with the hug, right? I don't ever start the hug because that would just freak him out… by me approaching them on where their comfort zone is, you feel the room change."

Not all adaptations occurred between sites from different national regions. One participant on the West Coast of the U.S. explained how an individual from the East Coast tended to exaggerate issues (e.g. *"more chicken little"* in the following quote) and to have an abrasive attitude, surprising everyone on their team:

"He's more abrasive than the rest of the team. He has a tendency to be louder than the rest of the team. He has a tendency to be more chicken little than the rest of the team… Any small thing ends up being a big crisis. (P-36)"

The participant attributed the differences to the individual's East Coast culture. The former was able to adapt and continues to expect similar attitudes from others who grew up in the region. Similarly, a participant based in Taiwan was able to adapt to his other Asia-based colleagues' behaviors by not taking such differences "personally" but rather adapted by *"factor[ing] that into the equation for future reference."*

Some participants were unable to cope with differences they perceived to be attributed to particular regions. One U.S.-based participant refused to work with teams from Malaysia because their practices of "saving face" meant that individuals who should have been fired were simply relocated to other sites. Those same individuals undermined work conducted by the participant by "dressing him down" during meetings and ignoring crucial e-mails that he sent. The participant used this experience as a cautionary tale for others collaborating with team members based in the region. Yet another U.S.-based participant described commitment issues in an Indian team and was surprised to find that the site committed to work they could not actually complete. He attributed this to the culture of the work site:

"...that seems to be the modus operandi for that site. They continue to get technology fed to them so they can become a center of dependence, so that their risk of being shut down diminishes."

This participant was unable to find a means to adapt and consequently severed the collaboration with that site and the region. An Israeli-based participant experienced similar encounters with other sites in Europe, where he found that his team members tended to "brighten things up". He reports that people tended to be "very careful in broad meetings" while others report that they adapted by compromising with their counterparts. They typically attributed such differences to the culture of the site or region while recognizing that such encounters are born of a need to secure work and create a dependency on the site, thus making the site indispensable.

In summary, we found several instances of individuals changing their behaviors when encountering differences with others in their team and some instances where participants responded to differences by refusing to collaborate with members of a certain culture. In both instances, they typically attributed these differences to a culture (e.g. the site, the region). We are not concerned with their attribution of behavior but rather the impact of encountering such differences have on the participants' sense of trust and whether they adapted to such differences. In most instances, some of which were reported in this section, we found that individuals typically adapted their behavior to enable a more effective collaboration with others in their team and that these adaptations spanned years. It should also be noted that participants of different genders, nationalities and sites (i.e. U.S., Taiwan and Israel) reported similar adaptations.

Conversational
Study participants reported changes in their spoken and written interactions with others in their team. In these instances, we again found that most participants reported that they were able to adapt to differences while others did not. Most participants explicitly communicated their understanding, or lack thereof, of differences during their interactions with their remote team members and requested clarifications either from their collocated team members (who have more experience with a certain culture, e.g. the Russian coconut analogy) or from the remote team members themselves. In each of these instances, we found that these differences had a negative impact on trust until the participant was able to adapt to these differences and adjust their expectations so that they could be met.

Some distinct examples of conversational adaptations were in response to a refusal by some team member to communicate with others. One female participant attributed the behavior to professional culture whereas the other female participant attributed the refusal to communicate to her male team member's religion. In both these instances, all team members were located in the U.S. Both participants reported they adapted to such differences by using non-synchronous communication, e.g. posting comments and information to each other through a wiki.

One participant, based in Ireland, described her encounter with her collaborators at a Malaysian site when they took the Irish team's comments too literally. She attributed this misunderstanding to the culture of the region and adapted by minimizing her feedback to her remote team members:

"...dealing with the people in Penang, I've come to learn that you can't – if you're asking for feedback, you can't give your own feedback; otherwise it might be perceived setting a direction." (P-31)

Another participant recalled the sensitivity she brought toward editing drafts produced by non-native English speakers. She was surprised by a Parisian colleague's misinterpretation of English law and realized she had to be sensitive to the ways in which they changed the draft. She attributed the differences to the culture of the region. She adapted by changing her communicative style so that it more closely resembled that of the remote team members.

We found that adapting to differences by articulating sentences carefully was a recurring theme. For example, several participants were surprised by the importance of saving face in Asian cultures. One U.S.-based participant recalled that she learned *"how to ask the questions in order to help them save face." (P-28)*

Such concepts were well understood by many of our participants, who referred to such occurrences as such. They also stated that they acquired such knowledge either through their continued interactions or through culture classes offered by the organization. Other U.S.-based participants described instances in which their adaptations influenced their conversational interactions:

"And so, when I am asking for something from somebody in Penang, particularly a manager, I don't want to do it in a way that puts them (sic) in a bad light because I'm afraid it would damage my relationship with him." (P-9)

A Chinese-based participant *(P-17)* observed that the failure to meet his expectations regarding quality led him to lack of trust. He adapted to such collaborations by explicating his understanding and due dates to affirm issues and deadlines.

We found that there were also instances where individuals did not adapt to differences. For example, one Polish-based participant *"stopped answering questions"* (P-34) in response to the aggressive conversational tone of her remote Israeli team members. She states that such interactions led her to feel that there she was in *"[an] exam, not being in a partnership working together"*.

It is important to emphasize again that some participants who had extensive experience often stated that they are narrating stories that occurred some time ago and often felt that they were rarely surprised anymore. A reflection on these representative conversational adaptations leads us to three principal observations. First, we find that these conversational adaptations were typically adopted in response to conversational differences. Second, most adaptations of this kind were based on the awareness of possible misinterpretations of conversational interactions. Finally, in most instances of conversational adaptation, participants describe a heightened sense of awareness of others in their team and this was again observed across genders, in addition to various professions, nationalities and sites.

Hybrid

We consider *hybrid* adaptations as adaptations that involve changes in both behavior and conversation when interacting with others of a different culture. Such changes typically occur as a result of encounters with team members who are of a different culture. We found these changes followed interactions that typically had a negative influence on trust. Consequently, participants sought to adapt to enable a more effective collaboration combining changes both internally (typically reflected in the way they think about events and interactions) and externally as they explicated their understanding of situations during their interactions. We should also note that there were more instances of *hybrid* adaptations than any other type.

One of our participants, based in Israel, recalled an instance when team members in Poland stopped working on a project without sharing that information with others in the team, in different locations. The participant attributed it to a fear of losing the project:

"Everybody's afraid [that] *if they say that they have problems, somebody will use it against them." (P12)*

The result of this experience led to his being skeptical of anything the Polish team says:

"To be cautious and also not to trust whatever they say. Interpret everything they say."

A U.S.-based participant narrated his adaptations within the context of his experience with his Israeli and Japanese team members. The participant was working with people from Japan and Israel and found himself in a difficult situation:

"We had to step in and it's like, "Wait a sec. What are the challenges of this? How far can we get on this one?" And we really p--sed [expletive] off the Israelis, because they thought they were close to agreement. But they were wrong. And the Japanese were getting extremely frustrated because they had this – this arrogant person on the phone—actually, people, on the phone, this arrogant culture on the phone—that was really pushing them to make a commitment that they were not comfortable with. The two cultures are not – they're not compatible" (P-30)

The participant attributed diversity of perceptions to the differences in the regional culture of the team members involved. He felt that the Japanese and Israeli cultures in particular were extreme opposites in characteristics. Fortunately, in this instance, the participant had taken language classes and attempted to seek conversational cues that he could interpret to understand what his Japanese counterparts were saying. Furthermore, he also actively sought to observe their body language cues to understand their reaction to the Israeli team members' conversation. He explains that he adapted his conversation and observes that *"ironically in these time[s]"* he became a *"peacekeeper"* for cross-cultural interactions in the company by adapting his behavior. Some of the adaptations were explicated through the class he took whereas others were internalized as mental checklists:

"If I'm working with the Japanese, here's how I act. Here's how I – you start meetings indirectly by asking how they're doing, what the weather's like; "Have those flowers bloomed? The Israelis, like, "We don't have time for that." You know? It's – you start off – you immediately just jump in with project status. "Here's the highlights." And I just developed the two different styles."

We found many instances in which participants attributed their adaptation to culture classes provided by AVTO. They used the information provided through these classes to adapt to "incompatibilities" between regional cultures, while others stated that they benefitted most from reading about regional cultural differences in their free time:

"... the first five or six years I was working at AVTO, I thought it was the person and I couldn't figure out how to uncouple the communication challenge. And after I took enough classes to learn about people and communications and relationships, it suddenly dawned on me that it isn't the person, it's something in their behavior that is rubbing wrong with my behavior that causes my perception of the difficulty or awkwardness. "(P-28)

Some participants detected behavioral differences in remote collaborators and adapted by seeking to understand their motivations. One example is reported by a male participant based in Mexico who was taken aback by the Singaporean team's renege on promises outlined in a previous business agreement. He later found out that another manager had overridden provisions in the document without telling him.

"... the people from the Orient has a different culture and different values, a different way of thinking." (P-15)

The participant adapted by identifying the decision-makers (behavioral adaptations) in future collaborations and interacting (conversational) with them directly. Other participants sought help in understanding others in their team. Their *seeking* others is a behavioral adaptation and their explicating their needs and implementing their suggestion leads us to conclude that such adaptations are a hybrid of both conversational and behavioral. In one instance, for example, a U.S.-based participant asked mutual colleagues to broker communications between them:

"I always work with what I call friend links. If someone invites me in to come in, I will take advantage of that and go and work and do a good job for them." (P-8, US)

As in previous types of adaptation, we also found instances where participants reported their failure to adapt and as in previous instances such a failure to adapt led to a breakdown in trust and collaboration. One example of such a breakdown is exemplified in a failure to deliver a product that remote team members were developing. They attributed this failure to a lack of trust:

"And we'd always get the commitment, "Yes, we were able to do that," "Yes, we could go this fast." But, we – and they'd always agree to those deadlines and goals, but they – we could never accomplish them. I was surprised. I thought the first impression is this person's incompetent, they just can't do it. And yet, I learned is we just hadn't built enough trust or the relationship – we weren't talking the same language." (P-18)

Other participants explained that the use of the term "the same language" referred to "cultural language"; the same terms did not have the same meaning in different sites and were often not understood in the same way. In other instances, participants discovered that a failure to deliver by a set deadline was sometimes because "next Friday" in one culture meant something else in another; alternatively failure to meet deadlines occurred because commitment was perceived differently within some cultures. In such instances of failure, we found that participants' adaptations consistently involved reiterating commitments and restating discussions to test the initial commitment response:

"I think you have to understand that just hearing yes isn't enough; you have to go a little deeper and maybe understand how they're going to do it. If someone says yes right away, then you've got to test it three, four – you have to ask three times, like, you have to test it more than once." (P-38)

Others not only reiterate their perception of commitments but also change their communication style:

"I become very crisp in my communication, very – I want to get everything in writing, be sure that there is perhaps not a language concern, that if it's written down are we all reading the same thing. I may be more specific. I want more details coming back. I – it borders on the micromanagement style." (P-37)

These instances illustrate some of the adaptations that involved both behavioral and conversational changes. Both types of changes led to relatively well-defined hybrid adaptations. We find that participants discussed internalized "check-lists" of acceptable behaviors and conversation starters, as was the case with U.S.-based participant's interactions with his Israeli- and Japanese-based team members. Others developed a process that they externalized through their iterations of commitments. The sources of these adaptations varied. Some reported that they sought colleagues to gain an understanding of how to adapt, while others sought cultural classes and books that discuss the various cultures.

A DISCUSSION OF EXPECTATIONS, ADAPTATIONS, AND TRUST

Our results suggest that trust judgments in culturally diverse teams are made from accumulated experiences that involve a sequence of cultural surprise, attribution, formulation of new expectations, and the application of new behaviors (adaptations) in new situations. Surprises typically violated participants' sense of trust toward others. Participants overwhelmingly attributed the surprises to external factors, such as the region or culture of the work site, rather than dispositional ones, i.e., the individual, suggesting that trust could be repaired [5]. Adaptations to those surprises were reflections of participants' expectations, or clarified sense of both cognitive and affective trust. To what extent they were able to adapt and repair their expectations determined the level of trust and consequently their ability to collaborate with others of different cultures.

We found that the participants are generally adept at learning from cultural surprises and making adaptations when needed. Some chose their words more carefully others developed checklists to improve cognitive trust in others. Furthermore, we found participants actively looked for social cues, and avoided causing loss of face to improve their sense of affective trust. While most participants adapted readily, a few approached new collaborations with skepticism and actively sought to collaborate with teams that were not of a certain culture. There were also instances where participants were rigid and made a clean break with their former collaborators, refusing to work in particular regions and thus failed to adapt. For many participants the path of adaptation ended at becoming so adept in their abilities to learn what to expect, that they could no longer recall instances of cultural surprises and adaptations had become ingrained in their everyday interactions with others of different cultures.

Participants also described instances where they found that the diverse cultural attributes within a single distributed team led to conflict during team interactions, as one subgroup failed to recognize the social cues of another. They found that some developers' cultural makeup lends itself to collaborating with certain cultures whereas others clashed (as in the Japanese-Israeli team and East-West US team). In some instances, the diversity had an adverse influence and the creation of a faultline, as the characteristics and accepted norms of behavior were distinctly different from each other.

We found a strong link between culture and trust, as trust is often defined in terms of meeting expectations, surprises occur when expectations are not met and, consequently, these surprises typically influence trust. In most instances, we found that surprise initially had a negative influence on trust in distributed teams. We also found, however, that our study participants typically modified their expectations such that they could trust others in their team because their expectations were subsequently met. Thus, we conclude that trust is born of shared experiences and perceived commonalities amongst team members which is consistent with Lau and Murnighan's [16] postulation that such knowledge of others' will fragment and weaken a group's initial faultline structure. We find participants are less likely to be "surprised" as they become more aware of cultural characteristics and it is therefore less likely that culture will influence trust towards others in their team.

Studying adaptations made by distributed team members yields insight into the ways in which individuals manifest their new expectations in everyday situations-in spite of violations of trust. Adaptations take place because the work still needs to get done, whether there is high trust or not. By categorizing adaptations into *behavioral*, *conversational*, and *hybrid*, we are able to unpack the types of adaptations people make, as well as offer a set of practical recommendations to individuals in situations that arise due to distributed development work.

Some types of adaptations may be more applicable in certain situations than others. For example, an individual is likely to watch (during a web- or tele- conference for example) for physical cues, when people speak, and understanding how to interpret certain attitudes they can use to guide their behavioral adaptations to perceived attributes. When meeting face-to-face is not possible, when communicating with a team member whose native language is not the same, or when meeting with cultures that value "saving face" individuals should consider conversational adaptations. In these instances, rephrasing sentences to establish shared meanings, as well as using non-critical rhetoric are useful strategies. Hybrid adaptations were more common in our data set than either behavioral or conversational alone; we conclude, therefore, they can be used in both situations.

RECOMMENDATIONS

Participants' response to team members' failure to meet expectations suggests the need to identify processes of adaptation that enable distributed teams to overcome the limitations of the distributions [25], such as:

- Identification of cultural knowledge sources: Explicitly asking for help from team members in different sites or from local colleagues who have had prior experiences interacting with remote sites to understand what is actually happening during interactions is recommended. We found seeking such sources allowed participants to develop a cultural awareness through others helps team members understand differences, which will allow them to adapt more readily (as with the participant's experience with Russian members who were described as coconuts by her colleague). Cultural awareness gained through other resources (e.g. novels, cultural courses) and explicit discussions of organizational cultural language are also practices which can decrease the likelihood of differences negatively influencing trust as team members can anticipate differences and modify expectations accordingly. However, a few participants noted that knowledge gained through classes is less effective, as it proved to be different from experiencing it firsthand.

- Explication of interactions: Establish practices in which proposals, conclusions and task assignments are explicitly articulated and documented at each location is recommended. Discussions should include detailed specifications of future actions and reification of such actions. Establishing these practices will allow team members to verbalize agreements and make an effort to discuss its nuances. It will also allow for caution and reaffirmation sought throughout the collaboration. A comparison of each location's understanding can then be conducted. Study data implies that reiterating expectations clearly and a call for reaffirmation of commitments during the ongoing collaboration are practices that can have a positive influence on the collaboration.

Inclusion of all sites: Including remote sites in policy and program development or discussions can lead to a perception of equality and greater transparency during interactions. Participants reported that some sites often "brighten things up" and commit to tasks they do not have the resources to carry out because they seek job security as in the Indian site that sought to be a center of excellence. Such sites were typically also reported as being fearful of losing the project (as reported of a Polish team) or excluded from decisions (as reported of a Mexican team).

RELATED WORK

Our work adds value to studies conducted by other researchers that show how distributed team members adapt during intercultural collaborations. Anawati and Craig [3] investigated how team members adapt their spoken and written communication, as well as allow for religious beliefs and time zone differences. They found that their participants adapted their language during their communications. The authors also report "behaviors of concern" experienced by their participants. We differentiate our work in two ways. First, we document specific surprises, attributions, and the ensuing adaptations to those particular surprises beyond written and spoken communication. Second, and more importantly, by framing surprises as violations of expectations rather than "behaviors of concern," we show the impacts of the surprises on trust.

In a controlled laboratory experiment, Wang et al. [29] also identified adaptations to communication. They observed that Chinese participants became as responsive as Americans in mixed-culture groups. We documented adaptations in communication as well, but observed other types of behavioral adaptations. In addition, we observed adaptations in real work settings. Our focus is on how the accumulation of surprise and attribution frame people's adaptations and future expectations rather than how communication media and national culture frame adaptations during the course of short-term tasks.

In a longitudinal study, Cramton and Hinds [6] document adaptations in distributed team members' practices in response to cultural differences embedded in local structures and practices. They characterize adaptation as a dialectical process by which tensions are managed and adaptation gradually occurs in response to initial "instantiation surprises". Our work documents specific adaptations narrated by our participants, rather than observing them over time, and linking them to specific instances of cultural surprise, attribution, and impacts on trust. In Cramton and Hinds' work there is an underlying assumption that surprises have a negative impact, but no explicit description of what it is. Where the former study does not consider attribution per se and assumes surprises are due to regional culture alone, we document different attributions made to different types of cultures. Our data suggest individuals can develop skill sets to use in their immediate day-to-day interactions rather than structural adaptations that would take weeks or months to have effect.

Adaptation has been described as response to *exceptions*, a term which has its roots in the vocabulary of organization theory. Exceptions are events that interfere with task completion, and require troubleshooting [18]. Orr and Scott [23] document institutional exceptions in large-scale global projects involving *regulative elements* such as constitutions and laws, *normative elements* such as norms, practices, and codes of conduct, *cultural–cognitive elements* such as shared beliefs, identities, and mental models. Exceptions involve three phases: *ignorance*, *sensemaking* and *response*.

Our findings enrich Orr and Scott's model of exceptions in two ways. First, we contribute to the *response* phase of their model by describing concrete adaptations to *cultural-cognitive* exceptions. Second, we extend their model by documenting the impact exceptions have on trust. *Adaptation* implies change in behavior that manifests from changes in expectations. Because we define trust in terms of expectations, the adaptations participants adopt tell us how their sense of trust toward others was impacted.

LIMITATIONS

Our research findings resulted from samples of interviews conducted with subjects located in the United States (34/43). We interviewed 9 individuals from non-US locations. As such, the extent to which we can generalize our findings across cultures is limited and may not hold in contexts influenced by other cultures. The study has several points in its favor, nevertheless. First, we observe the bias is not as severe as it may seem if spoken language is accounted for when considering regional cultures. We found 7 of the 34 participants from the US spoke multiple languages and languages other than English at home. Thus, a total of 16/43 spoke languages other than English at home. It is for this reason that we refer to participants as being "U.S.-based" as their location does not necessarily mean they are of that nationality or imply their cultural background.

Second, despite this bias in sample, we have an initial set of evidence that adaptations *do* extend across various cultures (e.g. professional, regional and gender). These were included where relevant in each section. Thus although our findings are grounded in a Western perspective, we believe that they may be extended across locations. We plan to further explore their generalizability in an ongoing study we are conducting of software development teams based in Brazil and their remote collaborators.

CONCLUSION

Our study was motivated by a need to investigate whether cultural differences influence trust in distributed teams and whether individuals attempt to counter-act this influence. We conducted our study within distributed development teams at a Fortune 500 organization and found that instances of behavioral, conversational adaptations in addition to adaptions that involved changes in both behavior and conversation. These adaptations were typically linked to interactions in which differences in culture emerged.

In this paper, we make two primary contributions. First, our analysis revealed the link between cultural differences and trust. Second, we document adaptations that individuals develop to avoid such differences influencing their trust and ultimately helped them to improve their expectations of others. We add value to previous literature on adaptations in intercultural collaborations by providing evidence of how people attribute specific differences and what the impact is on their sense of trust toward others.

ACKNOWLEDGMENTS

This work was supported by National Science Foundation awards #0943262, #0808783, and #1111446.

REFERENCES

1. Al-Ani, B., Redmiles, D. Supporting Trust in Distributed Teams through Continuous Coordination. *IEEE Software 99*, 1 (2009), 35-40.

2. Al-Ani, B., Wilensky, H., and Redmiles, D. An Understanding of the Role of Trust in Knowledge Seeking and Acceptance Practices in Distributed Development Teams. In *Proc. ICGSE 2011*, IEEE (2011), in press.

3. Anawati, D. and Craig, A. Behavioral adaptation within cross-cultural virtual teams. *IEEE Trans. On Professional Communication 49*, 1 (2006), 44-56.

4. Bos, N., Olson, J., Gergle, D., Olson, G., and Wright, Z. Effects of Four Computer-Mediated Communications Channels on Trust Development. In *Proc. CHI '02*, ACM (2002), 135-140.

5. Cramton, C. D. Attribution in distributed work groups. In P. J. Hinds, S. Kiesler (Eds.). *Distributed Work*, MIT Press (2002), 191-212.

6. Cramton, C.D., and Hinds, P. The dialectical dynamics of nested structuration in globally distributed teams. *Academy of Management Best Paper Proceedings*, (2009).

7. Furst, S., Blackburn, R., and Rosen, B. Virtual team effectiveness: A proposed research agenda. *Information Systems Journal 9* (1999), 249-269.

8. Gibbs. J. Culture as kaleidoscope: navigating cultural tensions in global collaboration. In *Proc. IWIC '09*, ACM (2009), 89-98.

9. Hall, E. T. *Beyond Culture*. Anchor Books/Doubleday, Garden City, NJ, USA, 1976.

10. Hantual, D., Kock, N., D'Arcy, J., and DeRosa, D. (2011). Media Compensation Theory: A Darwinian Perspective on Adaptation to Electronic Communication and Collaboration, In G. Saad (ed.), Evolutionary Psychology in the Business Sciences. Springer Publishing

11. Hofstede, G. Cultures *and Organizations: Software of the Mind*. McGraw-Hill, London, UK, 1991.

12. Holton, J. A. Building Trust and Collaboration in a Virtual Team. *Team Performance Management 7*, 3-4 (2001), 36-47.

13. Jarvenpaa, S. L. and Leidner, D. E. Communication and Trust in Global Virtual Teams. *Organization Science 10*, 6 (1999), 791-815.

14. Jarvenpaa, S. L., Knoll, K., and Leidner, D. E. Is Anybody Out There?: Antecedents of Trust in Global Virtual Teams. *Journal Manage. Info. Systems 14*, 4 (1998), 29-64.

15. Kittler, M.G., Rygl, D., and Mackinnon, A. Beyond Culture or Beyond Control? Reviewing the Use of Hall's High-/Low-Context Concept. *Int. Journal of Cross Cultural Management 11*, 1 (2011), 63-82.

16. Lau, D. C., and Murnighan, J. K. Demographic diversity and faultlines: The compositional dynamics of organizational groups. *Academy of Management Review 23*, 2 (1998), 325-340.

17. Lutters, W., and Seaman, C. Revealing actual documentation usage in software maintenance through war stories. *Information and Software Technology 49*, 6 (2007), 576-587.

18. March, J. G., & Simon, H. A. 1958. Organizations. New York: Wiley.

19. McAllister, D.J. Affect- and cognition-based trust as foundations for interpersonal cooperation in organizations. *Academy of Management Journal 38*, 1 (1995), 24–59.

20. McSweeney, B. "Hofstede's 'Model of National Cultural Differences and Consequences: A Triumph of Faith - A Failure of Analysis, Human Relations", (2002), 55.1, 89-118.

21. Nisbett, R.E. *The Geography of Thought: How Asians and Westerners Think Differently…and Why*. Free Press, New York, NY, USA, 2003.

22. Olson J., Olson, G. Culture surprises in Remote Software Development Teams. *ACM Queue 1*, 9 (2003), 52-59.

23. Orr, R.J. and Scott, W.R. Institutional Exceptions on Global Projects: A Process Model. *Journal of International Business Studies 39*, 4 (2007), 562-588.

24. Patton, M.Q. *Qualitative Research and Evaluation Methods*, 3rd ed. Sage Publications, Thousand Oaks, CA, USA, 2002.

25. Powell, A., Piccoli, G., and Ives, B. Virtual Teams: A Review of Current Literature and Directions for Future Research. *Database for Advances in Information Systems 35*, 1 (2004), 6-36.

26. Pyysiäinen, J. Building Trust in Global Inter-Organizational Software Development Projects: Problems and Practices. In *Proc. Int. Workshop on Global S.E.*, IEEE Computer Society (2003), 69-74.

27. Sabherwal, R. The role of trust in outsourced IS development projects. *Communications of the ACM 42*, 2 (1999), 80-86.

28. Samovar, L. A. and Porter, R. E. *Communication Between Cultures*, 4th Ed. Wadsworth Publishing, 1995.

29. Wang, H-C., Fussell, S. F., and Setlock, L.D. Cultural difference and adaptation of communication styles in computer-mediated group brainstorming. In *Proc. CHI '09*, ACM (2009), 669-678.

Offshoring Attitudes and Relational Behaviours in German-Indian Offshoring Collaborations: Reflections from a Field Study

Angelika Zimmermann

Loughborough University

Ashby Rd, Loughborouh, LE11 3TU, UK

a.zimmermann@lboro.ac.uk

+44(0)1509 2288445

ABSTRACT

Offshoring arrangements have become a common setting for intercultural collaborations. There is ample evidence that the success of these offshoring arrangements is influenced on the relational behaviours between offshore and onshore colleagues. However, it has not been questioned whether and how the attitudes that onshore colleagues hold towards offshoring affect their relational behaviours towards offshore colleagues. This paper draws together the literatures on offshoring and transnational teams, to argue for the importance of offshoring attitudes. It presents a qualitative case study examining the offshoring attitudes of German IT developers working with Indian colleagues in an Indian subsidiary of the firm. The inquiry revealed that respondents' offshoring attitudes were associated with their relational behaviours towards Indian offshore colleagues, namely whether Germans treated their Indian colleagues as fellow team members or as mere suppliers, how much effort they spent in communicating and transferring knowledge, and whether they supported or avoided the transfer of tasks to India. Importantly, these relational behaviours also had a reverse effect on the Germans' offshoring attitudes, creating vicious and virtuous circles of offshoring attitudes and relational behaviours. Certain departmental context factors were identified to explain the differences in offshoring attitudes and resulting vicious and virtuous circles. The findings demonstrate that researchers and practitioners have to pay more attention to offshoring attitudes in order to better understand relational behaviours between onshore and offshore members, and thereby achieve more successful offshoring collaborations.

Author Keywords

offshoring, transnational teams, global teams, attitudes, vicious circle

ACM Classification Keywords

J.4.3 [Computer applications]: Social and behavioral sciences – Sociology;

General Terms

Management

INTRODUCTION

Offshoring arrangements have become a common setting of intercultural collaborations, and they provide specific challenges to such collaborations. Offshoring commonly refers to the provision of goods or services, previously supplied inhouse, from subsidiaries or other firms in different countries [13]. Discussions about offshoring tend to revolve around economic and employment effects that offshoring bears on countries, industry, and employees. In contrast, little is known about the attitudes that Western, onshore members of an offshoring arrangement hold towards the transfer of tasks to the offshore destination, typically in a developing or emerging economy. In this article, I argue that such 'offshoring attitudes' can have a potentially crucial influence on the collaboration within offshoring arrangements in transnational teams (TNTs), because they influence how onshore team members behave towards their offshore colleagues. In what follows, I develop this argument in more detail, by referring to research on offshoring and TNTs. Whilst the offshoring debate does not examine team level dynamics, TNT studies have highlighted the importance of several relational behaviours in TNTs, such as subgroup formation and knowledge transfer, without considering the influence of offshoring attitudes.

These claims are supported by a qualitative study of German IT developers working in TNTs with offshore Indian colleagues, which captured offshoring attitudes in terms of perceived advantages and disadvantages that the transfer of tasks to India created for the firm, the team, and themselves. I identified factors that explained different attitudes, and examined how offshoring attitudes affected relational behaviours of Germans towards their Indian colleagues. The discussion highlights how this led to vicious and virtuous circles of offshoring attitudes and relational behaviours. To conclude, I provide recommendations for managing the offshoring process, in particular with regard to strategies of task distribution and ownership. I then outline limitations of the study and indicate directions for future research.

CONCEPTUAL BACKGROUND: OFFSHORING ATTITUDES AND RELATIONAL BEHAVIOURS IN TNTS

A lot is known on the potential benefits and risks of offshoring activities, such as cost savings, tapping on talent pools [20] on the one hand, and risks of loosing core competences and jobs in the onshore country on the other [2]. In contrast, we know little about the attitudes that employees working in offshoring arrangements hold towards the transfer of tasks to an offshore destination. Their views may be shaped by economic and political debates, but could also be based on other sources such as their own experience or socialisation through colleagues. From the public offshoring debate [20], it appears that TNT members are likely to evaluate the transfer with regard to consequences for the organisation, the TNT, and themselves. With regard to the organisation and the team, they may be concerned about cost advantages and performance. For themselves, they may see risks of additional coordination efforts and losing their own jobs. In support of this view, Cohen and El-Sawad (2007) demonstrate that British call centre staff perceived their Indian counterparts as threatening their own jobs. However, it has also been shown that TNT members can experience the international collaboration as a personally enriching opportunity for intercultural learning (Stah, Maznevski, Voigt, and Jonsen, 2009), independent of the offshoring debate. Hence, it is not apparent what range of attitudes are held by TNT members and how attitudes are associated with relational behaviours. Attitude research [1] even suggests that individuals can hold contradictory attitudes at the same time, leading to cognitive conflict. We therefore need to establish under what conditions TNT members develop certain offshoring attitudes.

When consulting the TNT literature, it becomes clear that offshoring attitudes are likely to have an impact on relational behaviours between onshore and offshore team members. In particular, team members' offshoring attitudes are likely to influence the strength and the dynamics of national subgroups. Subgroups are usually seen to emerge along 'faultlines', i.e. hypothetical dividing lines that create a split along team members' shared core attributes, which can become more or less salient in different contexts [15]. In TNTs, nationality and location tend to be such salient attributes, splitting the team into national subgroups [6].

Positive and negative offshoring attitudes may influence which attributes of members of another nationality in the team become salient. For example, onshore team members may perceive their offshore colleagues either as members of another culture who contribute interesting new insights and important support to the team, or as outgroup members who threaten their jobs.

Strong subgroups can have negative effects on relational behaviours, such as members withholding information from each other [4, 21]. As knowledge tends to flow along pre-existing social ties [8], it can be inhibited by strong subgroup divides [9]. Conversely, a strong shared team identity can motivate team members to contribute effort and knowledge to the team [8]. However, if subgroups are moderately strong and an inclusive atmosphere is maintained, subgroups can also promote knowledge sharing and team learning [9]. Hence, negative attitudes towards the offshoring collaboration are likely to reinforce negative intergroup dynamics, such as withholding information, whilst positive offshoring attitudes may go hand in hand with a more inclusive atmosphere that promotes knowledge sharing.

Importantly, the effect of offshoring attitudes on relational behaviours may not be straightforward, because attitudes are not necessarily consistent with behaviours [1]. We therefore need to establish whether and how offshoring attitudes influence relational behaviours, and what factors are responsible for this influence. On the basis of these theoretical considerations, this study aimed to explore:

- Offshoring attitudes of onshore TNT members; in terms of perceived advantages and disadvantages that the transfer of tasks created for the firm, the team, and themselves.
- Factors that caused these attitudes.
- Effects of these attitudes on relational behaviours towards offshore colleagues.

METHODS

This research examines offshoring attitudes and their effects on relational behaviours in TNTs, both complex and largely unexplored social phenomena. For this reason, a qualitative methodology was chosen [16]. The inquiry was guided by the initial expectations based on the offshoring and TNT literature, but was at the same time highly inductive.

Research setting and respondents

The fieldwork was conducted in a major German electronics firm outsourcing parts of its IT development to Indian subsidiaries. The main espoused reasons for offshoring of IT are cost savings and a shortage of qualified software engineers in Germany. This is a common organisational offshoring context, given that German firms are increasingly offshoring their software operations to

India, even in face of the recent economic crisis [18]. The company develops and produces automotive technology as its core business, followed by industrial technology, consumer goods and building technology, as well as engineering and IT services. The company has close to 300,000 employees worldwide, with about 300 subsidiary and regional companies around the world. In India, the company set up production plants as early as the fifties, and has built up software development sites rapidly since the early nineties, with an explicit aim of further offshoring in the future. The company now employs over 18,000 employees in India.

30 German IT developers were interviewed at German headquarters in Stuttgart (Germany), all working in virtual teams with Indian colleagues that were located in a wholly-owned subsidiary in Bangalore (India). I included only the German side and not their Indian counterparts, because Germans were bound to have a much better insight into their own and their German colleagues' offshoring attitudes.

Respondents had different levels of experience in collaborating with Indians, having worked with the Indian subsidiary from 1- 10 years. All of the participants were male, apart from one, like the vast majority of employees of this industry in Germany. Five organisational departments participated with three or more representatives in each (see Table 1). Additionally, I included nine other departments with one respondent each. These respondents could not be treated as representative of their department, but nevertheless allowed for a comparison of the emerging patterns across a broader range of departments.

Of the five main departments, Department 1 was tasked with developing and maintaining software functions for electronic control units (ECUs) to be implemented in car engines. Department 2 and Department 3 were responsible for the interface to different customers in the car manufacturing industry, and adjusted generic ECU software functions to particular customer needs. Department 4 produced software for new automotive safety systems. Department 5 was involved in software development for automotive safety systems as well, by generating electronic test methods and equipment. Each of the interviewed respondents worked in a different Indian-German team. The other nine respondents were involved in various tasks relevant to the German-Indian collaboration, including function development, customer support, managing the interface between software development and manufacturing sites, coordinating the collaboration with India for all ECU development departments, sales for an Indian customer, and software tool development for various firm-internal departments. Table 1 gives an overview of the departments and the numbers of respondents per department.

Department	Tasks	Number of respondents
Respondents in five main departments:		
1	Function development for electronic control unit (ECU)	3
2	Customer support for electronic control unit	4
3	Customer support for electronic control unit	6
4	Software development for automotive safety systems	5
5	Software test development automotive safety systems	3
Respondents in other departments:		
6	Function development for electronic control unit	1
7	Customer support for electronic control unit	1
8	Customer support for motor control	1
9	Interface between ECU development and manufacturing sites	1
10	Coordinator of the collaboration with India for ECU development	1
11	Sales department for Indian customer	1
12	Software tool development for various internal software departments	1
13	Software tool development for heavy motor vehicles	1
14	Software tool development for various internal departments	1

Table 1. Respondents per department.

Data collection

Data were collected by the author through semi-structured interviews that lasted between 40 and 70 minutes, with an average of 58 minutes. All interviews were conducted in German and tape-recorded. At the beginning of each interview, it was explained to all respondents that the research investigated respondents' attitudes towards their collaboration with Indian colleagues and how these attitudes affected the collaboration. They were informed that a feedback report would be written and sent to respondents, and that none of the respondents' names would be mentioned. All respondents were given identical starter questions. They were asked to state the number of German and Indian colleagues in their team and the tasks of each side. They were then requested to rate the performance of their German-Indian team using a scale developed by Gibson, Zellmer-Bruhn, and Schwab (2003). This scale uses a seven point Likert-type scale to assess goal achievement and effectiveness in terms of achieving team goals, team objectives, meeting the requirements set for the team, fulfilling its mission, and serving the purpose the team is intended to serve. Given the small respondent number, this rating served only to elicit attitudes towards performance, rather than as a statistical device.

Respondents were further asked to describe their offshoring attitudes in terms of perceived advantages and disadvantages that the transfer of tasks to India created for the firm, the TNT, and TNT members. Respondents were allowed to answer these questions with respect to themselves as well as their colleagues. Moreover, they were requested to describe relationships between Indians and Germans in their teams. If required, they were given more specific probes, for example with regard to team identity (how strongly colleagues felt they were part of one team) and knowledge transfer (how well information and knowledge was provided to the other side). To establish determining factors, respondents were further interviewed about what their attitudes depended on. They were also asked directly whether they thought that attitudes towards the collaboration affected the way in which Germans and Indians worked with each other, and what this depended on.

Although all of these points were covered in each interview, respondents were encouraged to speak freely about points of concern not included in the interview schedule, to allow for additional items to emerge. When additional items emerged in an interview, they were added as probes in subsequent interviews.

Data analysis

The interviews were transcribed and coded in German, using the NVivo 8 software and following a procedure of template analysis [14]. The initial coding tree was constructed from those initial interview items that had been maintained up to the end of the interviewing stage, and those that were added by respondents. During the process of coding, the tree was refined by merging similar codes, adding codes to capture emerging additional themes, and re-defining codes to better match respondents' explanations. Initially, the author coded half of the interviews to develop the coding scheme to some maturity. Then, two other academic, German researchers working on knowledge transfer in TNTs acted as second coders. They used the scheme to code three interviews. After each coded interview, the three researchers compared their codes and discussed differences. For the first two interviews, this led to some modifications of the codes to eliminate sources of misunderstanding and incorporate additional meanings observed by the second coders. No further code modification was seen as necessary for the third interview. The coding scheme was therefore deemed saturated and used for the analysis of all interviews.

Respondents' views on attitudes, effects on relational behaviours, and determining factors were analysed through node lookups and coding queries in NVivo. Respondents' reports were synthesised to gain summaries. Attitudes were categorised into overall positive, negative, and neutral. To transcend mere description, causal explanations were sought. The respondents' own interpretations were used as the primary source of explanation. Secondly, contrasting perspectives were compared, to establish determining factors from the researcher's perspective, and thus triangulate respondents' explanations. Thirdly, the five main departments were clustered into overall positive or negative in terms of their members' attitudes. For this purpose, a score was calculated by dividing all positive by all negative attitude summaries. A score below 1 was thus classified as negative and a score above 1 as positive. This clustering allowed for a useful comparison between departments, to determine the factors that could explain the different tendencies of these departments. This served as a further triangulation of the factors named by respondents and those identified by comparing individuals' attitudes. The analysis led to an explanatory model that captures attitudes, factors, and effects on relational behaviours across respondents and departments.

These methods follow Lincoln and Guba's (2002) recommendations to establish credibility of qualitative research. In particular, data coding was based on inter-rater agreements, and the findings were triangulated by drawing on participants' explanations as well as my own comparisons between respondents and departments. Moreover, I received participant confirmation of the results by sending a feedback report to all respondents, which outlined our main interpretations. Ten participants responded, all confirming that their views were represented in the report. In the results section, I will present extensive quotes to further support the study's credibility.

RESULTS

Most respondents held offshoring attitudes that could be classified clearly as overall positive or negative. However, some preferred to remain undecided, even when asked explicitly for their general evaluation. A number of respondents further differentiated between their own (typically more positive) and their colleagues' views. In the following, I will describe respondents' offshoring attitudes in relation to the factors that can explain them. I will then describe how these attitudes affected German employees' relational behaviours.

Offshoring Attitudes

Advantages and disadvantages for the organisation

Respondents named similar aspects of consequences of the transfer for the organisation, namely: costs, additional workforce, flexibility, and presence in the Asian market. However, respondents differed in their judgments of some of these effects.

Most respondents named cost benefits as the main reason for the organisation to transfer tasks to India. However, they differed in their views on whether this advantage was realised. The majority of respondents estimated that the organisation did gain a cost advantage. For example, some projects had been gained only due to a price advantage created through the transfer. The remaining respondents were more negative, estimating that there was no significant or no benefit for the organisation. Employees also stressed that at a higher level, managements' cost calculations were not transparent and employees could therefore not know the actual financial outcomes of the transfer:

"...Here you just have to say: 'How can that pay off?' Hardly any of us understand it. Then you content yourself with it and say: 'OK, someone has decided it, and hopefully they know what they are doing.'"

The overall cost benefit was seen to be tied to the TNT's perceived work performance, which is discussed in a later section. Most respondents further explained that the transfer created an additional workforce not available in Germany, because the firm had restricted its recruitment in Germany. Another perceived advantage for the organisation was increased flexibility due to different employment laws. Indian work hours were more flexible, allowing for longer hours in pressured phases of a project. Moreover, the Indian workforce could be increased or decreased more easily:

„Here in Germany, we have something like upper limits of personnel. That means even if I had the money, I can sometimes not increase my workforce, and that is a very, very big advantage of India... Within three months ...they build up any capacity for me. So that's an advantage:...this flexibility in building and de-building capacity, to deal with peaks."

A skilled local Indian workforce was by many seen to be necessary for supporting the increasing number of Indian and other Asian customers, therefore creating a competitive advantage:

„If you are in India and suddenly every Indian buys a car and you are in the market, then it is a massive advantage, again."

Advantages and disadvantages for TNT performance

The respondents described consequences of the transfer on team performance in terms of quality and efficiency, again arriving at contrasting evaluations. Many respondents stated that the quality of work produced in India was now satisfactory, whilst others pointed to severe quality problems, mostly in terms of software faults ('bugs'). In both positive and negative cases, participants emphasised that output quality depended on the complexity of the transferred task and the level of knowhow of particular Indian colleagues. Frequent support and monitoring were seen to be vital for achieving high quality. With regard to efficiency, most respondents found that it commonly took longer to get the same output from the TNT than from a purely German team. This was attributed mainly to coordination and communication efforts, and to insufficient knowledge and skills of Indian colleagues, particularly when employee turnover in India was high. Many Indians' lack of understanding of the software environment required Germans to answer queries, check the Indians' work, and rework results. Moreover, some respondents complained that too much time had to be spent on administration, task specification and documentation, and these procedures could take even longer than task completion itself:

„For one Indian colleague to do a task which is really only a flick of the wrist, I have to produce paper for hours over here for him to know what to do. ... this is in no longer in any proportion, the coordinative and planning effort and the actual task. ...The actual task, that's sometimes a matter of a few minutes - and we have to spend hours over here to organise it."

Another source of inefficiency was intercultural communication. Germans often learnt about problems only shortly before a deadline when it was too late to fix them. This was attributed primarily to language barriers, the Indians' indirect communication style, and Indians withholding information on difficulties. Most respondents explained that performance could improve over time, with increasing training and personal acquaintance with Indian colleagues, however only if employee fluctuation in India was not too high. Germans got to know their Indian colleagues primarily through training visits. During these visits, Indians worked alongside their German colleagues in Stuttgart for typically three months, and took part in shared social events, such as going out for evening meals. Many respondents also stated that their team was efficient only because Indians worked on routine, non-innovative tasks, requiring little coordination and communication.

Advantages and disadvantages for German team members

The transfer was seen to affect individual German team members in terms of workload, changes in work tasks, job security, professional learning, and intercultural experience. The respondents came to strikingly contrasting evaluations.

Many respondents thought the transfer had increased their workload, by creating additional tasks, such as coordination, support, and reworking Indians' results:

"In the end, you sit down and do everything yourself, and you are hopping mad that you have this burden on top of everything else."

Other respondents came to an overall positive calculation of such effort in comparison to the amount of time saved through delegating tasks to India. Moreover, respondents agreed that their work could no longer be done without Indian support, due to the shortage of new German recruits. The perceived workload depended on the same factors that determined work efficiency. For example, the amount of workload was seen to vary with the level of complexity of the transferred tasks:

> „If we hand something over to India, we always have the reservation that we can go only ... up to a certain degree of knowhow, and above that it gets difficult. Then people are concerned that it won't be done conscientiously, ... and this is leads you to say: 'If they end up inquiring about all sorts of things, then my workload is not decreased'."

The transfer of tasks to India also affected the nature of German employees' work tasks. Whilst half of the respondents saw the transfer as an opportunity for more interesting tasks, the other half perceived a threat to such tasks. About half of the respondents believed that despite the transfer, higher-end tasks would stay in Germany and new, conceptual tasks would be gained:

> "... given the increasingly scarce resources, we can concentrate on conceptual work, developing test concepts, plan tests, I'd like to call it test philosophy. There is the chance that you can offshore standard tasks or that you have more time for those tasks that go into more detail, require more experience."

In contrast, the other half of respondents complained that they increasingly had to pursue coordinative and fragmented tasks:

> "Well, our problem is that regarding tasks, we are pushed into a corner where we coordinate, check specifications, write a little bit. We do not create anything any more. If you were doing a craft: We are not building anything any more. No one over here writes a line of code any more or goes deeply into testing... That does frustrate us. ... occasionally you also want to see what it is that you are coordinating, or also do it yourself. This separation of different aspects is quite limiting."

These contrasting views can be explained by the amount of challenging, conceptual tasks available in different departments. In the department responsible for highly matured platform solutions (Department 1), Germans and Indians were competing for the few new development tasks. In contrast, many German customer departments (Departments 2 and 3) had to continuously find new software solutions in response to customer demands, and in the department for highly innovative safety systems (Department 4), respondents experienced a wealth of highly interesting new tasks for German employees. In the department responsible for testing (Department 5), the new focus was on developing innovative testing methods.

In addition, respondents' views varied with different individual preferences. Whilst some respondents were delighted to focus on more conceptual and coordinative tasks, others complained that they could no longer do the technical tasks they had been trained for. Moreover, over time, more experienced respondents had observed that higher end knowhow and complex tasks were not fully transferable, due to the high fluctuation in India, and this would secure German jobs. Where the task alternatives were less clear, respondents stressed that management had to provide very clear perspectives for the future of German tasks, and had to accurately allocate tasks between Indian and German colleagues.

The attitudes concerning interesting tasks were closely linked to perceptions of job security. About half of the respondents did not think German jobs were threatened at all. Most of them, particularly more experienced colleagues, explained that less new jobs would be created in Germany, but existing jobs were not in danger. In some cases, the cost benefits of the transfer were even seen to lead to additional projects, and to secure German jobs:

> "I do believe that in sum, this contributes to preserving jobs. ... I do think that it secures jobs over here. Not exactly the same tasks, as I said, but in total, we are better off."

On the negative side, respondents explained that German jobs would be increasingly threatened with the developing skills of Indian employees, causing a transfer of more demanding tasks. The perceived danger of losing jobs also seemed to depend on the recent growth or stagnation of the headcount in particular departments. A few respondents mentioned that with the recent economic crisis in 2008, the number of new projects and open German positions had decreased, and this had reinforced fears that jobs would be transferred. An unclear managerial strategy for preserving German jobs could reinforce insecurities about future jobs.

> "My people had fundamental fears: '... How much more will disappear? ... Will I still have my work the way I liked doing it? ... What comes next? There are partly no clear perspectives. It was only said: 'This and that goes to India. ... There was a bit of a hole ...'"

Despite such fears, some respondents perceived new opportunities for professional and intercultural learning arising from working in a TNT. Respondents described specific skills they had gained, such as coordinating and managing a larger, distributed team. The experience of working cross-nationally was regarded as an advantage when applying for jobs externally, and for progressing to leadership positions within the firm. The majority of respondents stated that they had benefited from practicing their English and interacting with another culture. For example, several respondents had been inspired by the greater enthusiasm of Indian colleagues at work:

> „... on the level of communication, I learn incredibly much, of course.... I also think it is good fun. I sometimes think, okay, there are good qualities that German colleagues have, but there are also good qualities that the other colleagues [Indians] have, which you can't learn from the Germans over here. ... ...I am for example really impressed by how disciplined they are and how eager

to learn, and that they simply rejoice when receiving further training."

At the same time, however, about one third of respondents pointed out that cultural differences led to difficulties, such as the aforementioned language barriers and lack of open communication about difficulties. The different focus on intercultural learning versus difficulties depended partly on individual preferences for speaking English and interacting with another culture. Moreover, those Germans who had got to know their Indian colleagues personally, particularly on visits to India, had developed a greater interest in intercultural encounters. The openness to communicate across cultures was also seen to increase over time, with growing intercultural experience.

Effect of Attitudes on Relational Behaviours

The respondents' offshoring attitudes had an impact on German team members' relational behaviours towards their Indian colleagues. More specifically, a combination of offshoring attitudes concerning performance and German employees affected the strength of national subgroups in some teams, with consequences for subgroup dynamics in terms of pinpointing mistakes, communicating and transferring knowledge, and avoiding task transfer. The attitudes concerning organisational effects of offshoring did not appear to have any impact on relational behaviours.

Some respondents explained that perceived performance problems and a frustration with the need to support Indians had led many Germans to prefer treating Indian colleagues as suppliers rather than equal team members, indicating a weak shared team identity and strong subgroups. This would allow them to request independent working, exert pressure when performance was not satisfactory, or even to blame Indians for mistakes:

„In the sense of: They have to deliver, and if it does not work, then it's India again who delivers bad quality."

Accordingly, it was mentioned that negative attitudes towards Indian performance, and the perceived threat to tasks and jobs led some Germans to judge Indian performance more critically than German performance, and pinpoint mistakes:

"There is criticism concerning efficiency, there is criticism concerning quality. However, ... only if you are looking for a scapegoat. ... If it comes to problems, you start to point a finger."

Some Germans who were frustrated about additional training and coordination needs, and those who feared intercultural communication, were seen to lack motivation to communicate and to transfer knowledge to Indian colleagues beyond the necessary. For example, they would not make new telephone appointments for those cancelled. Respondents also explained that fears of losing tasks or even their job could cause employees to block knowledge transfer:

„.... once ... people's substance is threatened, this influences the decision to support this transfer ... there must be someone who receives the knowhow, but there also has to be someone you hands it over, and a forced handover of knowhow does not work ..."

On the opposite end, several respondents described how employees who believed that the TNT could perform well spent huge amounts of extra effort on training Indian colleagues, for example by running workshops in India:

„Until one or two years ago, ... they identified the knowhow on the Indian side as a great problem. Then at that time, Mr. A. [pseudonym] flew over and conducted a week long training event. That had an incredibly positive effect on the collaboration. He does of course approach this with a generally positive attitude... That has a strong effect." / [Interviewer:] You think he would not have done that if he did not have such a positive attitude? / "Not in that form. He invested incredibly, that was very exhausting for him."

However, several respondents held the contradictory view that negative offshoring attitudes did not reduce employees' efforts of communication and knowledge transfer, because such effort was a condition for better future performance and therefore in all Germans' own interest.

Another consequence of negative offshoring attitudes was to counteract the task transfer. Some respondents had experienced that colleagues had avoided the transfer of tasks, if they believed the transfer caused worse quality, additional workload or threatened German tasks and jobs:

„Partly, colleagues have the desire to do everything themselves, and when this does not work any longer at all, to transfer what is left to India. I would attribute that to them thinking (1) you can do it better, over here and (2) fearing that the job will go off to India, completely.".

In a more subtle manner, other employees had reportedly formulated the task requirements in a way to ensure that Indians could not declare themselves competent to perform the task:

„... in some cases, people refuse to collaborate with India. You can do that in a very subtle way, of course. ... there are many possibilities to avoid it or to make sure that it does not happen. That is relatively easy. ... just by means of the task description, you can work towards getting the answer from India: 'We don't have anyone who can do this.'. There are many possibilities. It's easy."

Whether or not offshoring attitudes affected relational behaviours appeared to depend partly on the personal acquaintance between German and Indian colleagues, primarily through training visits. After such visits, some respondents perceived team cohesion to be strong and relationships between subgroups as friendly, despite problems of performance, workload, or threats to German tasks and jobs. Respondents also explained that after getting to know Indian colleagues in person, Germans were more self-critical and fairer in their judgement of Indian performance, and the fear of losing their job would no longer lead to reduced support effort.

Vicious and virtuous circles

The findings indicate that there was an interdependence between several offshoring attitudes and behavioural outcomes, implying that German employees' offshoring attitudes were tied into vicious and virtuous circles. In particular, negative offshoring attitudes regarding effects on performance and workload could cause Germans to avoid the transfer of non-routine, complex tasks, in order to reduce quality issues and additional workload. However, such a limitation of the task transfer also inhibited the development of technical skills on the Indian side, thereby setting boundaries to better future Indian performance, which in turn perpetuated negative attitudes and led to a continuing restriction of task transfer. Similarly, employees' frustration by performance, workload, and intercultural interactions could lead to decreased effort in communicating and transferring knowledge, making it impossible for performance to improve, workload to decrease, or intercultural competence to grow. This vicious circle was most apparent when it was intentional. For example, some Germans were seen to actively seek evidence for Indian mistakes in order to argue against the transfer:

„....and then you are always glad if the Indian colleagues have made a mistake, because then you can say: ‚Look, they have made a mistake, again.'. You have one more reason against having to work with them."

It was even reported that some employees contributed deliberately to Indian mistakes in order to promote their failure and reinforce their negative offshoring attitudes:

'Maybe you have noticed that he [the Indian colleague] hasn't really understood, but you do not tell him. Then he will take forever. You get no output, and in the end you do it yourself. That's the solution: "I'll just do it myself then, even if I work overtime." Then you will be able to say afterwards: "This doesn't work, does it.".'

By contrast, employees who believed in the Indian's ability to perform well and who spent extra amounts of effort in training did experience performance and workload improvements over time, which in turn reinforced their positive offshoring attitudes.

In two departments, opposite circles appeared to dominate. Different departmental context factors can serve to explain these contrasting offshoring attitudes and resultant circles. In department 4, responsible for developing software for automotive safety systems, respondents held overall positive views regarding all offshoring consequences, i.e. with regard to the organisation as well as team performance and German team members. These attitudes were tied into a virtuous circle, with positive relational behaviours in terms of a strong German-Indian team identity, fair criticism, great effort in communication and knowledge transfer, and active support of task transfer. For example, it was explained that the effort in communicating and transferring knowledge helped to achieve performance and workload improvements over time. It therefore co-occurred with positive evaluations of the transfer:

'... It cost us a lot of time and many trips to India. We are typically over there every quarter of the year for a week, but it was worth it. The project is now – the boss always says ‚"a success story", and we are now ... three months ahead of the time plan, which no-one would actually expect from a project like this.'

This virtuous circle was embedded in a combination of mostly conducive factors which can explain why positive offshoring attitudes predominated, resulting in the described virtuous circles. Due to the leading-edge product, the workforce was growing, and abundant new, innovative tasks were available to German employees, who were also keen to take on these new tasks. At the same time, primarily routine tasks were transferred to India, which matched Indian skills. The managerial strategy for the future task distribution was explicit and clear. German engineers had worked with their Indian colleagues in person on training visits, and they were interested in getting to know members of another culture. Respondents used varying degrees of monitoring, depending on the experience of their Indian colleagues. Germans had worked with Indians between one and three years, which can be classified as a medium length of experience.

Contrasting departmental context factors lead to opposite offshoring attitudes in department 1, resulting in vicious circles of offshoring attitudes and relational behaivours. Respondents in this department were overall undecided about the consequences of offshoring for the organisation. However, they came to clear overall negative evaluations with regard to consequences for team performance and German employees. Negative attitudes were interrelated with a weak German-Indian team identity and cases of pinpointing mistakes and avoiding task transfer. Employees' effort in communication and knowledge transfer was described as sufficient, but in some cases limited. In this department, hardly any new, challenging tasks were available for German employees, which was attributed to the mature product. New tasks tended to be coordinative, which did not meet the interests of German employees. More and more non-routine tasks had to be transferred to India to motivate the increasingly skilled Indian workforce. German employees had met their Indian colleagues in person, but some employees held reservations against the intercultural experience. The levels of monitoring were generally high. Germans had worked with Indian colleagues for up to ten years, a factor that would have supported positive attitudes if combined with other favourable conditions.

DISCUSSION

Research implications

This study is, to my knowledge, the first to examine offshoring attitudes of employees who are involved in and responsible for an offshoring collaboration. It is therefore the first study to show that the attitudes reported by individuals involved in offshoring collaborations can reflect many of the arguments found in the offshoring literature. Similar to the macro-level arguments for offshoring, respondents named costs, additional workforce, flexibility, and presence in the local market as the main potential organisational benefits [2]. The respondents' contrasting views concerning the future of German tasks and jobs corresponded to the macro level arguments for and against job benefits for employees in the country of origin [17, 13]. The results also support the claim that conceptual and high-tech tasks, as well as intercultural communication and virtual project management skills will become more important in the countries of origin [2, 20].

This study was further the first to reveal that offshoring attitudes can play a role for the strength of national subgroup divides. This was most apparent where Indian colleagues were treated as mere suppliers rather than team members. Moreover, subgroup dynamics were affected in terms of relational behaviours, namely creating a team identity, communicating, transferring knowledge, avoiding or supporting the task transfer, and in the extreme case even active contributions to Indian failure. Hence, offshoring attitudes influenced several relational behaviours of onshore team members, leading to vicious and virtuous circles. This finding of vicious and virtuous circles is particularly important, because it suggests that these circles perpetuate offshoring attitudes, and their impact on relational behaviours. This result therefore highlights how important is to take offshoring attitudes into account when designing offshoring arrangements to achieve offshoring success.

The findings thus add new components to previous models of offshoring success as well as global virtual team functioning. With regard to relational behaviours, Dibbern et al. (2008) describe their participants' perceptions on offshoring transaction costs, such as control and coordination costs, knowledge transfer costs, and specification/design cost. However, they do not consider that employees' perceptions of these transaction costs as such can, through behavioural consequences, impact upon offshoring success. Moreover, Govindarajan and Gupta (2001) identify major success factors of global virtual teams, including relationship aspects such as trust and communication, but do not take into account any perceptual influences.

Similarly, some of the factors responsible for offshoring attitudes resemble those that have previously been identified as relevant for TNT success, but previous research has not recognised their effect on offshoring attitudes and the related vicious and virtuous circles. For example, it is well known that the success of TNT's depends partly on the nature of the task. For instance, creative tasks have been suggested to benefit from cultural diversity of team members, whilst coordinative tasks may suffer from such diversity [12]. However, the importance of providing challenging tasks for TNT members' offshoring attitudes and, consequently, the circles of offshoring attitudes and relational behaviours, has not been recognised before. Moreover, it has been observed that a match between transferred tasks and the skills of offshore colleagues is necessary in order to achieve high performance of IT offshoring teams [11]. However, the consequences for offshoring attitudes have not been considered. Similarly, intercultural communication barriers [7, 12] and face to face meetings [e.g. 19] have often been highlighted as crucial for the functioning of transnational and virtual teams, but this study demonstrates another important function of personal acquaintance through face to face contact, namely to break the link between negative offshoring attitudes and behaviours.

Implications for practitioners

The findings on organisational, managerial, and individual factors suggest that the way the transfer is managed can affect employees' offshoring attitudes and therefore the success of the transfer itself. For this reason, managers in the onshore country have to reduce employees' fears of losing tasks or jobs, by providing clear and explicit plans for acceptable alternative tasks, the allocation of tasks between onshore and offshore colleagues, and for securing jobs. Managers can also highlight professional learning advantages by making successful offshoring management a condition for obtaining higher leadership positions.

Managers could further promote an exchange of best practice between departments. More experienced departments could advise others on successful task distribution between onshore and offshore locations and means of knowledge transfer. In this study, the same mistakes were seen to be made in different departments over time. Moreover, if managers are to take their employees' offshoring attitudes seriously and foster positive attitudes, they have to try to achieve as much ownership of the transfer as possible. For example, managers could listen to employees' fear of losing interesting tasks and negotiate acceptable future tasks. Through such discussions, members of the offshoring collaboration may become more conscious of their own offshoring attitudes and more able to suggest constructive solutions.

Limitations and suggestions for future research

This research had a number of limitations that raise questions for future research. Firstly, there were some indications that respondents' attitudes were situated, and would have been uttered differently in different contexts. A number of respondents differentiated between their own (typically more positive) and their colleagues' attitudes. This distinction suggests that in the interview situation, respondents may have presented a more rational, sensible evaluation of the transfer than in informal conversations with their colleagues. Accordingly, they would have been more familiar with the less rational views that their colleagues voiced in such informal situations, and therefore reported their colleagues' views as more negative. In addition, respondents may not have been as sure of their own evaluations as they appeared in the interview, but may have tried to come to evaluative conclusions when asked for it. This would again show a situational bias. These attitudes may thus have been a product of a process of social construction. I did not examine this process, but focused only on the resulting attitudes. Future research could examine the mechanisms of social construction, for example by using not only interviews, but also observations of meetings and social interactions between offshoring partners, and analyse the discourse that concerns offshoring and relational behaviours towards offshore colleagues. Such research should also consider several potential sources of social construction, such as the public offshoring debate, discussions with colleagues, and employees' first-hand experience.

This study aimed to establish offshoring attitudes, their determinants, and relational outcomes. For this purpose, it was sufficient to investigate perceptions of onshore team members only. Nevertheless, it would be interesting to explore the perspective of offshore team members as well, in order to understand how onshore members' relational behaviours are perceived and reacted to, which will determine the relationships between offshoring partners.

Finally, the study of vicious and virtuous circles can be advanced. Given the limitation to one organisational setting, we do not know whether the circles I found are typical, i.e. whether they apply across various organisational setting. However, given that the findings on factors, attitudes, and relational behaviours was derived from five different departments, it is possible that similar virtuous and vicious circles will emerge in other organisations. Future research needs to address such transferability of the findings.

REFERENCES

1. Ajzen, I. and Fishbein, M. The influence of attitudes on behavior. In: *The handbook of attitudes*, Albarracin, D. Johnson, B. T. and Zanna, M.P., eds., 173-221. Erlbaum, Mahwah, NJ, USA, 2005.

2. Bidanda, B., Arisoy, O. and Shuman, L. Offshoring manufacturing: Implications for engineering jobs and education: A survey and case study. *Robotics and Computer-Integrated Manufacturing, 22* (2006), 576-87.

3. Cohen, L. and El-Sawad, A. Lived experiences of offshoring: An examination of UK and Indian financial service employees' accounts of themselves and one another. *Human Relations, 60*, 8 (2007), 1235-1262.

4. Cramton, C.D. The mutual knowledge problem and its consequences for dispersed collaboration. *Organization Science, 12*, 3 (2001), 346-371.

5. Dibbern, J., Winkler, J. and Heinzl., A. Explaining variations in client extra costs between software projects offshored to India. *MIS Quarterly, 32*, 2 (2008), 333-366.

6. Earley, P.C. and Mosakowski, E. Creating Hybrid Team Cultures: An Empirical Test of Transnational Team Functioning. *Academy of Management Journal, 43*,1 (2000), 26-49.

7. Erez, M. and Earley, P.C. Culture, Self-identity, and Work. Oxford University Press, New York, USA, 1993.

8. Fulk, J., Monge, P. and Hollingshead, A.B. Knowledge resource sharing in dispersed multinational teams: three theoretical lenses. In: Managing multinational teams: Global perspectives, Shapiro, D.L., Von Glinow, M.A. and Cheng, J.L. (eds.), 155-188. Elsevier/JAI Press, Oxford, UK, 2005.

9. Gibson, C.B. and Vermeulen, F. A healthy divide: Subgroups as a stimulus for team learning behavior. *Administrative Science Quarterly, 48*, 2 (2003), 202-239.

10. Gibson, C.B., Zellmer-Bruhn, M.E. and Schwab, D.P. Team effectiveness in multinational organizations. Evaluations across contexts. *Group and Organization Management, 28* (2003), 444-474.

11. Govindarajan, V. and Gupta, A.K. Building an effective global business team. *MIT Sloan Management Review, July* (2001), 63–71.

12. Hambrick, D.C., Davison, S.C., Snell, S.A. and Snow, C.C. When groups consist of multiple nationalities: Towards a new understanding of the implications. *Organization Studies, 19*, 2 (1998), 181-205.

13. Harrison, A.E. and McMillan, M.S. Dispelling some myths about offshoring. *Academy of Management Perspectives, 20*, 4 (2006), 6-22.

14. King, N. Using templates in the thematic analysis of texts. In: Essential Guide to Qualitative Methods in

Organizational Research, Cassell, C. and Symon, G. (eds.), 256-270. Sage, Thousand Oaks, CA, USA, 2004.

15. Lau, D.C. and Murnighan, J.K. Demographic diversity and faultiness: The compositional dynamics of organizational groups. *Academy of Management Review, 23* (1998), 325-340.

16. Lincoln, Y.S. and Guba, E.G. Judging the quality of qualitative case study research. In: The qualitative researcher's companion, Huberman, A.M. and Miles, M.B. (eds.), pp. 205-216. Sage, CA, 2002.

17. Mankiw, N.G. and Swagel, P. The politics and economics of offshore outsourcing. NBER Working Paper 12389, 2006.

18. Mueller, O. IGCC Business Monitor: German companies in India upbeat on growth. *Indo-German Economy, 6* (2009), 5-7.

19. Oshri, I., Fenema, P. and Kotlarsky, J. Knowledge transfer in globally distributed teams: The role of transactive memory. *Information Systems Journal, 18*, 6 (2008), 593-616.

20. United Nations, World Investment Report, Transnational Corporations and the Internationalization of RandD. United Nations conf. on trade and development (2005).

21. Zimmermann, A. Interpersonal relationships in transnational, virtual teams – towards a configurational perspective. *International Journal of Management Reviews, 13*, 1 (2011), 59-78.

Domestic Artefacts:
Sustainability in the context of Indian Middle Class

Dhaval Vyas
Human Media Interaction
University of Twente, the Netherlands
dhaval_vyas@yahoo.com

ABSTRACT
Sustainability has become one of the important research topics in the field of Human Computer Interaction (HCI). However, the majority of work has focused on the Western culture. In this paper, we explore sustainable household practices in the developing world. Our research draws on the results from an ethnographic field study of household women belonging to the so-called *middle class* in India. We analyze our results in the context of Blevis' [4] principles of sustainable interaction design (established within the Western culture), to extract the intercultural aspects that need to be considered for designing technologies. We present examples from the field that we term "domestic artefacts". Domestic artefacts represent creative and sustainable ways household women appropriate and adapt used objects to create more useful and enriching objects that support household members' everyday activities. Our results show that the rationale behind creating domestic artefacts is not limited to the practicality and usefulness, but it shows how religious beliefs, traditions, family intimacy, personal interests and health issues are incorporated into them.

Author Keywords
Design, domestic settings, sustainability, developing countries

ACM Classification Keywords
H.5.m. Information interfaces and presentation (e.g., HCI): Miscellaneous.

INTRODUCTION
In the past decade, considerable efforts have been made to carry forward the 'green' agenda in the HCI research. For example, new paradigms and guidelines are developed for applying sustainability in interaction design [4], a set of field studies are carried out for informing the design of new technologies [8, 14, 25, 26] and new pervasive and ubiquitous technologies are designed for domestic settings that can inform users about energy usage in their homes [5, 10, 11]. However, most of this work has taken place within the developed world. In this paper, we will look at sustainability research from a developing world's point of view. We will provide an account of how women in India facilitate and enrich their daily household activities through sustainable practices. Our target group is the Indian middle class – a symbolic notion referring to a group of people whose population varies between 50 to 300 million [6, 20, 21]. Our focus is on their creativity and empowerment for supporting their family by reusing old things to genuinely support their everyday household needs.

We studied the everyday activities of ten household women belonging to the middle class in India. In this paper, we will provide the results of our ethnographic field study illustrating how sustainability is greatly intertwined with Indian household women's everyday housework. We particularly focus on their practices of reuse. From our field studies, we found that household women construct their home activities and home life in general by creatively and resourcefully appropriating, adapting and mixing existing and worn-out domestic objects to be able to support and enrich their everyday activities. We term these 'new' objects as *domestic artefacts*. Typically, any object found in a domestic setting such as a chair, TV, couch, table and so on can be termed a domestic artefact. However, in this paper, for the sake of our analysis, we use this term to refer to the artefacts that are created by the home dwellers in order to support their home lives. Our notion of domestic artefacts is similar to the conceptualization of everyday design by Wakkary and Maestry [24].

This work takes a slightly different approach, compared to the traditional ICIC works. We will study sustainable household practices in one culture (Indian middle-class) and develop important insights and lessons that can be used to support inter-cultural collaborations. Hence, we will not study the effects of inter-cultural interactions, as such, but provide implications for supporting intercultural interactions by studying one particular culture. In addition, we will use Blevis' [4] principles of sustainable interaction design (SID) as a lens to analyze our results. By utilizing Blevis' principles in the Indian context, we believe that several cultural-specific aspects of sustainability can be extracted and used for designing new technologies. We believe that not all of the sustainable practices that we draw from our results can be easily translated to the Western culture, or *vice versa*. However, several underlying phenomena can be used for designing sustainable products. Our contribution in this paper is threefold:

- Our results provide empirical evidence illustrating the role of women in household matters in the Indian middle class. In doing so, our results bring out several cultural and traditional practices of the Indian middle class that might be new for the HCI community.

- Our notion of domestic artefacts shed light on subjective issues related to family intimacy, care, religious beliefs and family traditions that should be taken into account when designing for sustainability in interactive technologies.

- Since we apply Blevis' principles, our result leads to new intercultural understandings on sustainability research.

In the rest of the paper, we will start by describing our motivations for focusing on sustainability and provide a brief introduction to the Indian middle class. Next, we will provide details of our field study, participants and their family dynamics. Then, we will describe our results and give examples from the field. Finally, we will discuss our findings and lessons for inter-cultural collaborations when designing for sustainability.

MOTIVATION

Sustainability

A majority of work towards dealing with sustainability in household matters, as seen in recent CHI and UbiComp literature, focus on developing technologies that can make home residents aware of their 'moral choices' on energy consumption and turn environmental action into a redirection of consumption patterns, for example. WaterBot [2] is a pervasive technology that provides ambient cues about water usage at a kitchen sink. The aim here is to motivate changes in people's behaviors while using water. Power-Aware-Cord [7] uses a dynamic glowing representation on a common electrical power strip that can display the amount of energy passing through it at any given moment. WattBot [19] is a residential electricity monitoring system that uses Apple's iPod and iPhone for allowing people to track their home energy usage and encourages them to reduce consumption. Researchers such as Bang et al. [3] have also attempted to create a game-like system called PowerAgent to provide information about energy consumption patterns in homes.

However, the environmental crisis is as much a cultural problem as a technical one. It is not just a simple matter of calculating energy and environmental costs of manufacturing, use, and disposal of one technology over another. It is important to understand people's attitudes [8], rationale [17], and their current efforts [26] towards sustainable practices, in order to guide the design of sustainable technologies. We believe that a deeper look into cultural practices and the role of individuals in household matters could lead to a much better understanding of sustainability. In particular, the prominent role of women (especially mothers) in everyday household activities cannot be ignored. We look at sustainability as a socio-cultural issue that should be dealt with using a bottom-up approach rather than a technological top-down approach.

In the West, the reuse and disposal of materials such as plastic, electronics and textiles poses a huge challenge. As an alternative approach towards dealing with sustainability, we believe that solutions to sustainability may be explored from cultures belonging to other parts of the world. Their consumption, reuse or recycling practices may provide an interesting perspective on sustainability.

We study sustainability in the context of middle-class India. In that, we look at household women's existing sustainable practices while carrying out their everyday housework. We believe that these domestic practices can greatly inform the design of new sustainable technologies. In particular, the study of middle class Indian households can be very important for HCI researchers for the following two reasons. 1) The increasing growth of the Indian middle class population would make this group one of the world's largest consumer groups. An understanding of their consumption practices would undoubtedly contribute towards the design of new sustainable technologies. 2) The financial and cultural situations in the Indian middle class have led to different ways of applying sustainability. These ways may be new to the West, but have always existed in this part of the world for a long time.

Indian Middle Class

Although the notion of class in India is *symbolic* and locally contested, and while there is no official definition of the middle class, the estimated population of the Indian middle class, according to the World Bank and other sources, ranges from 50 million to approximately 300 million [6, 20, 21]. According to a report by the Asian Development Bank, the middle class in India could touch the 1.2 billion mark (India's current population) in the next 20 years if recent economic growth is sustained [1].

Research into ICT for developing countries (in particular, India) has focused largely on rural areas (e.g. [9, 18]). While rural areas desperately need development, in India, it is the middle class that is growing at a much faster rate. The increase in the Indian middle class is due to economic growth in India and migration of low income and rural populations to big cities. As HCI researchers we need to pay more attention to this middle class, not only because, as we said, it is growing really fast, but because it will soon become one of the biggest consumer markets in the world. More importantly, we need to understand their consuming and sustainable practices in order to design sustainable technologies.

Even though, the middle-class in India is quite diverse, there are several cultural traits that are common to this group. In this paper we briefly summarize some of the important characteristics; for more details please refer to Varma's [23] book, titled *The Great Indian Middle Class*.

The Indian middle class have very strong family values. Middle class residents, traditionally, live in joint families, which include extended family members such as parents and/or in-laws. However, this trend is changing as more and more people prefer to live in single families. Families in the Indian middle class draw their incomes from administrative, knowledge-based and non-manual labor jobs in sectors such as banking, education, IT, and call centers. Typically, households in middle-class families prefer job security and higher education for their children. Financial stability is seen as an imperative and highly desirable factor in these families. Their children are constantly being motivated to study towards Bachelors' and Masters' degrees in medical, technical and financial fields. These households believe in saving as much money as they can rather than spending it on holidays or buying expensive things. In some cases, parents would give priority to spending money on their children's education, over their own needs. These families believe in value for money when buying new things.

THE FIELD STUDY

To collect a much deeper understanding of household women's sustainable practices and how these practices are connected to their everyday work, we carried out a field study in middle class Indian homes. We studied the everyday activities of ten household women, in the city of Ahmedabad, Gujarat. Table 1 provides details of our participants. We recruited them to have a variation in profession, age range and family dynamics (joint or single family). We believed that these choices would lead to a difference in their household activities and practices. Our participants belonged to the age range of 35 to 75. All the participants were married and had been living with their husband for at least 10 years. Participants included working professionals and housewives. Some of the participants lived in a joint family (with in-laws) and others mainly with their husband and children.

We used a combination of semi-structured interviews, in-home visits and observations during our fieldwork. In all cases, we kept our interaction with these household women longer than our initial visit. In some cases, we visited these participants' homes again and in others we prolonged our interactions via telephone calls. We focused our questions

No	Age	Work	Members in family	Family Dynamics
1	50-60	Working full-time in a Bank	2	Lives with her husband who also works fulltime. Has two children living abroad. Her parents-in-law died 20 years ago. The family has a decent income – towards a higher-middle class. She gets help from a maid for some domestic activities.
2	40-50	Housewife	4	Lives with her husband and two children. Husband runs a business and both children study. Her parents-in-law live separately. The family has a decent income – towards a higher-middle class. She gets help from a maid for some domestic activities.
3	30-40	Working full-time in a company	6	Lives with her husband, two children and parents-in-law. Husband works fulltime, children study at schools and parents-in-law are retired and stay at home. She leads in most of the household activities and her mother-in-law assists whenever she can, but is in bad health.
4	50-60	Working full-time in a Bank	3	Lives with her husband who is retired. She has two children, one living abroad and one still studying. Her parents-in-law died recently.
5	70-80	Part-time work	2	Lives with her husband who is retired. Has four children, all married and living separately. Her work involves going to a charity for a few hours a week.
6	50-60	Housewife	9	Lives with her husband and two sons – both are married and have their own children. Her husband and two sons work full-time. Her two daughters-in-law help her in the house. However, she plays a leading role in the household activities. The family has a large house and has a stable income.
7	50-60	Housewife	5	Lives with her husband, a son, a daughter and a daughter-in-law. Her husband is retired and her son, daughter and daughter-in-law work full-time. She gets help from a maid for some domestic activities.
8	50-60	Housewife	2	Lives with her husband. Both have health problems. Her daughter and son live separately. Her husband had a heart attack 2 years back and she recently had a knee replacement. She gets help from a maid for all domestic activities.
9	30-40	Part-time work	3	Lives with her husband and a son. The family income is very low as her husband has had no settled jobs. She teaches students and earns some money to help in the family.
10	40-50	Part-time work	4	Lives with her husband and two daughters. Husband works fulltime but has had health problems. Her elder daughter is finishing her medical education at university and her younger daughter goes to school. She gets help from a maid for some domestic activities.

Table 1: Details of our participants.

mainly to their reuse, but also took into account their everyday household activities. Considering the exploratory nature of our research, we appropriated qualitative methods to understand participants' subjective reasoning and choices in order to understand their practices of reuse. To understand how sustainability is practiced in home life by these participants, we paid particular attention to the artefacts that our participants created to support their household activities. Drawing on some established work in anthropology [13] and some recent attempts to study the use of artefacts in domestic settings [22, 25], we examined the practices surrounding these artefacts as a means of revealing how the home's social order is brought about.

RESULTS

Our field study generated a large amount of qualitative data, describing different sustainable practices. Figure 1 shows an elderly household who participated in this study. The space limitation will not allow us to describe all the practices in detail, hence in this section we will provide some general themes of reuse practices. In the following section, we will introduce our notion of domestic artefacts.

Figure 1: An elderly middle-class household.

General Themes

We explored the reuse of four types of reusable materials: 1) edible products, 2) paper-based goods, 3) textile and 4) plastic.

In *edible* products, we observed that rather than wasting parts of food products household women made use of it to support several household activities. In some cases unusable food products were processed further to make new edible items. In other cases, food products were reused in other household activities. For example, household women utilized leftover milk to make butter, buttermilk, cheese and home-made sweets. In some cases, sour milk was utilized to make hair oil. Some women utilized the water after boiling potatoes and rice to clean silverware. Whereas, used tea bags were reused as a fertilizer; and mon and orange peel were used to make home-made skin cream. *Paper-based goods* such as newspapers, calendar pages and so on were utilized as notebook covers and as covers for cupboard shelves to avoid dirt. In some cases, leftover pages from different notebooks were combined together to make a new notebook to be used as a diary or telephone book. *Textile-based goods* such as old clothes, curtains and bed sheets were repaired and reused for different purposes. For example, old clothes were modified to be reused as carry bags for grocery shopping; ripped bed sheets were used as pillow covers and covers for electronic appliances such as radios and TVs. Women's saris were sometimes modified to make other types of women's dresses. In some cases, a set of old saris were reused to make a dress utilizing important portions of the saris. *Plastic* bottles and containers were reused to store food related products.

We observed that there was multiple and multilevel reuse of certain things, for example, leftover milk. In addition, we found out that there is an industry of cheap laborers who modify or fix broken objects. For example, knife sharpeners go around the streets to sharpen blunt knives. Similarly, another type of laborers would fix plastic buckets and other objects. This clearly helps household women to prolong their use of old objects. Other trends also include making art pieces from unusable objects rather than recycling them. For example, we saw that old pieces of garments were framed and were used as a piece of art in homes.

An important characteristic of these sustainable practices is that they are not necessarily connected with an awareness to save the environment. In fact, several of our participants were more concerned about supporting an economical life. This does not mean that they were not concerned about the environment. The cultural aspects of middle-class Indian households and their reuse practices were inherently intertwined with each other.

DOMESTIC ARTEFACTS

In this section, we will discuss specific examples from the field that will illustrate sustainable practices of the middle class household women in India. Blivis' [4] principle *promoting renewal and reuse* is central to all these examples. These examples represent different reuse patterns that our participants created by appropriating, adapting and mixing existing, old and worn-out objects from their homes. We term these *new* objects as *domestic artefacts*. To protect the privacy of our participants, we will refer to them with pseudonyms.

A doormat

It is very common in Indian homes to see gunny sacks lying in the storage rooms. Gunny sacks (Figure 2a) are traditionally used for transporting agricultural food products such as wheat, rice and onions. A gunny sack is an inexpensive bag made from jute or other natural fibers. Gunny sacks can hold 20 to 50 kg of food products and are typically bought in a particular season (e.g. avoiding monsoons) to have it safely stored in the home. People in the Indian middle class tend to buy things in bulk, and they end up collecting several gunny sacks by buying a yearly quota of food products. Because of their strong, thick and dry texture, these gunny sacks are reused as a doormat, as a container for other things, and for other purposes in the storage room. We also saw highly creative use of these gunny sacks as fashionable carry bags and artistic show pieces for homes. In this paper, we will discuss the reuse of the gunny sack as a doormat.

Kinal is a housewife. She lives with her husband – who runs a business of engineering tools – and two university going teenagers. The family buys a good amount of food products in bulk and stores it in a safer place in the home, to be used for a long time. Kinal saves gunny sacks after putting food products such as wheat and rice away safely into large containers in her storage room. She uses some of the gunny sacks as a doormat at different places around her house. (The rest of the gunny sacks are stacked in the storage room for later use). She has kept these doormats at the backdoor entrance of her house (Figure 2b), in her kitchen, in the bathroom entrance and at the entrance of the storage room itself. When asked about why she does this, she answered:

"It is very important to enter the kitchen without shoes and with your legs clean. Similarly, in places such as the bathroom, storage room and toilets, one has to clean one's legs before leaving and entering. So, rather than buying new rags I just use these gunny sacks inside the home. Of course, for the main entrance a gunny sack would not look so nice. So, I have a nice welcome doormat there that I bought from a shop."

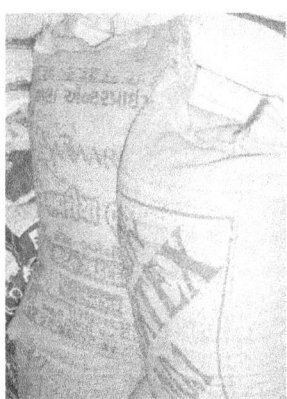 

Figure 2: (a) A bunch of gunny sacks, and (b) reuse of gunny sack as a doormat.

The kitchen is seen as a sacred place in middle-class Indian homes. One should to be clean before entering a kitchen. Kinal tries to keep a disciplined atmosphere in her home for her university going teenagers. With the use of gunny sacks as doormats, she keeps her house clean and as hygienic as possible. She also provided other useful insights into using this kind of doormats.

"In Hinduism, we do not use cotton materials as our doormats. Since, gunny bags are made from jute, it is natural and much holier than the cotton materials."

"This gunny sack is useful in all kinds of weathers. In monsoon, it soaks up water. So wet shoes and legs can be easily cleaned, and in a way useful to keep dirt away from entering the house. And because it is made of jute, it gives warmth in the winter. I normally keep a gunny sack on the kitchen floor where I can stand and do the cooking. So, I avoid standing on a cold floor."

Religious beliefs are important in Indian middle class homes. It is important that one enters the home clean. Normally, household members would clean their legs on these gunny sacks and then enter the house. Scientific literature has shown how different aspects of Hindu cultures and beliefs intersect with environmental values, and behaviors, with varying environmental consequences [12, 15, 16]. The example of a gunny sack as a doormat points to how sustainability and religious beliefs coincide. From Kinal's second quote, one can read the multipurpose character of gunny sacks. Climate plays an important role in people's everyday lives. In India, the climate is generally warmer compared to Europe and North America. Gunny sacks are seen to be very useful in these different weathers. Lastly, Kinal shows how purposefully she uses her gunny sacks to avoid dirt and keep herself warm while she cooks for her family.

This example refers to a number of principles and rubric of Blevis: *linking invention & disposal, promoting renewal and reuse, decoupling ownership & identity, salvage, reuse as is, and sharing for maximal use.* The use of jute for gunny sacks is inherently environmentally friendly, where after its original use it can be disposed of without making and worse impact on the environment. The material quality of a gunny sack allows multiple reuses, in addition to a doormat. Gunny sacks as such are inexpensive and do not get attached to any ownership, hence, they promote sharing for maximal use.

Inter-cultural insights for sustainability
- Religious beliefs are inherent in the reuse of objects.
- Health issues and family care are important in the reuse of household objects
- Specific areas in homes (e.g. kitchen) are treated differently while reuse of old objects.
- Practical needs and climate (e.g. cold floors in winters) encourage reuse.

A dress

Clothes have a significant value in Indian households, in particular, during marriages, religious gatherings, and other types of celebrations. For women in India, the sari is one of the traditional dresses. In the following, we provide an account on the reuse of an old sari by one of our participants. This is a particular example of how a mother's intimate and care-giving activity towards her daughter is intertwined with sustainability.

Mala works fulltime at a local bank as an officer and lives with her husband and two daughters. Her husband also works fulltime in a school as an administrator. Her elder daughter is about to finish her medical education and her younger one studies in a school. She reused her old sari to make a dress (Figure 3) for her daughter who is about to graduate. The following is Mala's account of how and why she reused her saris to make a dress.

"Over the years, I have bought several saris. I have a large collection of them in my cupboard. Sometimes the fashion goes away or a sari gets damaged after using it for years. Then we can either renovate the old sari with a professional tailor's help or make something else out of it. When I got married and came to live with my husband and in-laws in a joint family, my mother-in-law gifted me a very expensive brocade sari - [a sari used during marriages]. I have used it for 20 years for different celebrations and occasions and even though it is old I don't want to throw it away as it is part of our family tradition and family values. Now when my daughter is old enough I want to pass this on to her."

Figure 3: Daughter showing her 'new' dress made from mother's old saris.

What we see in Figure 3 is a dress made of Mala's old sari and other materials that could no longer be used. But as she suggested this sari is so important and valuable that she does not want to throw it away for recycling. Mala did not make this dress herself; she got help from a professional tailor in sewing the dress. (Unlike in the Western countries, tailor-made dresses are not expensive, because of the cheaper labor and skills). Mala selected a set of her old saris, including the gift from her mother-in-law, with different color combinations and explained the design to the tailor. The reason behind getting help from a professional was that the material of the sari was very expensive and the type of sari and its material was no longer available in the market. So, she wanted to make sure that the dress was made by a professional.

Importantly, the 'new' dress signifies both a family tradition of gifting an important object to the next generation and at the same time intimacy and love for a daughter by her mother. In Indian marriages, saris are commonly used for exchanging gifts between families. A gift of a sari to Mala from her mother-in-law was considered as a blessing and an auspicious object for beginning a new life in the hope of a long lasting marriage, when she joined her husband after the marriage. This was a family tradition to pass on such an auspicious gift to the next generation (with the same hopes and blessings). So, following the family tradition and taking into account her daughter's choice and the current day fashion, Mala chose to make a dress out of her old sari.

This example refers to the following principles and rubric of Blevis: *promoting quality & equality, salvage, remanufacturing of use, and achieving heirloom status*. This example shows how the practice of gift-giving of an auspicious object received the heirloom status. The cheap labor and antique qualities of the sari motivated the mother to remanufacture it to make a dress out of it.

Inter-cultural insights for sustainability

- Emotional objects pass through generations and original objects are remanufactured to convey family intimacy.
- Auspicious practices may enhance the sustainability of objects
- Family legacy and heirloom status [4] play an important role in supporting sustainability.

A flower pot

It is very common to see a large water jug made of clay in Indian middle class kitchens – commonly known as "Matki" (See Figure 4a). People use it to keep drinking water cold during summer time (temperatures typically go above 40° in the city of Ahmedabad). However, it is used throughout the year. These water jugs are made of clay which is environmentally friendly and can be easily recycled in their current form. We describe a case where a water jug was reused as a flower pot (Figure 4b) in the garden of one of our participants. The following example shows a typical water jug used in a kitchen and its reuse as a flower pot.

Figure 4: (a) A clay-based water jug used in kitchens and (b) An old water jug now reused as a flower pot in a garden.

Jayshree is a housewife who lives with her husband. Both of them are retired and are currently living on their pension money. Jayshree is fond of gardening and tries to look after the plants in her garden. Figure 4 shows an example where Jayshree has reused a used water jug for making a pot for plants. The following is her account on this pot:

"I have been using two clay water jugs in my kitchen. A smaller one (Figure 4b) got a crack one day. So, it was no longer useful as a water jug. I cut off its lid and started using it as a flower pot by growing a small plant in it. The use of clay water jug is as good as any other flower pots that you buy in the market. The body of the pot provides adequate air flow to the plant and lets the extra water out easily. I also decorated it a bit by coloring it. I like it when the pot looks beautiful; it is really pleasurable to water these plants."

The example shows Jayshree's resourcefulness and creativity to reuse a broken water pot. From a practicality point of view, this is very important. These kinds of water jugs have porous capabilities which are very important for the growth of the plant. Jayshree's awareness towards environmental issue is reflected in her choice for creating such a domestic artefact. Clearly, pottery would not be hazardous to the environment, the example, however, illustrates an activity that gives Jayshree pleasure to do her gardening. She also had some houseplants for which she reused nicely shaped whisky bottles. These plants do not need direct sun or porosity.

This example refers to the following principles and rubric of Blevis: *linking invention & disposal, salvage, reuse as is, and sharing for maximal use*. The use of clay for water jugs is inherently environmentally friendly, where after its use it can be disposed of without making a worse impact on the environment. The material qualities of the jug allows for reuse as a flower pot without much effort for remanufacturing.

Inter-cultural insights for sustainability
- Certain cultural practices such as use of clay water jugs have sustainability inherent in them, and also their reuse.
- Economical decoration for the home and thoughtful reuse.

Storage boxes
As we mentioned earlier, it is very common in Indian middle class families to buy groceries and food products in bulk. An example of a wheat gunny sack was given in a previous section, which can carry around 50 kg. of wheat. In this section, we will show how a steel oil box (Figure 5a) was modified to be used as a storage box for food products.

The practice of buying 15 to 20 kg. of food oil in a large steel container (Figure 5a) is very common in India. These steel boxes are used for easy transportation. They have a handle at the top to carry them around and a hole to pour the oil from. After use these steel boxes are either given out for manual recycling or reused for other purposes. We provide a very brief account of the reuse of a steel oil box by one of our participants. She modified the original oil box to use it for storing dry food products such as flour, wheat and snacks.

(a) (b)

Figure 5: (a) Food oil in a manufactured steel box, and (b) Flour stored in one of the boxes.

Kumud is a retired elderly lady who lives with her husband who is also retired. Over the years, she has bought several oil boxes and reused some of them as a container. She did not do this herself. There are professional welders who can modify oil boxes by cutting off the top and fixing a new lid onto it. Figure 5b shows Kumud's current use of her old oil box for storing flour (used to make 'roti' or 'chapatti' – a typical Indian bread). In her storage room, we found several of these reused boxes that were used for storing different food products. The oil box is a cultural object. People have been reusing it for years and over the years they have explored and appropriated different uses of this oil box. Although, not part of this study, we have seen the use of these modified steel boxes as travel bags by people in villages. They would store their clothes and other objects that are used in travelling.

This example refers to the following rubric of Blevis: *salvage, remanufacturing for reuse and achieving longevity in use*. The material quality of the oil box can be easily converted into a container box for storing food products. Its strong material qualities also offer multiple uses, not only as a storage box but also as a useful object for transportation.

Inter-cultural insights for sustainability
- The practice of buying food products in bulk and storing for longer periods encourages new ideas for reuse.

Carry bags
We already discussed reuse of clothes in a previous section, where a mother's sari was reused and modified to make a dress for her daughter. In this example, we will provide a more practical reuse of clothes. Figure 6 shows a set of carry bags designed by one of our participants from her grandchildren's jeans. The example shows the creativity of the participant and her active participation in the family activities.

Hansa is a housewife, who lives with her husband and nine other members in a large joint family. Her husband works fulltime in an insurance firm. Hansa has two sons who also have young children themselves. Hansa – a grandmother – is active in almost all the household activities such as cooking, cleaning and grocery shopping. She is well assisted by her two daughters-in-law, who are also housewives. Hansa's family is financially stable and she has a big house for her joint family. Hansa's grandchildren are growing fast and their old clothes are no longer in use. Hansa has a hand sewing machine at home and she designed carry bags reusing the denim material from her grandchildren's old jeans. The following is her account of these particular artefacts.

"When kids grow up, their clothes are not used anymore. I sometimes make use of the material from their old clothes for cleaning purposes. Sometimes, I make carry bags out of their clothes so that they can be used in grocery shopping or moving small things around. Here, I made these carry bags from the denim material. In the past, I used to make bags like these from synthetic material but those bags wear out easily. Denim is much stronger as a material. The good thing about these bags is that they are very easy to keep in cupboards, they are washable so can be used for a longer period. Importantly, these are good for travelling. And anybody in the home can use it and we don't have to spend money for buying bags. In one of the bags, I also did small embroidery on the bag so that it looks more attractive."

Figure 6: Carry bags made from old Jeans.

The above account shows how actively Hansa is involved in her large family's day-to-day matters. This example refers to the following rubric and principles of Blevis: *salvage, remanufacturing for reuse and de-coupling ownership & identity*. She made use of the denim material of the jeans and created carry bags that can be used by all the family members. The rubric *sharing for maximal use* is also an important aspect of this example. She knows about her grandchildren's clothing and remembers to reuse their clothes rather than throwing them away. Her particular interest is in practicality of household activities and having an economical lifestyle. Her personal interest in sewing also helps in creating these bags.

Inter-cultural insights for sustainability

- Shared use is common in large middle-class families, which encourages maximal sharing.
- Storage of used objects (e.g. jeans) allows people to find alternative reuse for future.
- Reuse is encouraged by collaboration among and between families
- Creativity and resourcefulness is inherent in the reuse of objects.

LESSONS FOR INTER-CULTURAL COLLABORATION

Our study provides a useful insight into how the cultural practices of women in the Indian middle-class are connected to supporting sustainability. Our paper shows that Blevis' principles and rubrics for sustainable interaction design are quite universal. Of course, certain principles and rubrics are more common and significant in the context of Indian middle-class. For example, the principle *promoting renewal and reuse* was the one seen in all the households, due to economical living standards. In the same way, rubric such as, *salvage, remanufacturing for reuse, achieving longevity of use* and *sharing or maximal use* were seen to be prevalent in the Indian middle-class. Similarly, due to a lesser individualistic culture, the same rubric played a significant role in supporting household sustainability.

We aimed to explore alternative approaches to look at sustainability research, which provided us some insightful results. It showed us how cultural, religious and traditional aspects related to households can shape sustainable practices. In the following, we discuss some important lessons for supporting intercultural collaboration when designing sustainable technologies in the context of the developing world.

- **Sustainability intertwined with culture:** One of the important aspects of our results is that through ethnography it brings the cultural issues to the fore and shows how the sustainable practices of household women are inherently intertwined with their culture. We showed how the reuse of a gunny sack as a doormat, for example, supported some religious beliefs and how modifying a mother's old sari into a dress for her daughter supported an ongoing family tradition, in addition to an auspicious belief. These religious beliefs and traditions are not limited only to the families in question. We believe that religious beliefs at large affect people's domestic lives and cannot be ignored while designing interactive technologies. A much detailed account on the role of religion on ICT use is provided by Wyche and Grinter [27]. Moreover, we saw a connection between the culture and trend of buying household products in large quantities (e.g. a 50 kg. gunny sack of wheat and 15 kg. steel can of food oil) and reusing the containers for other household activities. Women's roles have been central in this. They sustain the family needs and values by taking into account their financial situation. Household women would refrain from throwing food products in the garbage and rather make other uses of it. For example, using sour milk to make hair oil. Another cultural theme that was visible from our research was "home-made is better". For example, household women would rather make their own butter and buttermilk from their leftover milk than buy them from shops. This is one of the ways women nurtured their family members by providing them with home-made things. For designing interactive and sustainable technologies, one needs to take into account cultural and traditional values of different communities.

- **From reuse to enrichment:** An important aspect of our participants' sustainable practices was not the mere reuse of old and worn-out things, they in fact attempted to make their lives better and enrich their household activities. The example of the reuse of a mother's sari for making a dress for her daughter shows how an old fashioned but expensive sari that was part of a long family tradition was modified to make a new fashionable dress that a young daughter would appreciate shows that it is not about only reusing old things but make them suit the current needs and choices. It shows a woman's constant efforts and desire to improve the current life for herself and her family. And as we mentioned in an earlier section, there are professional tailors in India who would make a nice designer dress from old clothes. Similarly, the example of denim carry bags shows that it is about making a creative and much more practical reuse of old things. The carry bags made of denim material are strong (for carrying heavy things), foldable (to be kept in a woman's purse) and washable (for keeping them clean). From an interaction design point of view, we suggest that going beyond the principles such as *linking invention & disposal*, *achieving longevity of use* and *sharing for maximal reuse* [4], we need to think about how we can make a reuse valuable and an enhancement from its original use.

- **Creative & Intimate:** Two strong themes that came out of our research were household women's inherent creativity in their everyday work and intimacy towards their family. Examples of the flower pot, storage boxes and carry bags showed how household women creatively used broken and unusable things to make usable and practical things that can support different household activities. Their craving for making embroideries on carry bags and coloring the flower pot were examples of their personal satisfaction in doing these activities. Similarly, family intimacy was also inherent in the examples of the doormat and the dress. Taking the family hygiene in mind a participant reused gunny sacks in her kitchen and different parts of her home so that everyone could first clean his/her legs before entering the house. The example of the dress represented a mother's love towards her daughter, keeping the family traditions in mind.

As designers, we need to respect people's creativity, resourcefulness and appropriation capabilities for supporting their household activities including care giving and family intimacy. As a design philosophy, we propose to design technologies to support activities and practices that are already in existence in household lives, and not technologies that do these activities for them.

CONCLUSIONS

The population of the Indian middle class ranges from 50 to 300 million people, depending on how we define the middle class. It will be one of the largest consumer groups in the world, as it is growing rapidly. We as HCI researchers need to understand their consuming and reusing practices to be able to support intercultural collaboration with the West. Our notion of domestic artefacts gives an account of women's creativity and resourcefulness. Our results show that to support intercultural interaction, one should not have a limited focus on supporting practicality and usefulness, but also consider religious beliefs, traditions, family intimacy, personal interests and health issues.

ACKNOWLEDGMENTS

We would like to thank all our participants and Lynn Packwood.

REFERENCES

1. ADB. Asia 2050: Realising the Asian Century. A report compiled by the Asian Development Bank. http://www.asiandevbank.org/documents/reports/asia-2050/asia-2050.pdf (last accessed on 15/10/2011)

2. Arroyo, E., Bonanni, L. and Selker, T. Waterbot: exploring feedback and persuasive techniques at the sink. In Proceedings of the SIGCHI conference on Human factors in computing systems (CHI '05). ACM, New York, NY, USA, 631-639.

3. Bang, M., Torstensson, C., Katzeff, C. The PowerHhouse: A Persuasive Computer Game Designed to Raise Awareness of Domestic Energy Consumption. In: PERSUASIVE 2006. LNCS, vol. 3962, pp. 123–132. (2006) Springer, Heidelberg.

4. Blevis, E. Sustainable interaction design: Invention & disposal, renewal & reuse. In Proceedings of the 25th international Conference on Human Factors in Computing Systems. CHI '07. ACM, New York, (2007), 503-512.

5. Chetty, M., Brush, A.J., Meyers, B.R. and Johns, P. It's not easy being green: understanding home computer power management. In Proceedings of the 27th international Conference on Human Factors in Computing Systems. CHI '09. ACM, New York, NY, (2009), 1033-1042.

6. Donner, J., Rangaswamy, N., Steenson, M.W. and Wei, C. "Express Yourself" and "Stay Together": The Middle

class Indian Family. In J. Katz (Ed.). The Handbook of Mobile Communication Studies, Cambridge, MA, (2008), 325-338.

7. Gustafsson, A. and Gyllenswrd, M. The power-aware cord: energy awareness through ambient information display. In CHI '05 extended abstracts on Human factors in computing systems (CHI EA '05). ACM, New York, NY, USA, 1423-1426.

8. Hanks, K., Odom, W., Roedl, D. and Blevis, B. Sustainable millennials: attitudes towards sustainability and the material effects of interactive technologies. In Proceeding of the 26th International SIGCHI Conference on Human Factors in Computing Systems. CHI '08. ACM, New York, NY, (2008), 333-342.

9. Joshi, A., Welankar, N., Kanitkar, K., and Sheikh, R. Rangoli: a visual phonebook for lowliterate users. In Proceedings of the 10th international Conference on Human Computer interaction with Mobile Devices and Services. MobileHCI '08. ACM, New York, NY, (2008), 217-223.

10. Kappel, K. and Grechenig, T. "show-me": water consumption at a glance to promote water conservation in the shower. In Proceedings of the 4th international Conference on Persuasive Technology. Persuasive '09, vol. 350. ACM, New York, NY, (2009), 1-6.

11. Kim, S. and Paulos, E. inAir: measuring and visualizing indoor air quality. In Proceedings of the 11th international Conference on Ubiquitous Computing. Ubicomp '09. ACM, New York, NY, (2009), 81-84.

12. Kinsley, D. Learning the Story of the Land: Reflections in the Liberating Power of Geography and Pilgrimage in the Hindu Tradition, In L. E. Nelson (ed.) Purifying the Earthly Body of God: Religion and Ecology in Hindu India, New York: SUNY Press. (1998), 225—46.

13. Latour, B. Where are the missing masses? The sociology of a few mundane artifacts. In Shaping Technology/ Building Society: Studies in Sociotechnical Change, W. E. Bijker and J. Law (eds.). London: MIT Press, (1992), 225-258.

14. Mankoff, J.C.et al. Environmental sustainability and interaction. In CHI '07 Extended Abstracts on Human Factors in Computing Systems, CHI '07. ACM, New York, NY, (2007) 2121-2124.

15. Mawdsley, E. India's Middle Classes and Environment. Development and Change, 35 (1), (2004), 79-103.

16. Narayanan, V. Water, Wood and Wisdom: Ecological Perspectives from the Hindu Traditions, Daedalus, 130(4): (2004), 179–205.

17. Odom, W., Pierce, J., Stolterman, E. and Blevis, E. Understanding why we preserve some things and discard others in the context of interaction design. In Proceedings of the 27th international Conference on Human Factors in Computing Systems. CHI '09. ACM, New York, NY, (2009), 1053-1062.

18. Parikh, T.S., Javid, P.K.S., Ghosh, K. and Toyama, K. Mobile phones and paper documents: evaluating a new approach for capturing microfinance data in rural India. In Proceedings of the SIGCHI Conference on Human Factors in Computing Systems, CHI '06. ACM, New York, NY, (2006) 551-560.

19. Petersen, D., Steele, J., and Wilkerson. J. WattBot: a residential electricity monitoring and feedback system. In Proceedings of the 27th international conference extended abstracts on Human factors in computing systems (CHI EA '09). ACM, New York, NY, USA, 2847-2852.

20. Ravallion, M. The Developing World's Bulging (but vulnerable) Middle Class. The World Bank. Policy Research Working Paper. Report Number: WPS4816, January 2009. URL: http://go.worldbank.org/N15W7DSQO0 (Last accessed on 15/10/2011)

21. Sridharan, E. The growth and sectoral composition of India's middle class: Its impact on the politics of economic liberalization. India Review, 3(4) (2004), 405–428.

22. Taylor, A. and Swan, L. Artful systems in the home. In Proceedings of the 23rd International Conference on Human Factors in Computing Systems. CHI '05. ACM, New York, (2005), 641--650.

23. Varma, P.K. The Great Indian Middle Class. Delhi: Penguin. (1998).

24. Wakkary, R. and Maestri, L. The resourcefulness of everyday design, In Proceedings of the 6th ACM SIGCHI Conference on Creativity & Cognition. (C&C '07), ACM, New York, NY, (2007) 163-172.

25. Wakkary, R. and Tanenbaum, K. A sustainable identity: the creativity of an everyday designer. In Proceedings of the 27th international Conference on Human Factors in Computing Systems. CHI '08, ACM, New York, NY, (2009), 365-374.

26. Woodruff, A., Hasbrouck, J. and Augustin, S. A bright green perspective on sustainable choices. In Proceeding of the 26th International Conference on Human Factors in Computing Systems. CHI '08. ACM, New York, NY, (2008), 313-322.

27. Wyche, S. and Griner, R.E. Extraordinary computing: religion as a lens for reconsidering the home. In Proceedings of the 27th International Conference on Human Factors in Computing Systems. CHI '09. ACM, New York, NY, (2009), 749-758.

An Exploratory Analysis of Effective Indo-Korean Collaboration with Intervention of Knowledge Mapping

Indumathi Anandarajan
Indian Institute of Science
Bangalore-560 012, India
indumathi@mgmt.iisc.ernet.in
Phone: + 91 90 08 22 25 66

Prof. K.B.Akhilesh
Indian Institute of Science
Bangalore-560 012, India
kba@mgmt.iisc.ernet.in
Phone:+91 98 45 45 25 17

ABSTRACT

This paper presents an intervention of knowledge mapping towards effective Indo-Korean collaboration.

Author Keywords

Indo-Korean; Collaboration; Knowledge Mapping

ACM Classification Keywords

K.6.1. [Management of Computing and Information Systems]: Project and People Management - Management Techniques

INTRODUCTION

Collaboration provides an opportunity to work together. It's an effort towards perception of the parties. Perceptions are largely influenced by the information and stereotypes of what one has about the other. In this paper we argue that information on one's perception can be used very effectively to nurture and use the strengths, their cultural practices, outlook of each other etc. Korean company example has been illustrated to understand how managers do business in a cross cultural context and develop cooperation and collaboration. Korean organizations established branches in India to capture the Indian market. This kind of mix of both the domestic professionals (India) as well as foreign professionals (Korea) brings forth both opportunities and challenges; this is in accordance to what [4] has indicated that management practices and values differ from country to country due to each nation's unique culture and traditions.

METHODOLOGY

This paper is based on several interviews of Indian and Korean managers and knowledge professionals co-working in an Indian subsidiary of a Korean company. Around 150 knowledge professionals working in mobile, electronics and software field were interviewed; the interview lasted for around 30 to 40 minutes on an average, followed with filling of a questionnaire on various aspects. Questionnaire was used to study knowledge professionals "well being" and other knowledge management aspects. The aim was to identify the dominant cultures of both Korea and India through the interview process and its understood in relation to several work related aspects. Finally several interventions comprising of both technology enabled as well as other relationship enabling strategies are identified, while concentrating mainly on Knowledge Mapping as a core intervening strategy is suggested. What is being summarized and reported here should be pursued purely as an academic dialogue to see the possibilities of increasing collaborative effort between professionals of both the countries. Next set of arguments is an extrapolation of discussion with knowledge professionals belonging to both Korea and India.

IDENTIFICATION OF DOMINANT CULTURES

Dominant cultures for both Koreans and Indians who are co working in the same industry was identified.

Korea

It was stated by both the Indian as well Korean professionals in this study that Korean professionals are extremely hard working; they are willing to put their heart and soul to their work. This is further confirmed in the statistics mentioned by [10] studies on culture that Koreans worked on an average of 2390 hours per year. It was found out from the interview that when Korea decided to increase and improvise their national economy for the growth of the country, they unanimously decided that no other product of an outside country will be purchased by its citizens. And consequently all the Korean nationals worked really hard to possess technology and products which are being produced in their own country leading to exponential increase in its GDP. [2], states that "The key Confucian values of diligence and harmony have contributed to a relatively high work ethic."

An instance depicting their time consciousness and resilience was recalled by all the knowledge professionals in the interview when Korea successfully incorporated the automobile engineering technology which existed in another country, by observing its technology and attempting it themselves with several trial and error, Korea finally developed an even advanced technology of the same automobile engineering within a short span of time, purely because of their never say no attitude and to keep up to the competition.

India

Top Korean officials pointed out that in their field Indian knowledge professionals are good at understanding the process that goes into making any technology as well as to explain and express this process explicitly which is a lacuna in them, hence they branched out to India.

Korean professionals are of the opinion that Indian knowledge professionals have good analytical skills which they want to capture and have hence hired professionals for jobs involving analytics.

Korean Knowledge professionals also feel that the diversity that's existing in India makes the Indian knowledge professionals to get more adapted to all situations and helps them to look at solutions from new angles thereby arriving at unique and innovative solutions.

Korean knowledge professionals are hence of the opinion that Indian knowledge professionals are open to trying out new things and adapting to new procedures, reasoning out the mechanics involved in the technology, and they are also good at understanding the process that goes into developing the products or technology.

Three dominant cultures that can be identified from the aforementioned incidents between Korea and India are depicted in the table below:

Table 1. Dominant Cultures

KOREA	INDIA
Hardworking	Process oriented
Resilience	Analytical skill
Time conscious	Innovative

This cultural difference tends to have different consequences; we take an opportunity to understand this difference in both the cultural types through the interviews and by looking at several aspects of work revolving around knowledge professionals such as well being of professionals, work allotment, communication and dynamics in the team and performance appraisal.

Cultural Differences around Work Aspects

Well being

It was stated by the professionals that the well being of Korean knowledge professionals is high when they are able to perform successfully on challenging tasks. They are extremely hard working and stretch themselves to complete the task to get a sense of wellbeing. They are also time conscious and stick to their targets and deadlines.

As perceived by senior Korean managers Indian professionals have high well being when they understand the process that has gone in the challenging work. They are also good at clearly describing the process to others and hence help in transferring this knowledge to others. It was observed by Korean professionals that the Indian professionals tend to go in depth in the whole task and break down the strategies to achieve the bigger goal.

Work allotment

Korea follows a hierarchical structure; top management decides the task to be performed by others. The tasks are discussed with the superiors of each department, who in turn look into the project, form teams appropriately and each individual employee is assigned a set task to be performed. This finding is further proved by [6] contend that "Superiors tend to issue general directives, as opposed to specific and detailed ones. Subordinates then must use their own judgment about how to implement the directives."

Indian managers have the practice of asking all the knowledge professionals the skills they possess, their experience in working on similar projects and based on the obtained responses they are chosen for the project, and the work is finally allotted by the superiors on the basis of their skills, past experience and the need for the project.

Communication

In Korea formal communication is mainly along vertical hierarchies reflecting their high score on power distance. In this interview it was pointed out that Koreans value their superiors and tend to follow their instructions without disagreeing to what is being ordered to them. This is proved in the study by [2] "Koreans are reticent about open communication in formal meetings and have difficulty in airing their views, especially opposing ones."

Indian knowledge professionals tend to have good open communication with all the knowledge professionals, there is presence of top- down communication process and less of bottom up communication, i.e. information tends to get passed on from the superiors to the juniors via the managers but the opposite rarely takes place.

Performance Appraisal

Koreans are usually promoted based on hierarchy. The senior most in the ladder gets the promotion and pay hike, followed by the others in the hierarchy, which is in correlation with [2] findings. Well documented information, as well as the finding from this study shows that Koreans struggle and tend to work hard as they have to be in the higher ladder to prove themselves or they are considered to be worthless by the society.

In the Indian context, both rewards and promotion are based on performance appraisal, feedback from their superiors and their performance sheet will determine as to who gets promoted or rewarded.

Team dynamics

Team dynamics is very high amongst the knowledge professionals of Korea, as the larger culture i.e. economic, political, technical, and cultural climates in which the organization, the team, and the individuals operate are all willing to perform and achieve. This is further proved by [4] study that Korea has a low Individualism indicating that the society is collectivist rather than individualist.

Team dynamics is good with Indian knowledge professionals, as they are friendly by nature and good at interpersonal relationship leading to brain storming, innovation, exchange of ideas etc. [4] study also states that they are collectivist and this helps to work in teams.

This kind of cultural difference will make it difficult to work with, but if the organizations are able to collaborate, the advantages of both the cultures can be used to the maximum. Collaboration can be planned to bring the organizations with different cultures together and thereby to address the individual issues, the team issues, the effect of the different cultures on the organization, and also to look beyond the dominant stereotype, and hence here we present interventions to enhance collaboration.

INTERVENTIONS FOR ENHANCED COLLABORATION BETWEEN THE TWO COUNTRIES

The basic idea behind collaboration is to avail the strength and the power that both the countries possess and which both are willing to ask and share with one another for the benefit of all. Any collaboration to be effective between knowledge professionals from different countries there has to be an immense need to understand, believe and trust each other and the right attitude to explore feasible opportunities.

Collaboration between the two countries and people can be increased in several ways. There are several strategies that could be adopted to enhance collaboration which we just mention here such as: Augmented Reality technology leads to enhancement of information in a variety of workspaces. [1], Conceptualization is an abstract & Ontology is an explicit specification of a conceptualization, which is the statement of a logical theory. There is use of formal ontologies for specifying content-specific agreements for a variety of knowledge-sharing activities [3]. Twin the person approach where two individuals with different skill set and background work together, Interpersonal relations is to improve the interaction between the groups [7]. And in cross country collaboration there is collaboration across countries. We in this paper are focusing our attention mainly on Knowledge mapping and its application on both the cultures to build better collaboration.

Knowledge Mapping

Collaboration with the usage of knowledge mapping is effective between two countries. In the case of collaboration where the parent organization is located in a different country it will help in identifying where the key players of the organization are located and can be easily contacted to obtain their expertise.

Definition & Objective of Knowledge Mapping

Knowledge mapping is defined as a process of surveying, assessing and linking the information, knowledge, competencies and proficiencies held by individuals and groups within an organization [5]. It is a method of analysis to define the knowledge needed and the available knowledge to support an organization. The objective of knowledge mapping is to integrate the captured knowledge in the organization, transfer the knowledge to others and to make strategic plans for the development of the organization.

Knowledge mapping is an efficient tool for collaboration. It can be mapped at different levels, it makes it possible to map domain specific and core technology i.e. knowledge that is specific to each country or the technology that was developed by one country, its technological know- how and the procedures to operate can be mapped for future use. It's feasible to map the futuristic view of the stake holders i.e. the top management and senior professional, the demands of the customers, perspectives of competitors and suppliers etc. Best practices of the organization can be mapped; this will lead to cost effectiveness. All this knowledge can be mapped separately and used judiciously which will help in collaboration.

Benefits of Knowledge Mapping

Knowledge mapping has several benefits for the organization; it allows professionals to obtain the required critical knowledge in their respective field from where it is stored in the organization. As stated by [11] Knowledge mapping helps to understand the relationships between knowledge stores within projects and organizations. Knowledge mapping also helps in identifying the knowledge gaps. Knowledge mapping also tends to increase sharing of knowledge across the organization, and thereby faster knowledge acquisition. With the availability of knowledge it enhances the decision making process. Finally as stated by [12] knowledge maps are an interactive and open system for dialogue that defines, organizes and builds on the intuitive, structured and procedural knowledge used to explore and solve problems.

While collaborating between two countries there is lot of commonalities and differences in culture. Knowledge mapping will help in capturing different practices, perspectives, learning's they have acquired, different working patterns with respect to their culture and utilize it to integrate and work together. Knowledge mapping will help the organization with different cultural practices to develop formal communities of practice. It will help in people taking decisions and to make After-Action Reviews, based on the differences in their cultural practices.

Knowledge Mapping in relation to this Case Study

In relation to this case, knowledge mapping can be done by adopting the concept of Johari window [9] and we arrived at four quadrants. 1st Quadrant is where Knowledge is known to both Korea & India in a given organization, in 2nd Quadrant Korean generated knowledge is known to Koreans while not known to Indians, in the 3rd Quadrant Indian generated knowledge is known to Indians while not known to Koreans and finally last Quadrant comprises of Specific areas where both Koreans & Indians have to explore, debate and argue to arrive at knowledge. In this way Knowledge or schema is developed in terms of first set of known branches and sub branches specifically taking two broad routes one being on Indian side and the other on Korean side. This can remain separate but through knowledge mapping there is feasibility for exchange and sharing leading to mutual transfer of knowledge from one to the other. With knowledge mapping there is also feasibility to identify the knowledge gaps and hence an agreement between groups from both the countries where they have to work together. It is seen that some organizations tend to elaborately map knowledge, while some don't document, and yet others have good documentation but is not utilized as they lack the right attitude towards mapping. This kind of knowledge representation could be in the form of objects, causal linkages, standard operating procedures, standards, specifications, pictures & drawings, videos, documentation of conversation etc.

Knowledge mapping will help in identifying knowledge dependencies within cross functional work groups. As identified from the interview that the Korean professionals are hard working and tend to stretch themselves in their job, while Indian professionals are good at process oriented tasks. Knowledge mapping will help in mapping these different culture oriented traits and behavior. By adopting "twin the person approach" where in both the groups are brought together and encouraged to work on particular projects leading to exchange of their behavioral traits and practices. This exchange of traits and practices could be captured and mapped for the benefit of the organization.

Knowledge mapping can be used for task allocation, placement, performance appraisal, reward and continuous assessment of learning on the job. Transferring intricate knowledge will be easy with the help of knowledge mapping; formal communication irrespective of cultural difference will be feasible. It was identified through the discussions in the case study that the Koreans are people with few words; here professionals can obtain the knowledge through the help of knowledge mapping.

Therefore it can be concluded that knowledge mapping is a non-controversial mental procedure to build collaboration.

Inter cultural collaboration helps to dissolve the cultural stereotype, collaboration of the two countries lead to transfer of new ideas, new functions, disciplines, processes, which challenge and change the stereotypical way of functioning of their own respective countries. As [8] points out, "This cultural diversity because of collaboration leads to innovation, creativity and receptiveness to new cultural forms and relationships."

REFERENCES

1. Billinghurst, M., Kato, H. (2000) Out and About: Real World Teleconferencing. British Telecom Technical Journal (BTTJ), Millennium Edition.
2. Chen, M. (1995), Asian Management Systems, Routledge, London.
3. Convict Creations (2004) http://www.convictcreations.com/culture/southkorea.html#top
4. Gruber, T. (1993).Toward principles for the design of ontologies used for knowledge sharing. International Journal Human-Computer studies, 43 p 907-928
5. Hofstede, G. (1991), Cultures and Organizations, McGraw Hill, London
6. Hylton, A. (2002). KeKma-Training. http://www.kekmatraining.com/siteContents/course-materials/course-samples.htm
7. Morden, T., & Bowles, D. (1998). Management in South Korea: A review. Management Decisions, 36/5. MCB University Press. 316-330.
8. Self, R., Self, D.R. & Bell-Haynes, J., (2010). Intercultural human resource management: South Korea and the United States., EABR & ETLC Conference Proceedings.
9. Shenton, A.K., (2007) "Viewing information needs through a Johari Window", Reference Services Review, Vol. 35 Iss: 3.
10. UNESCO World Report "Investing in Cultural Diversity and Intercultural Dialogue", (2009) UNESCO Publishing.
11. White, D. (2002) Knowledge mapping and management, London, IRM Press
12. Wright, R. (1993). An approach to knowledge acquisition, transfer and application in Landscape Architecture. University of Toronto.

Knowing Me Knowing You: Exploring Effects of Culture and Context on Perception of Robot Personality

Astrid Weiss
Institute of Informatics/ICT&S Center
University of Amsterdam/University of Salzburg
Science Park 904, 1098XH/
Sigmund-Haffner Gasse 18
Amsterdam, The Netherlands/ Salzburg, Austria
a.weiss@uva.nl/astrid.weiss@sbg.ac.at

Betsy van Dijk, Vanessa Evers
Computer Science Department
University of Twente
PO Box 217, 7500 AE
Enschede, The Netherlands
e.m.a.g.vandijk@utwente.nl
v.evers@utwente.nl

ABSTRACT
We carry out a set of experiments to assess collaboration between human users and robots in a cross-cultural setting. This paper describes the study design and deployment of a video-based study to investigate task-dependence and cultural-background dependence of the personality trait attribution on a socially interactive robot. In Human-Robot Interaction, as well as in Human-Agent Interaction research, the attribution of personality traits towards intelligent agents has already been researched intensively in terms of the social similarity or complementary rule. We assume that searching the explanation for personality trait attribution in the similarity and complementary rule does not take into account important contextual factors. Just like people equate certain personality types to certain professions, we expect that people may have certain personality expectations depending on the context of the task the robot carries out. Because professions have different social meaning in different national culture, we also expect that these task-dependent personality preferences differ across cultures. Therefore, we suggest an experiment that considers the task-context and the cultural-background of users.

Author Keywords   Human-robot interaction; personality perception; cultural differences; task context.

ACM Classification Keywords
H.5.1 [Information Interfaces And Presentation]: Multimedia Information Systems - Evaluation/methodology;

General Terms   Experimentation; Measurement.

INTRODUCTION
Since the fictional play of Josef Capek on Rossum's Universal Robots (RUR) [1] it became popular belief that robots should perform a variety of "dull, dirty, and dangerous" tasks humans would rather not perform by themselves. Certainly, robots are suitable for these kinds of tasks as they are clearly definable, need to be fulfilled accurately, and must be performed exactly the same every time. A recent study by Takayama et al. [10] investigated what jobs people felt a robot should do and could show indeed that people prefer robots for jobs that require memorization, keen perceptual abilities, and service-orientation as long as robots work together with people and do not replace them. Robots move away from the simple and repetitive tasks they were originally designed for. It becomes more interesting to introduce robots in various environments, going beyond the work context, such as the domestic context, the health-care sector, and education. For all these interaction contexts it is important that robots will be socially accepted as sophisticated tools assisting humans or even as companions for the human.

Cultural factor research finds its way into Human-Robot Interaction research. The starting point was the interest into cultural differences in the perception of robots (see e.g. [8]). This research is mainly concerned with the question if and why people with Asians (in particular Japanese) cultural-background experience robots differently compared to people with a Western cultural-background. According to some researchers, a general retention of robots can be observed for Western cultures ([6]; [8]). However, more fine-grained studies, such as the cross-cultural study conducted by Bartneck et al. [2] with Dutch, Chinese, and Japanese participants could already show more subtle cultural influences in the attitude towards robots. They used the Negative Attitude towards Robots Scale to investigate people's attitude towards the interaction with robots. Interestingly, the Japanese participants did not have a more positive attitude towards robots, which was contrary to the authors' expectations.

Similarly, a study on the effect of cultural-background in human-robot cooperation, done by Evers et al. [4], showed that US and Chinese participants respond differently to robot advices. Moreover, they could show that assumptions from human-human interaction cannot universally hold true. A follow-up study by Wang et al. [12] showed that Chinese participants were more likely to comply to robots that communicated implicitly while US participants tended to comply with robots that communicated explicitly in a Human-Robot Team setting.

In this work in progress paper, we present a study design with which we want to investigate if the attribution of personality traits to an agent/robot is affected by the cultural-background of the user interacting with it. The study is currently in its data collection phase, but we will present the preliminary results of the first 31 valid participants. We base our work on three assumptions: (1) the attribution of personality traits towards a robot is affected by the task-context in which the human and the robot are interacting, and (2) the attribution of personality traits towards a robot is affected by the cultural-background of the user. In the following we will present related work in the area of socially interactive robots and personality trait attribution, followed by our study proposal for which we will describe in detail our research questions and hypotheses, study design, the manipulation, the participants, the procedure, and the preliminary results. We will close our paper with an outlook on expected results and future work.

SOCIALLY INTERACTIVE ROBOTS

A socially interactive robot can be considered as an embodied intelligent agent, which is designed especially for social interaction with humans. An interesting phenomenon is that users tend to perceive socially interactive agents as well as robots as having personality traits. Various assumptions exist, which try to predict human responses towards agents/robots with personalities, such as the media equation theory and the theory of attraction.

The media equation demonstrates that in many cases users tend to treat computing systems (but also TV and new media) in a social way, "just like interaction in real life" [10] which is a relevant theoretical precondition for our proposed study. The theory of attraction comprises the social similarity and complementary attraction rule, which can be considered as two equally compelling personality-based rules. The similarity attraction rule says that people like others more who are similar to their own personality traits. The complementary attraction rule on the contrary says that people prefer to interact with others whose personality characteristics are complementary to their own ones [7]. Isbister & Nass could show that for disembodied agents on the screen the similarity attraction rule holds true [7], however, for embodied virtual agents and for robots it could be demonstrated that the complementary attraction rule is supported ([7]; [9]).

We assume that it is not exclusively about the complementary or the similarity attraction rule why people prefer a specific personality of a robot, but about the task context and the cultural-background. The correlation between cultural-background and personality traits has already been acknowledged in social-psychology literature. For instance, Hofstede et al. [5] conducted a study, in which he classified over 40 nations according to 5 dimensions, namely power-distance, individualism, masculinity, uncertainty avoidance, and long-term orientation. Furthermore, Hofstede et al. also investigated the link between cultural dimensions and personality traits and could show that e.g. extraversion is positively correlated with individualism and negatively with masculinity [5]. In other words we can expect an influence on the preference of personality traits due to cultural-background.

However, research on personality traits and professions also shows the link between these two aspects. Barrick et al. [3] could demonstrate that managerial tasks correlate with extroversion personality traits, but that a surgeon's tasks and teachers' tasks correlate with introversion. This leads to our assumption that also the task context in which a robot interacts with the human has an influence on the personality traits attribution, besides the cultural-background. In the following we will describe in more detail how we want to investigate these assumptions.

EXPLORING ROBOT PERSONALITY TRAITS

The evidence for ambivalent assumptions on the correlation between robot's personality trait evaluation and the user's personality traits calls for a better understanding of predictors or mediators of a robot's personality evaluation. It is hoped that through a better understanding of the task context and the users' cultural-background as mediators for robot personality evaluation, the utility of personality cues for robots can be better realized for different task contexts.

We assume that trait-relevant situational cues (namely task context and cultural-background) moderate the evaluation/preference of the robot's personality. In other words, we assume that trait attributions are task- and culture-dependent. Thus, we hypothesize that participants will attribute personality traits to robots based on the task-context and on their cultural-background. To investigate this assumption we suggest a two-step study proposal to evaluate the impact of cultural context and task-context on the personality evaluation of robots. The first study will be video-based to get a first indication on our hypotheses (see Woods et al. [13] on the comparability of video-based and interaction-based studies in HRI). Based on the results we want to conduct an actual user study with the same robot and potentially iterated tasks and a different cultural-background distribution. In the following we will describe the design of the first video-based study in more detail.

FIRST STUDY

For the video-based study we use 6 pre-recorded scenarios with the Nao robot (see Fig. 1). We have a 2 (Nao personality: introvert vs. extrovert) by 2 (participant personality) by 3 (task context: introvert vs. extrovert vs. neutral) by 2 (cultural-background: Dutch vs. German) between-subject experiment.

Research Question and Hypotheses

By the means of the above described study design we want to investigate the following two research question and its according hypotheses.

RQ1: Will the assessment of a robot's personality be (a) task-dependent, be (b) culture-dependent?

H1: The task will mediate the personality evaluation of a robot and the user's personality traits.

H2: The cultural-background of the user will mediate the personality evaluation of a robot and the user's personality traits.

H3: The perception of the task context is cultural-background dependent.

RQ2: Will the assessment of interaction quality criteria for the robot (such as perceived enjoyment, intelligence, fun, trust, compliance, and willingness to spend time with the robot) be (a) task-dependent, be (b) culture-dependent?

Method

Our study should be based on 3 different tasks: a task that is particularly associated with extroverted personality traits [3], a task that is associated with introverted personality traits, and a neutral task (tasks not commonly associated with introverted or extroverted personality traits). We will use the Nao robot (see Fig. 1) to increase the potential that users interpret it as a robot that could perform meaningful tasks for/with humans. The tasks the robot will perform in the videos together with humans are based on the above-mentioned study from Barrick et al. [3] such as: teaching a student (robot as introvert teacher), caring about a patient (robot as ambivalent pharmacist, see Fig. 1), discussing the balance sheet of a company (robot as extrovert CEO).

Figure 1: Example scenery out of the video about the interaction with the caring pharmacy robot.

Manipulation

To simulate extrovert and introvert behaviour of the Nao robot, we manipulated verbal cues, namely loudness of voice and speech rate, as these aspects are associated with the judgment of extroversion/introversion. For the manipulation of nonverbal cues we focused on simultaneous manipulation of the moving angle and moving speed for gestures (the wider and faster the more extrovert) and more "autonomous/random" movements for the extrovert robot [9]. To simulate different task contexts (as mentioned above), teaching, caring, and management, we used different backgrounds for contextualization.

Procedure

In the video-based study, participants are asked first to state their age, gender, educational- and cultural-background. Afterwards, they watch one of the 6 different videos, in which the robot is either extrovert or introvert and performs one of the three tasks. Afterwards, participants are asked to answer several questions regarding the watched video. The survey is conducted online and the link is distributed via several student mailing lists of the University of Twente, The Netherlands.

Measures

The cultural-background of the participant for this first study is collected through a binominal self-reported category (Dutch or German). Please note that we are not measuring broad cultural value difference such as power distance or collectivism. We will investigate correlations between shared cultural values and responses in the follow-up study. Extroversion/ introversion of the participants, the perception of the extroversion/ introversion of the Nao robot and of the task context is measured by an index of the Wiggins personality adjectives items [14]. This index is composed of 8 adjectives for introversion (such as silent, shy, inward) and 8 adjectives for extroversion (such as outgoing, jovial, and perky). Furthermore, we added some questions to measure quality criteria, such as perceived enjoyment, intelligence, fun, trust, compliance, and willingness to spend time with the robot.

Preliminary Results

Up to now we could collect 31 valid cases for the online survey so far. Out of these 31 participants, 20 were male and 11 female, 28 were aged between 18 and 25, the other 3 were older. In total 9 introvert and 22 extrovert participants filled in the study, of which 21 participants indicated that they were Dutch and 10 that they were German. Clearly these sample sizes do not allow inferential statistics with meaningful results, however first trends could be found in the data. The videos with the extrovert task are so far rated more extrovert than the videos with the ambivalent task. Similarly, the videos with the ambivalent task were rated more extrovert, than the videos with the introvert task by both Dutch and German participants. There can be no clear tendency observed for the personality perception of the robot depending on the cultural background, however tendencies could be observed that Dutch participants would be less compliant with the robot, but trust it more and that Germans are willing to spend more time with the robot in general.

Similarly, for the robot perception depending on the task-context no significant tendency can be found in the data so far. However, the introvert CEO robot was rated as being the least introvert robot, but the pharmacist was more introvert than the teacher. The task does seem to have a potential effect on the way the participants perceive the introvert robot. During the pharmacist task the robot is perceived to be a lot more introvert and a lot less extrovert than during the other tasks. There is a significant interaction effect between the task and the robot's personality, on the perception of introversion of the robot, $F(3,34) = 3,703$, $p = 0.021$.

Regarding the quality criteria the extrovert robot is always rated better in terms of perceived enjoyment than the introvert one, but the task seems to have no effect. For fun the extrovert robot is rated better in the first two tasks, but during the teaching task it is rated quite similar to the introvert robot. However, the perception of intelligence differs greatly between tasks, but not in the expected way. The introvert CEO robot was perceived to be more intelligent than the extrovert one and the extrovert teacher was perceived to be more intelligent than the introvert one. A bigger sample size will enable us to conduct a deeper data analysis and based on that to inform the design of the second study in terms of the personality design of the robot and the choice of the task-context.

SECOND STUDY

The second study is considered to be a laboratory-based user study in which the users can interactively perform tasks with the Nao robot in similar tasks-context as in the previous video study. We will evaluate actual behaviour in order to assess user responses to the robot rather than self reported attitudinal data as collected in the study described in this paper. Moreover, for the user study we want to add measures for the cultural identity and for the persuasiveness of the robot for the laboratory-based study. For cultural measures we consider broad value differences to show that the cultural groups indeed differ in cultural value orientations, such as collectivism/individualism. For the persuasiveness of the robot we consider to increase the interactivity of the tasks, e.g. in the teaching task the robot could convince the user of a wrong information, in the caring task, the robot could convince the user to choose a specific medicine, and in the CEO task, the robot *could* convince the user to change financial numbers to the better. Additionally, we will use questionnaires to evaluate the persuasiveness of the robot. The model derived from the data of both studies, will offer a unique approach to understand personality evaluation and cultural embedding of tasks in Human-Robot Interaction.

CONCLUSION & OUTLOOK

In this paper we presented the study concept of a video-based study, which has the aim to explore task-dependence and cultural-background dependence of the personality trait attribution on a socially interactive robot. We expect that it is neither the similarity rule nor the complementary rule, but the mediation of the task context and the cultural-background that causes the specific evaluation of a robot's personality. The planned follow-up laboratory-based user study should offer us additional data to investigate these assumptions further. Our overall goal with a cumulative data analysis of both studies is to present a "user personality - cultural-background - task context –robot personality model" that explains under which specific task contexts and cultural pre-conditions the similarity attraction rule or the complementary attraction rule holds true.

ACKNOWLEDGMENTS

We would like to thank the students who participated in the Bachelor Class on Human-Media Interaction of 2011/2012: Bastiaan van den Berg, Kevin Leuwerink, Dennis Waalewijn, and Dennis Windhouwer.

REFERENCES

1. Capek J (1920). Rossum's Universal Robots. Prague, CZ.
2. Bartneck C, Suzuki T, Kanda T, A Nomura T (2006). The influence of people's culture and prior experiences with AIBO on their attitude towards robots. AI & Society The Journal of Human-Centered Systems 21(1).
3. Barrick, R., Mount, M. (1991). The big five personality dimension and job performance: A meta analysis. Personnel Psychology 44.
4. Evers, V. Maldonado, H., Brodeck, T., Hinds, P. (2008). Relational vs. group self-construal: untangling the role of national culture in HRI, Proceedings of HRI 2008, 255-262.
5. Hofstede, G., McCrae, R. R. (2004). Personality and culture revisited: Linking traits and dimensions of culture. Cross-Cultural Research, 38, 52-88.
6. Hornyak TN (2006). Loving the machine: The art and science of Japanese robots. Kodansha international, Tokyo, New York, London.
7. Isbister, K., & Nass, C. (2000). Consistency of personality in interactive characters: Verbal cues, non-verbal cues, and user characteristics. International Journal of Human-Computer Studies, 53, 251–267.
8. Kaplan, F. (2004). Who is afraid of the humanoid? Investigating cultural differences in the acceptance of robots. International Journal of Humanoid Robotics 1(3):465-480.
9. Lee, K. M., Peng, W., Yan, C., & Jin, S. (2006). Can Robots Manifest Personality?: An Empirical Test of Personality Recognition, Social Responses, and Social Presence in Human-Robot Interaction. Journal of Communication, 56, 754-772.
10. Reeves, B., & Nass, C. (1996). The media equation: How people treat computers, television, and new media like real people and places. New York: Cambridge University Press.
11. Takayama, L., Ju, W., Nass, C.(2008). Beyond dirty, dangerous and dull: what everyday people think robots should do. Proceedings of HRI 2008, 25-32.
12. Wang L, Rau PLP, Evers V, Robinson, P.K., Hinds, P. (2010). When in Rome: the role of culture & context in adherence to robot recommendations. Proceedings of HRI 2010, 359-366.
13. Woods, S.N., Walters, M.L., Koay, K.L., Dautenhahn, K. (2006). Methodological Issues in HRI: A Comparison of Live and Video-Based Methods in Robot to Human Approach Direction Trials. Proceedings of RO-MAN 2006, 51-58.
14. Wiggins, J. S. (1979). A psychological taxonomy of trait-descriptive terms: The interpersonal domain. Journal of Personality and Social Psychology, 37, 395–412.

Now That's News: Substitution and Culture in Electronic Newspaper Adoption in Scandinavia

Nicolai Pogrebnyakov
Copenhagen Business School
24 Porcelaenshaven, 1,
2000 Frederiksberg, Denmark
nicolaip@cbs.dk

Mikael Buchmann
Copenhagen Business School
24 Porcelaenshaven, 1,
2000 Frederiksberg, Denmark
mikaelbuchmann@gmail.com

ABSTRACT

This paper investigates the intent to use electronic newspaper in three Scandinavian countries. It explores the influence of perceived technology substitution, cultural factors as well as perceived ease of use and usefulness. Electronic newspaper is seen as a substitute to the printed kind that is distributed digitally on e-reader platforms. The data came from 1804 surveys administered in Norway, Sweden and Denmark. The results indicate that perceived substitution is the most important driver behind the intent to use of electronic newspaper, while culture has little or no effect. These results contribute to the nascent research on how the superiority of perceived substitutive functionality of one technological artifact over another may lead to the adoption of the superior artifact. It also calls into question the role of culture in technology adoption.

Author Keywords
Perceived substitution; culture; electronic newspaper; technology acceptance model

ACM Classification Keywords
I.7.4 [Document and Text Processing]: Electronic publishing; H.1.1 [Models and Principles]: Systems and Information Theory - Information theory;

INTRODUCTION
The newspaper industry is currently undergoing two major transformations: a transition to digital content distribution and an increasing use of mobile platforms. Entire business models in news, book, music and video distribution have been reassessed over the past several years. The increasing use of mobile technologies for content distribution reinforces this transition to digital. Access to media from mobile platforms is expected to overtake access from other platforms [6].

This paper focuses on the adoption of electronic newspaper. The transition to mobile digital content distribution in daily newspapers results in dramatic changes, including the emergence of new business models and the convergence of different media channels. Our contribution to existing research is threefold. First, it has been suggested that the effect of culture on technology adoption changes depending on the geographic location of the diffusion curve. We investigate a product before it is offered in the mainstream, allowing to broaden the understanding of culture's effect prior to launch. Second, we aim to integrate extant theories and perform theory testing in the context of mobile electronic newspaper adoption. To that end, we compare the influence of individual factors in adoption (using the technology acceptance model) with societal (national culture) and technology substitution ones. Third, we add to the research on technology substitution, which is a significant but somewhat under-researched topic.

CONCEPTUAL BACKGROUND
This paper builds on three theoretical perspectives: cultural dimensions, technology substitution and the technology acceptance model (TAM).

Technology Acceptance Model
The model measures the intent to use (IU) of a particular technology using the perceived ease of use (PEOU) and perceived usefulness (PU) as explanatory variables [3]; [19]. Revised versions of the model [22]; [17] add different constructs to expand on the underlying drivers behind the already established constructs. A similar approach was used in this study. National culture (CUL) and perceived substitution (SUB) were included to examine their effect on the IU (CUL and SUB) and PEOU on PU (SUB only).

Thus as has been shown in numerous earlier studies with the TAM, the original constructs of the model provide good causal explanations on technology acceptance. The TAM constructs and relationships between were therefore included in the research model in this study. However, because the goal here is not to test the TAM, no hypotheses were formulated with regard to that model.

Culture and Technology Adoption
It has been shown that national differences in technology acceptance can be attributed to cultural variations between countries [2]. Further, cultural variations have been shown to exert significant moderating effects both on the TAM

[13]; [17]; [23] and on high-technology product adoption in general [20].

As national culture may have an effect on the rate of technology acceptance, it has been included in this study. To conceptualize culture, Hofstede's five cultural dimensions have been measured through a series of questions which capture aspects of the respective dimensions [17]; [23].

Power distance (PDI). At the macro level, [20] and [16] found that a high PDI score has a negative influence on the country penetration of innovations.

At the individual level, [23] made a contrary finding. When studying online shopping in China, he found that high PDI had a positive effect on the intent to use. This finding has support in [18] and [24]. Because this study is also done at the individual level, this leads to the following hypothesis:

H1: Power distance (PDI) has a negative relationship with the intent to use (IU).

Individualism (IDV). High IDV scores have been found to positively influence adoption, albeit only for early adopters [20]. At the individual level [18] observe that higher individualism facilitates computer-based communication due to, in effect, the personal nature of technology. In spite of this appealing logic, neither [17] nor [23] found any significant relationship between IDV and any of the constructs in the TAM.

Despite the lack of a consensus on the effect of IDV on the intent to use of a new technology, the logic proposed by [18] suggests a positive influence. Thus, the following hypothesis is proposed:

H2: Individualism (IDV) has a positive relationship with the intent to use (IU).

Masculinity (MAS). Low MAS scores correlate negatively with adoption of technology [20]. Higher MAS scores entail personal traits such as the will to follow through on goals and higher self confidence [9]. As such they are more pronounced in individuals who are more confident that they will be able to use new technology to their advantage [13].

With regards to the TAM framework, [17] argue that perceived usefulness is related to the achievement of goals and professional mobility. These are traits typical for individuals with higher MAS scores, implying that a high MAS score positively affects the effect of PU on IU. Thus the following hypothesis is proposed:

H3: Masculinity (MAS) has a positive relationship with the intent to use (IU).

Uncertainty avoidance (UAI). The UAI score indicates how a society deals with uncertainty. Societies with high uncertainty avoidance have slower national adoption rate for innovations [16]. Further, societies with low UAI scores are less open to change [9], which may manifest itself as an inherent opposition to new technology and thus have a negative impact on the intent to use [18]. The following hypothesis is tested here:

H4: Uncertainty avoidance (UAI) has a negative relationship with the intent to use (IU).

Long-term orientation (LTO). Long-term orientation is a more abstract term compared to the other dimensions. It deals with subjects such as perseverance, thrift, future rewards and how people relate to them. [21] argue in favor of the importance of LTO in technology acceptance, as well as in perceptions of usefulness of a technology. The logic here is that individuals with lower LTO scores are less able to assess the advantages of a new technology when presented with it. This leads to the following hypothesis:

H5: Long-term orientation (LTO) has a negative relationship with perceived usefulness (PU).

Perceived Substitution

According to displacement theories (e.g. [11]), consumers must find a new way to allocate their time between the different media when a challenger enters the market [15]. Moreover, the functional-equivalence hypothesis which states that consumers will prefer media that offer the same product more easily or attractively [8], suggests that this perception plays a decisive role in the process of adopting new technology. This link has support in [4], where a clear substitution effect (significant negative relations) was found between Dutch users of online newspapers and printed newspapers.

Further, new media have been found to have displacement effects on older ones (see, e.g., [10]). When a new medium provides the same functionality as an existing medium, the new one is usually preferred if the content can be offered in an easier or more attractive way [5]; [15]; [12]. An example of this can be found in [4], who found a clear substitution effect of online newspapers on printed ones.

The functional-equivalence hypothesis suggests that superior usability and accessibility can lead to the phasing out of older media. If PU and PEOU are rated highly by the respondents, these constructs are arguably synonymous to usability and accessibility, giving grounds to propose the following hypotheses:

H6: Perceived substitution (SUB) has a positive effect on perceived usefulness (PU).

H7: Perceived substitution (SUB) has a positive effect on perceived ease of use (PEOU).

H8: Perceived substitution (SUB) has a positive effect on the intent to use (IU).

METHODOLOGY
Data Collection

Data for the study came from surveys conducted in three Scandinavian countries: Denmark, Norway and Sweden. Nationally representative samples were constructed based on age, gender and geographic location.

The survey questionnaire (available from authors upon request) contained four measurement items each for PEOU and PU. Two items for IU were included. The TAM items were constructed in the tradition of the original formulation of the TAM [3], which was used for clarity and simplicity in favor of later formulations, especially given that no explicit testing of the TAM was pursued here.

Questions for the cultural constructs (PDI, IDV, MAS, UAI and LTO) were modeled on those used by Yoon (2009) and contained three items each. Perceived substitution (SUB) also contained three items, which were constructed de novo following a review of the scarce literature on substitution and reasoning.

A total of 1804 completed responses were received. The total number of respondents was 594 in Norway (90.6% response rate), 601 in Sweden (91.2%) and 609 in Denmark (85.6%).

Path Modeling

Data from the surveys were analyzed with partial least squares regression (PLS), part of the family of structural equation modeling (SEM). There are two broad ways of performing SEM: covariance-based techniques such as LISREL, and variance-based techniques, out of which PLS path modeling is the most popular [14]. SmartPLS software was used in this study.

A two-step procedure described in [1] was followed. First, to avoid making generalizations based on wrong premises, the unidimensionality of the reflective measures must be assessed. As described in [7], the unidimensionality of each latent construct is assumed to exist only a priori and cannot be measured directly with PLS. Instead, what is measured is the discriminant and convergent validity of the reflective measures. Together they make up what is known as factorial validity, describing how well the measurement items relate to the latent constructs.

Second, after factorial validity has been confirmed, the path coefficients in the model were examined and interpreted. The path coefficients are created by the bootstrapping procedure which presents the paths in t-test values [1], allowing for straightforward analysis.

Three separate models were estimated, each with data for one of the three countries in the sample.

RESULTS AND CONCLUSION

For all three countries, factor reliability as well as tests for convergent and discriminant validity were conducted. As a result, some items were dropped from the cultural, technology acceptance and substitution factors.

The complete research model and path coefficients are shown in Figure 1. In the figure path coefficients are shown for Denmark. However, the results for all three countries tell a qualitatively similar story: the influence of perceived substitution on adoption constructs, including the intent to use, is statistically significant while the influence of cultural dimensions is not.

The results of this study bring new light to what drives consumer adoption. To the best of our knowledge, this study represents the first case where perceived substitution has been set in conjunction with the TAM. Based on the increase in explained variance of the perceived usefulness, future research applying the TAM in a similar situation might include and elaborate on this latent variable. There is an obvious potential to improve the construct's factorial validity, which should contribute further to even greater explained variance.

As for the intent to use the electronic newspaper, its perceived usefulness is highly influenced by the perceived substitution effect. The more the electronic newspaper can be made to have the characteristics of a traditional newspaper, with all the benefits of online access, the better are the chances of it succeeding. This is an important theoretical contribution, especially when compared with the lack of influence of cultural factors. Clearly, electronic newspaper offers additional functionality over printed newspaper, which may lead to mass replacement of the printed newspaper with electronic one. However, previous studies in the media domain have found substitution to moderately influence adoption while being complemented by other factors [12]. By contrast, our results indicate that

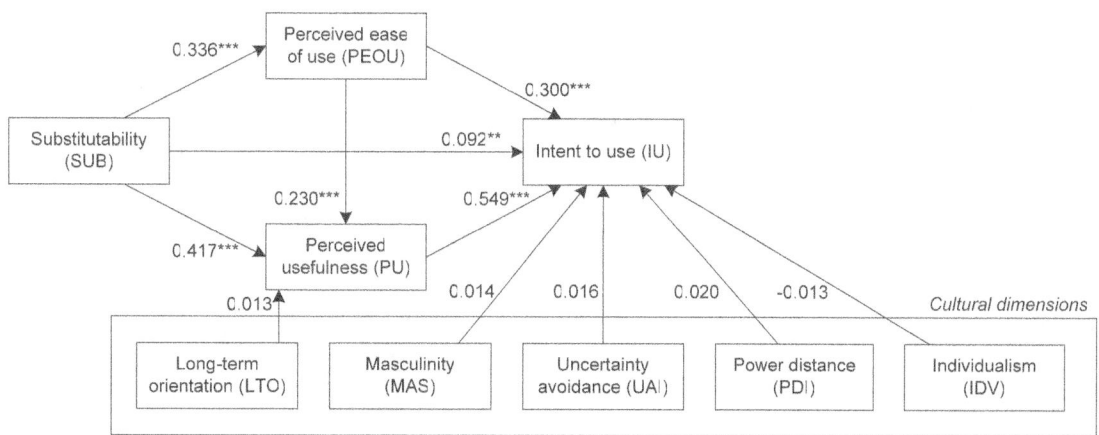

Figure 1. The research model with relationships between substitution, cultural dimensions and technology acceptance factors (path coefficients are for Denmark; $^{**}p < 0.01$; $^{***}p < 0.005$).

the intent to use of electronic newspaper is culture-invariant and is driven primarily by the desire to gain access to superior technology. This result calls for more research on the effect of perceived substitution on actual use, rather than the intent to use.

REFERENCES

1. Annear, K.D. and Yates, G.C.R. Restrictive and supportive parenting: Effects on children's school affect and emotional responses. *The Australian Educational Researcher, 37* (1). 63-82.
2. Daghfous, N., Petrof, J.V. and Pons, F. Values and adoption of innovations: a cross-cultural study. *Journal of Consumer Marketing, 16* (4). 314-331.
3. Davis, F.D. Perceived Usefulness, Perceived Ease of Use, and User Acceptance of Information Technology. *MIS Quarterly, 13* (3). 319-340.
4. De Waal, E. and Schoenbach, K. News sites' position in the mediascape: uses, evaluations and media displacement effects over time. *New Media & Society, 12* (3). 477-496.
5. Dimmick, J.W. *Media competition and coexistence: The theory of the niche.* Lawrence Erlbaum, London, UK, 2003.
6. Friedman, W. Nielsen: Mobile To Outpace Internet Growth, 2010.
7. Gefen, D. Assessing unidimensionality through LISREL: an explanation and an example. *Communications of the Association for Information Systems, 12* (1). 23-47.
8. Himmelweit, H.T., Oppenheim, A.N., Vince, P., Blumenthal, D. and Hetherington, H. *Television and the Child: An Empirical Study of the Effect of Television on the Young.* Oxford University Press, London, UK, 1962.
9. Hofstede, G. *Culture's Consequences (Second Edition): Comparing Values, Behaviors, Institutions, and Organizations Across Nations.* Sage Publications, Beverly Hills, CA, 2001.
10. Kayany, J.M. and Yelsma, P. Displacement effects of online media in the socio-technical contexts of households. *Journal of Broadcasting & Electronic Media, 44* (2). 215-229.
11. Lazarsfeld, P.F. *Radio and the printed page: An introduction to the study of radio and its role in the communication of ideas.* Duell, Sloan and Pearce, New York, NY, 1940.
12. Lin, C.A. Audience attributes, media supplementation, and likely online service adoption. *Mass Communication & Society, 4* (1). 19-38.
13. McCoy, S., Galletta, D.F. and King, W.R. Applying TAM across cultures: the need for caution. *European Journal of Information Systems, 16* (1). 81-90.
14. Ringle, C.M., Wende, S. and Will, A. SmartPLS 2.0 M3 (Beta), University of Hamburg, Germany, 2005.
15. Robinson, J.P. and Godbey, G. *Time for life: The surprising ways Americans use their time (Second Edition).* Pennsylvania State University Press, University Park, PA, 1999.
16. Shane, S. Cultural influences on national rates of innovation. *Journal of Business Venturing, 8* (1). 59-73.
17. Srite, M. and Karahanna, E. The role of espoused national cultural values in technology acceptance. *MIS Quarterly, 30* (3). 679-704.
18. Straub, D., Keil, M. and Brenner, W. Testing the technology acceptance model across cultures: A three country study. *Information & Management, 33* (1). 1-11.
19. Subramanian, G.H. A replication of perceived usefulness and perceived ease of use measurement. *Decision Sciences, 25* (5/6). 863-874.
20. Van Everdingen, Y.M. and Waarts, E. The effect of national culture on the adoption of innovations. *Marketing Letters, 14* (3). 217-232.
21. Veiga, J.F., Floyd, S. and Dechant, K. Towards modelling the effects of national culture on IT implementation and acceptance. *Journal of Information Technology, 16* (3). 145-158.
22. Venkatesh, V. and Bala, H. Technology acceptance model 3 and a research agenda on interventions. *Decision Sciences, 39* (2). 273-315.
23. Yoon, C. The effects of national culture values on consumer acceptance of e-commerce: Online shoppers in China. *Information & Management, 46* (5). 294-301.
24. Zakour, A.B., Cultural differences and information technology acceptance. in *7th Annual Conference of the Southern Association for Information Systems,* (Savannah, GA, 2004), 156-161.

A Conceptual Framework of Information Learning and Flow in Relation to Websites' Information Architecture

Ather Nawaz
Copenhagen Business School, Denmark
Howitzvej 60
an.itm@cbs.dk

ABSTRACT
Culture, information learning of users and knowledge domain shapes the experience of flow while interacting with websites' information architecture. This paper presents a conceptual framework of information learning and flow through extending person-artefact-task model. The paper attempts to relate the experience of flow when interacting with websites to information learning and website information architecture within the domain of HCI and usability.

Author Keywords
Information learning; Flow; Knowledge Acquisition; Information architecture; Human-Computer Interaction.

ACM Classification Keywords
H.5.m. Information interfaces and presentation
I.2.6. Learning

INTRODUCTION
With the adoption of technology and accessibility of a wide variety of websites worldwide, the users' conception of the website information architecture has become an important aspect of website structures. The aim of the paper is to provide an understanding that in addition to cultural background, how users' perception for information architecture is inspired by learning and usage of artefacts. Different cultures may have different levels of learning and usage of the artefacts which can impacts on the usability of the website in many ways. In addition to understanding user's cultural background, understanding the users flow can improve the usability of the websites. It is often a challenge for users to retrieve the information from the large complex websites such as e-commerce websites. The challenge may, however, not be the same in different countries and people with different information learning [1]. Yet the extraction of users' experience of flow when interacting with is a tough and challenging job. The flow and user's information learning can be understood through different factors such as users' language priority for websites, language fluency. In addition to language priority and fluency, it can be understood through users' priority for information presentation on websites and looking into the reasoning on why users perceive information into a particular order.

The experience of flow when interacting with artefacts highlights a number of abstract ideas (e.g., structure of the information in physical location). The abstract and subtle experience of things and culture shapes users thinking. The frequent visit of a grocery store can shape the people's conception of grouping in a grocery store. This experience may influence their thinking when search for grocery items on a website. The user's frequent use of websites and access to internet can also shape the users flow. An expert user who spends more time on the internet may tend to make more structured categories for website information structure in comparison to a novice user. On the other hand, these experiences are not easy to analyze. When the users search for items on a website, it can be influenced through the arrangement of items in the grocery store. From website structures perspective, it could be influenced though frequent visits of a grocery website and getting inspiration from arrangements of item on grocery store's website. Information finding skills, internet use and knowledge domain may shape a user's experience of flow when interacting with website information architecture. Information findability on a website is a kind of problem solving. It is governed by the way in which the problem solving space is structured by the users. One user may represent a problem mathematically, another visually, and still another metaphorically [2]. Understanding the users' perception of a website structure is becoming important because people are adopting e-commerce and websites to find products and services. This is associated with information learning and when interacting with websites information architectures. For example, a number of issue may arise when a novice user uses a website to search for, and buy products [3]. The lack of interaction of novice user with the website information architecture may result in finding it challenging to search for items on the website. A user may feel more challenged or captivated by searching information on a website that provides information in a single language. The person may spend more time to search for items on website structure which the user has not experienced before.

INFORMATION ARCHITECTURE AND CULTURE

The history of information architecture has evolved over a period of time. The term 'information architecture' (IA) was first used in 1976 by Richard Saul Wurman [4, 5]. The information architecture institute (IA Institute) has defined the practice of information architecture as: 1) The structural design of shared information environment; 2) The art and science of organizing and labeling web sites, intranets, online communities and software to support usability and findability [4, 6]. IA is an organization of information in such a way which can be manipulated efficiently by the users. On an abstract level, information architecture is a structure or map of information which allows others to find their personal paths to knowledge [7, 8]. Wurman describes Information architecture as a creation of structural and orderly principles to make something work [5]. Wurman defines IA generically which can be applied in different fields and genre of literatures. In this paper, we understand information architecture of websites as the placement of information on website at different levels.

National cultural differences are investigated by a number of researchers to understand to what level the users background effects on the websites [9, 10]. Kralisch and Yeo [11] investigated the impact of culture, language and medical knowledge on users' information categorization. The study suggests that whereas language predominantly affects the users' beliefs about ease of use and usefulness, culture broadly seen also influences the users' preferences in information categorization, their attitudes, and their behavior. The localization of contents not only covers the contents but it is a process of developing, tailoring and/or enhancing the capability of hardware and software to input process and output information in the language, norms and metaphors used by the community [12].

FLOW IN INFORMATION SYSTEMS

Flow is the holistic sensation which people feel when they act with a total involvement in an activity. It can be reflected through the users' exploration of searching information on a website or exploratory behavior on the internet. Flow theory has been applied to computer-mediated environments to study positive user experiences such as increased exploratory behavior, communication, learning, positive affect, and computer use [13]. The flow provides users with a view of the world within an activity to perform tasks in a certain way that they learn over a period of time through the flow. According to Csikszentmihalyi [14], a person experiencing flow, or achieving an optimal experience, will have clear goals, exercise control, lose their self-consciousness, and experience a distortion of time. In the e-commerce websites, the activities are broken into the tasks and artifacts, where tasks are the goals of activity and artifacts are the tools to complete the task. When a novice users search for an information such as a home appliance. The novice user might find it difficult to search for the information on the home appliances website and feels in the flow while using the telephone to call the company to know more information about the appliance, or newspaper advertisement that has the information of the appliance. It appears that the person do not have any problem in using the tools such as newspaper or telephone because the person has used these tools previously and feels in the flow to use it again. This assumption may not hold true when using websites to look for information. Depending on the person's experience with the websites and conception about the correct hierarchy of information architecture of products, it may differ for skillful users and novice users. The skillful users who spend more time on the internet and websites may find more flow while exploring and searching the information of an object on the websites and conversely may not find the flow when they use other means and tools to find information of an object. The person may tend to conceptualize the world in such a way which makes more sense to the previous experiences in a flow. In relation to a website, the expert users conceptualize the information and flow of information in connection to the previous website experience and the expectations are relevant to that experience. The users group the information in such a way which the users has experienced before, and the information clustering of a particular number of items is affected by the prior experience of interacting with the websites. Csikszentmihalyi [14] argues when experiencing flow 'self' becomes complex and person learns to become more than what (s)he was before. Flow model in information systems, on the contrary, is linked to activities where individuals have developed their skills efficiently enough to match challenges they are facing [15].

INFORMATION LEARNING, FLOW AND INFORMATION ARCHITECTURE

In the psychology, education and knowledge management literature, learning is commonly defined as a process which is influenced through the cognitive, environmental and contextual settings and it influences on the skills, values and word views of the users [16]. Information learning in this paper is defined as the skills and knowledge of information use that a user acquires over a period of time through studies, experiences, language, internet use and other learning. Some of these learning are explicit while other is implicit. These skills and knowledge shapes the users view of the world and help users to think about the structure of the websites in a certain way. Information finding on the websites requires some understanding and previous knowledge about the structure of the website to find the information effectively. It also takes learning and the experience of flow among the users into consideration. The learning and knowledge acquisition impacts on users' concepts and thus impact on information findability of the users [17]. Del Galdo, E., & Nielsen [18] expresses it though cultural learning differences in software user training.

PATUL – Person-artefact-task-usage and learning

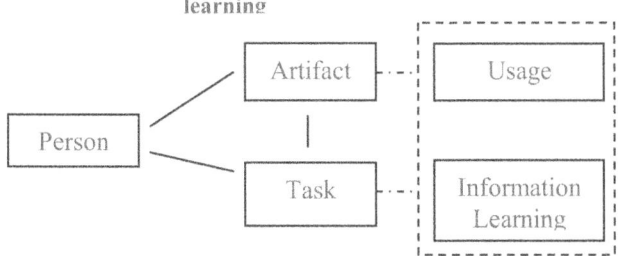

Figure 1. A person – Artefact – Task – Usage and Learning (PATUL)

The person- artefact- task-usage and learning (PATUL) (fig.1) is inspired from person-artefact task model (PAT). It is an intention to conceptualize about the person working on a computer-related activity and what factors can be influential to the flow experience of the person. The person may inspired through the previous usage of the artefact and performance of tasks [13]. A person may feel challenged and captivated by searching for information on the website that have not been experienced before. It can also be the case in the use of website languages in local language. There users find it easy to search for information on English language website because they have experienced the flow before. A native danish speaking user might find it easy to search for information in danish because he/she has experienced the danish website before. The learning and flow is anticipated for a native language speaker. The artefact plays an important role in the searching experience because artefact may influence the likelihood of an optimal experience. The task is the activity that a user performs on a website to look for information. The task may involve searching for an electrical trimmer on appliance's website or finding the contact information of the helpline for an organization on their website.

The users acquire knowledge with repeated attempts to use a system that portrays the properties similar to the one they are using. Parkinson et. al. [20] found that the time to search a menu frame and enter the response did improve with practice and learning from the practice. The practices related to the learning during the use of similar systems in their previous experience also provide users with the flow that helps in the outcome of an activity. In connection to the website use, the users' previous use of the websites and system is connected to their model of the website and its structure. The users' understanding about the structure of the websites can be understood by providing them with the website contents and ask them to sort the contents in a way which makes sense to them. By using the flow theory's approach, we can say that the users' learning and learning of the websites makes their conscious loose and improve their task time on a website to find items and information. We can collect the information related to their experience and learning though the questionnaire about the language and use of technology and websites.

CONCLUSION

This paper attempts to make a conceptual relationship between the information learning and flow by relating it to Person-artefact-task model. Regarding the learning and language, in spite of better fluency in the local language, users may prefer to use the websites in english because of their previous learning and usage of the website in the english language. It may also imply that the language fluency may not shape the choice of language of users for website. The paper provided an overview of how the information learning and usage of websites can possibly be related to each other to impact on the users flow for task performance or conceptualising information on the website. Most of the flow related studies in Information Systems are qualitative and measure the experience of the users using questionnaire. Measuring the flow itself can be challenging as it can be inspired from number of unrelated factors which users may not be able to explain or explicitly state.

REFERENCES

1. Scales, B.J. and E.B. Lindsay, *Qualitative assessment of student attitudes toward information literacy.* portal: Libraries and the Academy, 2005. **5**: p. 513-526.

2. Norman, K.L., *The psychology of menu selection: Designing cognitive control at the human/computer interface* 1991: Ablex Publishing Corporation.

3. Freudenthal, A., *The design of home appliances for young and old consumers.* 1999.

4. Mvugi, S., K.d. Jager, and P.G. Underwood, *An evaluation of the information architecture of the UCT Library web site.* South African Journal of Library & Information Science; 2008,, 2008. **Vol. 74** (Issue 2): p. p171-182, 12p.

5. Wurman, R.S., P. Bradford, and B.M. Pedersen, *Information architects* 1997: Graphis Press.

6. Institute, I. *Defining Information Architecture. Available online [http://iainstitute.org/].* 2009 June 2011].

7. Toms, E.G., *Information interaction: providing a framework for information architecture.* Journal of the American Society for Information Science and Technology, 2002. **53**(10): p. 855-862.

8. Wurman, R.S., *Information anxiety* 1989: Doubleday New York.
9. Hofstede, G.J., *Cultures and organizations: Software of the mind* 2005: McGraw-Hill Publishing Co.
10. Yeo, A. and W. Loo, *Identification and Evaluation of the Classification Schemes: A User Centred Approach.* Designing for Global Markets, 2004. **6**: p. 8-10.
11. Kralisch, A., A. Yeo, and N. Jali, *Linguistic and cultural differences in information categorization and their impact on website use*, 2006, IEEE. p. 93b.
12. Hussain, S. and R. Mohan, *Localization in Asia Pacific.* Digital Review of Asia Pacific 2007/2008, 2007: p. 43.
13. Finneran, C.M. and P. Zhang, *A person-artefact-task (PAT) model of flow antecedents in computer-mediated environments.* International Journal of Human-Computer Studies, 2003. **59**(4): p. 475-496.
14. Csikszentmihalyi, M., *The flow experience and its significance for human psychology.* 1988.
15. Karppinen, P., *Flow Models in Information Systems: Is Learning the Missing Element?*, in *The 34th Information Systems Research Seminar in Scandinavia – IRIS 2011* 2011: Turki, Finland.
16. Illeris, K., *Transformative learning in the perspective of a comprehensive learning theory.* Journal of Transformative Education, 2004. **2**(2): p. 79.
17. Vosniadou, S., *Knowledge Acquisition and Conceptual Change.* Applied Psychology, 1992. **41**(4): p. 347-357.
18. Del Galdo, E. and J. Nielsen, *International user interfaces* 1996: Wiley New York.
19. Nawaz, A., T. Clemmensen, and M. Hertzum. *Information Classification on University Websites: A Cross-Country Card Sort Study.* in *Information Systems Research Seminar in Scandinavia (IRIS)*. 2011. Turku.
20. Parkinson, S.R., N. Sisson, and K. Snowberry, *Organization of broad computer menu displays.* International Journal of Man-Machine Studies, 1985. **23**(6): p. 689-697.

Networks in Equity and Sustainability: A Preliminary Tool for Intercultural Analysis and Discussion

Arlene Ducao	Alex Simoes	Ilias Koen	Henry Holtzman	Cesar Hidalgo
MIT Media Lab	MIT Media Lab, 77	The DuKode Studio	MIT Media Lab	MIT Media Lab
77 Massachusetts Ave,	Massachusetts Ave,	166 7th Street,	77 Massachusetts Ave,	77 Massachusetts Ave,
E14/E15, Cambridge,	E14/E15, Cambridge,	Brooklyn, NY	E14/E15, Cambridge,	E14/E15, Cambridge,
MA, 02139, USA	MA, 02139, USA	11215, USA	MA, 02139, USA	MA, 02139, USA
arlduc@mit.edu	simoes@mit.edu	ikoen@dukode.com	holtzman@media.mit.edu	cesar@media.mit.edu

ABSTRACT

Some of the world's most pressing problems can be traced to inequity between people, both in the present and over time. Long periods of inequity can lead to both social and environmental degradation. In its 2011 Human Development Report (HDR), the United Nations incisively examines some of the complex relationships between socioeconomic equity and environmental sustainability. Members of the MIT Media Lab and The DuKode Studio created "Networks in Equity and Sustainability," a visualization tool that shows, via a network graph, how nations are multi-dimensionally linked. Examining linkages with this tool can illuminate potential partnerships between cultures. As the tool is expanded in the future, it will support intercultural discussions in the global effort for a world that is more equal today and more sustainable over time.

Author Keywords

United Nations; Human Development Report; network graphs; visualization; DuKode; MIT; Equality; Equity; Sustainability.

ACM Classifications

H.5.m. [Information Systems]: Information interfaces and presentation (I.7)] – Miscellaneous;

General Terms

Human Factors; Design; Economics.

INTRODUCTION

The United Nations' annual Human Development Report (HDR) provides a wide array of data that compares nations in several major dimensions. This data includes nation-by-nation information on income, gender, education, poverty, health, birth rates, mortality rates, and environmental sustainability. Each year, HDR also provides a comprehensive series of analytic articles based on a timely theme. The HDR 2011 theme is *Sustainability and Equity: A Better Future for All* [1]. The HDR's articles make the compelling point that sustainability and equity must be addressed together, for sustainability is the same as equity over generations. Unsurprisingly, the world's most disadvantaged people suffer the most in terms of both environmental sustainability (resource depletion) and economic equity. However, the HDR highlights positive synergies within and between nations working to improve systems that support sustainability and equity.

The handful of example synergies highlighted in the HDR were our starting point as we developed "Networks in Equity and Sustainability" [2] (Figure 1), a tool to visualize important dimensions of the HDR 2011 dataset. Inspired by these synergies, we aim to make a tool that could highlight both actual and potential synergies between nations, via nearest neighbors in a network graph. For each nation, we show the most similarly performing nations in sustainability, economic equity, gender equity, and income. In showing nearest neighbors, we want to suggest both predictable and unexpected intersections for intercultural exchange between nations working to improve and sustain human development. In addition to highlighting potential inter-nation synergies, we also present ways to examine larger regional and continental patterns through a system of data-activation switches.

PRECEDENTS

The UN HDR includes detailed datasets and calculations printed pages of the HDR document. While deeply extensive, these documents do not dynamically show relationships for any given country. As a result, interested parties must spend time sorting through the printed to find specific countries and extrapolate specific relationships. In recent years, the UN HDR has included an interactive online component [3,4]. Most of these components have had limited interactivity, allowing limited access to nation-by-nation and relational data.

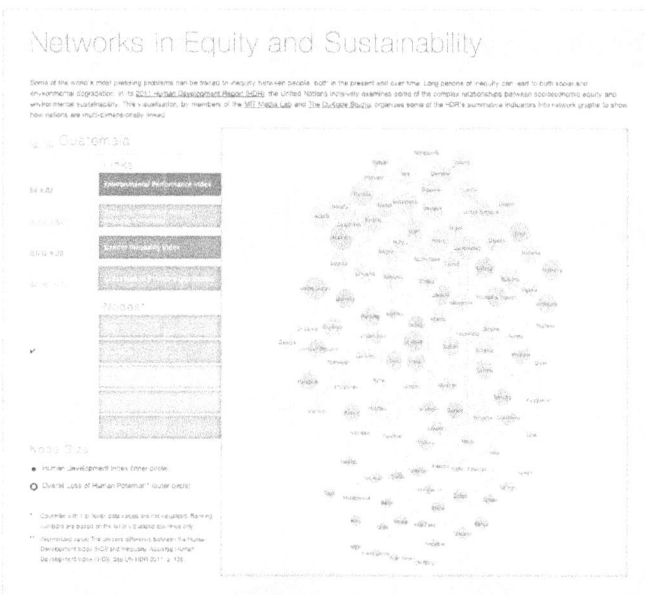

Figure 1. Visualization Screenshot.

The UN HDR 2011 presents a highly extensive, flexible set of data tools and visualizations for analyzing many facets of HDR data [5]. These tools are particularly useful for examining detailed information on individual countries, examining large global patterns, and examining time-based changes in long-lived UN HDR indicators (human development, education, health, and income). While these tools provide much information, they do not provide visually intuitive relational data between countries, especially for newer UN HDR indicators like the Environmental Performance Index.

The web site Visualizing.org [6], a repository of data visualizations sponsored by General Electric and the Seed Media Group [7], recently held a competition for visualizations of UN HDR 2011 data. Our visualization, which was entered in this competition, is unique in presenting relational data for a number of key indices and indicators, including the new Environmental Performance Index.

CONSTRUCTION AND USER INTERFACE

"Networks in Equity and Sustainability" was constructed using HTML, CSS, SVG, and d3.js [8], a Javascript library that allows for fast-performing, vector-based, data-driven documents. The d3 Force module is primarily used to construct a network graph of colored nodes, colored links, and spatial sorting.

UN HDR Data is visualized as follows: Countries are represented by nodes. Node size is represented by an inner and outer circle: the inner circle maps to the Human Development Index, and the outer circle maps to Overall Loss in Human Potential (the percent difference between the Human Development Index (HDI) and Inequality-Adjusted Human Development Index (IHDI)) [9]. Node color is segmented by continent.

4 link colors are mapped to the Environmental Performance Index (EPI), Inequality-Adjusted Human Development Index (IHDI), Gender Inequality Index (GII), and Gross National Income (GII). The IHDI index is adjusted by the Multidimensional Poverty Index of health, education, and living standards. Users can activate 1 or more link types and can activate 1 or more country colors.

Of the UN HDR datasets, those chosen for this visualization were selected to reflect composite calculations for equity, sustainability, gender, development, and income. Of the chosen metrics, a higher number indicates a comparatively positive status. The only exception is the Gender Inequality Index (GII), in which lower numbers indicate positive status. Some of the metrics are too new to analyze temporally; for instance, the Environmental Performance Index was first calculated in 2010. As a result, this visualization is not time-based. Also, countries with one or fewer data values are not visualized.

In addition to toggling links and continents, users can see a nation's nearest neighbors for any activated link type by rolling the cursor over that nation's node (Figure 2). A nation's next-smaller neighbor is indicated by a thick line, while its next-larger neighbor is indicated by a thin line. Rolling the cursor over a nation's node also result in a display of specific data values and rankings for every indicator (EPI, IHDI, GII, and GNI) being visualized. Ranking numbers are based on the list of visualized countries only.

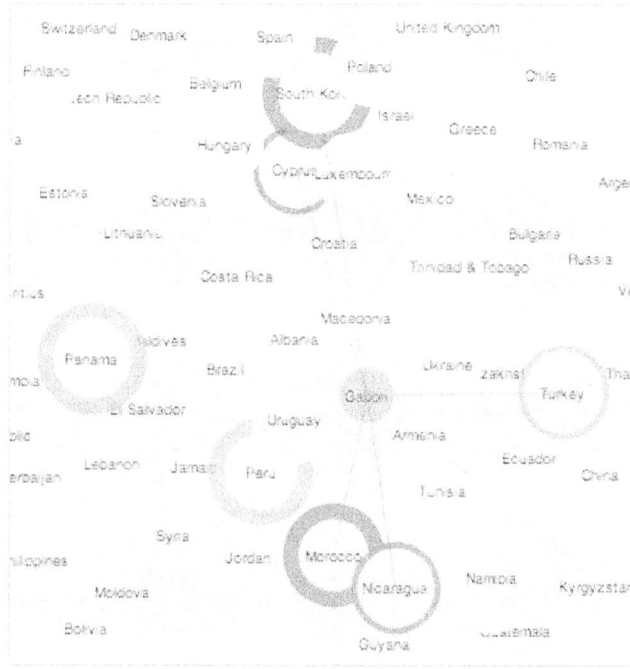

Figure 2: Node with Nearest Neighbors Highlighted.

EXAMPLE USE CASES

National-, regional-, and subject-based practitioners can use the "Networks" visualization tool to spark research or even just simple conversations in an intercultural setting:

1) Practitioners focused on a particular nation can activate all network links (edges) to see a nation's nearest neighbors in all of the visualized indices (i.e. Figure 2 above).

2) Practitioners focused on a particular region can toggle node colors on/off for countries in a specific continent.

3) Practicioners in a particular subject—for instance, environmental sustainability—can activate relevant network links (edges) to see the linear progression and nation-neighbors of a particular index.

FUTURE WORK

One apparent feature for increasing collaboration and communication with this tool is to implement mechanisms for user input, comments, and discussion. As new indices mature, a time-based element can be added to the visualization as well. Currently, we are discussing the advantages of adding gameplay to the visualization system in order to incentivize potential users to participate.

We are also interested in integrating non-UN data that more broadly reflects culture and living situations. This includes language, religion, and climate data. Datasets currently being explored include the UNESCO Interactive Atlas of the World's Languages in Danger [10].

Next steps for this visualization include user testing with diverse human development professionals to evaluate the use of this tool for intercultural collaboration. The ACM ICIC and the United Nations may be relevant settings for these tests. During the tests, it will be important to examine what kinds of intercultural questions are best explored by this visualization tool.

ACKNOWLEDGMENTS

We thank CHI, ICIC volunteers, all publications support and staff, our colleagues at MIT Media Lab and DuKode, and additional colleagues who provided feedback.

REFERENCES

1. UN Human Development Report 2011. Available at http://hdr.undp.org/en/reports/global/hdr2011/

2. Networks in Equity and Sustainability. Available at http://hdr.media.mit.edu/.

3. UN Human Development Report 2009. Available at http://hdr.undp.org/en/reports/global/hdr2009/

4. UN Human Development Report 2007-08. Available at http://hdr.undp.org/en/reports/global/hdr2007-8/

5. UN HDR Data Tools and Visualizations. Available at http://hdr.undp.org/en/statistics/

6. Visualizing.org. Available at http://www.visualizing.org/

7. Seed Media Group. Available at http://seedmediagroup.com/

8. d3.js. Available at http://mbostock.github.com/d3/

9. UN HDR 2011, p. 138. Available at http://hdr.undp.org/en/media/HDR_2011_EN_Complete.pdf

10. UNESCO Interactive Atlas of the World's Languages in Danger. Available at http://www.unesco.org/culture/languages-atlas/

Cultural Differences across Governmental Website Design

Nitesh Goyal
Cornell University
ngoyal@cs.cornell.edu

William Miner
Cornell University
wgm6@cornell.edu

Nikhil Nawathe
Cornell University
ngn9@cornell.edu

ABSTRACT
In this paper, we study the relevance of Hall and Hofstede's works to the web design beyond traditional domain areas like e-commerce, and advertising. Existing theories explain how design may be affected by cultural differences, and we explore how those differences can be seen in the government website design across Brazil, Russia, India, China, and US. We describe our findings confirming that differences exist, more so between China and US than the rest, and point out where cultural theories fail to explain the results, in particular for Brazil, Russia and India and finally, focus more on the differences between China and US.

Author Keywords
Culture; website design; design.

ACM Classification Keywords
H.5.2 [Information Interfaces And Presentation]: User Interfaces - Interaction styles;

General Terms
Human Factors; Design; Measurement.

INTRODUCTION
In 2001, Jim O'Neil, the chairman of Goldman Sachs, coined the acronym "BRIC". Expanded as "Brazil, Russia, India, and China" [13], the term is used to group four of the world's largest and fastest growing economies. By the year 2012, the world's population is expected to crest the 7 billion mark [16]. Almost 45% of these people are projected to live in BRIC countries [9]. As these countries continue to technologically develop, their presence and influence on the Internet will continue to grow.

Currently, the Internet is a decidedly western system. While, over 50% of the World Wide Web is written in English, only 27% of Internet users speak English as a first language [6]. These users, come from diverse geographic, ethnic, and cultural backgrounds and undoubtedly, expect different things and interact with the web in different ways. Many theories suggest that people behave differently in different situations due to their established cultural identity. Hofstede's "Software of the Mind" theory [8] and Halls' theory [7] discuss the implications of cultural backgrounds.

In this paper we explore how these cultural differences affect the visual and informational design of the websites. More specifically, we are interested in how the design of the websites by the Governments of different cultures appears different.

This cross-cultural analysis of websites is in the form of a visual structural comparison of a single genre of websites. In other words, we compare different webpages of a single genre: Government websites and look if there are distinctive differences that correspond to the culture of the origin country. These comparisons involve multiple entities like the colors, the information flow, the navigational structure, and other elements described later.

This paper evaluates the validity of some of the established cultural theories as a source of explanation of how these cultural differences are reflected in the Government's designers' perspectives of the website designs of publicly accessible websites, hosted by the Governments. Hence, the contribution of this work is to discuss the variance of content layout, navigational structure, and use of multimedia elements across Governmental websites of five countries: Brazil, Russia, India, China, and US.

STUDY OF CULTURE IN WEB DESIGN
There has been some work in the direction of cross-cultural website visual layout comparison. For example Zhang et al. [17] puts forward design principles of Chinese websites by focusing on the following three graphic design language characteristics: systematic relationship equilibrium and symmetry; line is grace and curve is force; and unification of form change and stability. Cyr et al. [5] focused on color treatments across three culturally distinct viewer groups for their impact on user trust, satisfaction, and e-loyalty. To gather data, a rich multi-method approach was used including eye tracking, a survey, and interviews.

Marcus and Alexander [11] derived five cultural dimensions and design components based on questionnaires. Overall, they gave an understanding of the relationships linking the amount of white space, color, layout and imagery for specific countries when designing websites. In an article by Cook & Finlayson [3], the authors speak about the fact that different types of websites (e.g. news, social networks, business, etc.) should have different design principles after factoring in culture. Kim and Kuljis [10] focused on an investigation of web site design differences between two very different cultures (South Korea and United Kingdom). This article also looked at how the "collectivist" nature of the Korean society was reflected on their web bulletin boards.

Barber and Badre [1] devised a set of "cultural markers" in web design that can be used to describe the difference in design. Building on this, Zhao [18] conducted a comparative analysis of websites originating in China and United States. The measures took two categories, "design measures" and "content measures". The content measures evaluated things such as personalization (e.g. use of words such as 'I', 'my', 'you' and 'your"), organizational history, and organizational achievements. The design measures evaluated things such as low- and high-context communication (e.g. how direct or explicit the communication methods were). Overall, these articles and others like it provide a solid framework to build a relevant and robust evaluation method.

Following on the possibility of personalization is the ability to change and choose specific language as the mode of communication between the website owner or designer and the viewers. Besides the choice of the languages available in a website, quality is also an important factor for the language translation from the originally intended to the localized version for the users. Robbins and Stylianou [14] found that the Latin American websites studied by them offered a translation into at least one international language, while a much lower number from the websites studied from US/Canada offered a translation into another language.

The layout of the webpage elements like banners, menu placement, or search functions has been shown to vary according to the cultures. Marcus and Gould [12] have shown that organization and location of the pictorial information on a webpage can be related to the direction of the written script of the readers. Further, Sun [15] has found that low-context cultures like Germany prefer a structured and a logical layout, much like France as shown by Barber and Badre [1], which prefers a centered layout.

The Hall's dimensions can be further used to show the richness of communication media chosen by different cultures to exchange information online. High context cultures can be expected to prefer multiple, personal or richer modes of communication like face-to-face or online video, audio chat or telephone. On the other hand, low context cultures can be expected to use lesser personal mode of communication like e-mails. Robbins and Stylianou [14] have found significant difference between the Nordic countries (lower-context) and Japanese (higher-context) in choice of e-mail as the preferred mode of communication. Nordic countries were shown to have a higher preference (100%) for e-mails than Japan (80%).

Bernard [2] has shown that a clear and facilitated path to information using navigational aids or navigational structure is important for users to not get lost on the websites. This ties well with Hofstede's dimension of uncertainty avoidance, as evidenced by Marcus and Gould [12]. According to him, users from a high uncertainty avoidance culture would be unable to accept and deal with the unstructured, and unfamiliar information, norms, and rules. Thus, they would require a structured navigational layout, with navigational aides, of the websites. Conversely, low uncertainty avoidance cultures will be lesser affected by the lack of navigational structures and aides.

Marcus and Gould [12] have found that materialistic culture designers are more likely to use graphics and multimedia. This may be connected with Hofstede's dimension of masculinity as described by Cyr [4]. According to her, the more masculine societies would prefer more multimedia while lesser masculine societies would prefer lesser multimedia elements like videos, sound, or animation.

METHOD

We chose to study BRIC countries (Brazil, Russia, India, and China) and compare them with US because of their growing economic clout, and subsequently the increasing use of Internet across these countries at a rate higher than the rest of the world. It is, hence, imperative to understand the implications of design decisions made by the Government, and how they perceive their websites should look for the consumption by not just the users in those countries but also the expat population.

There are multiple reasons for choosing Government websites: Firstly, governments are empowered and may have the necessary financial freedom to create and maintain the websites. Secondly, government websites reflect a single genre of website designs which aim at information dissemination to the citizens of the respective countries. Thirdly, while it cannot be said with complete surety, it is highly likely that the government websites will not be outsourced for creation to external countries/cultures due to the sensitive nature of the information and for internal information control and security.

Next we created a coding scheme to extract relevant information from the raw data sources. The coding scheme is based on the one described by Cyr et al [17] and extended with other variables like number of pictures, and use of currency symbols. For easier data handling, the 45 metrics were classified into 8 categories: Language, Layout, Symbols, Content Structure, Navigation, Links, Multimedia and Color. Three Websites from three countries: Germany, Canada, and Japan were used as the training coding set by the 2 coders. The inter coder reliability, Chronbach's Alpha was found to be high (0.93). Next we looked for a set of 10 websites from each country belonging to the same departments/ministries of the government to hold the validity in the data set. The categories are Main portal, President's page, Supreme Court's page, Congress/Senate/Parliament/Upper House, Treasury/Finance, Department of State/Foreign Affairs, Military, Commerce, Tourism, and Education. Of all the multiple departments held by the governments, only a few had a functional website. Thus, we chose these common 10 departments, which had a webpage and could be compared with each other. The results of coding these five countries (50 webpages) are shared next.

RESULTS AND DISCUSSION

Figure 1 Count of Images (left) and Links (right)

As shown in Fig 1, China leads in the number of images used across the web pages. The higher context cultures depend upon the verbal and non-verbal cues to communicate effectively, represented by higher number of non-textual elements like images. China is categorized as high context culture, and the Fig1 (left) agrees with it. US on the other hand is categorized as low context culture, also evident from Fig 1 (left) with lower number of images. However, while Brazil, Russia, and India are higher-context cultures, the number of images the Government in these countries uses to communicate with its citizens is much lower to agree with this classification, unlike the results from Zhao [18]. Same holds for the number of internal links on a page seems to be far higher in China and Brazil vs. Russia, USA, and India. This could be because of growing westernization of the cultures, and reflecting in the design.

While Brazil, Russia, and India do not completely fit the suggested classification, China provides the strongest differences, most notably against USA. Brazil and Russia have English translations of their websites translated using Google and reflect the original layout, agreeing with Robbins and Stylianou [14]. China has websites reflecting the US website structure for their English versions, significantly different from the Chinese version, as shown in Fig 2. We believe that this is an important evidence to show how one culture (Chinese) finds it imperative to change its look to control the perception by others. On the other hand, it might be possible that the English webpage is newer and is hence designed using newer technologies. However, both the websites show the usage of exactly the same technologies: HTML, CSS, AJAX, and FLASH.

Figure 2 Comparing China's Chinese and English websites

The amount of uncertainty avoidance explains the difference in the number of nested tables and links in Chinese websites as compared to USA. In Figure 3, it is evident from the information architecture map of the main Government website of US & China, that US website prefers a different navigational structure than Chinese websites from the sparse Blue-dots representing links on a page, no tables represented by red-colored dots, scarcer images represented by pink dots. While this ties well with Bernard [2] and Marcus and Gould [12], does this reflect the Chinese Government's wish to communicate with its citizens using a relatively complicated and highly uncertain navigational structure as opposed to a simpler one in US?

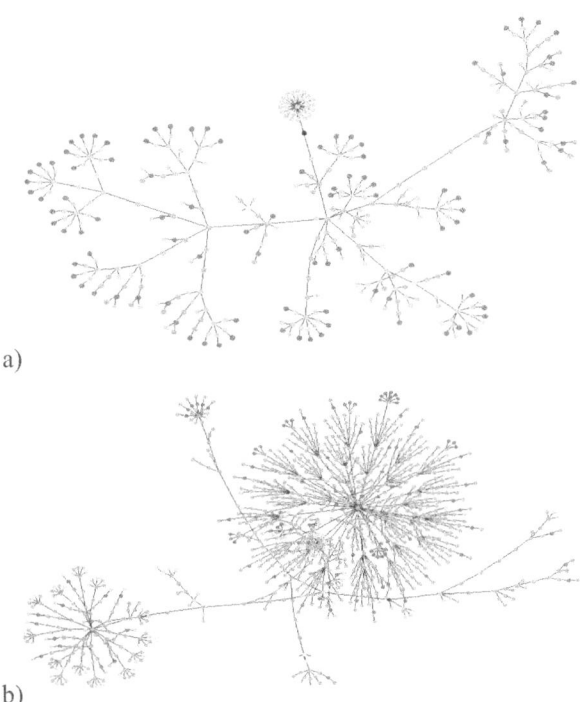

Figure 3 Navigational Structure and Linkage between US (a) and China (b), links being Blue, Tables being Red, Images being Pink, and <Div> tags being Green

In high context cultures, higher bandwidth is needed to communicate. One can see this difference in the quantity and nature of information on the main portal of the Chinese and US Government, As shown in Figure 4, it is evident that US websites are shorter in length and give more specific textual information, compared to a longer length of links, providing a much lower context.

Figure 4 Comparison of left-rotated main portal of USA (left) vs. China (right) in terms of amount of text, and nature of text

CONCLUSION

In this paper we have shown how Hall and Hofstede's work can be used to compare website designs across governmental websites across multiple cultures and explain the differences, like information architecture and multiple language versions, that exist between them and found the strongest differences between Chinese and US government websites as compared to the other countries. Also, some other differences like use of images, and links have not found a suitable explanation in the previous research and needs further probing.

LIMITATIONS AND FUTURE WORK

We gathered our data from a restricted data set of 10 Government websites per country. So, one must be cautious when generalizing beyond the same. Also, the data has been collected only from the websites. This means that we cannot be completely sure about the culture and value system of the designers – while it is highly likely that the cultures and values should be compatible due to security issues. To counter this, we would like to do user studies with designers from China and USA and derive from interviews how the website designs might vary. Finally, we restricted our work to find explanation in Hall and Hofstede's works, ignoring to draw on the greater body of research to base our claims in explaining the differences, which we would like to pursue in future.

ACKNOWLEDGEMENTS

We would like to thank Gilly Leshed and Eric Baumer for their constant guidance and help with editing previous versions.

REFERENCES

1. Barber, W. & Badre, A.N. Culturability: The merging of culture and usability. in 4th Conference on Human Factors and the Web, 1998
2. Bernard, M. Criteria for optimal web design (designing for usability), 2002. Available: http://psychology.wichita.edu/optimalweb/print.htm
3. Cook, J. & Finlayson, M. The Impact of Cultural Diversity on Website Design. Advanced Management Journal, 70(3), 15–23, 2005
4. Cyr, D., Trevor-Smith, H. Localization of web design: an empirical comparison of German, Japanese, and US website characteristics. Journal of the American Society for Information Science and Technology 55 (13), 1–10, 2004
5. Cyr, D., Head, M., and Larios, H. Colour appeal in website design within and across cultures: A multi-method evaluation. International Journal of Human Computer Studies. 68, 1-2, (2010, January)
6. "Distribution of languages on the Internet". Retrieved from http://www.netz-tipp.de/languages.html, 2002
7. Hall, E. & Hall, M. Understanding cultural differences. ME: Intercultural Press, 1990.
8. Hofstede, G. (1991). Cultures and Organizations: Software of the mind (1991). McGrawHill, New York, 1991
9. Internet Usage Statistics, 2010, December 12. Retrieved from http://www.internetworldstats.com/stats.htm
10. Kim, I. & Kuljis J. Manifestations of Culture in Website Design. Journal of Computing and Information Technology, Vol 18, No 2, 2007
11. Marcus, A. & Alexander, C. User validation of cultural dimensions of a website design. In Proceedings of the 2nd international conference on Usability and internationalization(UI-HCII'07), Nuray Aykin (Ed.). Springer-Verlag, Berlin, Heidelberg, 160-167, 2007
12. Marcus, A., & Gould, E.W. Cultural dimensions and global web user-interface design. Interactions, July/August, 33-46, 2000
13. O'Neill, J. Building better global economic BRICs. Global economics paper 66. The Goldman Sachs Group, New York, 2001
14. Robbins, S.S. & Stylianou, A.C. Global corporate web sites: an empirical investigation of content and design. Information and Management, 40, 205-212, 2002
15. Sun, H. Building a culturally-competent corporate web site: An explanatory study of cultural markers in multilingual web design. SIGDOC '01,October 21-24, 95-102, 2001
16. World Population: 1950-2050. U.S. Census Bureau, Population Division (2010, December). Retrieved from http://www.census.gov/ipc/www/idb/worldpopgraph.php
17. Zhang, Y., Huang, X., and Wang, H. Computer-Human Interaction: The Principles of User Interface in Chinese Website Design. In Proceedings of the 2009 International Conference on Multimedia Information Networking and Security - Volume 02 (MINES '09), Vol. 2. IEEE Computer Society, Washington, DC, USA, 46-49, 2009
18. Zhao, W., Massey, B.L., Murphy, J. and Liu, F. Cultural dimensions of web site design and content. Prometheus, Vol. 21 No. 1, pp. 75-84, 200

Detecting Value Differences behind Intercultural Meetings

Naomi Yamashita
NTT Communication Science Labs.
Kyoto, Japan
+81 774 93 5115
naomiy@acm.org

Hideaki Kuzuoka
University of Tsukuba
Ibaraki, Japan
+81 29 853 5258
kuzuoka@iit.tsukuba.ac.jp

ABSTRACT
Even when people participate in the same meeting and reach a consensus, their interpretations of its content might be quite different due to different cultural backgrounds, roles, values, and so on. This could be problematic later when people realize that discrepancies exist between their recognized roles and others' expectations; they might have different understandings and/or priorities. It would be quite beneficial if we could notice such differences soon after meetings. In this paper, we propose a method that enables us to detect such discrepancies among attendees.

Author Keywords
Detection method; values; meetings; preferences; expectations

ACM Classification Keywords
H.5.3 [**Group and Organization Interfaces**]: Computer-supported cooperative work.

General Terms
Human Factors; Measurement.

INTRODUCTION
According to Geert Hofstede [1], the core of culture is formed by values, which he defines as "broad tendencies to prefer certain states of affairs over others." However, since values cannot be discussed or directly observed by outsiders [1], research exploring the values of various cultures tends to be conceptual and/or discussed only at the "style" level rather than the "content" level. For example, CSCW/HCI/CMC researchers have explored how value differences between collectivism and individualism are reflected in participant communication patterns and how different media affect those patterns [2].

While such previous research has deepened our understanding of intercultural communication and the effects of various technologies on it, it cannot identify which meeting content is subject to value differences among meeting attendees. Detecting where and how the interpretations of meeting attendees differed would be quite beneficial.

In this paper, we propose a method that detects the different values held by attendees about meeting contents. The method's basic idea is that all attendees take minutes of the same meeting and generate a prioritized ToDo list for themselves as well as expected ToDo lists for all other attendees. Since the prioritized ToDo lists reflect each attendee's values (i.e., how they emphasize each of the things discussed in the meeting), comparing the prioritized ToDo lists among meeting attendees allows us to identify how each attendee interpreted the meeting. The expected lists of the other attendees help us spot the discrepancies between an attendee's self-recognition and the expectations of others.

Note that the purpose of our study is *not* to identify the causes of different interpretations among meeting attendees. They might be caused by a mixture of factors, including differences in cultural and organizational norms, second-language abilities, personalities, and so on. Instead of providing attendees with general ideas for avoiding misunderstandings (e.g., teaching the differences in their collaboration styles based on cultural differences), we provide attendees with feedback about how other attendees actually interpreted the meeting contents and what expectations they placed on other attendees. By providing meeting attendees with such feedback, they will have a chance to discuss and accommodate their recognitions before problems occur.

In the remainder of our paper, we explain the details of our method and report a pilot study that investigated the value differences between two meeting attendees. Our method effectively detected value differences, even when their meeting minutes were very similar to each other, because their ToDo lists sometimes appeared quite different from the ToDo list expected from the other attendee.

In future work, we will implement a system that allows meeting attendees to easily capture the differences between their minutes as well as their ToDo lists. We will further investigate how to resolve such discrepancies between meeting attendees. As we accumulate instances of many meetings and analyze the similarities/differences between people's values, we hope this bottom-up and contents-based approach adds a fresh dimension to tackle intercultural collaboration.

Permission to make digital or hard copies of all or part of this work for personal or classroom use is granted without fee provided that copies are not made or distributed for profit or commercial advantage and that copies bear this notice and the full citation on the first page. To copy otherwise, or republish, to post on servers or to redistribute to lists, requires prior specific permission and/or a fee.
ICIC'12, March 21–23, 2012, Bengaluru, India.
Copyright 2012 ACM 978-1-4503-0818-2/12/03...$10.00.

PROPOSED METHOD

Many values are basically unconscious to those who hold them. Therefore, "values cannot be discussed, nor can they be directly observed by outsiders. They can only be inferred from the way people act under various circumstances [1]." If so, how can we detect differences in people's values?

Our method attempts to bring them to the surface by having meeting attendees (1) prioritize their tasks and (2) clarify their expectations of other attendees. By looking through each member's prioritized ToDo lists, we can infer what items are valued by each attendee. Furthermore, by comparing each attendee's prioritized ToDo list with those expected by other attendees, we can identify the discrepancies between the attendee's self-recognition and others' expectations.

Note that the different values spotted by our method cannot be detected by analyzing meeting conversations. Our method incorporates two factors that are rarely discussed in meetings: priority among the topics discussed in multiple meetings and attendees' expectations of other attendees.

Priority among Multiple Projects/Tasks

The prioritized ToDo lists contain not only the topics discussed in a single meeting but also those discussed in other meetings: other tasks/projects being handling over the same period. By taking multiple projects into account, a prioritized ToDo list reflects how the list holder values certain items over others (Figure 1).

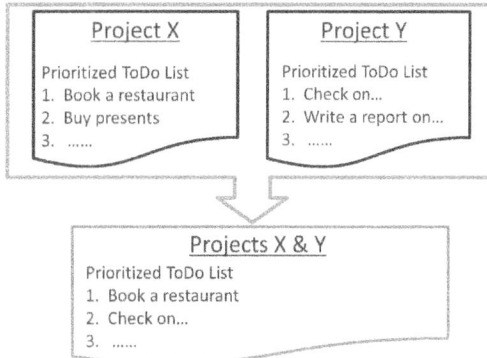

Figure 1. Eliciting values through prioritized ToDo lists of concurrently running projects/tasks

Inclusion of Others' Expectations

Since people rarely discuss their priorities among multiple projects, it is usually difficult to assess the priorities of other attendees. Certain things discussed in a meeting might even be forgotten if they are valued low. However, when people reach a consensus in a meeting, they tend to act as if they also shared their values and expect that other attendees will act according to their estimations.

Our method detects such discrepancies between meeting attendees (e.g., attendees A and B) by comparing A's prioritized list with B's expectation of A's prioritized list (Figure 2).

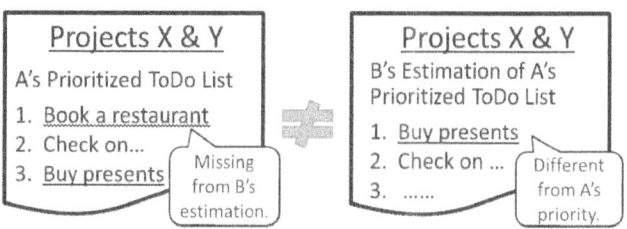

Figure 2. Detecting discrepancies between values by comparing their prioritized ToDo lists

Novelty of our Method

Most intercultural/cross-cultural studies have generally taken one of three approaches: ethnographic, psychological (i.e., controlled experiments [2] or scenario-based studies [3]), or data mining [4] (i.e., comparing communication patterns between populations). The biggest difference among these approaches and our method is that ours allows meeting attendees to realize the differences/problems themselves, but the previous approaches involved an outsider as an analyst. Furthermore, our method does not form a hypothesis like in the psychological studies. Nor does it require attendees to participate in regular communication tasks (e.g., map navigation tasks) like in the data mining approach.

PILOT STUDY

In our pilot study, we explored the potential of our proposed method to see if prioritized ToDo lists serve as an index to detect value differences between meeting attendees. As an initial trial, we studied meetings between two people.

Participants

Four pairs (three Malaysia-Japan pairs and one Cambodia-Japan pair) of students of the University of Tsukuba were recruited and paid for their participation. Since the Malaysian and Cambodian participants had been living in Japan for more than four years and were daily exposed to Japanese, they could clearly understand everyday conversations and reading/writing tasks in Japanese.

Study Overview

The pilot study consisted of three phases:

In the first phase, participants answered demographic questionnaires including their cultural backgrounds (e.g., countries they were raised and places they've lived) and language use (e.g., their native languages and second-language fluency).

In the second phase, pairs sat across the table and discussed the role sharing of two fictional projects:

Project 1 [Report Assignment]: Pairs must hand in a report in ten days. In the report, pairs must present the findings of the elder-care situations in their home countries and evaluate the similarities/differences.

Project 2 [Party Planning]: Pairs must plan a Christmas party in ten days to promote exchange between Japanese and international students. The

male-female ratio and Japanese-foreigner ratio were both fifty-fifty.

Participants were given 30 minutes to discuss the specific tasks for each project and to decide on the division of roles. During the discussion, they were allowed to take notes but were told to not share them with their partners.

In the final phase after the discussion, participants answered post-task questionnaires about their priorities in their ToDo lists and their expectations of their partners.

Prioritized ToDo Lists

In the post-task questionnaires, participants (i) itemized the main points discussed in the meeting (i.e., summarized their minutes) based on their notes, (ii) listed their responsibilities within ten days in preferential order (i.e., their own prioritized ToDo lists including both projects), and (iii) listed the things they think that their partners have to do within ten days by order of importance (i.e., an estimated prioritized ToDo list of their partners including both projects). Last, participants were asked about their confidence in their estimations and guessed how well their partners would estimate their prioritized ToDo lists.

RESULTS

To determine whether our method detected the value differences between pairs, we took the following steps: First, we compared their minutes to see if there were any comprehension problems; if the minutes differed substantially, perhaps misunderstandings or language issues existed in grasping the main points of the discussion. Second, we compared each participant's prioritized ToDo list with the prioritized ToDo list estimated by his/her partner.

Concordance Rate of Minutes within Pairs

To evaluate the similarities/discrepancies between the minutes of the pairs, we calculated the concordance rates in each pair (participants A and B) and categorized each item in the minutes as "matched" or "unmatched" to reflect whether it was contained in their partner's minutes. Then we calculated the concordance rate based on the following formula:

$$\text{Concordance Rate between A and B} = \frac{(\text{\# of matched items in A's list}) + (\text{\# of matched items in B's list})}{(\text{\# of items in A's list}) + (\text{\# of items in B's list})}$$

Note that the numbers of matched items in A's list and in B's list are not exactly the same when the granularity is different; for example, an item in A's list might correspond to two items in B's list.

Table 1 shows the concordance rate of the minutes in each pair. The first and second rows show the concordance rate of the minutes for report assignment and party planning. The third row shows the concordance rate for all the meeting minutes for each pair.

Table 1. Concordance rate of minutes in each pair (M: Malaysian, C: Cambodian, J: Japanese)

	M-J 1	M-J 2	M-J 3	C-J
Report Assignment	0.98	0.92	0.9	0.79
Party Planning	0.77	1	0.87	0.86
Overall	**0.85**	**0.96**	**0.88**	**0.83**

The results in Table 1 show that, in most cases, the items recognized as key points by meeting attendees were also considered key points by their partners. However, we can also see some small discrepancies in the presence/absence of items about deadlines, the need to reach others, and alternative ways to achieve their goals.

Concordance Rate between Self-aware ToDo List and Partner-estimated ToDo List within Pairs

Attendee A's self-aware ToDo list must meet the expectations of his/her partner B's estimated ToDo list. Without the order of priorities, a problem could occur if an item expected by B doesn't appear on A's ToDo list.

To find out the chances for such instances, we calculated the concordance rate of self-aware ToDo lists and partner-estimated ToDo lists within pairs. Similar to the calculations of the concordance rate between minutes, we categorized each item on a participant's ToDo list into either "matched" or "unmatched" depending on whether it was contained in his/her partner's estimated ToDo list. Then we calculated the concordance rate based on the previously noted formula.

Table 2 shows the concordance rate between self-aware and partner-estimated ToDo lists within pairs. The first row shows the concordance rate between a Malaysian/Cambodian participant's estimated ToDo list and his/her Japanese partner's ToDo list for report assignment. The second row corresponds to the concordance rate between a Japanese participant's ToDo list and his/her Malaysian/Cambodian partner's estimated ToDo list for report assignment). The third and fourth rows show the concordance rates of the ToDo lists for party planning.

Table 2. Concordance rate between self-aware and partner-estimated ToDo lists in each pair ([R.A.]: Report Assignment, [P.P.]: Party Planning)

	M-J 1	M-J 2	M-J 3	C-J
M or C's estimated list vs. J's list [R.A.]	0.71	0.75	0.5	0.39
J's estimated list vs. M or C's list [R.A.]	0.71	0.75	0.5	0.39
M or C's estimated list vs. J's list [P.P.]	0.38	0.71	0.35	0.4
J's estimated list vs. M or C's list [P.P.]	0.38	0.67	0.35	0.5
Average	**0.55**	**0.72**	**0.43**	**0.42**

By comparing the concordance rates between the minutes (Table 1) and ToDo lists (Table 2), we conclude that the concordance rates between the self-aware and partner-estimated ToDo lists were much lower than the concordance rate between the minutes. Even though pairs reached a consensus in their meetings and had relatively good understanding of the discussions (i.e., the concordance rates of the minutes were relatively high), the future actions of the participants reflected in their ToDo lists were quite different from those expected by their partners.

When focusing on different items between self-aware and partner-estimated ToDo lists, we realized that two types of items caused discrepancies: (a) self-aware ToDo items that were not recognized by partners, and (b) partner-estimated ToDo items that were not recognized by themselves. The latter case is more problematic than the former because failing to meet the expectations of others could breed distrust. Exceeding the expectations of others is less problematic, although it could also be frustrating in some cases.

To investigate how much participants failed to meet the expectations of others, we classified each item into the (a) or (b) classes discussed above and calculated the ratio between them.

Table 3. Discrepancy caused by items on partner-estimated ToDo list but not on self-aware ToDo list.

	M-J 1	M-J 2	M-J 3	C-J
On M or C's expected list but not on J's list	0.2	0.5	0.54	0.6
On J's expected list but not on M or C's list	0.5	0.5	0.42	0.25

Table 3 shows that roughly half of the ToDo items that constituted the discrepancies between self-aware and partner-estimated ToDo lists were those expected by partners but not recognized by themselves. Such items were mainly concerned with contacting others (e.g., interviewing elderly people, booking a restaurant, notifying party attendees about what to wear at a party, etc.) and things to do on the deadlines (e.g., emceeing the Christmas party and writing a report on the deadline date).

Priority differences

Last, we compared each participant's prioritized ToDo list with his/her partner's estimated prioritized ToDo list. No one accurately estimated his/her partner's prioritized ToDo list. In fact, they were very different from one another, regardless of their confidence in their estimations indicated by the post-task questionnaires.

Below, we provide a case example where a considerable difference was found within a pair (M-J 1). After their discussion, the Malaysian participant considered it particularly important to contact the party attendees to ask about their food preferences because she was conscious that some Malaysians don't eat pork. This ToDo item was valued as the second most important item on her whole ToDo list. But this item was not even on her partner's list. The Japanese partner expected her partner (i.e., the Malaysian) to contact the party attendees and tell them about the party's formal dress code. This item was rated as the most important thing to do, although it was not found on the Malaysian's list.

CONCLUSION

We proposed a method that detects value differences among meeting attendees regarding meeting contents. We showed how different meeting contents can be when reflected into future actions as a ToDo list; although pairs reached a consensus in their meetings and listed similar issues as the main points of the discussion, the concordance between self-aware and partner-estimated ToDo lists turned out to be quite different. By applying our method to many real meetings and accumulating data on the similarities/differences between attendee's values, we might be able to discover a new feature that sheds light on value differences between cultures.

REFERENCES

1. Hofstede, G. Culture's consequences: international differences in work-related values. Sage, 1980.
2. Setlock, L., Fussell, S., and Neuwirth, C. Taking it out of context: Collaborating within and across cultures in face-to-face settings and via instant messaging. *Proceedings of CSCW'04*, ACM Press.
3. He, Y., Zhao, C., and Hinds, P. Understanding information sharing from a cross-cultural perspective. *Proceedings of CHI Extended Abstracts'10*, ACM.
4. Eisenstein, J., Smith, N. A., and Xing, E. P. Discovering sociolinguistic associations with structured sparsity. Proceedings of the Annual Meeting of the Association for Computational Linguistics, 2011.

An Intercultural Study of HCI Education Experience and Representation

José Abdelnour-Nocera, Mario Michaelides, Ann Austin, and Sunila Modi
Centre for Internationalisation and Usability
School of Computing and Technology, University of West London
St Mary's Road, Ealing. London, W5 5RF
{Jose.Abdelnour-Nocera, Mario.Michaelides, Ann.Austin, Sunila.Modi}@uwl.ac.uk

ABSTRACT
The discipline of human-computer interaction has become a subject taught across universities around the world, outside of the cultures where it originated. However, the intercultural implication of its assimilation into the syllabus of courses offered by universities around the world remains under-researched. The purpose of this ongoing research project is to provide insights for these implications in terms of the student and teacher experience of HCI. How this subject is socially represented across the different universities studied is a key question. In order to develop intercultural awareness of these questions universities from UK, Denmark, Namibia, Mexico and China are collaborating in a multiple case study involving students and lecturers engaged in evaluation and design tasks. Findings will then be used to propose an international HCI curriculum more supportive of design for intercultural collaboration. This paper describes the initial steps of this study and some preliminary findings from Namibia.

Keywords
HCI education; culture; design; evaluation; cognitive styles

ACM Classification Keywords
K.3.2 [Computers and education]: Computer and Information Science Education – computer science education.

INTRODUCTION
Human-Computer Interaction (HCI) is a well-established and important subject in computing, technology and design in universities across the world. HCI is taught in order to explore, understand and aid in improving the usability and user experience of interactive systems and products. Though each educational community refers to similar methodologies and frameworks in order to teach this subject, little is known of the student experience and how local perspectives have influenced their content and approach to teaching. In addition, different levels of 'maturity' in the adoption of HCI among different countries suggest that its representation and experience can take many forms. Therefore, a current challenge for this discipline is explicating the possible tensions created between local cultures and the assumptions, priorities and values embedded in HCI concepts and methods mainly developed under particular paradigms.

This project proposes to explore how HCI is socially represented, taught and experienced in different institutions spanning four continents in China, Namibia, Mexico, Denmark and the United Kingdom. The project will begin by investigating how each educational community perceives what a usable system is through observation, discussion, and interviews in the context of a common evaluation and design task. An international and multilingual science education portal supporting middle school children will be focus of these activities. These will provide data on their benchmarks for what they view as good usability as well as identifying similarities or differences with other institutions and their attitudes to this subject.

The project will then progress to investigate their teaching approaches and methods, gathering data on all aspects such as the structure of their modules, the learning outcomes, the content, choice of literature, assessment methods, use of technology and their conduct in day-to-day teaching. Close attention will be paid to their perception on how HCI issues such as colour and metaphors are delivered, which will also offer data on the influences culture has had on their delivery.

The short duration of this project and its methodological design make it impossible to report on longitudinal accounts of appropriation of HCI by teachers and students. However, we hope to provide insights on the nature of HCI education as an intercultural encounter and the opportunities this can bring to locally validate, question and enrich some of its key concepts and methods. Including these insights into an international HCI curriculum will form designers better prepared to support intercultural collaboration.

HCI EDUCATION IN DIFFERENT COUNTRIES
Though there are numerous articles on HCI education and a few in relation to a country's delivery of the subject, there is no substantial body of literature which offers a thorough investigation into the influence that culture has on its delivery and in comparison with other countries/cultures. There are however other studies that discuss HCI education in certain countries such as New Zealand [17], Sweden [16], South Africa [17], Brazil [20] and Costa Rica [2].

These studies offer a brief view into HCI education. Sharkey & Paynter [17] investigated the need and coverage of HCI in relation to their educational courses in New Zealand. Their research came to the conclusion that the use of design tools was the most common topic followed by task analysis. This contrast with Sweden [16] where design principles, processes and cognitive psychology are the two subjects deemed to be the most important. Both countries had different approaches in their decisions but it would be interesting to investigate this factor especially regarding the time lapsed since these papers were published. Also, students in Costa Rica [2] offered their view that HCI should include more graphical design and heuristic evaluations, which the institution amended to accommodate.

In Brazil, a multicultural and developing country, challenges such as illiteracy and digital illiteracy impact on how HCI is implemented and ultimately how it is taught without discriminating against their fellow citizens being a important issue [20]. De Souza confirms semiotics has had a stronger influence, unlike traditions in Europe and North America, and that along with social inclusion are the two key areas that define Brazilian attitudes towards HCI. They are however disadvantaged in the fact that Portuguese HCI educational material is limited and is hindering understanding and development of this subject, a complaint shared by Gulliksen & Oestreicher [16] and [2] in regards to Sweden and Costa Rica.

Kotzé [11] looks at HCI education in South Africa, which in many ways shares cultural similarities with Brazil in terms of the range of ethnic, cultural, language and educational background issues. Kotze argues that HCI is a critical subject that needs to be taught but South Africa has been slow to embrace it. This is due partly to the ICT industry, which is characterised by systems development with little consideration for human factors. There seems to be a problem with institutions and cultures taking HCI seriously. This is echoed by Smith et al. [18] who indicate that in India where a large IT industry exists, HCI education has been neglected which is having an effect on the population and on India's global marketability. Though India produces high-class engineering graduates, very few courses address HCI. However, over the last few years the HCI community in India has grown and the topic begins to be addressed at national level through events such as the India HCI conferences taking place annually since 2010.

With the need for HCI apparent in order to aid the usability of systems at home and abroad, what are best strategies for teaching this subject? Smith et al. [19] suggest that western HCI tools and techniques might not be effective in developing countries and that some degree of localisation or adaptation are required. Lazar [12] has utilised community-based projects to enhance HCI education in Canada and has discovered that if students are involved with users they are in a better position to appreciate their needs.

Ultimately the literature available offers glimpses into HCI education in different environments though the papers vary in depth, content and publication dates. An aim of this project is to add consistency and contemporary analysis to this body of research, and to make sense of cross-country variations, convergences and emergences from a cultural perspective. In the next section we describe the main theories driving this perspective for us.

CULTURE AND COGNITION.

An area of consideration when discussing teaching and learning is that of the individual cognitive style of the learner. Cognitive, or learning style theory is a complex and contentious subject area with many conflicting theories and very many instruments to determine the different perspectives of cognitive style [3,4] and in addition, the cultural background of an individual may affect the outcome of any cognitive test [22]. However, researchers in the fields of culture and cognitive styles have identified a correlation between cultural characteristics and the holistic or intuitive versus analytical dimensions of cognitive style [8,15].

Nisbett's investigations into the relationship between culture and cognition investigate the cultural differences between East Asians and people from the Western world [5,14] and discuss how an inclination towards holistic or analytic reasoning is influenced by cultural identities. Building on Witkin's definition of subjects as 'field dependent' or 'field independent' [21] Nisbett differentiates between holistic and analytic reasoning, defining holistic thought as 'an orientation to the context or field as a whole' and analytic thought as 'detachment of the object from its context'. [5:19]. A later study that further focused on attention and perception discovered that the exposure of the subject to particular cultural icons or practices influenced the analytic versus holistic perception, particularly amongst bicultural subjects, concluding that the relationship between culture and cognition is not fixed, but flexible and dynamic [14].

Hayes and Allinson tested the hypothesis that culture would account for differences in learning style in a study involving managers from East Africa, India and the United Kingdom. Using Hofstede's [10] four dimensions of Power Distance, Uncertainty Avoidance, Individualism-Collectivism and Masculinity-Femininity, and the Theorist/Pragmatist and Activist/Reflector scores of Honey and Mumford's Learning Style Questionnaire, Hayes and Allinson identified two dimensions of learning style, Analysis and Action [9]. Further work in this area resulted in Allinson and Hayes' Cognitive Style Index (CSI) [1], a compact questionnaire which is designed to test whether individuals tends more towards an intuitivist (right brain dominant) or analyst (left brain dominant) approach.

METHODOLOGICAL STRATEGY AND INITIAL ANALYSIS MODEL

The case study in each country includes a visit to a university where a group of around 20 undergraduate HCI students will be asked to engage in a heuristic evaluation and evaluation task of a science education portal for primary school children. The activity given to students will act as a cultural probe [6] as it contains elements with different cultural affordances, e.g. heuristic evaluation as stimulating analytic thinking and prototype sketching as stimulating holistic thinking. The visit will also include meetings and interviews with lecturers and staff in charge of curriculum design. In addition, documents and course materials produced by the university will be analyzed.

Quantitative data on culture for each student group will be collected using Hofstede's VSM94 instrument, and Hayes and Allinson's CSI survey will be used to situate each student in an intuitive-holistic scale. We acknowledge the limitations of Hofstede's model on national culture [13] and are very careful not to make stereotypical interpretations or generalizations from the data collected. Even more we are not expecting students to match the national culture scores 'predictions' for their country. However, we still believe that it will be useful to find out the mean scores for each group on each cultural dimension, e.g. power distance, masculinity and collectivism, to enrich our comparative analysis of quantitative and qualitative data. Qualitative data will be analyzed for manifestations of national culture dimensions [10], cognitive styles [14] and high and low context cultures [7]. While these different cultural models give us a top-down framework for analysis, a bottom up analysis of this data will also be developed. The aim will be to uncover cultural patterns, themes and dimensions exclusively emerging from the HCI education domain.

Data gathering can be structured in three levels looking at different types of culture markers per group:

Student experience will be studied through completion of VSM 94 and CSI surveys, individual 'expert' evaluation and interface design tasks producing quantitative and qualitative data on students' performance and views on the use of heuristics, scenario and persona development richness and content, usability and user experience goals; focus groups aimed at exploring perceptions of the task given to them and HCI concepts and tools in the local context. Students' evaluation and design rationale statements and sketches will be analyzed in terms of the dimensions holistic-analytic, high and low context, and through emergent themes.

Teacher experience will be studied through interviews and analysis of HCI course materials. We expect to obtain information on their role as HCI educators, the challenges and indigenous perspectives on the discipline. Qualitative data obtained at this level will be analyzed in terms of the dimensions holistic-analytic, and high and low context as well through development of emergent themes.

HCI in the curriculum: through interview and document analysis quantitative and qualitative data will be obtained with a view to find out about how HCI as a subject is represented in the course offer and discourse of each university. The teaching and assessment methods used and their rationale will also be studies and analyzed. We will look for evidence of holistic-analytic dimensions, high and low context and through development of emergent themes.

These activities will help us answer the following questions:

a) How does culture influence delivery of HCI education?
   i. How is selection of teaching material influenced by cultural differences?
   ii. Which topics do an institution choose to deliver in HCI curriculum – why? Any correlation to Hofstede dimension scores for the country and/or cognitive styles found?
   iii. Institutional perception/representation in computing curriculum of HCI education.
   iv. What is the HCI teacher perception?
b) How does culture influence the experience of studying HCI?
   i. What is the Student perception of HCI tools and concepts?
   ii. How do cultural dimensions and cognitive styles correlate with students' preferences for learning HCI?
   iii. What are the perceptions of HCI tools and methods vis-à-vis findings for cultural markers?
   iv. What is the community's understanding of what constitutes a usable system?

The answers from question a) and b)i,ii will help us to prepare an international framework for HCI education. The answers from question b)iii,iv will enable us to enrich the curriculum to help HCI students develop an awareness of intercultural collaboration issues for design.

PRELIMINARY FINDINGS FROM NAMIBIA

At the time of writing data gathering for Namibia has been completed. While a full analysis of data is not available, there are some findings worth noting at this stage.

The mean scores for the VSM94 survey indicate the group is slightly individualistic with very low power distance. This is contrast to with Hofsetde's scores for Namibia and most of sub-Saharan Africa indicating collectivistic societies with a tendency to a high power distance. This might be an indication that globally HCI students will show less cultural variability along certain dimensions due to increased exposure to technology and similar learning situations.

The CSI survey indicates that most students are of adaptive nature. This suggests they do not have a strong preference for either intuitive or analytic modes of information processing. They are comfortable drawing on both, in whatever combination seems appropriate at the time, in order to improve their understanding of a situation and make decisions about how to act. This is echoed in their engagement with the HCI evaluation and design tasks: all of them attempted to complete the design and evaluation tasks, which contained intuitive and holistic components. However, most of them expressed difficulties in applying the heuristic to assess particular aspects of the website they were asked to work with. Detailed observations in scripted heuristic evaluations, as the one used in this research, are more compatible with very analytic cognitive styles. This is in contrast with the authors' experience of UK HCI students who tend to feel more comfortable in applying heuristics.

CONCLUSIONS

In summary, this project intends to enhance our international knowledge of HCI Education to support intercultural perspectives. It aims to find opportunities and challenges for the dissemination and enrichment of this discipline through eliciting and assessing the importance of local, disciplinary, national and HCI cultures. It does so by exploring the context, performance and views of stakeholders involved in learning and teaching.

This project is limited by the short duration of data gathering in each country and by not being able to observe first hand experience of HCI education happening over a period of time. Nevertheless, this study provides a unique, and probably the first, opportunity to systematically compare and analyze data obtained from four continents. We are aware that it stands in different epistemological positions as it looks, on one hand, at performance and, on the other hand, at meanings used to represent and experience HCI. However, we see this as an opportunity for triangulation, co-validation and enhanced understanding of HCI education in a multicultural context.

REFERENCES

1. Allinson, C.W. and Hayes, J. The Cognitive Style Index: A Measure of Intuition Analysis For Organizational Research. *Journal of Management Studies 33*, (1996), 119-135.
2. Calderon, M. Teaching Human Computer Interaction: First Experiences. *CLEI Electronic Journal 12*, 1 (2009).
3. Cassidy, S. Learning styles: An overview of theories, models, and measures. *Educational Psychology 24*, (2004), 419-444.
4. Coffield, F., Moseley, D., Hall, E., and Ecclestone, K. Should we be using learning styles? What research has to say to practice. *Learning and Skills Research Centre, London*, (2004).
5. E Nisbett, R. and Norenzayan, A. Culture and cognition. *Stevens' handbook of experimental psychology*, (2002).
6. Gaver, B., Dunne, T., and Pacenti, E. Design: cultural probes. *interactions 6*, 1 (1999), 21–29.
7. Hall, E.T. *An anthropology of everyday life: An autobiography*. Doubleday, 1993.
8. Hayes, J. and Allinson, C.W. Cultural differences in the learning styles of managers. *Management International Review*, (1988), 75–80.
9. Hayes, J. and Allinson, C.W. Cultural differences in the learning styles of managers. *Management International Review*, (1988), 75–80.
10. Hofstede, G. *Cultures and organizations: software of the mind*. McGraw Hill, Berkshire, UK, 1991.
11. Kotzé, P. Directions in HCI education, research, and practice in Southern Africa. *CHI'02 extended abstracts on Human factors in computing systems*, (2002), 524–525.
12. Lazar, J. Using community-based service projects to enhance undergraduate HCI education: 10 years of experience. *Proceedings of the 2011 annual conference extended abstracts on Human factors in computing systems*, (2011), 581–588.
13. McSweeney, B. Hofstede's model of national cultural differences and their consequences: A triumph of faith-a failure of analysis. *Human relations 55*, 1 (2002), 89.
14. Nisbett, R.E. and Miyamoto, Y. The influence of culture: holistic versus analytic perception. *Trends in Cognitive Sciences 9*, 10 (2005), 467–473.
15. Nisbett, R.E. and Norenzayan, A. Culture and cognition. *Stevens' handbook of experimental psychology*, (2002).
16. Oestreicher, L. and Gulliksen, J. HCI education in Sweden. *SIGCHI Bulletin 31*, 2 (1999).
17. Sharkey, E. and Paynter, J. Computer Human Interaction Education in New Zealand Universities. (2004).
18. Smith, A., Ghosh, K., and Joshi, A. Usability and HCI in India: cultural and technological determinants. *HCI International (Crete*, (2003).
19. Smith, A., Joshi, A., Liu, Z., Bannon, L., Gulliksen, J., and Baranauskas, C. Embedding HCI in developing countries: localizing content, institutionalizing education and practice. *Human-Computer Interaction–INTERACT 2007*, (2007), 698–699.
20. de Souza, C.S., Baranauskas, M.C.C., Prates, R.O., and Pimenta, M.S. HCI in Brazil: lessons learned and new perspectives. *Proceedings of the VIII Brazilian Symposium on Human Factors in Computing Systems*, (2008), 358–359.
21. Witkin, H.A., Lewis, H.B., Hertzman, M., Machover, K., Meissner, P.B., and Wapner, S. Personality through perception: an experimental and clinical study. (1954).
22. Witkin, H.A. A cognitive-style approach to cross-cultural research. *International Journal of Psychology 2*, 4 (1967), 233–250.

Author Index

Abdelnour-Nocera, José	157	Holtzman, Henry	145	Pogrebnyakov, Nicolai	137
Adamson, David	67	Ishida, Toru	57	Rau, Pei-Luen Patrick	87
Akhilesh, K.B.	129	Koen, Ilias	145	Redmiles, David	97
Al-Ani, Ban	97	Kulkarni, Ranjitha Gurunath	47	Rosé, Carolyn Penstein	47, 67
Anandarajan, Indumathi	129	Kuzuoka, Hideaki	153	Rudnicky, Alexander I.	67
Austin, Ann	157	Li, Hui	87	Shah, Hina	77
Baljko, Melanie	39	Li, Ye	87	Simmons, Erik	97
Bjørn, Pernille	21	Mädche, Alexander	87	Simoes, Alexander	145
Buchmann, Mikael	137	Mayfield, Elijah	67	Suresh, Tushar	47
Cervantes, Ruy	11	Michaelides, Mario	157	Trainer, Erik	97
Ducao, Arlene	145	Michan, Renée Korver	21	Trivedi, Gaurav	47
Evers, Vanessa	133	Miner, William	149	van Dijk, Betsy	133
Fischlmayr, Iris	31	Modi, Sunila	157	Vyas, Dhaval	119
Gluesing, Julia	1	Nardi, Bonnie	11	Weiss, Astrid	133
Goyal, Nitesh	149	Nawathe, Nikhil	149	Wen, Miaomiao	47
Hamidi, Foad	39	Nawaz, Ather	141	Yamashita, Naomi	153
Harrold, Mary Jean	77	Nersessian, Nancy J.	77	Zheng, Zeyu	47
Hautasaari, Ari	57	Newstetter, Wendy	77	Zimmermann, Angelika	107
Hidalgo, Cesar	145	Philippart, Nancy	1		

www.ingramcontent.com/pod-product-compliance
Lightning Source LLC
Chambersburg PA
CBHW080938300426
44115CB00017B/2873